BACHELORS OF A DIFFERENT SORT

GENERAL EDITOR:
Christopher Breward
and
Glenn Adamson

FOUNDING EDITOR:
Paul Greenhalgh

also available in the series

Bringing modernity home
Writings on popular design and material culture
JUDITH ATTFIELD

Design and the modern magazine
EDITED BY JEREMY AYNSLEY AND KATE FORDE

The culture of fashion
A new history of fashionable dress
CHRISTOPHER BREWARD

Stained glass and the Victorian Gothic Revival
JIM CHESHIRE

The British country house in the eighteenth century
CHRISTOPHER CHRISTIE

'The autobiography of a nation'
The 1951 Festival of Britain
BECKY E. CONEKIN

The culture of craft
Status and future
EDITED BY PETER DORMER

Material relations
Domestic interiors and the middle-class family, 1850–1910
JANE HAMLETT

Arts and Crafts objects
IMOGEN HART

Representations of British motoring
DAVID JEREMIAH

Interiors of Empire
Objects, space and identity within the Indian Subcontinent, c. 1800–1947
ROBIN JONES

The Edwardian house
The middle-class home in Britain 1880–1914
HELEN C. LONG

The birth of modern London
The development and design of the city
ELIZABETH MCKELLAR

Interior design and identity
EDITED BY SUSIE MCKELLAR AND PENNY SPARKE

Dress and globalisation
Identity and the tactics of encounter
MARGARET MAYNARD

The material Renaissance
MICHELLE O'MALLEY AND EVELYN WELCH

Chinoiserie: Commerce and critical ornament in eighteenth-century Britain
STACEY SLOBODA

Establishing dress history
LOU TAYLOR

The study of dress history
LOU TAYLOR

Bachelors of a different sort

QUEER AESTHETICS, MATERIAL CULTURE AND THE MODERN INTERIOR IN BRITAIN

John Potvin

Manchester University Press

Copyright © John Potvin 2014

The right of John Potvin to be identified as the author of this work has been asserted by him in accordance with the Copyright, Designs and Patents Act 1988.

Published by Manchester University Press
Altrincham Street, Manchester M1 7JA, UK
www.manchesteruniversitypress.co.uk

British Library Cataloguing-in-Publication Data is available

ISBN 978 1 7849 9109 8 *paperback*

First published by Manchester University Press in hardback 2014
First published by Manchester University Press in paperback 2015

This edition first published 2018

The publisher has no responsibility for the persistence or accuracy of URLs for any external or third-party internet websites referred to in this book, and does not guarantee that any content on such websites is, or will remain, accurate or appropriate.

Printed by Lightning Source

to my two beloved companions in life, aesthetics and domesticity,
the doctor and the earl

Contents

List of figures — viii
Preface — xiv

1 Men of a different sort: the seven deadly sins of the modern bachelor — 1

I Wilde spaces

2 'God Save the Queen': Lord Gower, idolatry and the cult of the *bric-à-brac* diva — 39
3 Vale(d) decadence: Charles Ricketts, Charles Shannon and the Wilde factor — 81

II Country living

4 Askesis and the Greek ideal: Edward Perry Warren and Lewes House — 131
5 Of art and irises: Cedric Morris, Arthur Lett-Haines and the decorative ideal — 161

III Stage design for living

6 Coward in the room: interwar glamour and the performances of a queer modernity — 199
7 Cecil Beaton: artifice as resistance — 246

8 Conclusion: manifesto for a queer home of one's own — 286

Select bibliography — 290
Index — 307

List of figures

Every reasonable effort has been made to contact or trace copyright holders. No harmful or malicious intent was intended in the reproduction of images, and if any errors have been inadvertently made, please contact either the publisher or the author so any corrections might be made for subsequent editions.

    Cover: *Cedric Morris and Lett-Haines with Rubio the parrot*, c. 1930–36. Courtesy of The Tate.

2.1	Camille Silvy. *Lord Ronald Charles Gower Sutherland-Levenson-Gower*, 15 July 1865. Courtesy of the National Portrait Gallery.	40
2.2	Cover page from *Bric À Brac* by Lord Ronald Gower, 1888. Private Collection.	41
2.3	Edward Dossetter. Frontispiece, *Bric À Brac*, featuring Lord Ronald Gower's *Old Guard* and façade of Gower Lodge, Windsor. Private Collection.	42
2.4	Edward Dossetter. *Old Guard* outside Gower Lodge, Windsor. *Bric À Brac*. Private Collection.	45
2.5	Queen Victoria. 'Sketch by the Queen of one of H. M. Bridesmaides and given to my Mother when she was Mistress of the Robes'. *Bric À Brac*. Private Collection.	50
2.6	Edward Dossetter. Chimney in the Saloon. *Bric À Brac*. Private Collection.	51
2.7	Edward Dossetter. Sitting room on the ground floor. *Bric À Brac*. Private Collection.	52
2.8	Edward Dossetter. Sitting room. *Bric À Brac*. Private Collection.	53

List of figures   ix

2.9   Edward Dossetter. Sitting room. *Bric À Brac*. Private
      Collection.   54

2.10 Napoleon Sarony. *Oscar Wilde*, 1882. Courtesy of the
      National Portrait Gallery.   61

2.11 Napoleon Sarony. *Lord Ronald Charles Gower Sutherland-
      Levenson-Gower*, c. 1884, published 1902. Courtesy of the
      National Portrait Gallery.   63

2.12 Edward Dossetter. Marie-Antoinette Relics, *Bric À Brac*.
      Private Collection.   68

3.1   Charles Hazelwood Shannon. *Self-Portrait*, 1897. Oil on
      canvas. Courtesy of the National Portrait Gallery.   82

3.2   Charles Hazelwood Shannon. *Charles de Sousy Ricketts*,
      1898. Oil on canvas. Courtesy of the National Portrait
      Gallery.   83

3.3   George Charles Beresford. *Charles Ricketts and
      Charles Shannon at Yeoman's Row, Brompton Road, London*,
      October 1903. Courtesy of The Fitzwilliam Museum,
      Cambridge University.   84

3.4   George Charles Beresford. *Charles Shannon*, 13 October
      1903. Courtesy of the National Portrait Gallery.   87

3.5   George Charles Beresford. *Charles Ricketts*, 13 October
      1903. Courtesy of the National Portrait Gallery.   88

3.6   Dining room, The Vale. Courtesy of The Fitzwilliam
      Museum, Cambridge University.   98

3.7   Interior view of Lansdowne House, featuring cabinets of
      curiosity. Courtesy of The Fitzwilliam Museum,
      Cambridge University.   103

3.8   Charles Shannon in his private studio, Lansdowne House.
      Courtesy of The Fitzwilliam Museum, Cambridge
      University.   105

3.9   Dining room featuring the lapis lazuli tabletop dining
      table, Spring Terrace. Courtesy of The Fitzwilliam Museum,
      Cambridge University.   108

3.10 Charles Ricketts seated in front of part of his picture
      collection, Lansdowne House. Courtesy of The Fitzwilliam
      Museum, Cambridge University.   109

3.11	Charles Ricketts at work amidst his treasures, Lansdowne House. Courtesy of The Fitzwilliam Museum, Cambridge University.	110
3.12	Charles Shannon. *Portrait of Ricketts/The Man with the Greek Vase*, 1916. Courtesy of the Leamington Spa Art Gallery and Museum.	111
3.13	Charles Ricketts as the decadent Aesthete. Courtesy of The Fitzwilliam Museum, Cambridge University.	112
3.14	Oscar Wilde relaxing on the (plush) divan during his lecture trip through America, 1882. Courtesy of Corbis and the Condé Nast Archive. Courtesy of the National Portrait Gallery.	115
4.1	Edward (Ned) Perry Warren and John Marshall with their dogs, c. 1890s. Courtesy of Edward Reeves Photography.	135
4.2	Edward (Ned) Perry Warren, John Marshall and St. Bernard, c. 1890s. Courtesy of Edward Reeves Photography.	137
4.3	One of Lewes House's studios. Courtesy of the Lewes House Archives, Lewes District Council.	145
4.4	One of Lewes House's studios. Courtesy of the Lewes House Archives, Lewes District Council.	146
5.1	Cedric Morris and Arthur Lett-Haines with Rubio the parrot, c. 1930–36. Courtesy of The Tate.	164
5.2	Cedric Morris, the image of the bohemian artist in Paris, c. 1920s. Courtesy of The Tate.	167
5.3	Sir Cedric Morris. *Self-Portrait*, 1930. Courtesy of the National Portrait Gallery.	169
5.4	The Pound at Higham with sculpture by John Skeaping in foreground, c. 1940–50. Courtesy of The Tate.	179
5.5	Group shot of students with Cedric Morris: 'Belton, Boo, Jan, Self, Mildred, Cedric' c. 1930–36. Courtesy of The Tate.	180
5.6	Sir Cedric Morris, c. 1920. Courtesy of The Tate.	182
5.7	Benton End, n.d. Courtesy of The Tate.	183
5.8	Arthur Lett-Haines takes some sun, c. 1930–36. Courtesy of The Tate.	187
5.9	Sir Cedric Morris. *Iris Seedlings*, 1943. Courtesy of The Tate.	190

List of figures xi

6.1	Howard Coster. Noël Coward in front of the window in the sitting room of his 17 Gerald Road, Belgravia, home, 1939. Courtesy of the National Portrait Gallery.	203
6.2	Noël Coward reclined on an Art Deco sofa in the newly decorated 111 Ebury Street flat, London, 1 September 1927. Courtesy of Getty Images and the Hulton Archive.	206
6.3	Noël Coward working in bed in his by then standard Chinese silk robe. *The Sketch*, 29 April 1925. Courtesy of the University of Bristol care of ArenaPal Images.	207
6.4	Radclyffe Hall influenced by Noël Coward's manner of dress with Lady Una Troubridge (cut off), undated. Courtesy of the National Portrait Gallery.	209
6.5	Maurice Beck and MacGregor. Double portrait of Noël Coward and friend and set designer Gladys Calthrop, c. 1924. Courtesy of Lebrecht Music and Arts and the Richard Bebb Collection.	216
6.6	First page of an article by Joan Woollcombe in *Homes and Gardens's* feature of Noël Coward's 17 Gerald Road home. *Homes and Gardens*, February 1937, p. 313. Courtesy of *Homes and Gardens*, IPC Southbank Publishing.	219
6.7	Views of Noël Coward's 17 Gerald Road home. *Homes and Gardens*, February 1937, p. 314. Courtesy of *Homes and Gardens*, IPC Southbank Publishing.	220
6.8	Views of Noël Coward's 17 Gerald Road home. *Homes and Gardens*, February 1937, p. 315. Courtesy of *Homes and Gardens*, IPC Southbank Publishing.	221
6.9	Views of Noël Coward's 17 Gerald Road home. *Homes and Gardens*, February 1937, p. 316. Courtesy of *Homes and Gardens*, IPC Southbank Publishing.	222
6.10	Howard Coster. Noël Coward with personal secretary Lorn Loraine in the sitting room of his 17 Gerald Road home, 1939. Courtesy of the National Portrait Gallery.	225
6.11	Vandamm Studio. Gertrude Lawrence and Noël Coward on sofa in *Private Lives*, Times Square Theatre, New York, 1931. Courtesy of the Billy Rose Theatre Division, New York Public Library for the Performing Arts.	229
6.12	Lynn Fontane, Alfred Lunt and Noël Coward in *Design for Living*, Ethel Barrymore Theatre, New York, 1934. Courtesy	

	of Lebrecht Music and Arts and the Gwen Watford Collection.	232
6.13	Lynn Fontane, Alfred Lunt and Noël Coward in *Design for Living*, Ethel Barrymore Theatre, New York, 1934. Courtesy of Corbis and the Condé Nast Archive.	233
6.14	Vandamm Studio. The set for the original Broadway production of Noël Coward's *Design for Living*, Ethel Barrymore Theatre, New York, 1933. Courtesy of the Billy Rose Theatre Division, New York Public Library for the Performing Arts.	236
6.15	Moderne-styled advertisement for the Exhibition of British Industrial Art in the Home London, 1933, *Homes and Gardens*, July 1933, p. xviii. Courtesy of *Homes and Gardens*, IPC Southbank Publishing.	237
6.16	Howard Coster. Wells Wintemute Coates, 1937. Courtesy of the National Portrait Gallery.	239
7.1	Peter North. Cecil Beaton, c. 1920s. Courtesy of the National Portrait Gallery.	249
7.2	Attributed to Cecil Beaton. Self-Portrait, 1927. Courtesy of the National Portrait Gallery.	251
7.3	'Aesthetics versus Athletics', *Illustrated London News*, 17 March 1883. Private Collection.	253
7.4	Cecil Beaton sitting in his student residence, Cambridge, 1922. Courtesy of the Cecil Beaton Studio Archive at Sotheby's.	255
7.5	Cecil Beaton. Self-Portrait in drag as Lady Mendl (Elsie de Wolfe) for Elsa Maxwell's costume party at the Waldorf, New York, 1 May 1934. Courtesy of the National Portrait Gallery.	259
7.6	Millar and Harris. Cecil Beaton posing outside Ashcombe, 1930. Courtesy of the National Portrait Gallery.	268
7.7	Millar and Harris. Cecil Beaton posing outside his studio at Ashcombe, 1930. Courtesy of the National Portrait Gallery.	269
7.8	Cecil Beaton in Tyrolean suit posing in front of the bedroom murals, Ashcombe, early 1930s. Courtesy of Corbis and the Hulton Deutsch Collection.	271

List of figures

7.9   Possibly by Baron George Hoyningen-Huene. Cecil Beaton
      in his bed designed by friend and artist Rex Whistler,
      Ashcombe, 1930. Courtesy of the National Portrait Gallery.   272

7.10 Cecil Beaton siting on a white sofa in his all-white studio,
      Ashcombe, early 1930s. Courtesy of Getty Images and the
      Hulton Archive.   273

7.11 Cecil Beaton in Tyrolean suit, standing in his bathroom
      surrounded by the hand outlines of his many friends who
      visited Ashcombe, early 1930s. Courtesy of Corbis and the
      Hulton Deutsch Collection.   277

7.12 Cecil Beaton and Rex Whistler painting *en plein air* on
      Ashcombe's grounds, c. 1930s. Courtesy of the National
      Portrait Gallery.   281

Preface

In December 2010, in front of friends and family and in the domestic spaces of our closest friends, I married my husband. Our choice to marry was a public declaration that our relationship, companionate, sexual and domestic in nature, would be recognized, that, it would become part of the public record and that despite an ever-increasing neo-liberal and conservative world, we would not be silenced. Our choice of location was as much political as it was practical. We chose to be married in a domestic setting, the site of our cherished community, the location of friendship, love, heated debates and laughter. Given that the men in this book have been with me for some time now, some longer than others, I was repeatedly reminded of them in the many days leading up to, during and long after the day of our wedding. I thought about how their lives, whose partial stories fill these pages, were in various ways and to varying degrees silenced through the closing of their homes' doors, the painful and deafening sound of time marching on. The fact I was able to stand before my husband, in front of friends and family, speaks to a long, and long from over, struggle many are all too familiar with; a struggle I hope my friends' children will not have to bear, but will also never forget.

In many ways the contents of this book resemble my own design for living in which life, work and aesthetics are so tightly interwoven they become inseparable, one never valued over the other. While I may have gotten married in the process of writing this book, I have certainly not set out to valorize neither one form of domesticity over others nor a particular or singular expression of sexual identity over the myriad forms queer sexuality takes. Some of the men in this book maintained domestic relationships with each other for over 50 years, often within the fraught and permissive space that an open relationship offers. Some were tragic in their love affairs, finding solace in their work and domestic havens, while others were forced into despair and exile from their objects of desire, both human and material. Common amongst my collected group of *bachelors of a different sort* is how they defied and overcame experiences, moments and expressions of shame to design, for themselves, not a room, but an *entire home of one's own*. Given that the book ends loosely around 1957 with the publication of the Wolfenden Report, it might seem obvious to state that none of the men featured in this book was married to or entered into a civil union with another man. This fact, I suggest, remains an important one, especially in our period of more progressive laws and seeming tolerance: as a result we tend to take much for granted. It is precisely for this reason that I have dared to briefly insert myself here; not as a way to elevate my own status, but to include one more, nascent form of sexuality, one these men never could have fathomed or even perhaps would have desired for themselves. Perceptions of sexuality and identification with its signs and codes change as rapidly as industrial and interior design does today. The future offers, I hope, uncharted design and sexual territory, which will yield richly textured and challenging narratives.

I am grateful to the memories of the men I have included in this book as much as to those who helped along the process of researching, writing and producing it. My research and the ability to reproduce images in this book has been greatly enabled by staff at the National Art Library and the Design Archives of the Victoria and Albert Museum (London), the Tate (London), the Billy Rose Theatre Division of the New York Public Library for the Performing Arts, the British Library, The Fitzwilliam Museum (Cambridge University), National Portrait Gallery (London), Leamington Spa Art Gallery and Museum, the University of Bristol, the Cecil Beaton Studio Archive at Sotheby's, Maggi Hambling of the Estate of Cedric Morris and the Lewes House Archives, Lewes District Council. I owe a special debt to all those not listed above who also kindly granted me permission to reproduce the beautiful images which help to enliven the spatial narratives and material cultures of the men in this book.

I will always be indebted and immensely grateful to Amelia Jones, Matt Cook, Penny Sparke, Dirk Gindt and Joseph McBrinn for their insightful and thoughtful comments at various stages of the process. There were others who have also shared much for which I am honoured: Anne Anderson for her baffling knowledge of all things Victorian as well as for many of the images which help illustrate Lord Gower's interiors, Penny Sparke for her continuous inspiration, encouragement and incomparable devotion to the study of the modern interior, Janice Helland for her support over the years and Emma Brennan of Manchester University Press and the Studies in Design series editors Christopher Breward and Glenn Adamson for their patience and diligence. I am, as always, eternally indebted to Hugh MacPherson for his technological wizardry and for his willingness to lend a helping hand. Finally, I am very grateful to the Social Sciences and Humanities Council of Canada as well as The Paul Mellon Centre for Studies in British Art Research, which, through their generosity allowed me to conduct the necessary research in London and further afield.

Parts of Chapter 3 have appeared in the following forms in two different volumes: 'The Aesthetics of Community: Charles Shannon and Charles Ricketts and the Art of Domesticity', in Jason Edwards and Imogen Hart (eds), *Rethinking the Interior: Aestheticism and the Arts and Crafts Movement, 1867–1896* (Aldershot and Burlington: Ashgate, 2010), and 'Collecting intimacy one object at a time: material culture, perception and the spaces of aesthetic companionship', in John Potvin and Alla Myzelev (eds.), *Material Culture in Britain, 1750–1920: The Meanings and Pleasures of Collecting* (Aldershot and Burlington: Ashgate: 2009). As well, part of Chapter 4 appeared as 'Askesis as Aesthetic Home: Edward Perry Warren, Lewis House and the Ideal of Greek Love', in *Home Cultures: The Journal of Architecture, Design and Domestic Space*, vol. 8, no. 1 (March 2011).

John Potvin
Toronto/Stockholm/Montreal

1 ✧ Men of a different sort: the seven deadly sins of the modern bachelor

THE BACHELOR has long held an ambivalent, uncomfortable and even at times an unfriendly position in society. As late as 1977 Alan G. Davis and Philip M. Strong published what is surely one of the oddest sociological surveys ever performed in the postwar era, in which they investigate the 'social problem' commonly referred to as the bachelor. The authors note how the world of the bachelor – the social institutions that catered to and aided his lifestyle – had long since dissolved. As a result, the contemporary bachelor 'experience[s] many occasions when he is alone and known in public settings'.[1] They suggest that given both the figure's 'biographical deficiency and the stereotypes … they must do their best to "pass" as a normal person … They cannot rely on someone who "really" knows them to help interpret the puzzles of everyday life … Given these difficulties; no one with whom to rehearse their identity; no one to explain and evaluate others' behaviour.'[2] By war's end, the figure of the bachelor had become a social pariah, an odd misfit of pity and suspicion, a figure clearly out of its depth when it concerned quotidian and social customs. Perhaps this apparent lack spoke less to the nature and condition of the bachelor than how it betrayed a social structure that privileged heteronormative companionate coupling. Their study underscored how marriage guaranteed, as it still largely does today, social knowledge, navigational skills and entrance into society. This sociological portrait is in many ways a logical extension of the one that emerged and developed in popular consciousness throughout the long nineteenth century. First and foremost, the bachelor was a lover of luxury and comfort, an aspect of his personality, which, if we were to take Davis and Strong's characterization at face value, was the cause of his apparent social awkwardness. As a result, the bachelor was also often thought of as similar to if not the same as the connoisseur, the eccentric and free-loving globetrotter, unbound and unrestricted, unfettered by familial obligations in his search for the exotic and the novel; a man driven only by his self-centred needs, drives and pleasures.

One of the earliest and perhaps the most complete exposition of the bachelor as a distinct typological entry in the encyclopaedic quest of the Enlightenment Project remains *Old Bachelors: Their Varieties, Characters, and Conditions* (1835) in which its anonymous author underscores the importance of this (anti)social type. Two entire volumes were required to elucidate the type's numerous sub-species and traits. While the homosexual was not 'called into being' until 1869 and the term would not gain social currency until the end of the nineteenth and early twentieth centuries, the bachelor was identified as a decidedly queer type, one whose gender performances and sexual identity were at best dubious and at worst immoral given how he reneged on his obligations to serve wife, home and nation. According to the tract's author, a 'man who voluntarily devotes himself to a Bachelor's life, has undoubtedly a wrong estimate of humanity. There is a disposition implanted in all of us for the companionship of woman; we must have some being upon whom we can pour out our affections, and no stoicism can ever eradicate this portion of our common moral nature.'[3] It is not surprising that in a social order that attempted to register and control every typological and social difference, an anatomical characterization became a necessary means to visually ascertain the bachelor's inner character through surface bodily readings. The 'most effeminate of his tribe', the bachelor was a 'poor, lanky and anatomized creature' driven by his insatiable passions and a feverish 'impure imagination' which causes 'his *moral* sense' to descend 'into the *animal* sense of the savage'.[4] In a chapter devoted to the 'Rakish Bachelor', the author claims this sub-species to be one which indulges too much 'in sensual gratification' and is therefore marked as 'one of the most brutalizing agencies that can be brought to bear upon humanity'.[5]

Bachelors were also said to be preoccupied with the chief occupations of 'freedom, luxury, and self-indulgence', and hence lacked a true and honourable vocation in a world in which market capitalism, bourgeois morality and the Protestant work ethic saw this idle lifestyle as anti-masculine and anti-national. In short, bachelors removed themselves from the realm of production[6] and contributed nothing to the health of the nation. Eve Kosofsky Sedgwick identified an important transition that occurred in the nineteenth century from the bachelor as a transitional stage in the development of adult masculinity (leading to full maturity consummated in the union of marriage) to the bachelor as an identity or typological entity; now a corporeal object to be scrutinized and monitored. This marked shift underpinned a period of crisis for hegemonic masculinity in which the transition from developmental stage to fixed identity was also collapsed into a medical discourse that progressively decried and associated masturbation as the cause for the condition of *spermatorrhea*, popularly referred to as the 'bachelor's disease'.[7] While no such disease existed in reality, it nonetheless proved an effective discursive formation around the medical and social threat the bachelor as a type began to pose to the health and future of the nation. All and every sexual activity that did not lead to procreation became increasingly conflated with an ever-expanding definition of homosexuality, and gradually the once seemingly innocuous term bachelor was progressively deployed as an index pointing to homosexuality. In an article from 1909 in the short-lived men's magazine *The Modern Man*, T. B. Johnson questioned how a bachelor should spend his leisure time. Given the associations between non-productive and non-procreative tendencies that were grafted on to the identity of the modern bachelor, the author was quick to point to the solid and socially acceptable goal of making money, even when pursuing leisure activities. In addition to this noble pursuit, all other leisure time should be devoted to 'reading works connected with his own line of business and thus making his position more certain, his usefulness to his employer greater and his prospects better'. Clearly for Johnson the bachelor was a bourgeois – and not an aristocratic – man. The final goal of this use of time, it was clearly stated, 'would only help the bachelor when he ceased to be one of the unattached'.[8] As Katherine V. Snyder insists,

> the bachelor disrupted the proper regulation that defined home economics throughout the nineteenth century and into the twentieth. The disorderly potential of the bachelor may well indicate the susceptibility of this home economy to elements that many would have wanted to consider extrinsic to it … Representations of bachelors at home, living in or visiting other people's houses … the discourse of bachelor domesticity itself provided opportunities for bachelors to go out of bounds.[9]

Bachelors like Joris-Karl Huysmans's infamous anti-hero Jean Des Esseintes commit to, reside and indulge in the realm of the sensual, excess and artifice; a queer use of time and space. Within the interior worlds men like Des Esseintes designed, it was held that too many of the senses were activated simultaneously, a destabilizing force to a healthy human body and pure soul.[10] The figure of the bachelor precipitated a cultural and moral war that privileged mind, reason and intellect over pleasure, delight, the senses and the body itself. For, as the anonymous author of *Old Bachelors* claimed: 'Men who give themselves over to these kinds of enjoyments lose sight of the great truth that the body is but the slave of the mind:-- with them the body is omnipotent; the mind is the servant'.[11] In this light, the bachelor was the anti-hero in the Cartesian *cogito*, which pits mind against body, the latter a vacant and flawed handmaiden to the former.[12] While not all aesthetes were homosexuals, nor were all homosexuals bachelors, the associations were at times so profound and easy to construe that the figures became one and the same in the threat to social, cultural, economic and racial stability. By the end of the nineteenth century, through their perceived excessive, immature, unnatural and antisocial needs and desires, the twin figures of the bachelor and the homosexual were all too often conflated as equally deviant and queer characters. Bachelors, not unlike homosexuals, were seen to occupy 'remarkable bedrooms and other spaces [that] were often located either dangerously close to or threateningly far from, sometimes, even simultaneously within and beyond, the "civilised residences" of married people and families'.[13] The real threat, then, was that they lived among everyone else. *They* were the threat from within.

This book carefully considers the myriad and complex relationships between queer male masculinity and interior design, material culture and aesthetics in Britain between 1885 and 1957 – that is *bachelors of a different sort* – through rich, well-chosen case studies. The domestic, and not the public domain, I suggest, was the landscape in which the battles over masculine identity and male sexuality were waged. The cases as I have positioned them here affirm a commingling of sex, gender and design as it cuts across fictional, embodied, performed and lived-in spaces. The seven deadly sins of the modern bachelor, as I have identified them and to be discussed later in this chapter, comprise a contested site freighted with contradiction, vacillating between and revealing the fraught and distinctly queer twining of shame and resistance. In a more recent context, gay shame for David Halperin and Valerie Traub refers to those 'queers that mainstream gay pride is not always proud of, who don't lend themselves easily to the propagandistic publicity of gay pride or to its identity-affirming functions'.[14] However shame is neither new nor particular to contemporary internalized expressions of disgust and sexual identity. Rather, like discursive and community-based practices they boast long and storied histories. Compromising a separate chapter, each case study provides evidence of unique and parallel queer expressions of sexuality and masculinity within the spaces of the modern interior. Given I view queer as multifaceted and polyvalent, in no way do I wish to conclude that one queer mode of expression is either better, 'good' or even queerer than another. Importantly, the bachelors I discuss, whether in a long-term stable or open relationship or non-committal series of relationships, developed entire material and aesthetic programmes as a result of or by way of their queer masculinity.

All the bachelors whose aesthetic lives comprise this book were middle- and upper-class men of the creative arts, whether as writers, collectors, playwrights, actors, designers, antiquarians, sculptors, painters, photographers and/or illustrators. In each and every case, the domestic realm and interior design, that is, the material conditions and products of these men's creativity, have largely been ignored in traditional surveys of their work, with the notable exception of Charles Shannon and Charles Ricketts (the subjects of Chapter 3). In her thoughtful investigation of the domestic conditions of some key literary figures Diana Fuss cogently states that 'creative genius is idealized as unfettered imagination, transcending base materiality, something cut loose from the mere bodily act of putting pen to paper – a mechanical gesture'.[15] With an eye toward a post-Cartesian blueprint that seeks to recognize that creative, intellectual minds require and are products of embodied praxis, the projects and projections of interior space also become inseparable from cultural production itself. Following from Fuss's conclusion that domestic interiors form a vital force in the creative processes of writers, I too wish to question how domestic space and interior design inhabit the work of these men as much as to explore the phenomenological and sensory affect engendered by the men who created, lived and loved in these spaces.[16] In this connection I summon the posthumous publication of E. M. Forster's recollection of the sensory affect his visits to the home of homogenic, socialist activist Edward Carpenter and his long-term companion George Merrill had on the writer, which by his own admission led directly to the creation of his beautiful and highly acclaimed novel *Maurice* (1971). Here it is worth quoting his interactions, sensations and conclusions at length as they reveal much in the way of the complicity between space, sensual physicality and creativity for the queer bachelor. Of his time with the two men, Forster wrote:

> It must have been on my second or third visit to the shrine that the spark was kindled and he and his comrade George Merrill combined to make a profound impression on me and to touch a creative spring. George Merrill also touched my backside – gently and just above the buttocks. I believe he touched most people's. The sensation was unusual and I still remember it, as I remember the position of a long vanished tooth. It was as much psychological as physical. It seemed to go straight through the small of my back into my ideas, without involving my thoughts. If it really did this, it would have acted in strict accordance with Carpenter's yogified mysticism, and would prove that at that precise moment I had conceived.
>
> I then returned to Harrogate, where my mother was taking a cure, and immediately began to write *Maurice*. No other of my books has started off in this way. The general plan, the three characters, the happy ending for two of them, all rushed into my pen.[17]

Forster equates his unlikely and unfamiliar sensation to a missing tooth, a now phantom body part, a prosthetic device for sensate memory. 'Base materiality' inspires and serves to enliven and ensure his creativity. In this passage he also admits to the important causal relationship between body, creativity and queer domestic space in his marked experience. Finally, it is also important to note the movement and migration that necessarily took place for the burst of creativity to occur, revealing how both time and space are vital ingredients in the erotic and even phallic nature of the swelling pen of creation. Here fiction, creativity itself, was the very real and material result of the exemplary and, for some, coveted domestic lifestyle Carpenter and Merrill shared.

Memorializing the interior
Penny Sparke and Susie McKellar have importantly argued that there is a 'disjunction between the heavily documented idealised interiors and ephemeral and poorly documented *lived-in* interiors'.[18] In the case of aesthetic bachelors, fact and fiction, lived-in and idealized spaces are never too far apart, however. This book attempts to map the actual, visual, material, aesthetic and spatio-sexual cultures of the dwellings these bachelors fashioned. The work of one particular scholar still, almost two decades later, stands out as exemplary in this regard. In her groundbreaking volume *Sexuality and Space*, Beatriz Colomina compels her reader to consider how architecture, or more exactly space, is 'a system of representation' and forces us to pay heed to the idea that space is already a part of the history and realities of sexuality and the multiplicity of its performances. As I will argue throughout, space as a 'system of representation' codes the reception and perception of interiors, defined by way of those you pass through it or stand outside peering in through the lens of social control.

I wish to avoid vagueness and generalization, and as a result I pay close attention to particular homes and domestic interiors of Lord Ronald Gower, Alfred Taylor, Oscar Wilde, Charles Shannon and Charles Ricketts, Edward Perry Warren and John Marshall, Sir Cedric Morris and Arthur Lett-Haines, Noël Coward and Cecil Beaton. In order to best achieve a more holistic portrayal of these men's practices of design, aesthetics and sexuality, the complete human sensorium is taken into account where possible and plausible to invoke the sounds, sights, smells, touches and tastes of dwelling; one could refer to these as the sensory landscape of identity. These spaces are symptoms of and enable orientation along this landscape, and, like the way 'we reside in space, then sexual orientation might also be a matter of residence, of how we inhabit spaces, and who or what we inhabit spaces with'.[19] By offering 'cognitive maps'[20] phenomenology advocates we move, act and perceive the world through the objects that occupy spaces: these are the very objects that help situate our own embodied experiences of being-in-the-designed-world. The design of space powerfully evokes sensate recollections and enlivens inchoate sexual formulations. When John Addington Symonds recalled his birthplace at 7 Berkeley Square, London, he described these spaces and their decorative details as loci that depressed and stifled him. He retold how 'a dingy dining room and a little closet leading through glass doors into a dusty back garden' were amongst the most oppressive in the 'suffocating atmosphere of a narrow sect … resembling … a close parlour'.[21] Space can be an orientation toward pleasure as much as toward pain, fear or threat, resistance and shame.

Representations, whether visual, textural, sensory, textual or literary, regardless of whence they come, possess an equivocal relationship with actual, lived practices and the totality of their experiences, but they serve a useful purpose nevertheless. They are, after all, all that remain. The narrative of the senses is largely informed by and formed through a Proustian *mémoire involontaire* as much as *mémoire volontaire*, and as a result, as with photographs of no longer extant spaces, we must also bear in mind the implicit and tacit mediation which necessarily occurs in sensory representations. They are vital here as they reveal, in varied ways, the manner in which memory holds traces of the gendered and sexual identity of interiors. Photographic images, while vital to reconstructing or understanding the way these men fashioned themselves through their interiors, do nevertheless engender a distance between the viewer/researcher and the embodied spaces explored. 'Visual representations of interiors are not simply transparent to spatial referents, even if such spatial referents exist; representations construct interiors on a two-dimensional surface as much as practices of decoration and furnishing construct interiors spatially.'[22] Personal diaries are equally mediated, self-edited and rehearsed expressions of social control and expectations, themselves representations on a par with visual imagery. Autobiography and biography, subjective recollections, play an important part in this project for they help to conjure links, values and important associations for a community. Auto/biographies also help to form important mental pictures of the interior and, like photographs, act as mediations of embodied experiences that orient our perceptions of historically bound lived-in space. Memories, reminiscences and memoirs are the product of an attenuation over time, a deferral tempered or aggrandized by time itself and life's events. Memoirs and recollections are heavily relied upon in certain chapters. Biographies are only partial glimpses, however; perceptions based solely on a position as outsider, a sort of interloper within the spatial culture of the home. Autobiographies, on the other hand, provide different knowledge of the interior. The text of life-writing tends to reinforce the spatial aspect of the interior, in as much as it acts as a textual reinterpretation of one's own awareness or illiteracy of the interior; a self-conscious re-imaging or even denial of the experiences and expressions of the interior. Finally, literary reminiscences are both abstract and tangible as they reveal, describe and memorialize the experiential, phenomenological and aesthetic culture of lived-in space. It seems rather fitting, therefore, that I should begin (Gower) and end (Beaton) with chapters devoted to men who memorialized the interiors of their most cherished country estates through the publication of a book. While the interior played a formidable role in the life and creative output of all the bachelors included here, Gower and Beaton took it one step further by memorializing their homes in both words and images. Language provides a mediated and not unproblematic experience of the senses and spatial perception. The middle classes have always been all too eager, after all, to ensure and maintain a certain type of representation that was in keeping with their ideals and notions of self-fashioning, rather than the realities of their day-to-day machinations (realities that often blurred the boundaries demarcating class distinction above or below their social station). Representations in their myriad forms and functions, then, can only ever partially boast a holistic look into the queer expressions of space and design. Taken together they can help to recreate as much as is possible interiors and the embodied practices which enliven them.

I am interested in and intrigued by the different ways various forms of representations help to narrate the perceptions and chorography of the domestic landscape as these become spaces for the formation of identity, community and cultural production. I seek to open up, where possible, a metaphorical dimension to the study of domestic interiors, that of the human subjective, whose identity and identification with these spaces create meanings because and in excess of their three dimensions. After all, sexuality and aesthetics are not the sole purview of opticality and visual culture but are formed through the polyvalent experiences of the human sensorium, group and personal perceptions, and social and cultural codes in excess of actual physicality. Historical scholarship is fundamentally an act of giving or renewing a voice that has been silenced. This is especially true and vital for those operating on the margins, whose stories have doubly been silenced. As is often the case with histories exploring marginalized groups, archival, pictorial and textual resources are scarce, fragmentary and opaque at best. The task of rebuilding is not an easy one.

As a result, my various cases in differing ways highlight the methodological quagmire that a project of this nature necessarily enlists. By this I aim to suggest the various types of objects and materials admitted into the frame of this investigation. No pictures remain, for example, of Alfred Taylor's, Oscar Wilde's or Sir Cedric Morris and Arthur Lett-Haines's respective homes. All that can be deployed are court proceedings, media reportage or numerous contemporary reports by colleagues and friends in diaries and journals. This seemingly unbalanced picture, which at times appears to privilege textual over visual or material sources, is, however, a sign of the technological, social and cultural conditions of these men's lives. On the whole, I rely on photographs, diaries, journals, periodicals, recollections, treatises and auto/biographies as tools toward achieving my goal. Given the varied nature of the queer bachelors I explore in this book, I have elected to deploy an equally diverse, queer methodology akin to Judith Halberstam's investigation of female masculinities inasmuch as I use literary, visual and material culture analysis, auto/biographies, contemporary commentaries, archival research, popular criticism and historical survey when and where necessary though never exclusively. My avoidance of confining myself to one particular method allows a freedom to honour the variance of the cases and is itself a 'refusal' to conform 'to methodological consistency' and patriarchal norms.[23] The book, then, develops a varied methodological and theoretical framework for each chapter to stay as 'faithful' to the unique, eclectic and idiosyncratic expressions of the modern interior.

Queer time and space

Halberstam argues that '[i]f we try to think about queerness as an outcome of strange temporalities, imaginative life schedules, and eccentric economic practices, we detach queerness from sexual identity and come close to understand [Michel] Foucault's comment in "Friendship as a Way of Life" that "homosexuality threatens people as a 'way of life' rather than as a way of having sex"'.[24] Part of what distinguishes the bachelors in this book as queer and defines the parameters of the book itself is their alternative and subversive relationships to space, materiality and time. Queer life does not follow an ideal blueprint. How could it, when none exists? Nor does it adhere to the socially sanctioned heteronarrative in which key defining markers of space and time punctuate a subject's life, namely marriage and procreation, which help to define normalizing temporal scripts of interiors and habitation.[25] These normalizing scripts of temporal development and social progress are premised on the notional separate spheres that are in turn divided along the lines of gender and labour. Cross-sex relationships act as socially acceptable purveyors of longevity, progeny and stability as they develop along a narratological model that sees a so-called natural progression of things which privileges genetic offspring over cultural legacy. In his often neglected yet poignant interview, 'Friendship as a Way of Life', Foucault pointed to the problems of characterizing male same-sex intimacy by posing the following series of questions: 'How is it possible for men to be together? To live together, to share their time, their meals, their room, their leisure, their grief, their knowledge, their confidences? What is it to be naked among men, outside of institutional relations, family, profession, and obligatory camaraderie?'[26] Expanding on Foucault's critical enquiry, this book seeks out similar lines of questioning while extending into the arena of aesthetics, space and material culture and their effect on male bonds, filiation and sexual identity. It investigates how interior design provided an ideal opportunity for the formation and coding of a queer masculinity and how, in turn, these interiors could be informed by the ways men re-imaged and re-imagined the home, sharing their lives separate from and yet imbricated in dominant, normative definitions of domesticity and masculinity. We must ask ourselves what are the aesthetic, cultural, social, economic and political implications of interweaving one's life with another person of the same sex? How did the domestic realm as a stage for the performance of masculinity as well as the perception and reception of same-sex relationships function as the embryo for the formation of productive communities on the one hand and steadfast stereotypes still in circulation today on the other? The object is to devise a blueprint, not universal but case-specific, through which to re-evaluate the role the home played for men in their cultural production, collaboration and partnerships moving beyond the active/passive, dominant/submissive axis. After all, queer lifestyles are so much more a product of alternative modes, orientations, expressions and articulations of the everyday, than outcomes purely resulting from the practices of sex.

To achieve this broad intellectual concern, *Bachelors of a different sort* has three primary theoretical, historical and historiographic threads of inquiry that intersect at a defining moment in British cultural history. First and foremost is a need to insert a broad definition of desire, pleasure and shame into the history of domestic interior design and the decorative arts. This need also acknowledges how domestic spaces and objects highlight the commitment of their inhabitants to desire, intimacy, domesticity and community. As a parallel phenomenon to the first, the second thread references the spatially defined and circumscribed homosexual as a type that shifted emphasis away from random acts of intimacy to acts constitutent of a specific and identifiable identity. Taking off from previous scholarship on queer identities and the history of homosexuality, I wish to cross the threshold moving from the public arena (where sex acts took place and communities were formed) into the home wherein intimacy, identities, design, collecting and communities provided shelter, care and space to materialize the tensions of modernity itself.

Broad in its implications, the third and final issue, which pulls the previous two threads tighter together, exposes how sexuality itself as well as the domestic sphere raises the question of historiography and methodology. In simple terms, the formidable character of Wilde has tended to dominate the scholarship on British male homosexuality and in large measure has also helped to define queer identity for the general public in the English-speaking West ever since his demise. Scandalous and sensational, the case of Wilde (in particular) and his cohort Taylor (by association) have remained central in the public and scholarly mind. In contrast, lifelong companions Ricketts and Shannon, friends and associates of Wilde, led an 'exemplary' bourgeois (both aesthetic and middle-class) existence and have subsequently and interestingly been largely overlooked by a generation of modernist scholars invested in avant-gardist (heterosexual and masculinist) modern art movements, which have all too easily and conveniently been pitted against the perceived excess and decadence of Victorian visual and material culture. The varied experiences of male homosexuality *vis-à-vis* the public and private spheres suggest that certain facts, people and places go unnoticed while others continue to affect and define sexual identity, scholarship, the histories of sexuality and aesthetics, and public perception.

In this introductory chapter I set out to: first, chart a man's fraught and tense place within the home; second, underscore the discursive history and conceptual parameters of the bachelor as these collided with queer sexualities through social and cultural perceptions; third, align the fraught terrain (sexual and otherwise) of the queer bachelor, that is, *bachelors of a different sort*, with ideals of material culture and the domestic realm; and, fourth, elucidate what I identify as the seven deadly sins of the modern bachelor, terms which simultaneously mark sites of derision and shame and sources of empowerment and liberation, antagonistic forces in the experience and expressions of embodiment. This introduction leads us off to explore the first and deadliest of sins, queerness. At its most basic queer is that which binds the men included in this book together. In the very least, apart from an acute inclination toward and heightened sense of the aesthetic, these men possessed a rather queer sense of the interior, material culture, aesthetics and, of course, sexuality. While many of these men lived out their lives in several homes and interiors, each chapter does not pretend to offer complete life histories of each man or couple, but reveals fragments that best offer us settings to further understand queer spaces of the modern interior. Like coming out of the closet (itself a product of modernity), the modern interior is a space always in process, never complete, never static.

A man's home
If the Industrial Revolution sought to revolutionize and rationalize labour, production and industrial performance, it also inadvertently transformed the way people lived, loved and performed their gender.

In his investigation of the nineteenth-century interior, a spatial as much as conceptual constellation, Charles Rice contends that 'the interior emerged in a domestic sense as a new topos of subjective interiority, and ... practices of self-representation in the context of domestic life'.[27] Heterosexual masculinity was formed in and informed by its relationships to wife and children, identities and relationships coded by the purportedly confining strictures of the domestic sphere. As a result, men began to understand their public function and private role very differently; the spatial centre of their masculinity forever gravitated toward the necessities and allure of the public domain, a masculinity increasingly over-determined by the conflicting needs of a separated home life and a thirsty empire. Since the early part of the nineteenth century, men, like women in entirely differing ways, have held conflicting and ever-evolving relationships to the domestic realm with equally fraught expectations placed upon them; these expectations have shaped, defined and codified their social worth. Men's relationship to the domestic has only more recently come to bear on the history of gender. Historian John Tosh in particular has been at the forefront of charting men's dubious relationship to this private realm beginning in the nineteenth century. He notes how with every passing decade, 'domestic routine grew more comprehensive and more constraining'.[28] In large measure, the rhetoric and structures (discursive and actual) of domestication were also a response to the intensifying phenomena of rapid urbanization and industrialization increasingly taking their toll on traditional notions of masculinity and the familial unit, moving both into new territory. The 1880s and 1890s in Britain marked a period of contrasting and competing forces that increasingly mapped out a blueprint that separated domestic narratives from work life. The growing separation of men from a more complete experience of the home's cultural life resulted when they began to labour and toil outside its walls, and women increasingly became unaware of and uninvolved in the work environment of their mates. Prior to this men often sought out women within the same profession, who added to the household income and mental and physical force. The last quarter of the century also witnessed men carving out meaningful lives outside of companionate marriage either by maintaining a lifestyle premised on all-male society or just simply by postponing marriage, forcing 'the characteristically Victorian culture of domesticity' into 'a new phase'.[29] By the interwar period the supposed sexual liberation of a new generation informed the increased independence from the traditional and more mundane ideals attributed to the domestic realm. The plethora of treatises, manuals and essays on conduct and domestic management did not simply refer to the home as a constellation of physical and spatial features, but rather set out to establish definitive and requisite moral codes, a limited assortment of possible behaviours for men and women understood in terms of companionate marriage.[30] Throughout the nineteenth and well into the twentieth century masculinity was indelibly tied to public destiny and empire-building, particularly the 'preferred forms of masculinity'. Even the term bachelor as a domestic possibility included a decidedly colonial flavour with expressions like 'baching it', and 'bachelorizing' referring to those living in the colonies, with men establishing themselves in the 'new world'.[31] The so-called 'true Englishman' dominated the 'conception of masculine identity' and suggested a vital collusion between heroism and nation-building, through either free-market enterprise or colonial expansion.[32] The rise of colonial conquests and the need to serve Crown and country additionally bestowed on many men an alternative, suitable and honourable vocation, shifting their attention to an all-male culture, and reinforced the gender divide associated with the domestic realm. If the colonies served to intensify and aggrandize the link between masculinity and empire, then they also ensured to forever sever the bond that might have flourished between masculinity and domesticity in the modern era.[33] For hegemonic masculinity, colonial outposts and the domestic sphere became equally uncharted, unknown and possibly threatening territories.

The gulf between men's antagonistic and fraught relationship with the domestic sphere and the home itself would only accelerate throughout the twentieth century. As a result of the increasing codification of both the so-called separate spheres and sexual difference, men progressively turned to alternative spaces and sought out venues in which homosociability was welcomed, celebrated and even expected. Large numbers of men, particularly in London, actively sought out the desires and pleasures of same-sex companionship and began to transform spaces and places to accommodate them. Venues such as boarding schools and clubs allowed men of all ages to escape the constraints of domestic servitude. Various institutions accommodated male homosociability politically, culturally and economically and equipped men to forestall marriage and hence the purportedly constricting confines of the home. As Amy Milne-Smith demonstrates: 'Men's retreat to homosocial spaces and activities thus signalled not only an escape from the tyranny of the Victorian home but also a search for a new form of emotional life'.[34] However, it is also important to make note of the contradictory and contrasting moral codes, which tacitly suggested that, although the number of bachelors in the city increased with every passing decade, beginning in the 1860s such a choice or preference was viewed with contempt and suspicion because it wilfully reneged on the patriarchal ideals of lineage, a stabilizing familial, economic and political force.

In his *The Wilds of London* from 1874, a collection taken from a serialized column, James Greenwood devoted a chapter to 'the comforts of home' in which he questioned what was meant by the term *home*. Did it 'simply comprehend a cheery room, happy faces, cosy hearthrug, tea-and-toast, and that sort of thing', he queried. Greenwood remarks that these might be found in any location one might travel to, and, however good in quality and cheerfulness in temperament these might prove to be, they fell short of what it truly meant to be at 'home'. The exercise to determine one's place was to 'go no farther than [one's] window. Where are the familiar faces, and sights, and sounds that tend to the perfection of that tranquillity and repose expressed in that magic little word of four letters?'[35] However, who or what constituted the objects within the landscape of the home one fashioned through the mind's eye? Greenwood evokes the issue of class and those who comprised the domestic landscape when he called into doubt what to make of 'that muddy boy, with his straight red hair sprouting like early crocuses through his tattered cap, and who blithely carols "Hop light, Loo," as he trudges home with a stumpy birchroom on his shoulder? ... You are familiar with his appearance – he is a recognized object in your "home" picture; tell us something about him".'[36] Within the delightful and personalized representation one constructed of one's home, its labour-intensive maintenance was objectified, and necessarily altered the memories of the home. The men who laboured in the gentleman's home remained complete strangers to its master, he knew nothing of their lives or work. In silence and near invisibility, these men conspired to fashion a home for their master. Greenwood concludes by reifying the national ethos that a man's home is his castle:

> In reality your house is your world, and your sympathies are bound by the four walls of it. The familiar faces and things visible from the loopholes of your castle may conduce to your enjoyment of home as the sight of falling snow or accumulated ice enhances the worth of a glowing grateful of Wallsend coals; but as far as your real knowledge of the passers to and fro is concerned, you might as well look out on a desert.[37]

Greenwood's prose reminds us of the fundamental detachment by which the middle and upper classes live out the spaces of their homes and the disembodied memories these evoke. Rob Shields has more recently identified 'topophilia' as 'human's affective ties with their environment which couples sentiment with place'.[38] Topophilia takes on a decidedly unique quality in the British context, embodied either in the migration Oxford and Cambridge graduates undertook from the idealized hallowed halls of academia to their new homes or in the British traveller who attempted to adapt local environments to suit English domestic ideals. In both instances, men attempted a cultural and spatial translation in which they aimed for the familiar amidst the foreign.

The establishment of a 'household creates the conditions for private life, but it has also long been a crucial stage in winning social recognition as an adult, a fully masculine person; until women were admitted to the political process, to speak for one's family in the public arena conferred weight which was denied to the single man'.[39] Not only was private life denied to the single man, the implications were undeniably heteronormative. By the end of the nineteenth century, queer men were increasingly searching out their own expressions of safety, comfort and productivity within the inner sanctum of hearth and home. The comfort and design of the home was something altogether different. Deemed feminine, the care for the home stood foursquare at odds with the goal of getting on with the business of the nation. As Synder reminds us: 'Bourgeois domesticity as an ideology was not based on marriage *per se*, but on the gendered division of labour and the construction of a private realm as the locus of true selfhood, a realm different from that of the marketplace'.[40] We would do well to remember that the emergence of domesticity as an ideal was connected to 'the rise of industrial capitalism and imperialism',[41] and I would importantly add the development of modern sexual typologies.

Decoration, as Thad Logan points out, 'does ideological work'. It does so by announcing the home's 'difference from the public world, to mark [its] separation from the marketplace, to mask the fact of [its] participation in the narrative of capitalism'.[42] Not only are the myriad objects displayed in the home a product of the accumulation of capital, but so too is the bourgeois notion of property a by-product of capitalism, the idea that a man has the right to ownership of his own home whatever form this may take. As Sharon Marcus has noted, '[d]omesticity was too costly for working-class families, since it required not only having a home but also possessing sufficient household income to pay for *bric-à-brac* and multiple rooms with separate functions'.[43] Interesting is how *bric-à-brac*, the objects of consumptions, the effects of capitalism, factor into the qualities and necessities of domesticity in Victorian Britain. While the less-is-more ethos would not define the British modern home until the 1930s, the careful and thoughtful accumulation of objects would remain a constant in the definition of bourgeois domesticity. In her article, 'Furnishing a Man's Room: A Woman's View of the Problem' for *Homes and Gardens*, Clarice Moffat attended to the dilemmas associated with providing bachelors with a proper and adequate home when she wrote that

> [f]urnishing and decorating a man's room presents problems that are all its own. Heaven knows, it is not indifference to his surroundings that the average man evinces. No one who has tried to find a home for some

unwanted ornament by placing it in the room of husband or brother; no one who has tried to bring order out of chaos by the removal of junk which, once gone, is bitterly referred to as property of priceless practical and sentimental worth; no one who has listened to the subsequent frenzied complaints and accusations will ever accuse a man of indifference. No, it is rather a too detailed category of like and dislike which greets the would-be planner: space for books and wireless, a wardrobe that combines the functions of tailor and storage emporium, places not only clothes but also for all those unclassified and unclassifiable possessions which clutter tables, chairs and jacket pockets.[44]

Moffat concluded that there was also a clear gendered divergence in what was understood as a necessity to properly furnish one's home with. She remarked: 'Ask the average man to state consciously what he wants in the way of furnishing, and he will say briefly: "No frills, nothing impractical, nothing odd." Seemingly simple requirements, but there is a vast discrepancy between the masculine and feminine classification of such things. Take lighting, for instance. Those little bedside lamps so dear to a feminine heart, with their adjustable shades and neat gadgets, arouse no responsive echo in the masculine.'[45]

However, by the mid-1920s bachelor flats were perceived as not conducive to the display of *bric-à-brac*, a result of trying to accommodate a man within increasingly tighter quarters, but also a means towards the re-virilization of the single man in a period of increased adherence to the dictates of modernism and its staunch anti-Victorian stance. In an essay from 1925, *House and Gardens* claimed that

> [o]ur Victorian forebears had the unfortunate knack of making everything ill proportioned. Their rooms have invariably the fault of being too high in proportion to their area or too square to their height, or possessing some undesirable feature which renders satisfactory decoration a very difficult task unless drastic structural alterations are resorted to … There being but one living-room in these bachelor chambers, it became imperative to resort to a weeding-out process, with the result that the quality of the small collection gradually improved and became more interesting, until, after a lapse of many years' patient hunting and discrimination, something approaching finality was arrived at … The contents of the room are nondescript as regards period. 'Period' rooms are always inclined to be stiff and formal. A more interesting and pleasing effect can be achieved by the association of pieces which, although dating from varying periods and having many contradictions in point of style, yet possess a certain harmonious relationship.[46]

Men were no longer meant to be connoisseurs of the specific, but rather discreet accumulators of objects meant to harmonize across time, place and style; a nod to the modernist zeal which pitted period rooms as old-fashioned and moribund against a trans-historical, universalizing aesthetic. By the 1930s, *Homes and Gardens* was declaring everyone, men and women alike, to be a 'small collector'. Consumption and collecting have traditionally been conceptualized as antagonistic, valued differently along the line of gender. Collecting, nonetheless, 'allows both genders to participate in the feminine world of consumption in a way that simultaneously supports the masculine world of production'.[47] The best setting for objects of choice was no longer the perceived moribund display cases of the Victorians; 'no attempt made to treat them only as rare and depressing, museum pieces. In this way too, their presence provides that individual touch by which the personality of their collector is expressed'.[48] The careful choice and accumulation of objects destined for the limited spaces of a bachelor's home collectively functioned at once as both emblems of taste and status as well as totems to ward off the encroaching severity of industrialization and modernization lurking in the streets of the city. Yet at the same time the home and its interiors were meant to embrace modernity not simply as an aesthetic ideal, but as all-encompassing lifestyle and identity. Following the Second World War the neologism of the 'bachelor pad' took on a decidedly hetero-masculinist tone and ideal, largely fuelled by men's magazines and Hollywood films. As Bill Osgerby has evocatively shown, in the postwar period in the USA, what emerged 'was a man who was affluent and independent, with a sense of individuality crafted around fashionable display and the pleasures of commodity consumption – yet this was also a man who took care that his aesthetic tastes marked him out as avowedly heterosexual and resolutely "manful"'.[49]

Historian George Chauncey sees bachelor subcultures in New York as anti-domestic, '[e]mbodying a rejection of domesticity and of bourgeois acquisitiveness alike'.[50] While this is likely to have been the case for those men whose economic bracket impelled them to live in small lodging houses and rooms, it is certainly not the case for the men I present in this book. These British bachelors were astute collectors, men who sought to redefine the parameters of domestic life and fashion a new cultural order. In the United States, as Elizabeth Collins Cromley argues, the bachelor question was 'quite insistently posed by the explosion of popular magazine writing about bachelors in the second half of the nineteenth century, and particularly these writings lavished on the bachelor home and on such bachelor homemaking activities as interior decoration and cooking'.[51] As recurrent characters, bachelors were often socially perceived and interpolated into literary narratives as 'threshold figures that marked the permeable boundaries that separate domesticity, normative manhood, and high-cultural status, from what was defined as extrinsic to these realms'.[52] The emergence and growing popularity of the bachelor flat on the cusp of the twentieth century, in large measure, underlined one of many fears of a modernizing age. The modelling of the bachelor's home and its interior design forced late Victorians to rethink and re-imagine the home in entirely novel ways, supported by consumption and new theories about the display of *objets d'art*, leaving many to feel uncomfortable.

Defining the modern home

In his study of the Haussmanization of Paris (1852–70) and the processes of modernization which gripped the City of Lights, Walter Benjamin wrote how 'the bourgeois has shown a tendency to compensate for the absence of any trace of private life in the big city. He tries to do this within the four walls of his apartment.'[53] This modernizing zeal coupled with a constant and unnerving shock of urban development with its destabilizing chaos forced those who could afford its trappings to seek refuge in an idealized bourgeois interior. Bourgeois ethics led to the creation of a perfect, honourable domain, a domesticated realm entirely of the bourgeois' own devising; a complete and collective design enterprise in artificiality by an entire class subsumed within a rhetoric of individuality. The ethics of design and the codes of gender and sexuality were indelibly linked as a result. By the nineteenth century, the bourgeois home stood as the embodiment of the nation, its borders rendered sacred and fortified by the ever-increasing gender divide. British art and cultural critic John Ruskin wrote that the home was the

> place of Peace; the shelter, not only from all injury, but from all terror, doubt, and division. In so far as it is not this, it is not home; so far as the anxieties of the outer life penetrate into it, and the inconsistently-minded, unknown, unloved, or hostile society of the outer world is allowed by either husband or wife to cross the threshold, it ceases to be home.[54]

The fictional, though powerful, notional public/private divide was symbolically and architecturally delineated by way of the threshold and maintained through the ideals of individuality that in turn could be visualized and materialized in the objects collected, consumed and displayed in the home. To blur, sully or destroy the threshold was to threaten hearth and home as well as the people and even objects that populated it. The home became a complex mapping device for the individual, a world of his/her own divining. But what to make of those men who were forced, compelled or who desired to locate home outside of the landscape of cross-sex familial relations?

Men had to find their own way through a burgeoning domestic architecture and broadening landscape of domestic lifestyles. In the industrial metropolises of New York, Paris and London new types of dwelling spaces began to appear in the latter half of the nineteenth century to accommodate a new and emerging breed of man of varying classes who sought and acquired work in the offices and factories of empire. Building single-dwelling flats for single women in the last quarter of the nineteenth century proved to be a more difficult endeavour, particularly in cities like New York, where it remained socially unacceptable for the so-labelled fairer sex to reside alone within the dangerous landscape of the metropolis.[55] Social stigma for young men, on the other hand, could be avoided. By 1870 New York, for example, claimed 125,000 bachelors living in the country's largest city. While hotels were an ideal and at times preferred option for the wealthy, affordable accommodations for middle- and working-class bachelors were in short supply. In 1876 architect E. T. Littell suggested bachelor units with a parlour, without dining room or kitchen, premised on the belief that most bachelors ate out in clubs and restaurants or with their friends. In this way, buildings that accommodated bachelor flats could be run like a club with membership fees to eat in the communal dinning room.[56] In these early days of bachelor living, the average flat had only two rooms: the bedroom and the parlour.

In the latter half of the nineteenth century, English men began to seek out their own flats, apartments, lodgings and boarding homes. However, according to Marcus, '[a]llmost no purpose-built apartment houses were constructed in London before the 1880s: there were sets of chambers for single men, a moderate number of "model dwellings for the working classes," and fewer than ten buildings offering "luxury flats"' suited to the all-consuming social season of the city.[57] Notably, chambers such as those in Henry Ashton's Victorian Street Apartments (1853), Belgrave Mansions (1867), Albert Mansions (1870), the Queen Anne's Gate near St James's Park (1874), F. Butler's Victoria Street flats (1877) and New Kent Road flats (1876) were small and were formed as hybrid spatial networks that straddled accommodation types of, on the one hand, hotels with their amenities and services (meal preparation and cleaning) and solitary dormitories, on the other. The famed Albany, for example, also had purpose-built chambers to accommodate bachelors and became so fashionable, and equally fascinating, that it formed the backdrop to such popular literary characters as those found in Marmion Savage's *The Bachelor of Albany* (1847) and Wilde's *The Importance of Being Earnest* (1895), although in Wilde's case he clearly envisioned a larger space. Many of the apartments built in the last decades of the nineteenth century were believed to provide shelter for no one distinct group; a troubling ambiguity for social commentators. They were created in the hope of attracting an 'indefinite group' that ultimately did not come from a social set that demanded and grew up in luxury or from the 'precarious trades and professions, a class which [could scarcely] afford higher rents than from £70 to £150 per annum'.[58]

Domestic decorum and propriety in property did not simply refer to one's own home but its location within the urban topography; the choice of location was as important a factor to consider as any. Unlike the Parisians and New Yorkers, Londoners were quite reluctant to adopt apartment living, fearing, among other things, closeness to their neighbours. England prided itself on and cultivated an identity premised on a clear sense of distinction and isolation; likewise, urban inhabitants were meant to follow suit.[59] Spatial boundaries between rooms and between people were vital in the proper functioning of modern spaces for British domesticity. J. J. Stevenson remarked that, unlike in a French home where rooms flowed into each other, the distinctly English characteristic of rooms must see each divided with pre-established boundaries and thresholds. If not, then a 'room loses its value to us if it is a passage to another. The dining room must be capable of being shut off from the rest of the house, communicating during dinner only with the kitchen. The dinner should not have to be carried past the drawing room door, or through the hall and public passages, and the kitchens must be so placed that their smells and noise not invade the house.'[60] Within his formulation of the various component spaces that comprise the unifying whole of a home it was the topography coupled with the phenomenological experiences of its parts that stand out as the most essential. The modern British house, for Stevenson, possessed a number of key characteristics: isolation; unity; convenience; compactness and simplicity; light and air; warmth; and architectural effect.

Immanuel Kant once declared the home to be 'the only rampart against the dread of nothingness, darkness, and the obscurity of the past … The man without a home is a potential criminal.'[61] Throughout the nineteenth century, lodgings and boarding houses in particular were seen as a threat not simply to a man's privacy but to social order itself. As of the 1840s it was commonly held that because lodging houses 'are not let by floors or even by sets of rooms; they are dovetailed into each other. All who have had practical experience of such interiors cannot hesitate to admit, that in the majority of them, the worst features of life in common as it was practiced [sic] centuries ago have been preserved; the best have been irrevocably forgotten.'[62] The implication was that the various lodgers (complete strangers) would come into contact with each other, blurring boundaries of propriety and property. Tracts decrying London's city life abound in which the lodging home embodies its ills and evils.[63] Also at issue was space, or the lack thereof, which it was believed led to all sorts of evils, namely sexual promiscuity and looseness. In his book *The Pauper, the Thief, and the Convict: Sketches of Some of Their Homes, Haunts and Habits* from 1865 Thomas Archer went so far as to equate the common lodging with the brothel.[64] Flats were seen as a more ideally suited alternative to lodging houses for those of good breeding as well as for elderly people and those of the poorer classes, as these are then 'enabled to live in pleasant surroundings'.[65] Flats, it was held, would be better able to uphold the domestic twin pillars of privacy and comfort. However, the tenants of flats were considered 'very dirty people', and as a result it was recommended that 'a distempered wall is preferable to a wall paper'.[66] Flats were also better equipped to withstand the seeming transience and constant movement of urban life, a product of rapid urbanization and the conditions of modernity itself. Themselves products of a modern thinking, flats embodied a precarious refutation of family life as well as the ideals of generational attachments to hearth and home, inheritance and property. Flats would eventually be rejected by the middle classes and taken up by the very wealthy and bachelors of the city, the latter believed to embody this refutation of family life and its coeval ideals.

The concern for class in Britain also extended itself to the incursion of trades people into the private homes of its respectable citizens. By the twentieth century it was made clear that in 'London the reason for excluding service staircases is generally the desire to keep tradesman's boys out of the house, and to avoid the uncontrollable "back door"'.[67] While service lifts replaced the need for comings and goings, one cannot help note the emphasis and sexual subtext of the 'back door' reference, signalled out by quotation marks by the author. As Leonore Davidoff argues, 'back stairs of the home became a euphemism for anus: exit for waste products and objects of disgust'.[68] The supposed 'uncontrollable' nature of the back door tacitly refers to the uncontrollable nature of the labouring classes, unable to contain their urges and propensity towards social disruption. The subtext is once again made clear, that class ambiguity and ambivalence coupled with the omnipresent threat of social evil and dubious hygiene must be controlled spatially when it concerns any home or public housing. Sydney Perks noted in 1905 that

> [i]n looking through old newspapers, it is interesting to see the objections then made to flat; one was the risk of illness from infectious diseases, another was the objection to servants in flats, and a third was, strange to say, the great risk of burglary. Time has shown, with regard to the second and third objections, that a flat has an advantage over an ordinary house, and also that there is cause to fear infection.[69]

Proper design, then, of self-contained flats, apartment buildings and homes was not simply a question of aesthetic comfort and taste, but remained a question of social and physical health in the service of respectability and class structures befitting domestic space and to Britain itself. After all, as Rice notes, the domestic interior took on a clear identity 'through decoration', that is, 'the literal covering of the inside of an architectural "shell" with the "soft" stuff of furnishing'.[70] The modern interior is designed and decorated to accommodate the aesthetics of identity and cultures of power.

The sexual landscape of space
Bachelors of a different sort focuses closely on a relatively short period of time in British history marked by rapid developments and wholesale change in every facet of cultural, aesthetic and social life. The book explores the parallel experiences of modernity, modernism and modern art and design in their uniquely British experience. These importantly coincided with the naming and further policing of sexuality and subsequent related identities as much as they paralleled the emergence of commodity culture as part of identity formation and the fashioning of the modern interior. The loose timeframe for this book is largely predicated on two important benchmark moments in the history of homosexuality in Britain that implicitly, though inadvertently, characterize the manner in which the queer bachelor necessarily negotiated the privacy and publicity of the domestic sphere: the Labouchere Amendment (1885) and the Wolfenden Report (1957).

What the book recounts therefore, if only in part, is what I call the Labouchere generation, the bastard children – or bachelors – that British courts felt needed to be regulated as much in their homes as in public. The interiors these men designed and/or appropriated were not escapist in the sense of removing oneself from the world, but rather were interventions in the everyday expressions of what it meant to be queer in a hostile and ever-changing, modern world. The 1885 amendment not only defined what constituted indecent and degenerate behaviour in the public domain, but more significantly shifted the court's and the public's attention to the private, domestic sphere. It claimed that:

> Any person who, in private or public, commits, or is a party to the commission of, or procures or attempts to procure the commission by any male person of any act of gross indecency with another male person, shall be guilty of a misdemeanour.[71]

It is worth remembering that the Labouchere Amendment was also commonly referred to as the blackmailer's law. As a result, one could never truly be comfortable, even within one's own home. The implications were that the safety and purity that the threshold provided could be sullied by criminal and sinful activity, no longer simply by aberrant sexual activities, but also in terms of a tainted act of blackmail which stood to threaten the inherent ideals of the class system itself. The period was plagued by sex scandals, which helped to precipitate a policing of the private as much as the public. The much-publicized case of the 1889 Cleveland Street scandal, for example, involving high-ranking government officials and members of the royal family in the indecent activities of a homosexual brothel, as well as the Wilde trials of 1895 decisively added a physical, tangible and, more strikingly, spatial dynamic to homophobic panic and pointed to the precariousness of the perceived privacy of the domestic realm, an arena neglected by current scholarship.

The second bookend date refers to the aftermath of the Second World War, which offered very different cultural registers for masculinity and domestic space. In Britain, in an era of increased repression, the homosexual, as a type to be feared and exposed to the authorities, was conceptualized as a direct threat to the definition and stability of domesticity. A Law Society memorandum directly removed homosexual men from within the spaces of the home by simply, though profoundly, asserting that 'male persons living together do not constitute domestic life'.[72] Now, not only were homosexual, gay or queer men meant to perform closeted identities in the public domain, but they were also meant to be invisible within the supposed safety of their home. The love that dared not speak its name also dared not cohabit, reminding us once again that the domestic realm is far less private than it is public, despite our best efforts to carve out some sort of spatial privacy and intimacy.[73] Sparke has argued that 'the boundaries, between the "separate spheres" were fundamentally unstable and it was that instability, rather than the separation per se, that, I will suggest, defined modernity, and by extension the modern interior, reflecting the constant shifting identities and the increasingly fragmented experiences of the inhabitants of the modern world'.[74] The so-called and largely mythologized 'separate spheres' were also largely defined and coded through gender, which in turn prescribed the performances and understandings of sexuality. After all, gender performances are often less about gender per se and more often than not expose the cultural and social expectations placed on sexual identity, which largely services national interests. The Wolfenden Report asserted that, in terms of criminal law, the government could be concerned only with public decency and concluded that 'it is not in our view the function of the law to intervene in the private lives of citizens, or to seek to enforce any particular patterns of behaviour'.[75] There was, according to the report, already a distinction made in British law between sin and crime; in the report these distinctions were made along the public/private spatial axis.[76] While the report went some way toward the decriminalization of homosexuality in Britain, it nevertheless maintained that it was a social and public menace and that a 'happy family home' would provide the necessary antidote for a homosexual 'propensity'.[77] In most spaces, places, conditions, contexts and situations, straightness is taken for granted, assumed and more often than not preferred. For this reason, we must be aware of and investigate how queer subjects negotiated what we today label as heteronormativity and the heterosexual matrix. This spatial alienation and queer dislocation have been, I assert, reaffirmed and perpetuated in contemporary scholarship.

While this book seeks to move away from the medico-juridical premises of sexuality, British courts, nonetheless, have had an important impact on policing the borders and performances of gendered identity, spaces of sexuality, parameters of public perception and experiences of resistance and shame. The use of these two significant historical documents (Labouchere Amendment and Wolfenden Report) does not simply coincide with my case studies, but importantly help to assert and redefine homosexuality and queer identity in distinctly spatial terms along the private/public axis. If, as Matt Houlbrook argues, the city is the site of liberation and freedom as much as it enables the realization of a homosexual identity, it is, as he also notes, the location of fear, alienation, isolation, police raids and imprisonment.[78] Moreover, with the numerous homosex scandals that plagued the last quarter of the nineteenth century, public perception shifted to understand that immorality, degeneracy and sexual perversion could easily traverse the porous borders marking the domestic from the public realm. With this research, then, I seek to shift the attention away from how men could be together in public to how men could sustain a life (whether as a solitary or coupled bachelor) in private, a vital and yet decidedly neglected dimension of current scholarship on sexuality and design histories of the period. The attainment of domestic perfection, often debased and derided for its purportedly feminine nature, constituted an economy understood in terms of non-productive expenditure – a conclusion convincingly called into question by more recent scholarship. By exploring the alternative, bohemian and modern cross-sex community of the Bloomsbury Group, Christopher Reed has convincingly argued that domesticity (read: feminized) and modernism (read: masculinized) have been constructed, after the fact, as antagonistic patterns. As he extensively demonstrates, there exist notable examples of those who fashioned their own identities and cultural production outside of and in response to this opposition.[79] I, too, wish to move beyond such steadfast divisions and binary formulations. What my case studies expose is not simply the facile and arbitrary use of such binary oppositions developed in their own time and maintained by scholars today, but also how they confused the supposedly inherent qualities of domesticity, cultural production and sensual identity.

Discussions of queer space usually begin and end with public expressions of male eroticism, reaffirming men's public (rather than domestic) role as well as reifying the notion that queer men had no real relationship (erotic or otherwise) to the domestic. If the infamous pornographic novel *Teleny* (1893) revealed anything about the spatial aspect of late nineteenth-century queer sexualities, it was that the domestic formed an integral part of erotic desire and even everyday, quotidian pleasures. As Marcus cogently draws out, the novel 'dared to portray a gay desire for domesticity and highlighted the painfulness of gay alienation from homes organized around heterosexuality'.[80] Discussions of queer domesticity then should not, cannot, begin and end exclusively with the erotic. In *Queer Space* Aaron Betsky too easily conflates queer space with eroticism by defining queer space as 'a useless, amoral, and sensual space that lives only in and for experience. It is a space of spectacle, consumption, dance, and obscenity. It is a misuse or deformation of a place, an appropriation of the buildings and codes of the city for perverse purposes.'[81] The ultimate *raison d'être* of queer space for Betsky lies exclusively in orgasm.[82] Queer, for him, distinguishes itself solely through the libidinal. Furthermore, 'queer space finds its origins in the closet' for Betsky.[83] *Bachelors of a different sort* views queer identity and queer space as neither limited to sex acts, orgasm and genital pleasure nor the outcome of a shaming closet, a post-Stonewall concept which had no bearing on the actual lived experiences of men and women prior to the Second World War. Rather, I seek to purposefully cross the threshold into spaces that accommodated cultural, social, sexual and aesthetic difference. How might we think about, along Foucault's terms, men sharing their spaces and lives together, beyond while not denying sex/uality? What to make then of queer couples like Shannon and Ricketts, who for all intents and purposes aligned themselves with a distinctly bourgeois notion of domesticity while transforming and translating its interiors to suit their own queer purposes? Betsky continues the falsehood that the ideal divide along the line of gender (perpetuated by manuals, institutions and domestic practitioners) was borne out in actual day-to-day practice. He asserts that queer experiences of space were also determined along the ideal divide that was maintained through sexual difference: the city (public space) was 'rewritten by men cruising and refusing to accept its strictures', while on the other hand, '[i]nside the domestic environment itself, queer women were sloughing off the bonds of conventions. They turned the layers of accumulated self-definition into the all-white world of Elsie de Wolfe, where machinery and decoration fed on each other to create a sensible and sexual setting for women only.'[84] According to him, homosexual women were sequestered to setting up house and home in private while homosexual men achieved sexual pleasure (supposedly without lasting bonds) in public spaces and places. In short, by claiming that whether designed by women or appropriated by men queer space 'is free from outside constraints'[85] Betsky negates all too easily the impact of such social forces as the Labouchere Amendment and the Wolfenden Report as well as how queers managed, with varying success, to straddle multiple life-worlds simultaneously (normative, queer and/or otherwise).

Marcus highlights the significant research published on Victorian lesbian couples, to which I would add the ground-breaking work on female same-sex culture in the interwar period, 'because the couple form is what makes lesbian sex visible'.[86] However, she also importantly underscores how no such study exists on British men. While this book embraces male same-sex couples, it also extends the parameters by exploring how queer men, broadly conceived and in various forms of relationships, negotiated, designed and performed domestic space. As Marcus asserts:

> [w]hile same-sex couples never typified its social norm, domesticity was also defined by features that lesbians and gay men could and did embrace: interiority, an identification of self, couple, and family with a home understood as more than a physical space, as an expression of personality, shared tastes, and emotional bonds; aestheticism, the association of the home with comfort, pleasure, and beauty, embodied in material objects and design principles; privacy … attachment, intimacy, and love.[87]

There are a number of excellent and thoughtful studies on the intersection of homosexuality and the spaces of the public realm particularly among scholars of British cultural history.[88] And while there are also a plethora of smart books and volumes attending to the geographies of sexuality, it seems like a glaring lacuna that few scholars see the domestic as a landscape – or geography for that matter – which plays host to and locates sex/ualities.[89] The result is a sort of reification of the public/private divide by scholars fascinated by the public domains of civility, culture and community and who, through a collective silence, render the home seemingly unintelligible, feminine and inconsequential.[90]

Seven deadly sins

> It seems to me that in these days the term 'interior design' covers a multitude of sins.
> Derek Patmore (1935)

Here I wish to appropriate and reassign the once infectious notion of the seven deadly sins to what I identify as the highly suggestive negative qualities or characteristics attributed to the bachelor type. The seven deadly sins (lust, envy, gluttony, greed, wrath, pride and sloth), as they were conceived in early Christendom, are seen as the origins of all other sin. Their significance lay in the fact that they lead the sinner down the path of evil, away from grace. These seven deadliest of sins reside at the core of the aberrant, or sinful, type that the homosexual, man of aesthetics and bachelor held in common. They are, as I distinguish them here, not merely instrumental to identity formation but fundamental to the interpellation of the queer subject in the narrative of the modern interior itself. The seven deadly sins of the bachelor are: queerness (sexual and socio-spatial aberration); idolatry (the unhealthy worship of a female diva, which today has intensified into celebrity culture); decadence (the excessive drive of luxury and sensory stimulation); askesis (the unnatural training of the self); decoration (feminine propensity toward the ornamental and non-functional); glamour (the over-stimulated attraction toward one's self, body or environment); and finally, artifice (superficial indulgence in the realm of unnatural aesthetics). Within Catholic doctrine deadly sins can be purged by the penitent through confession within its attending space of the confessional, a private interior devoted to shame, guilt and remorse. In much the same way, the sins of the modern bachelor require their own confessional box, here metaphorically and spatially transformed into the proverbial closet, an important subtext running throughout this book. However, unlike the confessional, I do not seek to attribute guilt to the interior spaces these men fashioned. Rather I see them as exposing a constant tension between resistance and shame. Each chapter, beginning with this one focused on queerness, deploys one of the seven deadly sins of the bachelor as a guiding principal. While the seven deadly sins function as the theoretical and methodological structure for the book, I do not suggest that each chapter's character(s) possessed only one characteristic trait. On the contrary, all the men exhibited many or all of these markers of excess that lead away from the path of (social) grace and normativity. My use of queer for this project is derived from and indebted to the work of Eve Kosofsky Sedgwick and David Halperin, who each posit it to be a positionality at odds with normative gender and sexuality and the normalizing ethos of the mainstream and dominant ideology of a given time and place. 'As the very word implies', Halperin argues, '"queer" does not name some natural kind or refer to some determinate object'. Rather, 'it acquires its meaning from its oppositional relation to the norm. Queer is by definition whatever is at odds with the normal, the legitimate, the dominant.'[91] Sedgwick, on the other hand, proposes queer as 'the open mesh of possibilities, gaps, overlaps, dissonances and resonances, lapses and excesses of meaning when the constituent elements of anyone's gender, of anyone's sexuality aren't made (or can't be made) to signify monolithically' much in the same way that the interiors functioned for the men discussed here.[92] Queer also distinguishes itself as being in excess of a normative and preferred gender and sexuality, but which nevertheless does not point to one determinate or homogenous identity.[93] Queer provides an ever-shifting space for and means of resistance, whether consciously or otherwise; in short, a space *in* excess to the normative.

Excess is not simply a social or cultural attribution but also importantly a discursive designation, one marked out by the simple word 'too', that is, either *too* much or even *too* little; a conclusion necessarily arrived at by way of setting in relief objects, spaces or people against a backdrop of the normative. This short word, I submit, serves as an important linguistic indicator for the seven deadly sins. For example, bachelors were seen as either too miserly or too luxurious in their economy; either too antagonistic to or too enthralled by the ideals of the domestic.[94] Sedgwick also comments on the contradictory existence of the bachelor when she notes how he 'is at least partly feminized by his attention to and interest in domestic concerns. (At the same time, though, his intimacy with clubland and bohemia gives him a special passport to the world of men, as well).'[95] As the site and sight of social contradictions and cultural superstitions the bachelor was forced into a no-win situation, and was characterized as residing in no-man's land, neither here nor there, neither this nor that, a figure lurking in the shadows of the threshold. Excess, then, is distinguished by an imbalanced masculinity that only further guarantees hegemonic masculinity's supposed rightful honorific position of power. R. W. Connell has importantly asserted that

> [o]ppression positions homosexual masculinities at the bottom of a gender hierarchy among men. Gayness, in patriarchal ideology, is the repository of whatever is symbolically expelled from hegemonic masculinity, the items ranging from fastidious taste in home decoration to receptive anal pleasure. Hence, from the point of view of hegemonic masculinity, gayness is easily assimilated to femininity. And hence – in view of some gay theorists – the ferocity of homophobic attacks.[96]

It is easy to enjoy the assumptions of a camp gay decorator, but at what cost? To what space of dwelling does the camp gay decorator retire after a long day of work for the privileged few? While my investigation here is not of the professional 'gay' decorator, queer theory, as Thad Logan has advocated, would prove exceptionally beneficial to unpacking the history not only of professional interior design,[97] but of the aesthetics, domesticity and interior design more broadly understood for men more generally who dared not marry or perform ideal, preferred and/or hegemonic heterosexual masculine identities.

This is a book about queer bachelors (the first deadly sin) and the fashioning of their homes, material cultures and embodied selves. In this book I want to revel in the stereotype of the queer bachelor and frolic gaily in the spaces he created over the decades. I want to appropriate or re-appropriate the numerous negative representations (those seven deadly sins I have identified) and deploy them as entries into the sophisticated life-worlds they have dared to fashion. Often the spaces they created engendered a pedagogical network, and thus their homes lend a certain spatial dimension to this acquisition of knowledge for us years after the fact. Many of the men, especially those who began their careers in the nineteenth century, followed the era's Uranian[98] pedagogical pattern of adopting younger men and educating them. This also had a distinctly queer initiative, an erotic education, not necessarily sexual, but one in which desire and pleasure within and beyond knowledge factor into the relationship between the older and younger man. I highlight the domestic as the facilitator of this special sort of pedagogical initiative, for it is within the spaces of the modern interior, rather than the alienating public sphere, that culture of this nature could actually take place.

The remaining six deadly sins are presented here as a unique conceptual force attached to a specific case study as a means to facilitate the material: idolatry (Gower); decadence (Ricketts and Shannon); askesis (Warren); decoration (Morris and Lett-Haines); glamour (Coward); artifice (Beaton). I not only wish to interject these so-called seven deadly sins into the various disciplinary traditions in a decidedly queer manner, but I wish to appropriate them towards positive and productive intellectual ends, that is, as a collective act of resistance. Indeed, they are, as is this text, the site of a social and intellectual polemic in a neo-conservative age of naming, assimilating and ultimately repressing difference through subtle acts, modes and apparati of shaming into submission. The case studies have been divided into three sections, with two chapters each. The first section attends to the affective omnipresence of Wilde, who travelled through spaces, polluting and threatening them with his excess, or in the very least the collective perception of it. While volumes have been written about Wilde, less attention has been paid to the material culture he engendered. Through his omnipresence he remained a particularly important shadow figure to both Gower and Ricketts and Shannon in different yet similar ways. The Irish playwright, poet and theorist is not here given his own chapter, but rather forms the backdrop against which Gower and Shannon and Ricketts are illuminated. As a shadow figure, an all-pervading threat to the wellbeing and hygiene of the spaces he occupied and visited, Wilde is purposefully deployed as a foil, as he was subsequently perceived in the late nineteenth and early twentieth century following his unfortunate demise.

The men in these first two case studies were not only colleagues and friends of Wilde but were men whose material cultures, social identity and/or queer aesthetic were the result of or had an impact on Wilde. In these two chapters, I also wish to scrutinize the notion of guilty by association (as much as guilty by design), how these men handled scandal or avoided it altogether and how this affected their material culture, collecting practices and interior spaces.

A collector's home to the core, Gower Lodge housed Lord Gower's numerous treasured objects; its crowing glory was his formidable collection of Marie Antoinette memorabilia. The collection housed in the lodge served as the impetus and material basis for his book *Bric À Brac* (1888). Somewhat self-indulgent, at least at first view, this lavish, well-illustrated text serves at once as a celebration of Victorian pleasures of consumption while cataloguing historically significant objects expressive of lineage, personal memories and familial legacy. Ricketts and Shannon, who were perhaps better known as collectors than as artists, also created an entire interior and domestic programme centred on the highly bourgeois ideal of acquisitiveness, though in their case it was greatly tempered by both financial means and intellectual sophistication. Their respectable middle-class domesticity provided a veil or threshold of protection from the hostility represented by the outside public arena, symptomatic of homophobic anxiety and retribution. Aesthetic bachelor homes became in large part safe spaces of concealment, seemingly removed from the ever-expanding police surveillance and public scrutiny and yet fertile ground for a creative community to flourish openly.

In addition to the public/private divide, there is also the assumption of a city/country divide in the exploration of queer men's lives. The assumption is that most homosexual men ran off to the city to live alone, or with other like-minded men in single dwelling homes away from family. With her lens focused exclusively on contemporary American culture and case studies, Halberstam nonetheless importantly concedes that while 'queer subcultures [do indeed] thrive in urban areas', she 'contests the essential characterizations of queer life as urban'.[99] Given how many of the case studies explored here emerge from the rural and at times geo-political margins of the centre of London, this book asserts the belief in the importance, plausibility and significance of queer lives and queer subcultures managing themselves within the pastoral confines of rural Britain. This book seeks to dispel the assumed and implied urban-centric nature of queer life embedded in contemporary scholarship on male (homo)sexuality and design history. The second coupling of chapters, as a result, emphasizes lives set in distinct opposition to London and attends to the much neglected country life of queers.

Fundamentally the entire book cuts across the steadfast binary between country and metropolis and argues for the importance of the former in queer lives and networks. The realities of queer life in the countryside, the gay pastoral scenes of queer creative and cultural production has figured rarely in current scholarship. In this section, I focus on the spaces and Uranian writings of American collector Edward Perry Warren and his obsessive search for an antique-styled community in Lewes House, Sussex. In his three-volume *Defence of Uranian Love* (1928), written under the pseudonym of Arthur Lyon Raile, Warren falls within a specific literary tradition of queer authors since the eighteenth century who turned back to Ancient Greece as a preferred exemplary Uranian society in which an older male figure who took a younger male under his tutelage and protection guided him to adult life. Warren practised what he wrote, and numerous were the young men who benefited financially, socially, culturally and even sexually from a relationship with him. The second case study delves into the intimate communal spaces of painting *en plein air* that Sir Cedric Morris and Arthur Lett-Haines enlivened for their countless friends and students. With Morris and Lett (as he was affectionately referred to) the garden became a crucial addition to the spatial conceptualization of their domestic union as much as a locus for creative production and domestic tension. The garden was for Morris what certain parts of the home's interiors were for Lett, and what ensued over the many decades of their rich, though tumultuous, relationship was a spatial landscape that betrayed their complicated sexual and social choreography.

Long after Wilde's infamous fall from grace, the book's third and final section with its emphasis on the heyday of jazz and the 'Bright Young Things' of the interwar period positions the domestic interior as a stage set for modern sexualities and gender performances. My first case enters into the theatrical and personal spaces of playwright and actor Noël Coward. The simultaneously camp and closeted humour of Coward's plays are set in relief to his reputation as a sartorial trend setter as well as the modernity of his domestic design both on and off the stage. In the final chapter devoted to an equally famous and infamous cultural actor, I seek to unravel the glorious artificial life-world constructed by Cecil Beaton. With Ashcombe, Beaton's first country estate, he entered into a deep and long-lasting love affair which ended tragically when he was forced to give up the lease. In the numerous renovations to and modernizations of the estate, Ashcombe was unabashedly conceived as at once a theatrical stage and a haven of refuge, a bi-polar space which paid witness to his highest highs and lowest lows. For Beaton Ashcombe was, as with all the domestic landscapes discussed here, a home all his own.

Notes

1. A. G. Davis and P. M. Strong, 'Working without a Net: The Bachelor as a Social Problem', *Sociological Review*, vol. 25 (25 April 1977), p. 113.
2. *Ibid.*, p. 121.
3. *Old Bachelors: Their Varieties, Characters, and Conditions* (London: John Macrone, 1835), Vol. 1, pp. 1–2.
4. *Ibid.*, p. 287.
5. *Ibid.*, p. 280.
6. W. R. Greg, 'Are Women Redundant?' *National Review*, Vol. 14, No. 28 (April 1862), p. 452.
7. K. V. Snyder, *Bachelors, Manhood, and the Novel* (Cambridge: Cambridge University Press, 1999), p. 32.
8. T. B. Johnson, 'Bachelor Leisure', *The Modern Man* (16 January 1909), p. 22.
9. Snyder, *Bachelors*, p. 33.
10. See for example M. Nordau, *Degeneration* (New York: D. Appleton and Company, 1905).
11. *Old Bachelors*, pp. 288–9.
12. Here I have purposefully deployed a female and labour designation to underscore how the body was perceived as flawed and female in nature as a foil to the male and masculine power of the mind and culture, which has long dominated Western culture and philosophy. The result, as is clear by now, is how the bachelor's masculine identity was feminized and vilified owing to his desire to give in to his sensual, bodily drives.
13. Snyder, *Bachelors*, p. 19.
14. D. M. Halperin and V. Traub (eds.), *Gay Shame* (Chicago and London: University of Chicago Press, 2009), p. 9.
15. D. Fuss, *A Sense of an Interior: Four Writers and the Rooms that Shaped Them* (New York and London: Routledge, 2004), p. 1.
16. See *ibid.*, p. 2.
17. E. M. Forster, *Maurice* (London and New York: Penguin Books, 1971), pp. 215–16.
18. P. Sparke and S. McKellar (eds.), *Interior Design and Identity* (Manchester: Manchester University Press, 2004), p. 2.
19. S. Ahmed, 'Orientations: Toward a Queer Phenomenology', *GLQ: A Journal of Lesbian and Gay Studies*, vol. 12, no. 4 (2006), p. 543.
20. R. Shields (ed.), *Places on the Margin: Alternative Geographies of Modernity* (London and New York: Routledge, 1991), p. 25.
21. Symonds in S. Marcus, 'At Home with the Other Victorians: The History of Homosexuality as the History of Domesticity', *South Atlantic Quarterly*, vol. 108, no. 1 (winter 2009), p. 129.
22. C. Rice, *The Emergence of the Interior* (London and New York: Routledge, 2007), p. 19.
23. See J. Halberstam, *Female Masculinities* (Durham, NC: Duke University Press, 1998).
24. *Ibid.*, p. 1.
25. J. Potvin, *Visual and Material Cultures Beyond Male Bonding, 1880–1914: Bodies, Boundaries, and Intimacy* (Aldershot and Burlington: Ashgate, 2008), p. 150, note 82.
26. M. Foucault, 'Friendship as a Way of Life', in P. Rabinow (ed.), *Ethics: Subjectivity and Truth: The Essential Works of Michel Foucault, Volume One* (New York: The New Press, 1997), p. 136.

27 Rice, *The Emergence of the Interior*, pp. 2–3.
28 J. Tosh, 'The New Man? The Bourgeois Cult of Home', *History Today* (December 1996), p. 13.
29 *Ibid.*, p. 146.
30 S. Marcus, *Apartment Stories: City and Home in Nineteenth-Century Paris and London* (Berkeley, Los Angeles and London: University of California Press, 1999), p. 90.
31 Snyder, *Bachelors*, p. 34.
32 G. Dawson, *Soldier Heroes: British Adventure, Empire, and the Imagining of Masculinities* (New York and London: Routledge, 1994), pp. 1–2.
33 J. Tosh, *A Man's Place: Masculinity and the Middle-Class Home in Victorian England* (New Haven and London: Yale University Press, 1999), p. 175.
34 A. Milne-Smith, 'A Flight to Domesticity? Making a Home in the Gentlemen's Clubs of London, 1880–1914', *Journal of British Studies*, no. 45 (October 2006), p. 798.
35 J. Greenwood, *The Wilds of London* (London: Chatto and Windus, 1874), pp. 180–1.
36 *Ibid.*, p. 181.
37 *Ibid.*, pp. 182–3.
38 Shields, *Places on the Margin*, p. 29.
39 Tosh, *A Man's Place*, pp. 2–3.
40 Snyder, *Bachelors*, p. 21.
41 H. Heynen, 'Modernity and Domesticity: Tensions and Contradictions', in Hilde Heynen and Gülsüm Baydar (eds.), *Negotiating Domesticity* (New York: Routledge, 2005), p. 6.
42 T. Logan, *The Victorian Parlour* (Cambridge: Cambridge University Press, 2001), p. 204.
43 S. Marcus, 'At Home with the Other Victorians: The History of Homosexuality as the History of Domesticity', *South Atlantic Quarterly*, vol. 108, no. 1 (winter 2009), p. 120.
44 C. Moffat, 'Furnishing a Man's Room: A Woman's View of the Problem', *Homes and Gardens* (January 1939), p. 278.
45 *Ibid.*, p. 278.
46 W. M., 'When a Man's Single: How a Bachelor Has Furnished His Chambers', *House and Gardens* (May 1924), pp. 421–2.
47 R. W. Belk and M. Wallendorf, 'Of Mice and Men: Gender Identity in Collecting', in Susan M. Pearce (ed.), *Interpreting Objects and Collections* (London and New York: Routledge, 1994), p. 251.
48 M. Lubbock, 'Collections as Decoration', *Homes and Gardens* (May 1939), p. 459.
49 B. Osgerby, 'The Bachelor Pad as Cultural Icon: Masculinity, Consumption and Interior Design in American Men's Magazines, 1930–65', *Journal of Design History*, vol. 18, no. 1 (spring 2005), p. 100.
50 G. Chauncey Jr, *Gay New York: Gender, Urban Culture and the Making of the Gay Male World. 1890–1940* (New York: Basic Books, 1994), p. 79.
51 E. C. Cromley, *Alone Together: A History of New York's Early Apartments* (Ithaca and London: Cornell University Press, 1990), p. 249.
52 Snyder, *Bachelors*, p. 7.
53 W. Benjamin, *The Arcades Project* (Cambridge, MA, and London: The Belknap Press of Harvard University, 1999), p. 19.

54 J. Ruskin, *Sesame and Lilies* (New Haven and London: Yale University Press, 2002 [1865]), p. 122.

55 Cromley, *Alone Together*, p. 14.

56 *Ibid.*, p. 115.

57 Marcus, 'At Home with the Other Victorians', pp. 87–8.

58 F. T. Verity, E. T. Hall, G. C. Horsley and W. S. Sparrow (eds.), *Flats, Urban Houses and Cottage Homes: A Companion Volume to 'The British Home To-Day'* (London: Hodder and Stoughton, 1906), pp. 82–3.

59 Marcus, 'At Home with the Other Victorians', p. 84. In a number of the cases I explore in this book, privacy is ironically neither relevant nor a chief concern, despite an ever-increasing purview of the legal and medical institutions which continued to survey the sexual aberrant, even in his *natural* habitat. Rather, community, alternative forms of pedagogy and cultural outreach are the hallmarks of many of the spaces explored.

60 J. J. Stevenson, *House Architecture*, Vol. II: *House Planning* (London: Macmillan and Co., 1880), p. 48.

61 Kant in M. Perrot (ed.), *A History of Private Life: IV From the Fires of Revolution to the Great War* (Cambridge, MA, and London: The Belknap Press of Harvard University Press, 1990), p. 342.

62 W. H. White, 'On Middle-Class Houses in Paris and Central London', address to the Royal Institute of British Architects, *Sessional Papers, 1877–78* (19 November 1877), p. 30.

63 Marcus, 'At Home with the Other Victorians', pp. 101–2.

64 T. Archer, *The Pauper, the Thief, and the Convict: Sketches of Some of Their Homes, Haunts and Habits* (London: Groombridge, 1865), p. 98.

65 Verity et al., *Flats, Urban Houses and Cottage Homes*, pp. 81–2.

66 S. Perks, *Residential Flats of All Classes Including Artisan's Dwellings: A Practical Treatise on the Planning and Arrangement* (London: B. T. Batsford, 1905), p. 60.

67 Verity et al., *Flats, Urban Houses and Cottage Homes*, p. 84.

68 L. Davidoff, *The Family Story: Blood, Contract, and Intimacy, 1830–1960* (London and New York: Longman 1999), p. 166.

69 Perks, *Residential Flats of All Classes*, p. 27.

70 Rice, *The Emergence of the Interior*, p. 3.

71 J. Weeks, *Coming Out: Homosexual Politics in Britain from the Nineteenth Century to the Present* (London: Quartet Books, 1977), p. 14.

72 Cited in M. Houlbrook, *Queer London: Perils and Pleasures in the Sexual Metropolis, 1918–1957* (Chicago and London: University of Chicago Press, 2005), p. 110.

73 See also E. K. Sedgwick, *Epistemology of the Closet* (Berkeley: University of California Press, 1990).

74 P. Sparke, *The Modern Interior* (London: Reaktion Press, 2008), p. 11.

75 It is important to note that decriminalization did not follow until well after the Wolfenden Report. In G. Kinsman, *The Regulation of Desire: Homo and Hetero Sexualities* (Montreal, New York and London: Black Rose Books, 1996), p. 214.

76 *Ibid.*, p. 215.

77 See *ibid.*, p. 216.

78 Houlbrook, *Queer London*.

79 C. Reed (ed.), *Not at Home: The Suppression of Domesticity in Modern Art and Architecture* (London: Thames and Hudson, 1996).

80 Marcus, 'At Home with the Other Victorians', p. 121.

81 A. Betsky, *Queer Space: Architecture and Same-Sex Desire* (New York: William Morrow, 1997), p. 5.

82 Ibid., p. 17.

83 Ibid., p. 21.

84 Ibid., pp. 12, 13.

85 Ibid., p. 21.

86 Marcus, 'At Home with the Other Victorians', p. 121. On lesbian couples and the domestic realm see for example: S. Marcus, *Between Women: Friendship, Desire, and Marriage in Victorian England* (Princeton: Princeton University Press, 2007); M. Vicinus, *Intimate Friends: Women Who Loved Women, 1778–1928* (Chicago: University of Chicago Press, 2004); S. Koven, *Slumming: Sexual and Social Politics in Victorian London* (Princeton: Princeton University Press, 2004); S. Jackson, *Lines of Activity: Performance, Historiography, Hull-House Domesticity* (Ann Arbor: University of Michigan Press, 2000); R. Vanita, *Sappho and the Virgin Mary: Same-Sex Love and the English Literary Imagination* (New York: Columbia University Press, 1996); M. Elliman and F. Roll, *The Pink Plaque Guide to London* (London: GMP Publishers, 1986); L. Doan, *Fashioning Sapphism: The Origins of a Modern English Lesbian Culture* (New York: Columbia University Press, 2001); B. Elliott, 'Housing the Work: Women Artists, Modernism and the *Maison d'artiste*: Eileen Gray, Romanie Brooks and Gluck', in Bridget Elliott and Janice Helland (eds.), *Women Artists and the Decorative Arts, 1880–1935: The Gender of Ornament* (Aldershot and Burlington: Ashgate, 2002); L. Doan and J. Garrity (eds.), *Sapphic Modernities: Sexuality, Women and National Culture* (New York: Palgrave Macmillan, 2006); T. T. Latimer, *Women Together/Women Apart* (New Brunswick: Rutgers University Press, 2005); K. Marra, 'A Lesbian Marriage of Cultural Consequence: Elisabeth Marbury and Elsie de Wolfe, 1886–1933', *Theatre Annual: A Journal of Performance Studies*, no. 47 (fall 1994).

87 Marcus, 'At Home with the Other Victorians', p. 121.

88 See for example: N. Bartlett, *Who Was That Man? A Present for Mr. Oscar Wilde* (London: Serpent's Tail, 1989); M. Cook, *London and the Culture of Homosexuality, 1885–1914* (Cambridge: Cambridge University Press, 2003); M. Houlbrook, *Queer London: Perils and Pleasures in the Sexual Metropolis, 1918–1957* (Chicago and London: University of Chicago Press, 2005); J. Potvin, 'Vapour and Steam: The Victorian Bath, Homosocial Health and Male Bodies on Display', *Journal of Design History*, vol. 18, no. 4 (winter 2005); A. Stephenson, 'Staging Authenticity: Tourist Spaces and Artistic Inscription in Inter-war English Art', *Visual Culture in Britain*, vol. 4, no. 1 (2003); A. Stephenson, 'Precarious Poses: The Problem of Artistic Visibility and its Homosocial Performances in Late Nineteenth-Century London', *Visual Culture in Britain*, vol. 8, no. 1 (summer 2007).

89 See D. Bell and G. Valentine (eds.), *Mapping Desire: Geographies of Sexualities* (London: Routledge, 1995); D. Bell (ed.), *Pleasure Zones: Bodies, Cities, Spaces* (Syracuse: Syracuse University Press, 2001); J. Binnie, *The Globalization of Sexuality* (London: Sage, 2004); M. Blindon, 'Jalons pour une géographie des homosexualités', *Espace Géographique*, vol. 2, no. 37 (2008); M. P. Brown, *Closet Space: Geographies of Metaphor from the Body to the Globe* (London and New York: Routledge, 2000); F. Browning, *A Queer Geography* (New York: Noonday, 1998); L. Johnston and R. Longhurst, *Space, Place and Sex: Geographies of Sexualities* (Lanham: Rowman and Littlefield, 2010); R. Kitchin, 'Sexing the City: The Sexual Production of Non-Heterosexual Space in Belfast, Manchester and San Francisco',

City, vol. 6, no. 2 (2002); N. Oswin, 'Critical Geographies and the Uses of Sexuality: Deconstructing Queer Space', *Progress in Human Geography*, vol. 32, no. 1 (2008).

90 I am not suggesting that there are not excellent studies on male sexuality and the interior. Rather, I simply and importantly want to highlight the current imbalance that privileges the public domain over the domestic realm. The study of the interior in many disciplines has come into its own only in the past two or so decades. For important queer readings see for example: M. Camille, 'Editor's Introduction', *Art History Special Issue on Queer Collecting*, vol. 24, no. 2 (April 2001); M. Cook, *Queer Domesticities: Homosexuality and Home Life in Twentieth Century London* (London: Palgrave, 2014); J. Edwards, 'The Lessons of Leighton House: Aesthetics, Politics, Erotics', in Jason Edwards and Imogen Hart (eds.), *Rethinking the Interior: Aestheticism and the Arts and Crafts Movement, 1867–1896* (Aldershot and Burlington: Ashgate, 2010): M. Hatt, 'Space, Surface, Self: Homosexuality and the Aesthetic Interior', *Visual Culture in Britain*, vol. 8, no. 1 (summer 2007): P. McNeil, 'Crafting Queer Spaces: Privacy and Posturing', in John Potvin and Alla Myzelev (eds.), *Fashion, Interior Design and the Contours of Modern Identity* (Aldershot and Burlington: Ashgate, 2010); C. Reed (ed.), *Not at Home: The Suppression of Domesticity in Modern Art and Architecture* (London: Thames and Hudson, 1996); C. Reed, 'Imminent Domain: Queer Space in the Built Environment', *Art Journal*, vol. 55, no. 4 (winter 1996b); C. Reed, *Bloomsbury Rooms: Modernism, Subculture, and Domesticity* (New York: Yale University Press, 2004); C. Reed, 'Design for [Queer] Living: Sexual Identity, Performance, and Décor in British *Vogue*, 1922–1926', *GLQ*, vol. 12, no. 3 (2006).

91 D. M. Halperin, *Saint Foucault: Towards a Gay Hagiography* (Oxford and New York: Oxford University Press, 1995), p. 62.

92 E. K. Sedgwick, *Tendencies* (Durham, NC: Duke University Press, 1993), p. 8.

93 *Ibid.*; Halperin, *Saint Foucault*.

94 Snyder, *Bachelors*, pp. 31; 19.

95 Sedgwick, *Epistemology of the Closet*, pp. 189–90.

96 R. W. Connell, *Masculinities* (Berkeley: University of California Press, 1995), p. 78.

97 Logan, *The Victorian Parlour*, p. 235.

98 A term from the nineteenth century to designate the homosexual as a third sex. The term took inspiration from Ancient Greek mythology and comes from the German word *Urning*.

99 J. Halberstam, *In a Queer Time and Place: Transgender Bodies, Subcultural Lives* (New York and London: New York University Press, 2005), p. 15.

I ✧ Wilde spaces

2 ✧ 'God Save the Queen': Lord Gower, idolatry and the cult of the *bric-à-brac* diva

BORN IN the majestic Stafford House, Lord Ronald Charles Sutherland Gower (1845–1916) seemed as if to belong to another, more romantic era, one in which the aristocracy still ruled and sexual scandal never posed a real threat. As the fourth and youngest son of George Granville, second Duke of Sutherland (the largest land owner in Britain) and Lady Harriet Howard (Mistress of the Robes to Queen Victoria), Gower was well educated at both Eton and Trinity College (Cambridge), though he left the latter before completing his degree. As Dr George Charles Williamson once explained: 'Few men came into more intimate and personal contact with the important persons of the Victorian era'.[1] He was on friendly terms with Queen Victoria, who was counted among his most cherished relationships, despite his jealousy of the woman, who he insisted, too often monopolized his mother's time.[2] From his youth he was considered 'a welcome visitor at the great houses of England, good-looking, popular, courteous; a typical member to power and to attention'.[3] He was a Liberal politician who served Parliament (1867–74), and it was only after the death of his mother in 1868 that he realized that art, rather than politics, was his true vocation [Figure 2.1]. It was while working in the studio of sculptor Matthew Noble (1818–76), supervising preparations for his mother's tomb, that Gower decided to throw himself completely into art. It was also after her death when Gower associated himself more readily with homosexual communities and a so-called bohemian lifestyle.

In addition to being a politician and sculptor he was also an avid collector, historian and writer, charged by many as a dilettante and fascinated by times long lost. In the summer of 1876 Gower acquired a house in Windsor, near Cliveden, where his parents also had a home favoured by his mother. Gower Lodge was the result of cherished memories and regal attachments to the numerous divas who filled his life, namely his mother, Queen Victoria and the former queen of France, Marie

2.1 Camille Silvy. *Lord Ronald Charles Gower Sutherland-Levenson-Gower*, 15 July 1865.

Antoinette. Gower constructed a 'treasure house'[4] that best reflected his unique sense of queer time and place. At Gower Lodge he installed the collection he had built up through the 1870s and 1880s, and in 1888 memorialized his renovated home, its interiors and the various objects

"BRIC À BRAC"

OR

SOME PHOTOPRINTS

ILLUSTRATING ART OBJECTS AT GOWER LODGE, WINDSOR

DESCRIBED BY

LORD RONALD GOWER, F.S.A.

A TRUSTEE OF THE NATIONAL PORTRAIT GALLERY

LONDON

KEGAN PAUL, TRENCH & CO., 1 PATERNOSTER SQUARE

MDCCCLXXXVIII

2.2 Cover page from *Bric À Brac* by Lord Ronald Gower, 1888.

they contained with the neglected and long since forgotten publication of *Bric À Brac or some Photoprints Illustrating Art Objects at Gower Lodge, Windsor* [Figure 2.2]. Exhibited at the Royal Academy in 1877 along with his statue of Marie Antoinette, Gower placed one of his most celebrated sculptures, *Old Guard*, outside the front door, faithfully guarding it and marking the property as a product of his own aesthetic devising [Figure 2.3].

2.3 Edward Dossetter. Frontispiece, *Bric À Brac*, featuring Lord Ronald Gower's *Old Guard* and façade of Gower Lodge, Windsor.

Gower was deeply loyal, committed and sentimental about his upbringing and the familial home. In the two volumes of his *Reminiscences* (1883), Gower's self-narrative begins with the place of his birth, a space that clearly affected his first and deepest impressions, betraying his own passion for domestic interiors. These reminiscences are both affirmative and nostalgic, and Gower, born in Stafford House, claimed to have been raised in an 'art palace' surrounded by St James's Palace, Green Park and the Mall. He recalls how 'Rogers, the bank-poet, the friend of Byron and Moore, said that, although he has seen all the palaces of Europe, he preferred Stafford House to any of them. "I have often said," he added "that it is a fairy palace, and that the Duchess is the good fairy!"' Queen Victoria made numerous visits to Stafford House and each left a deep and long-lasting impact on the impressionable young Gower. According to him, she paid perhaps the highest compliment, once also paid by Louis XIV: 'I have come from my house to your palace!'[5]

Together the practices of space and interior design are the resulting matrix of aesthetic, cultural, social, psychological and memorializing registers in the life of queer men, for not only do they initiate and inform gender performances and sexual codes, but so too do they mark the domestic as a site for the enactment of a difference. Together the furniture and collections that filled Gower's Windsor home compel us to search out the narratives that *bric-à-brac* at once enliven and expose well beyond the shadows of the endless and meaningless accumulation late Victorians were said to been have afflicted by. These narratives are to be found in the material mappings of identity formation and subjectivity. More often than not research pertaining to homosexuality and collecting has gravitated toward questions of homoeroticism or the sexual nature of objects. However, this chapter as well as the one that follows seeks to question what exists beyond the, at times, obviousness of the homoerotic and the restrictive associations attributed to what might constitute a truly queer collection and domestic design. As Michael Camille perfectly asserted in his introduction to a special issue on queer collecting for *Art History* (2001), 'there has been relatively little exploration of the relationship between collecting and even more hotly contested terrains of difference in contemporary culture – gender and sexuality'.[6] While the contributions to his special issue certainly went a long way in addressing this lacuna, there still remains, nevertheless, much to be discovered and questioned. In this and the following chapter I wish to question what might constitute a queer collection. Is it simply the sexual nature of the objects themselves or the identity of the collector? What do we make of the performative, sensual, edifying, phenomenological and embodied practices of collecting for men within the domestic realm? Certainly, as I hope to show, it is a number of things, but I suggest it is more importantly a conjuncture of competing forces at work that compel either the collector to see things queerly or the visitor to perceive things as being queer. In this instance, then, queer stands in at once as both a mode of empowerment and source of derision, and in its wake confirms its duplicitous, fluid and ambivalent nature.

Although this chapter focuses its lens on the writings, interiors and collections of Gower it will also briefly entertain important diversions into the early aesthetic theories and domestic practices of Oscar Wilde (1854–1900), initiated while a student at Magdalen College (Oxford) and developed in the first residence he took up with Frank Miles in Tite

Street. Not unlike but to a lesser extent than with Charles Ricketts and Charles Shannon (the subjects of the following chapter), for Gower, Wilde played a shadowy figure who lurked in the nebulous interstitial crevices between aesthetics, class and sexuality where he often found himself, not without problem. In *Who Was that Man? A Present for Mr. Oscar Wilde* Neil Bartlett importantly deduces that 'each of Wilde's characters is a collector, a connoisseur. They love to do nothing more than to recite the list of their treasures, to sort and catalogue them'.[7] In effect, *Bric À Brac* functions as a similar sort of narratological performance in which Gower listed and narrated the importance of each *objet d'art* in an attempt to reify their collective significance to both history and the story of his life. Gower's highly idiosyncratic collecting programme in addition to his interiors materialized an alternative to the heteronormative understanding of heritage, lineage, progeny and inheritance, ideals that assured, as Graham Dawson has shown, the steadfast relationship between heroism, nationalism and 'preferred forms of masculinity'. What this engendered in turn was a desire as much as a need for a 'dominant conception of masculine identity' identified as the 'true Englishman'.[8] Gower performed and understood these ideals on his own terms; his alternative masculinity embodied a life-world in which *bric-à-brac* and idolatry, specifically the diva worship of the tragic heroine, conspicuously diverged from the social perceptions and cultural expectations of the preferred performances of masculinity premised on heroism, militarism and chivalric idealism. Gower's unique collection was certainly not overlooked by Wilde. It has long been suggested that not only did Gower serve as inspiration for Lord Henry Wotton in Wilde's *The Picture of Dorian Gray* (1891), but so too did his dubious social circle provide the Irish playwright and poet with a blueprint from which to pen *The Portrait of Mr. W. H.* (1889).[9] Gower owned two rare books bearing the gilt coat of arms of Marguerite de Valois, possessions of a woman included in Wilde's litany of objects found in Lord Henry Wotton's Mayfair house (specifically a copy of *Les Cents Nouvelles* bound for her by Clovis Eve). Here fact and fiction cohere to form a perverse domestic space in which the collector is found guilty by his (material) associations. With this in mind, I wish to explore more closely this queerest of collectors who set out to create a domestic blueprint immortalized in a published catalogue of his treasures (as memorial and act of devotion), at whose centre was the allegorical figure of the diva-queen who served as the personification of both sexual identity and class affiliation. The diva-queen and the material culture associated with her, I posit, was the perfect embodiment of an alternative expression of and conduit for the ideals of heritage, lineage, progeny and inheritance so important to Gower's interior design and life story.

2.4 Edward Dossetter. *Old Guard* outside Gower Lodge, Windsor. *Bric À Brac.*

Filling in the spaces

Gower Lodge was transformed from half-timber cottage into a collector's haven filled with antique *bibelots*, pictures, books and regal memorabilia, not too unlike how his parents decorated Stafford House, though on a decidedly grander scale.[10] As he himself admitted, 'the defiant bronze figure of my "Old Guard," would easily find room at the foot of the staircase of Stafford House' [Figure 2.4].[11] The home of one's parents, the domestic spaces of one's upbringing, serves as an important locus of memory and can often influence the design blueprint for one's own home. This was certainly evident in Gower's case, especially as the familial home also engendered myriad associations with aristocratic legacy and familial heritage, affective attachments and affiliations that played themselves out in the objects he collected to fill his lodge. The politician-cum-sculptor described his lodge as 'homelike and comfortable look[ing], with its large gable, mullioned windows, and its creepers around the porch'.[12] *Bric À Brac* was a testament to its author's love affair with the spaces he constructed and the *objets d'art* that surrounded him daily. As a *catalogue raisonné* of his most prized possessions, the book was the product of a series of photographs taken of the lodge by Edward Dossetter in the summer of 1886, which according to the author himself were 'the excuse for this publication'.[13] Dedicated to journalist George Augustus Sala (1792–1828), himself an earnest bibliophile noted for elaborating a complex system to house his more commonplace books,

Gower's book was a fitting tribute from a man who claimed *bric-à-brac* as a 'humble form of art'. In both cases it was material culture rather than high art which formed a coveted and much respected collection. Gower's text vacillates between humility and pride and in it he demonstrates how

> [t]hose who think it necessary to possess a priceless assemblage of *bric-à-brac* in order to issue a *catalogue raisonné*, may smile contemptuously at the smallness of my little gathering. Let me, however, remind those that great wealth is rarely combined to real love of art, or even ensure good taste in such matters. There is nothing to my mind more depressing than to find a large house filled with an indiscriminate jumble of precious 'curios' and art treasures, brought together for no better reason than to display the wealth of the owner. People who really love art for its own sake derive often as much, if not greater, pleasure from the least expensive things ... Fortunately it does not require to be a millionaire to form a collection of art objects, which may be of permanent use and interest to others as well as the owners.[14]

For Gower a collection was not dependent on wealth or monetary merit, but rather on aesthetic interest and passion, the true calling of the aesthetic collector. By cataloguing his preferred objects and by making public his private passion through the publication of the book, he not only assured each object its merit and value in perpetuity, but also aligned himself through acquisitiveness with the importance, lineage and heritage of certain objects and their provenance. While his achievements as a collector (a hunter in the primeval sense of the term, a decidedly male prerogative) are immortalized in this book, so too is his identification with a refined aristocratic lineage ever more in disrepair with the continued emancipation of the middle class. One commentator noted in 1875 that the collector 'will prefer rarity to beauty if the latter happens to be so common as to carry with it no special value'.[15] In Gower's case, particularly as it concerned his assortment of Marie Antoinette memorabilia, to which we will return in the final section of this chapter, both rarity and beauty were tantamount for a collector whose pedigree, fascination and discrimination helped equally to guarantee the worth, merit and significance of each object and the collection as a whole.

Williamson characterized Gower as a collector who

> had all the collector's *flair*, good discriminative ability, the eye for a fine object, whether it was a book, a miniature, or an engraving, and fortunately for himself, the ability to obtain what he wished. His passionate ardour for colour and of form led him to appreciate many a little treasure that a less cultured collector would have passed by. A fragment of a Roman glass, glowing with superb purple and gold, a broken fragment of a Greek marble figure, a gem or an engraved stone, perhaps imperfect, but none the less delightful, a mass of radiant crystal, a Greek Tetradrachm, a Roman

Sestertius, or a short length of old French brocade, each appealed to him in its varied excellence, and he eagerly added them all to his collection.[16]

In his brief exposition on the merits and concerns of the relatively new phenomenon of *bric-à-brac*, theorist and writer James Grant Wilson preoccupied himself, to the point of obsession, with the monetary worth of such objects and their future return as investments. So new was the phenomenon of *bric-à-brac* that Wilson claimed to be unable to locate the term in any dictionary.[17] Wilson, however, was certainly not alone in his obsession with the monetary or economic value of collected objects. In his *A Plea for Art in the House*, clergyman and prolific writer John Loftie anxiously propounded the need for men 'to collect judiciously'.[18] He asserted that collecting was to be conducted only during a man's leisure time using funds allocated expressly for the pursuit of leisure; the implication was that the man to whom he referred was decidedly *not* an aristocrat, a member of the so-called 'leisure class'.[19] For Loftie economy of time and economic thrift should be evident in equal measure in the formation of a proper collection. However, he also importantly recognized consumption as a legitimate pleasure when he asserted that an object held two distinct pleasures for its owner. The first lay 'in the act of buying itself' while the second existed 'in the subsequent possession of the object bought. But if the object be one which soon loses it value this second pleasure is gone with it'.[20] Accordingly, value, possession and pleasure became inextricably linked within the affective registers of a collection. Ultimately inherent value, of which monetary worth must be included, was endemic to any pleasure associated with a collected object. For male critics like Loftie and Wilson an object seemingly cannot possess any other equally noble *raison d'être* or instigate 'other' forms of pleasure.

For his part Clarence Cook, the rather acerbic critic of the *Tribune* in New York, exhorted the merit of decorative art objects beyond mere curios: 'Our senses are educated more by these slight impressions than we are apt to think; and *bric-a-brac*, so much despised by certain people, and often justly so, may have a use that they themselves might not be willing to admit'.[21] Avid collectors of these objects, *bric-a-bracquers*, belonged to a class of wealthy men Wilson designated as '*dilettanti* rather than to men of learning, or the general public'. As a term, dilettante smacks of disdain, particularly when pitted against a longstanding image of a man of learning, who, through his contemplative and critical analysis, elevates the subjects (or objects) of his study. The material culture these so-called *dilettanti* assembled provides us with important and unique glimpses into the cultural histories of notable people, places and things. According to Wilson, 'the antique gem or coin, or the characteristic piece of pottery and porcelain, often brings us a closer and more accurate knowledge of the real life of a community or nation than a formal history can do, just as we learn much more concerning the illustrious men of their time with whom they were acquainted from the pages of Pepys and Evelyn, and the gossip of James Boswell, than we can from the volumes of the more dignified biographer'.[22] Gossip, traditionally seen as a base or crass network for the acquisition of knowledge and information, is rendered akin in its potential value and social significance as *bric-à-brac*, as both share a form of acquisitiveness, a hoarding of trifle objects and factual or fictional tidbits collected for one's own personal delight. Biography, on the other hand, and presumably the higher arts, remain firmly within the realm of the learned. Wilson was not alone when he made clear that what he described designated a hierarchy that positioned contemplation over action (and subsequently collecting over consumption); *bric-à-brac* fell into the latter increasingly maligned and suspect category. Through this association the dilettante was obliquely feminized and marginalized within the socio-cultural codes attributed to sexual difference. This perception constructed a narrative of difference, a position located outside, made separate and distinct through simple, yet highly meaningful, acts and acquisitions. Identity was legibly guaranteed through objects: a collector acquires and projects his dreams, aspirations, desires, self-worth, pleasures and sentiments on to his prized objects. These, in turn, are said to reveal a so-called image, or identity, one in constant formation through acquisition – or consumption – one that is perceived outside the life-world of things the custodian has constructed for himself.

According to Loftie

> it may fairly be argued, and, indeed, has several times been pointed out already, that it is the duty of every one who is so fortunate as to possess a home and to be the head of a family, to endeavour, so far as he can, to make his family happy by making his home beautiful ... Too many men collect only for their own private gratification; and it may be as well as before we go further to draw a sharp line between the man who gathers objects in which he alone is interested, and the man who desires to beautify his house with what he buys. My concern here is with the latter only.[23]

Loftie asserted an important distinction between two different types of men who collect, evidently privileging one over the other. The implication was that a collection should be not simply self-serving, but rather in the service of one's family, a task orchestrated by its (male) head. For Gower a collection did not provide interest simply to its owner, but should also be of benefit to the community, a set of people who populate the domestic landscape. Gower, however, does not restrict those who might benefit from his collection to members of his family, and as such falls somewhere within the breach Loftie elucidates. In Gower's case two constituencies, at once both aspirational and concrete, crossed the threshold of his home. Presumably these would have been from the more genteel classes; that is, queers and aristocrats who, by the end of the Wilde trials, would become too easily conflated in the public perception.

Although finances are of concern to the collector, at the heart of any collecting programme, according to Gower, was 'to take up a line, and to follow that line steadily, with industry, and with patience'.[24] Focus and resolve stood as the ultimate hallmarks of a good and honourable collecting practice. For Gower these central tenants materialized through the acquisition of *bibelots* (or *bric-à-brac*) once owned by the former queen of France Marie Antoinette and the images and objects of great female aristocratic luminaries. Gower's pride over his relics of the queen shines through when he admitted that these objects form the core of his collection against which all else was judged. He wrote: 'The set of medals, illustrating many events in the career of Marie Antoinette, is, I believe, the most perfect collection in existence, and is certainly historically interesting ... These will, I hope, serve as an excuse for introducing less interesting art objects, as well as the views of the little house which contains my *bric-à-brac*.'[25] Loftie similarly postulated that '[b]y forming a collection he [the collector] does good work for the knowledge of art, and he increases the value of each individual specimen in his collection ... But collecting involves more than this. It implies what phrenologists call "comparativeness". The collector must endeavour to ascertain the comparative excellence and rarity of the objects he collects. This is especially the case with prints.'[26] The man most interested in including his family in the joys and outcomes of his endeavours as a collector 'will prefer pictures or prints, which can be hung on his walls, to anything else', concluded Loftie.[27] Of the twenty-one portraits in any medium listed among Gower's chief possessions, three were self-portraits of male artists (Reynolds, Gainsborough, Downman), while a significant fifteen were of women. Among the most notable of the identified sitters were those of fashionable aristocratic women who collectively held a place of honour within Gower's constellation of diva figures. Chief among these were: a sketch by Queen Victoria of one of her bridesmaids and given to his mother when she was Mistress of the Robes [Figure 2.5]; Lady Georgina Spencer, Duchess of Devonshire (Sir Joshua Reynolds); Constance Gower, Duchess of Westminster (Sir J. E. Millais), Maria Siddons (Sir Thomas Lawrence); Lady Georgina Charlotte Bertie (John Downman); and finally Georgina, Duchess of Devonshire and Queen Charlotte (both by John Downman). However, in confidence, Gower admitted to friend and novelist Mrs Marie Adelaide Belloc Lowndes to having only 'three women in [his] life, and one of them died fifty years before [he] was born'.[28] The tacit

2.5 Queen Victoria. 'Sketch by the Queen of one of H. M. Bridesmaides and given to my Mother when she was Mistress of the Robes'. *Bric À Brac.*

allusion made here is to his beloved Marie Antoinette who alongside his mother and Queen Victoria formed the three graces of his life. Lowndes also recalled how '[a]ll over his country house were paintings and engravings of his mother. I remember a small replica of Leslie's painting of the Coronation, where the radiantly lovely young Duchess of Sutherland is seen standing immediately behind the Queen.'[29]

2.6 Edward Dossetter. Chimney in the Saloon. *Bric À Brac.*

The portraits of these beautiful young women, along with the other possessions he listed and described in *Bric À Brac*, were generally scattered between the saloon and three sitting rooms of Gower Lodge. Not part of the original structure and constructed as an afterthought, the saloon boasted a specially commissioned chimney and fireplace designed by A. Y. Nutt (noted as architect to the Queen) featuring inset casts by Brucciani of the angelic choir by Donatello located in Padua [Figure 2.6]. Installed in the central compartment was a low-relief plaster medallion by the Scottish Pre-Raphaelite sculptor Alexander Munro of Constance, Countess Grosvenor (later Duchess of Westminster), Gower's much-cherished sister. The tops of the various tables in the room were littered with books and precious *'bibelots'*.[30] In the ground-floor sitting room, Gower kept to the preferred wall colour of the day, a dull pale green akin to the colour of a goose egg. According to the author, the choice of colour 'harmonises admirably with the gilded cornice, door, and mirror frames and outer frame of the fireplace, which formerly served as frames to the set of English historical pictures relating to the seventeenth century, painted by Benjamin West, formerly at Grosvenor House, and which are now panelled in the library at Eaton Hall'. On either side of the fireplace were bas-relief casts of *La Force* (*Power*) and *La Foi* (*Faith*) from Germain Pilon's works in the Louvre [Figure 2.7]. Like

2.7 Edward Dossetter. Sitting room on the ground floor. *Bric À Brac.*

the casts in the saloon, these decorative personifications demonstrate an important aesthetic dimension in which objects from the past could be adopted and then 'adapted to harmonize even with the surroundings of a cottage' in the present.[31] Additionally, they were also able to merge seamlessly with the overall material culture Gower painstakingly constructed, helping to further demonstrate the image of the home as a composition.

An additional two sitting rooms were located on the first floor. Again for rooms such as these, dull green, deep red and purple were suggested as the ideal backdrops against which to display pictures (whether mezzotints or engravings) to best effect. For the first of these two sitting rooms, Gower covered the walls with a rich, deep purple damask to better highlight paintings that included Italianate views of Linton, a copy by E. M. Ward of John Everett Millais's portrait of Lady Ormonde (located above the door), a copy of Gainsborough's portrait of Princess Elizabeth (on the door), and to the right of the door Sir J. Millais's 'Kit-Cat' oil painting of Constance, Duchess of Westminster, the latter reproduced in his catalogue. In the second of the two sitting rooms, the fireplace took centre stage over which he placed Sir Joshua Reynolds's portrait of Georgiana Cavendish, Duchess of Devonshire, as a child, who as an adult would become renowned for her trend setting

'God Save the Queen'

2.8 Edward Dossetter. Sitting room. *Bric À Brac*.

style and political activism. He placed E. M. Ward's sketch of Marie Antoinette as Dauphine to the left of the fireplace and below was the fan belonging to the ill-fated Queen, part of the assortment of memorabilia included in Gower's memorializing catalogue [Figure 2.8]. In this room, various *bric-à-brac* was spread out in a space that was the 'least lived in of any in the house'. However, Gower remarked that it often seems that the 'the largest room in a very small house tends toward vacancy, or the occasional visitor, who is often ushered into such a room, cold and cheerless; but in this sitting room there are many things to occupy the attention of any caller, if at all artistically inclined'.[32] It was there, in this the final room he described, that the most coveted prizes of his collection, the *bibelots* (or more aptly relics) of the diva-queen herself were assembled. Here provenance and legacy commingle with pleasure, historical accuracy with a collector's zeal. 'The bibelot as *objet d'art* became a sign of superiority, marking both social and financial success: in the old regime possession by the nobility conferred cachet upon the work; in the bourgeois world it is the other way around.'[33] These objects stand at the precipice of two opposing worlds, one lost and longed for by Gower, the other one in which he found himself. Gower devoted a separate and lengthy entry on his relics of Marie Antoinette, worth quoting in its entirety here.

2.9 Edward Dossetter. Sitting room. *Bric À Brac*.

On this page I have grouped together a few objects connected with Marie Antoinette. The fan was given by the young Archduchess to the leader of a company of maidens who welcomed her at Strasburg. Religiously cared for by her descendants, it came into the possession of Madame la Princess d'Henin, who kindly made me a present of it many years ago in Paris. In the centre is the little bust of Marie Antoinette in alabaster, mounted on a 'Giallo antico' and white marble stand, which was given me by the Empress of the French at Chislehurst in 1877. It is eight inches high. Below and on either side are miniatures and medallions of the Queen and Louis XVI, the latter in marble, Sevrès [sic] 'biscuit', and Wedgwood ware, collected in different places, in Paris, at Amsterdam, and Brighton. The two books belonged to Marie Antoinette, whose arms they bear. One is a book of devotion, the other of fashions. The 'lunette' is of ivory, and belonged to the Queen; it was given me by Arthur G. L. Gower. On the back of the little octagonal profile miniature of the Queen is engraved, 'Pleurez et vengez la'. I got this miniature in Windsor; it had evidently served as a brooch to some Royalist lady; but how or when it found its way to Windsor, I know not.[34]

In this entry, Gower perfectly exposes the way possession, passion and value cavort seamlessly in the cataloguing of a series of treasured though decidedly queer objects, which formed the centre of his collection. For Gower, his collection was a means to ward off the desecration of the memory of Marie Antoinette and that which she represented for Gower, pride for his aristocratic heritage and the links he shared, through his family, with the royalty of both France and Britain. He also believed, for example, to have shared in common with Queen Victoria a mutual love for Scotland, his native land. 'Lord Ronald never forgot for a moment that he was a Scot, and he was exultantly proud that through his mother he was descended from Belted Will.'[35] Familial ties formed an integral part of Gower's queer sense of lineage and heritage, but these are seen through the prism of his own forms of cross-identification and material expressions of identity.

Mania: the feminizing cultures of bric-à-brac

Bric-à-brac remains a special and unique specimen within the history of collecting, inhabiting an ambivalent position somewhere between high art and mundane practicality. In 1875 an anonymous critic noted how 'the position and surroundings of furniture are of more importance than the furniture itself'.[36] The spaces created between and betwixt each piece of furniture and *bibelot* conjures phenomenological impressions, orientations toward inchoate ideas, thoughts, expressions, sentiments and experiences. These are powerful affects that the decorator-collector may or may not be aware of in the design of his domestic comfort, but do reveal themselves over time. As the same critic also importantly noted: 'Houses are furnished by their owners. They represent the taste, not of such and such a firm, but of those who have to live in them.'[37] While we have long taken for granted the notion that a home represents, even embodies, the identity of its owner, in the last quarter of the nineteenth century in Britain it took on important currency within the cultural and heavily gendered landscape of the separate spheres. Increasingly, then, the dwelling place of collected objects was not simply a question of crass materiality and filling in space, but one conditioned by temporality, an accumulation over a period of time that exposed and incited carnal desires, sensualist pleasures, familial pressures, social obligation and the political will of the collector. We might say, these objects thicken space itself.

Since the Industrial Revolution, morality and judgement have held sway in the historiography of collecting and consumption. Antiquarian Louis Hertz, who penned such self-help books as *Antique Collecting for Men* (1969), claims that '[w]omen usually collect with decorative values or a definite decorative purpose in mind; men, for study from a technical or historical standpoint'.[38] What happens in the case of bachelors, especially those of a different sort like Gower? These, I suggest, had to perform both functions, to the detriment of gender codes that dominated the domestic sphere well into the late twentieth century. Russell W. Belk and Melanie Wallendorf also question the cultural signification of collecting through the gendering of purpose, that is, the 'societal functions' collections hold for members of a particular gender. They argue that

> [w]omen's collections tend to represent achievement in the feminine world of connection to other people–achievement of sentiment ... Here, the powerful achievements of masculine control over nature are exemplified through the killing of wild beasts, the conquering of the West, and the fighting of fires. In such ways collections perform the societal function of gendering achievement worlds while celebrating the societal importance of achievement. [Another] societal function of collecting is reification and integration of gender dialectics. Through collecting culture is made visible. Intrapersonally, collecting permits experimentation with androgyny as an individual participates in the masculine hunt for additions to the collection, as well as feminine nurturance in curating the collection.[39]

Although their analysis centres less on historic realities than on contemporary beliefs, Belk and Wallendorf are correct to underscore the gendered differences attributed to the narratives of collecting. However, we would do well to remember also that the so-called curating of a collection has traditionally fallen on to the shoulders of 'men of learning' and not women, for as the authors point out women have traditionally been seen as mere consumers, a designation that implies a lack of intellectual discernment necessary for curation.

Collections, like autobiographies, open up gaps, some purposeful, others inadvertent. These gaps are filled with the memories, meanings, desires and pleasures attributed to them by the object's current owner. In this way, subjectivity and a collection's formation are indissoluble.[40] Collections help to situate the subjective self within the world of things and people. As Susan Pearce argues: 'The imaginative link which holds material together may be purely personal or may engage the wider world'.[41] Writing in the same year as the Labouchere Amendment on Lord Frederic Leighton's infamous spell-binding home, Wilfrid Meynell contended that '[t]he artist lives his whole life under his own roof, and every room bears witness to his presence ... every room is therefore, in some sense an epitome of his history'.[42] The question is what secrets do a collection and each room portend to reveal about those who dwell with and within them? The language used to condemn the homosexual was not dissimilar to that used to vilify the aristocrat, both destined to fulfil the role of neglectful, unproductive degenerate that the middle classes and the mass media had established for them. However, the aesthete, perfectly embodied in the figure of Wilde, was also conflated with the figure of the homosexual, a queer figure who shrugged off his masculine duties to home (understood as a family dwelling) and empire. William Holman-Hunt declared that aesthetes were by nature 'self-conscious', always describing their own exquisite emotions or 'egotistical excesses'.[43] Harry Quilter further denounced the aesthete as 'neither true artist nor true man, but a sort of aesthetic hybrid, able to work himself into a phrenzy of irrational admiration about anything which is sufficiently old, obscure or grotesque'.[44] Anne Anderson posits that '[c]osseted within the House Beautiful or Palace of Art surrounded by precious relics, the aesthete would be accused of living in selfish isolation, threatening both productivity and progress'.[45] For physician and arch-conservative social critic Max Nordau, '[p]oetry and music, pictures and statues, amusement and travel, became his [the collector's] idols, and cultivation his substitute for the plain duty of patriotism'.[46] In these terms, it is no wonder that the privacy of the interior also needed to be policed.

Avid collector Edmond de Goncourt coined the term *bricabracomania* in his much-referenced *La Maison d'un artiste* (1881), where he also noted that the condition was the result of a 'psychology of accumulation'.[47] He equated the condition to that of a contagious disease while compatriot Paul Bourget claimed it to be 'the diseases of the nervous sensibility [that] led man to invent the factitious passion for collecting because his interior complexities made him incapable of appreciating the grand and simple sanity of things in the world around him'.[48] Yet another critic asserted that '[s]ociety disintegrates under the corrosive action of a deliquescent civilization [weighed down by] refinement of appetites, of sensations, of taste, of luxury, of pleasures; neurosis, hysteria, hypnotism, morphinomania, scientific skulduggery, extreme schopenhaurism'.[49] However, no one critic was more scathing, totalizing and unrelenting than Nordau in his attacks of the aesthete, collector and degenerate alike. According to him:

> The present rage for collecting, the pilling up, in dwellings, of aimless *bric-à-brac*, which does not become any more useful or beautiful by being called bibelots, appear to us in a completely new light when we know that Magnan has established the existence of an irresistible desire among the degenerate to accumulate useless trifles. It is firmly imprinted and so peculiar that Magnan declared it to be a stigma of degeneration, and has invented for it the name 'oniomania' or 'buying craze'. This is not to be confounded with the desire for buying, which possesses those who are in the first stage of general paralysis. The purchases of these persons are due to their delusion as to their own greatness. They lay in great supplies because they fancy themselves millionaires. The oniomaniac, on the contrary neither buys enormous quantities of one and the same thing, nor is the price a matter of indifference to him as with the paralytic.[50]

For Nordau the collector was not simply charged with an affliction, but guilty of a pathological disease, suffering from compulsive behaviour to consume coupled with delusions of grandeur, terms ascribed to the queer figure well into the twentieth century. For Nordau the collection provides a cover (one is tempted to say a closet) for the disease of consumption lurking below the surface of the victim, the evidence of which was provided by the very interiors he fabricated to house himself and his collections. Quite simply, he accumulated *too* much.

Health and medical reform also fuelled the growing antipathy toward excessive *objets d'art*. In 1884 the International Health Exhibition advocated that people put away their clutter. Even in the pages of *The Lady*, for example, critics admonished its readers against 'trumpery *bric-à-brac*', instilling the notion of saving up for one good piece over the regular purchasing of not good pieces, thus reducing the number of objects filling a home.[51] While interior design remained the privilege of men until the 1890s, *bric-à-brac* was considered a woman's delight and trifle and not something to be considered serious by men.[52] The introduction of electric light, rooms heavily populated with furniture and of course *bric-à-brac* made late Victorian homes, with their dark walls and fabrics, appear dingy and morose.[53] The new lighting technology also exposed the dirt within the home that posed a threat to its inhabitants.[54] Health and domestic reform went hand in hand as Britain and Europe ushered in a new century, and by 1910 most *bibelots* became a thing of the past, relegated to the attic, or worse to the proverbial, metaphorical and actual closet.

The late Victorian desire for eclecticism increasingly became suspect as the century drew to a close. Although the complete look was generally not highly regarded either, its opposite, a taste for the eclectic, did require, it was noted, the 'bold genius of a master mind and hand.' One critic from 1876 argued that the 'purity of style which insists on every article, even to the time-piece and fire-irons in a room, having the same points of family likeness, is a dull, narrow, uncongenial thing, and those who advocate it fail to recognise the broad principles underlying all true art whatsoever'.[55] Deborah Cohen maintains that in the 1890s, even before Wilde's highly public demise, men's relationship to interior design was being called into question at a time when the eclecticism that had governed Victorian taste up until that point was progressively deemed effeminate. She also notes how Mrs Talbot Cook, for example, writing in *Hearth and Home* in 1893 made a clear distinction between a 'real man' whose love of sport and the outdoors placed him in higher esteem and an unmasculine 'handy man' able to make his own draperies.[56] The *bric-à-brac* which had once fuelled the electric interior was now being condemned for its 'effeminate' characteristics by heroic, often male architects and designers who staunchly 'advocated the virtues of simplicity, authenticity, and integrity, contrasting these sober and "virile" qualities with the sentimentality, ornamentation, and ostentatious pretensions associated with eclecticism'.[57] These objects would collectively stand foursquare as the material index of Victorian and effeminate excess, emblems of idle, meaningless accumulation by twentieth-century modernists who rejected the material attachments of sentimentality, heritage and posterity in their overzealous rejection of all and any links to their fathers and forefathers. Modernity was largely presented 'as a heroic pursuit of a better life and a better society, which is basically at odds with stability, tradition, and continuity … To be modern thus means to participate in a quest for betterment of oneself and one's environment, leaving behind the certainties of the past.'[58] Gower's modernity, on the other hand, was predicated on talismanic objects of affective affiliation with a collective, shared identity that provided a sense of attachment with the past and its luminaries, tragic or otherwise. The goal was not to renounce the past, but rather to ensure its continuity, especially Gower's own direct association with it.

Establishing connections
Walter Hamilton, the first to chronicle the history and development of the Aesthetic Movement, noted in 1882 how

> Wilde occupied some fine old wainscoted rooms over the river in that college [Magdalen] which is thought by many to be the most beautiful in Oxford. These rooms he had decorated with painted ceilings and handsome dados, and they were filled with treasures of art, picked up at home and abroad, and here he held social meetings, which were attended by numbers of the men who were interested in art, or music, or poetry, and for the most part practices [sic] some one of these in addition to the ordinary collegiate studies.[59]

The Rt Rev. Sir David Hunter Blair who attended Oxford in those *wild* days recalled the Irishman's 'bonhomie, good-humour, unusual capacity for pleasant talk, and Irish hospitality, exercised much beyond his modest means'.[60] It was as a result of this hospitality that Wilde soon developed a following and community centred on regular Sunday evening soirées in his rooms to which all friends were always welcome. Blair noticed how on several occasions 'cheerfulness degenerated into a scuffle or romp, to the imminent danger of our host's *bric-à-brac*'. According to Blair, Wilde's rooms were 'pleasantly' well furnished, but were not as Thomas Seccombe described them, 'notorious for their exotic splendour [sic]'. Blair's dismissal of Seccombe's 'absurd' comments regarding Wilde's student rooms was based on first-hand knowledge; for, unlike Seccombe, Blair had not only known Wilde in his undergraduate days, he also helped him with the furnishing of his interiors. Seccombe, on the other hand, did not know Wilde at the time.[61] Here, personal memory and direct experiential knowledge trump idle gossip. Seccombe's comments were the product of reading the identity of a space through the lens of events and identifications after the fact; premised entirely on a guilty by association ethos. Wilde's later identity (based solely on an aesthetic of sexual deviance) served to conjure spatial narratives that in no way fit the perceptions of his Oxford contemporaries.

It was, however, during his Oxford days that Wilde met Frank Miles (1852–1891), two years his senior; a meeting that was to unravel a series of relationships and a chain of events that led to his eventual fall from grace. Miles and Wilde met in 1874 or 1875, and in 1877 the two began staying in Miles's lodgings in Salisbury Street, off the Strand. There, Wilde had his panelled walls painted white and amassed a small but conclusive array of *objets d'art*, including his famed blue-and-white china, Tanagra figures, Greek rugs and hangings and Damascus tiles. Wilde referred to their home in Salisbury street as 'this untidy but romantic house'.[62] Edward Williamson Godwin (1833–1886), regarded by Wilde with the highest esteem and reverence for his work, was commissioned in 1877 by Miles to design a studio house for himself, and ostensibly Wilde, at 1 Tite Street, Chelsea (since renumbered 44), into which they moved in August 1880. With Miles, Wilde entered into what was in reality his first domestic partnership. As Mark Girouard points out, history has been unfavourable to Miles, often a footnote to the early life of the playwright. By the time of the commission, Miles had already gained a considerable reputation as an artist and, as Girouard notes, 'sponsored Wilde's arrival in London society rather than the other way around. Miles had the moneyed background, social connections and artistic success that Wilde initially lacked.'[63]

Upon completion of his studies the following year Wilde 'permanently' settled in with the artist. It was also through Miles that Wilde developed his knowledge of and interest in flowers. Years later, in his first lecture in North America, Wilde commented on the true value that the lily and sunflower possessed for the movement and dispelled the erroneous suggestion that these were vegetal forms of sustenance for a young aesthete. '[T]hese two flowers', he claimed, 'are in England the most perfect models of design, the most naturally adapted for decorative art – the gaudy leonine beauty of the one and the precious loveliness of the other giving to the artist the most entire and perfect joy'.[64] Flowers proved to be a source of joy through good design as much as a queer mode of communication amongst like-minded men. It was also through Miles that Wilde met Sarah Bernhardt, Lillie Langtry and Constance, Duchess of Westminster (Wilde devotee and Gower's sister). Miles was widely reputed to have facilitated Langtry's entrée into celebrity. Among Wilde's prized possessions at Salisbury street was a portrait of Langtry by Edward Poynter in which she sits reclined in a red chair holding a rose delicately

2.10 Napoleon Sarony. *Oscar Wilde*, 1882.

to her bosom, absorbed in her own thought world, wearing a golden-yellow dress.⁶⁵ The two men, particularly Miles, held a profound fondness for the young actress, verging into the fanatical. The artist produced a series of drawings that were turned into postcards; a material and visual culture that helped to solidify her social cachet and attractiveness and served as the impetus for the diva-worship that necessarily ensued.

Miles and Wilde entertained often and invited friends for 'Tea and Beautie's' whose centrepieces were Miles's numerous portraits of beautiful women like Langtry, bright stars in the celestial plane of celebrity. According to Gower, by the time the two met in 1876, Miles's obsession with Langtry was already in full bloom, claiming: 'Frank is quite in ecstasies about her'.⁶⁶ Miles and Wilde's goal, according to Neil McKenna, 'was to establish themselves as arbiters of taste among the more relaxed, more exciting and fashionable society of writers, artists, and poets. Oscar once remarked that there were only three ways to get into society: feed it, amuse it or shock it. He used all three tactics simultaneously.'⁶⁷ It was also through Miles that Wilde (then still an undergraduate) met his friend and patron Gower on 2 June 1876 when the two went up to visit the playwright in his rooms located at the cloisters on the ground floor of Magdalen College. In his diaries, Gower had this to say about his meeting with Wilde: 'By early train to Oxford with F. Miles … There I made the acquaintance of young Oscar Wilde, a friend of Miles's. A pleasant cheery fellow, but with his long-haired head full of nonsense about the Church of Rome. His room filled with photographs of the Pope and of Cardinal Manning.'⁶⁸ Soon after he was introduced to Gower, Wilde paid regular and frequent visits to Windsor Lodge, which he declared to be 'one of the most beautiful houses I ever saw'.⁶⁹ Along with Miles, Gower also introduced Wilde to numerous important ladies of society, who could serve as possible patrons.⁷⁰ Among these, as already noted, was Constance, Duchess of Westminster, with whom Gower, Miles and Wilde had tea on 14 March 1877.

Shame, stigma and scandal

For some, however, Gower's dubious reputation extended to the domain of religion and moral influence. Blair asserted, without doubt, that Gower had a negative influence on Wilde. It was due entirely to his questionable moral inclinations, according to Blair, that Gower kept Wilde away from Catholicism. In his memoirs, he described him in the following manner:

> I cannot here omit mention of another friend of Oscar Wilde, one quite outside the circle of his Oxford intimates, who exercised on him an influence entirely antagonistic to Catholicism. This was Lord Ronald Gower, the well-known art critic, writer, and sculptor, himself a Trinity (Cambridge)

'God Save the Queen' 63

2.11 Napoleon Sarony. *Lord Ronald Charles Gower Sutherland-Levenson-Gower*, c. 1884, published 1902.

man, and a dozen or so years older than Wilde and myself. Possessed of genuine artistic attainments, handsome, nobly born, and passably rich, he was a notable and popular figure in the society of the 'seventies' ... Whenever they met he would use the weapons of ridicule and sarcasm, at which he was fairly adept, to laugh his friend out of his Catholic proclivities.[71]

Perhaps most fascinating about Blair's depiction of Gower's negative influence is how it deterred what was, according to him, Wilde's 'natural bent toward Catholicism'.[72] Obliquely through religious affiliation, Gower's reputation was put into question.

Gower was also said to have introduced Wilde to London's sexual underworld. Gower's association with the seedier side of London circulated widely among the city's queer artistic set and well beyond. John Addington Symonds came to know Gower by 1887, and his gondolier boyfriend Angelo Fusato disapproved of him, claiming that Gower 'goes from love to love–with jack today and Tom tomorrow — [and] sinks deep into the mire, loses respect, and ends in degradation'.[73] In a letter from September 1891 to Edmund Gosse, Symonds also complained about Gower, who was staying with him at Davos. In the letter Symonds criticized how he was 'a dreadful man to live near, though very interesting' because he 'saturate[s] one's spirit in Urningthum of the rankest most diabolic kind'.[74] The following year he also wrote that Gower 'knows everybody, from the cabbies, corporals & carabinieri up to the painters, princes and plenipotentiary envoys'.[75]

In May 1878 Gower left England, after which, in *The Man of the World*, journalist Williamson Mackay published an article making 'shocking, imputations upon some member of the aristocracy of "refined tastes" and "studious habits"', who was also an 'artist of more than ordinary ability' – these were the words Gower used in the subsequent suit against the newspaper.[76] However, by year's end, his closest, high-ranking friend, the Prince of Wales, accused him of 'being a member of an association "for unnatural practices"'.[77] Furthermore, a decade later, in 1888, when he had completed his statue of *The Prince Hal* depicted as a young man trying on his father's crown, 'an ideal of lithe youthfulness', rumours began to circulate of the suicide of the troubled model, Raoul Perrin, who had allegedly posed for the sculpture. Gower was represented as having used the young man, rejecting him in his time of need. Although Gower did come into contact with Perrin, there is no evidence to suggest that the model actually posed for the statue that was one of five sculptures forming his much-celebrated *Shakespeare Memorial*.[78] In his two-volume *Reminiscences*, Gower made a significant connection between himself at the moment of his controversy and Marie Antoinette.[79] As art historian Whitney Davis concludes, 'Gower survived scandal, though probably by the skin of teeth, because his prevarications, though convenient, were accepted: in the end he gave Society what Society expected of him. Considering his position and achievements, and perhaps mindful of his subtle lesson on hypocrisy, Society let him alone. Hindsight has come to prefer Wilde's to Gower's social and artistic pose, both as politics and as art.'[80]

Collecting: beyond anality
Undoubtedly collecting is a form of controlled passion. After all, the objects that surround us on a daily basis are 'objects of a passion' of some sort.[81] However, the homosexual art collector has long been tied to notions of sublimation. Even Wilde himself toyed with this notion with Dorian Gray, for whom the 'treasures, and everything that he collected in his lovely house, were [to him] a means of forgetfulness, modes by which he could escape, for a season, from the fear that seemed to him at times to be almost too great to be borne'.[82]

Collections and their objects can also become indices for the hidden, the obscured and the closeted. Jean Baudrillard in a more contemporary context equates a perverse sexuality with the collector. He asserts that 'a correlation with sexuality can generally be demonstrated, so that the activity of collecting may be seen as a powerful mechanism of compensation during critical phases in a person's sexual development. Invariably it runs counter to active genital sexuality, though it should not be seen as a pure or simple substitute thereof, but rather a regression to the anal stage, manifested in such behaviour patterns as accumulation, ordering, aggressive retention and so forth.'[83] Collecting, within his postmodernist and quasi-Freudian formulation, can only ever be infantile, regressive and underdeveloped, rather than evidence of a sophisticated language through which to communicate meaning replete with historical value and signification. The clear subtext of Baudrillard's relegation of the collector to the anal stage refers to his propensity for possession, and ultimate lack of development within the progressive schema Freud set out nearly a century earlier. Baudrillard's theorization of the collector is also markedly akin to the heroic masculinist modernity of his predecessors who saw *bric-à-brac* as effeminate and a hindrance to progressive development and sought a disavowal of the past along with supposed moribund systems of valuation. Provenance for men like Gower was acquisition not simply through the proper artistic channels, but rather through association and affective affiliations with historical personages he held in high esteem, the very sentimental debris loathed by modernists who saw this as a distinctly reactive force. Long before Freud developed his theories, homosexual men were associated with anality and the decay of hygiene: 'As a symbol of anality, positioned near the public toilets, they [homosexuals] also take part in the lowness of animal life … the odours of the pederast, an amateur of strong perfumes, show the olfactory proximity between musk and excrement.'[84] The senses and identity commingle in a specific way according to critics who sought to identify a phenomenological blueprint of deviance.

Authentication and other such aspects of collecting evoke a paean to the culture versus nature debate, a way for the aesthetic bachelor to rise above and authenticate his own importance and status as superior dilettante in terms of both acquisition through consumption and astute knowledge as a collector. If we subject the notion of sublimation tacitly expressed and profoundly maligned by Baudrillard to further scrutiny we might also agree that the manifest and artificial culture engendered by the collector rises above and controls nature (his sexual nature that is), by channelling his passion and physical energy into the hunting and gathering implicated in the culture of collecting. While this is surely part of some collectors' endeavours, we cannot stand still in the space of sublimation alone for it divests the collector of any real sense of personal and cultural agency. The collector, Gower himself, was very much in control at a time when sexologists were defining the so-called homosexual as an aberrant type. The collection is less about anality and sublimation and more a means to exert control over one's own domain in a period of loss of control. This conjuncture also collided with the remnants of the Enlightenment project and its zealous quest to order the universe into discrete categories and typologies. In this schema the homosexual was the first to be 'called into being' against which normality and heterosexuality itself would be set into relief. In this way, the homosexual was always a cast shadow, something to avoid, but never shaken off in the light of day.

In his revealingly personal writings on diva prose and worship Wayne Koestenbaum provocatively queries: 'In a culture without closets, would I have adored divas?'[85] Indeed, I suggest that the need for the surrogate diva-queen, the allegorical figure which simultaneously embodies our hopes, desires and fears, is necessary in a world in which the queer collector as allegorist communicates through the secret language of things; a far more sophisticated mode of communication than is assumed in Baudrillard's postmodernist readings and Freud's anal stage. Objects, the material culture of our lives, often stand in to communicate when words cannot or should not express desires, meanings or affiliations, especially when it concerns that *love which dare not speak its name*. Objects speak to us as much as for us. They comprise a language known only to those engaged in the transactions associated with these objects. In this way they become opaque, discernible only to those in the know, structured by codes of a community. As Camille brilliantly posits, it is less important to locate sexuality and gender 'as things we see *in* images … than as inherent in the very structure of relations through which images have been inherited, bought, sold, exchanged and enjoyed'.[86] The fear is that by acknowledging the exchange of objects as a revelation of sexuality and gender implies there is a network or system at play, leaving many vulnerable to its agents and denied access to knowledge. The mania for *bric-à-brac* was identified by the 1870s and sustained in popular literature such as Mrs Burton Harrison's collection of fairy tales *Bric-a-Brac Stories* (1885). These stories expose the fantastical 'secret life of things'.[87] This secret life of things marks the bond that exists between private collectors as queer figures. As Camille has astutely pointed out, 'it is not just that the unmentionable nature of same-sex desire has often meant that the subject had to communicate the "secret" in a coded language, but the fact that this language was a system of objects'.[88]

Benjamin wrote: 'in every collector hides an allegorist, and in every allegorist a collector. As far as the collector is concerned, his collection in never complete; for let him discover just a single piece missing, and everything he's collected remains a patchwork, which is what things are for allegory from the beginning'.[89] Like the queer figure, the collector holds close his stories, revealing only to a privileged few parts, tidbits that are as opaque and fragmentary as the archives. *Bric-à-brac* functions in a similar way, as it is often only scraps, lonely and lost parts of a perceived whole whose former glory has since passed. Queer narration works much in the same way, for it too can only ever reveal itself in parts, spurts and bouts. Objects in a collection are never simply about provenance, but are often about the desires and performances of the collector in the acquisition (hunting and gathering) and curation (nurturing) of his collection. In the literary and certainly within the pictorial and decorative arts, allegory has long held an important and revered place of honour. Allegory works itself out through a layering of meaning, a text or image meant to stand in for something else, something deeper hidden within. It is, by its very nature, duplicitous, as on the surface it provides only a partial revelation, a queer circumvention of leaving meaning open to one and all. Allegory then provides a shield, a boundary, a protective armature. With its long respected traditions in numerous disciplines, I see allegory's use as far more compelling and empowering than sublimation in a discussion of collecting and a collector's identity. As I see it, Gower was a queer allegorist, piecing together the secret life of things within the confines of his home as both a collector and a queer man, these two facets of his social and personal identity rubbed together in the material legacy of Marie Antoinette, who stood in as *the* quintessential allegorical figure, the diva-queen. For Gower she served as index for his sexual identity as much as for his class affiliation.

'Off with her head': a queer castration

Aristocrat and author Lowndes would spend two to three days a week with Gower on a regular basis, to which her husband never objected. When she knew him, she recalled, Gower

> owned the finest authentic collection of relics of the last Queen of France in the world ... I remember the lovely little fan which had been presented to

2.12 Edward Dossetter. Marie-Antoinette Relics, *Bric À Brac*.

the then Austrian Archduchess when she first stepped on the soil of France at Strasburg, and I have sometimes wondered who now owns that fan. Lord Ronald's devotion to Marie Antoinette was the reason why the Empress Eugenie gave him a small alabaster bust which the Queen had presented to one of her ladies-in-waiting; and he was also given by a French friend her tiny gold thimble.[90]

Here provenance, of an object passed down through affiliation and association, enriches the narratological development and subsequent gravitas of Gower's collection and obsession with the diva-queen. Others also noted his important and precious relics of the Queen. One writer remarked how '[i]n the lovely drawing-room of Lord Ronald's London house is to be found an interesting and moving collection of his heroine's relics, including a quaint inlaid fan given by the Girlish Dauphine to the spokeswomen of the first deputation of maidens who welcomed her as a bride on to French soil at Strasbourg, and presented to its present owner by the Princess d'Henin'.[91] His collection was not merely personal, but also culturally significant.

It was in 1876 that Gower caught his 'cult' for the queen which began while studying in Paris, when in February he took up a studio with his assistant Luca Madrassi in 4 rue Candolle. It was in this studio that he created two life-size sculptures exhibited at the Royal Academy one year later.[92] The first was a standing figure of *Marie Antoinette leaving the*

Conciergerie on her way to Execution, while the second was the already mentioned reclining though alert *Old Guard* that remained on guard outside Gower Lodge. In the summer of that year Gower had the plaster figure turned into a life-size marble, which was soon acquired by the Duke of Westminster.[93] The former was based, in part, on an unflattering pen and ink sketch by Jacques-Louis David (1748–1825) of the Queen seated in a tumbrel on her way to her inevitable fate at the hands of the revolutionary zealots (1793). Despite his reference to David's work, Gower made clear how the French painter's 'participation in some of the bloodiest scenes of that time will render his memory ever odious'.[94] David, after all, was one of the three men who cross-examined the Queen's children. The sculpture was also influenced by the recollections of Gower's dance master from the early 1860s, an older Frenchman who, as a child in 1793, 'had seen Marie Antoinette on the way to the scaffold … with her grey hair cut short, her hands tied, seated in a cart, still retaining her calm demeanour as the mob shouted and mothed around her'.[95] The statuette would also serve as the prototype for the version displayed in Madame Tussaud's much-visited wax museum. What is important about the creation is the manner in which so-called first-hand, eyewitness accounts (a mere sketch and gossip) assist Gower to conjure this fateful moment in the life of his heroine, in less than an ideal diva pose. These accounts do not simply help to recreate, as it were, the event, through the guise of representation, but more importantly lend a greater proximity between himself and his diva-queen. The intense desire and need to associate himself with and connect through direct material and historical affiliations with the Queen was also guaranteed ever more directly through his grandmother, who was the wife of the English Ambassador at the court of Louis XVI, herself a friend to the French queen. Their friendship, we might conclude, provided a mere two degrees of separation between Gower and the diva-queen. As Williamson claimed in his memorial tribute to the artist, his interest in Shakespeare and Marie Antoinette was 'hereditary', implying a link between obsession, nature and lineage.[96] Talia Schaffer, however, argues for the notion of 'symbolic genealogy' as a lineage the connoisseur fashions for himself. Through this symbolic genealogy inheritance is not necessarily guaranteed through genetic affiliation (though it can be), but is largely fashioned culturally. As such its patterns or systems might refer us back to Foucault's seminal notions of genealogy and archaeology, which acknowledge the plurality and contradictory origins of meaning, a conflicted past that simultaneously leaves traces of power, resistance and pleasure.[97]

Gower published texts he had written on France's most beloved female figure, Joan of Arc, as well as its most maligned and detested, Marie Antoinette; both having fallen victim to the machinations, histories and recordings of men. Williamson noted that 'all the idolatry of his young mind was poured out towards two of his heroines, Marie Antoinette and Joan of Arc'.[98] Idolatry is complicated by a cross-sex identification process in addition to aristocratic lineage and cultural patrimony in a world now determined by bourgeois morality, the heterosexual matrix and the illusory parameters of the separate spheres. In both instances, Gower took great pains to visit all the important and relevant pilgrimage sites of his heroines. As one writer noted, '[h]aving always had a special interest in Marie Antoinette, he for some years made it his chief business to visit those places consecrated by her presence. He travelled all over Europe in search of documents and letters shedding light on her tragic story, and gathered together a unique collection of Marie Antoinette medals and relics.'[99] The author's choice of words underscores the pseudo-religious devotion Gower maintained through his acts of pilgrimage (hunting), writing and curating of his acquired relics (nurturing).

In *Last Days of Marie Antoinette: An Historical Sketch* Gower waxes soulfully how

> [a]s the clouds of adversity gathered around, Marie Antoinette displayed a patience and a courage in unparalleled sufferings such as few saints and martyrs have equalled. The pure ore of her nature was but hidden under the dross of worldliness; and the scorching fire of suffering revealed one of the tenderest hearts and one of the bravest natures that history records. To this is owing, I believe, the universal interest felt in her life and in her misfortunes.[100]

His acutely detailed account of the Queen in the last remaining days of her life spent in the confines of prison was one premised on the pitiful material culture of the spaces she was forced to endure. Included in his sketch were the few and simple objects she was allowed to keep in her cell, awarded to her by the Revolutionary Tribunal. According to the devotee, the Queen kept a personal inventory 'of her linen, marking it down with a pin on the wall. Rosalie, her faithful maid, adds that she had also scratched some other things on the wall; but after her death these were all painted over with a thick coat of whitewash.'[101] Gower wrote of how she had no furniture at her disposal, and, as a result of not being 'allowed a chest of drawers, she placed her clothes in a paper box that Rosalie brought her, which she received, says Rosalie, as if it had been the most beautiful piece of furniture in the world'.[102] Gower's prose is neither detached nor distanced, but intensely sympathetic and painfully personal. Koestenbaum surmises how writing by the diva worshipper fulfils myriad functions in the life of the queer devotee: 'I write diva prose if I am weak but want to pretend to be strong, if I want to cut off opposition, if I want to feign beauty while knowing I'm plain, if I want to bully but seem polite, if I want to praise myself lest no one else praise me. Diva prose is the style of the outsider who has arrived inside, but still fears the sentries.'[103] Identification with the diva-queen is profound. Gower understood first-hand the trials and tribulations of being misjudged, the emotional debris from the scandals that plagued his life, and later in life when he was subjected to selling and dispersing the collection he had so lovingly assembled. Gower recalled how:

> I can never remember a time when the life of Marie Antoinette did not interest me beyond all other subjects; it has been an ever-increasing attraction, this feeling of sympathy for one of the bravest, although most womanlike characters in modern history. Perhaps, too, having also had something hard to ensure oneself, of having had to live through detraction and calumny, has made this interest and sympathy (for one whose life, so bright as its outset, was so soon rendered a long martyrdom by the foulest and cruellest lies that were ever shaped upon the head of queen and woman long before her physical sufferings commenced) stronger.[104]

His idolatry through diva prose or, more profoundly, his identification with the ill-fated Queen is palpable to the point of the visceral. Collecting these objects embody simultaneously mourning and identification as the site of pleasure and identity formation. As Susan Stewart argues, the collector replaces the 'narrative of production' with the 'narrative of the collection … the replacement of the narrative of history with the narrative of the individual subject–that is the collector himself'.[105] These purposeful acts of replacement–or displacement–serve the collector well in his diva prose, a writing style that eloquently unmasks the secret of things.

The 'demonized' diva, as Koestenbaum describes her, 'is associated with difference itself, with a satanic separation from the whole, the clean, the contained, and the attractive. Mythically, she is perverse, monstrous, abnormal, and ugly',[106] a description not entirely unlike those used to vilify Marie Antoinette, and later to condemn the homosexual. The final act in the drama of the French diva-queen's life, the one Gower chose to immortalize in marble and prose, was a violent and graphic act of othering, differencing and most significantly of silencing, an act that would facilitate, even if only symbolically, the ascendancy of the bourgeoisie. By the end of the nineteenth century, the aristocrat and the homosexual alike were vilified in a similar manner. Unproductive, enfeebled, degenerate, neither figure, it was commonly held, could assist in the betterment and future of the nation. The homosexual, moreover, lacked the possibility to contribute to the heteronormative and capitalist system of narratological progression through to procreation. Marie Antoinette's consumption (provided as *the* reason for the downfall of France) or that of the queer aristocratic collector, obsessed with the demonized diva, are equally marked as the source of ultimate and unbridled excess. Cutting off the head is an act of dismemberment that is not simply an act of murder, but a symbolic and Freudian subtext of removing the voice, a castration that disavows power. Both were rendered silent, whether through her death or his scandals. Luxury then becomes a locus for escape and pleasure and cannot be dismissed as mere frivolity but a political strategy of empowerment and the displacement of the centre of that power – distinctly away from bourgeois morality.

Pain, memory and loss: material culture and the cycles of a queer collector's life

In Honoré de Balzac's novella turned novel *Le Cousin Pons* (1847), the main character Sylvain Pons, a bachelor, is at once a collector and a gourmand. He shares his home with Wilhelm Schmucke, a musician like Pons, with whom he pools his meagre resources and lives out an entirely domesticated and intimate existence. Sharon Marcus notes that what significantly differentiates Pons in the late 1840s from other bachelors is that he lives with another man.[107] His gourmand side leads him to dine regularly with his wealthier cousin M. Camusot de Marville (a lawyer) and his wife who treat Pons to continuous gastronomic surprises and tasty novelties. His gratitude is such that he elects himself responsible to locate a suitable husband for the couple's only child Cécile. His efforts are in vain and result in Pons being rejected from the family and denied access to their luxurious family home. Mme Camusot, however, soon learns of Pons's priceless art and plots to secure his collection for the family as a dowry for their daughter. In addition to the family, others (including Pons's landlady Mme Cibot) conspire to rid Pons of his beloved collection, which, once their plot is exposed, leads to the bachelor's death in misery and agony. However, it is his beloved companion Schmucke to whom he bequeaths all that remains of his collection and worldly possessions. Schmucke is quickly shamed into handing over his inheritance to the de Marville family, an act that not only denies the legacy of the two men's relationship, but also leads to him dying alone, longing for his dear departed companion who was *his* only true passion. While the story reveals Balzac's disdain for bourgeois morality, it nevertheless highlights the lengths to which the heterosexual matrix maintains boundaries and cohesion to the detriment of queer time and space. The lone figure of the queer bachelor, precisely because of his collection, his solitary pleasure, falls victim to the overriding needs of compulsory heterosexual unity and its requirements on class identity. Schmucke too also suffers at the hands of the family through acts of denial and coercion. As Judith Halberstam contends, '[t]he time of inheritance refers to an overview of generational time within which values, wealth, goods, and morals are passed through family ties from one generation to the next. It also connects the family to the historical past of the nation, and glances ahead to connect the family to the future of both familial and national stability.'[108] Inheritance and lineage are reinstated through progeny rather than affective affiliation.

Later in life, Gower adopted the much younger Frank Hird, with whom he was romantically entangled. Upon learning of their unique relationship Wilde famously quipped: 'Frank should be seen but not Hird'.[109] While the two remained faithful companions until Gower's death in 1916, Wilde's sardonic comments infantilize Hird as much as rendering him Gower's own 'eye candy'. Wilde's witty attack removes Hird's voice and seemingly reinforces the silence that *the love which dare not speak its name* intimated. Little of their intimate life together is known; however, we do know how Gower was 'cared for with increasing devotion by Mr Hird, he passed the last few remaining years of his life – although martyred by suffering and burdened with trouble – in a gentle atmosphere, fittingly corresponding to his own nature'.[110] Although Gower adopted Hird,[111] a queer appropriation of the familial structure that guarantees legitimacy to one's heirs, an act that ensured an alternative form of lineage and legacy, Gower had little left to bequeath his young companion. Balzac's tragic novel presages Gower's and Hird's relationship, and the parallels of their narratives are uncanny; chief among them is how these men, like most of the men in this book, created what we might characterize as 'counter-intimacies', sites of resistance to preferred expressions and normative structures of bonding, filiation and intimacy, opening up for themselves a non-normative, or queer, conjugal, companionate domesticity.[112]

In his weighty, though unfinished *Arcades Project*, Benjamin discussed the collector as a nest-builder.[113] The narrator in *Le Cousin Pons* described his relationship with his companion in the idealized terms of romantic love and notes how they mutually turned their backs to the outside world, creating their own ideal life-world, or nest. Their domestic realm and apparent, though unassuming, bliss was interrupted only by Pons's culinary retreats to his cousins, acts that would forever infect the queer couple's domestic harmony and its longevity. Equally fascinating is how the narrator claims that food and Pons's collection act as substitutes for women: 'Good food and *bric-à-brac* were the equivalents of a woman for him'.[114] Pons's collection is akin to a 'lover' who adores 'his beautiful mistress'.[115] Balzac's formulation of equating the collector to a lover and his collection to his mistress implies a distinctly heterosexist application, and does not take into consideration a queer appropriation of this sort of transference, desire and pleasure. Rather, Balzac's not surprising formulation of a collection as an act or system of sublimation reifies cross-sex desire and heterosexual companionship. Gower's collection of *bric-à-brac* not only problematized Balzac's not uncommon cross-sex theorization of a collector's passion, but more importantly his queer mistress was none other than the diva-queen herself, an allegorical rather than sublimated figure of sexual identity as much as class affinity.

It was in his splendid student quarters that Wilde, as legend goes, pronounced his infamous performative dictum: 'Oh, would that I would live up to my blue china!'[116] Wilde's words would not only come to underpin the lofty ideals established by the Aesthetic Movement to create a complete lifestyle premised uniquely on aesthetics, but so too did it make an important claim for the indelible relationship between art, life and the body. This performative utterance, symbolic more than actual, exposes the nature of identity *vis-à-vis* a collected, material object. Here the transformative potential of altering oneself to suit one's furniture and/or décor underscores how the 'House Beautiful' was not simply yet another artistic movement but an entire moral philosophy and lifestyle. Years later, rector of St Mary's (Oxford) Dean Burgon castigated the man who claimed to desire to live up to his blue and white, asserting that 'when a young man says not in polished banter but in sober earnestness, that he finds it difficult to live up to the level of his blue china, there has crept into these cloistered shades a form of heathenism which it is our bounden duty to fight against and to crush out'.[117] Material objects for Wilde as much as for the angered Oxford Dean exposed an ethical tug-of-war; a struggle for the moral wellbeing of the modern man in a free-market economy. First and foremost, the home and its interior design stood as the true register of life itself for Wilde, even until the apocryphal moments of his death in Paris, when he sorrowfully pronounced: 'My wallpaper and I are fighting a duel to the death. One or the other of us had to go.'[118] As we know, the wallpaper won out. In Wilde's final dictum on design, the wallpaper was as much a case of bad design as it served as emblem of how the decorative triumphs over the human body, that is, more exactly nature itself. It is worth singling out how these two now legendary epigrams service as bookends to the life led by the Aesthetic Movement's greatest (and queer) oracle. Both mark punctuated moments in the narratological development of aesthetic life; that is, first to become the object, to transform oneself into the aesthetic ideal the blue china embodied, and second to extinguish life at the hands of bad design. The latter is a cunning metaphor for Aestheticism's supposed demise when Wilde was jailed and later forced into exile. Here the cycle of life is made possible through design itself. In the epistle *De Profundis*, written while imprisoned, Wilde made clear that it was through his relationship with Bosie, Lord Alfred Douglas, that he was forcibly evicted from his home. Seeped in nostalgia, he longed to return to the interiors of his fashioning and the objects of familiarity.

There are clear, near universal, themes attached to collecting: 'desire and nostalgia, saving and loss, the urge to erect a permanent and complete system against the destructiveness of time'.[119] In short these various relationships amount to a collector's life. Pain, memory and loss, albeit at a distance, tinged the final episode of Wilde's life as much as they did for Gower. Swindled in 1910 by a businessman of ill repute, Captain Frank Sheckelton, of whom little is known,[120] like Wilde before him, Gower was forced to liquidate his hard assets, his inherited furniture and exquisite regal relics. 'In his later years of pathetic anxiety', recalled Williamson,

> one of his hardest tasks was accomplished, when he had to part with the choice collection of treasures concerning Marie Antoinette, which he had given the best years of his life to collect; and those of us who have seen him handling her fan, her glove, her books, her lorgnette, her medals, and many of the little treasures which had belong to her, and which were of inestimable value for him, still shrink from remembering how painful it was for him to part from these things, and to let them go over the seas when his trouble came upon him.[121]

Despite his best efforts, Gower could not guarantee the vestigial remnants of the Queen's material culture he had gathered neither for a subsequent generation nor for his adopted heir Hird. Not only was Gower forced to live out his remaining years in conditions he was less than accustomed to, but so too was he forced to sell his *objets d'art* and the memorabilia he had lovingly and painstakingly collected, leaving his beloved heir with little in the way of inheritance. Gower's gleeful pride of naming, enumerating and writing the material history of his collected objects – reliquary remnants – made him so happy that he wrote and published a book to commemorate his role in their history for future posterity. In the writing of these objects, he queerly interpolates himself into this history, material legacy and lineage, and by extension their cultural patrimony. Allegory, appropriation and identification were the means by which Gower was allowed to delight in his own queer forms of legacy, provenance, posterity and affiliations. While these provided an immeasurable source of pride, he could not financially sustain his life's work and fell victim to what he surely saw as an unjust death sentence when his *bric-à-brac*, the very embodiment of his diva-queen, was forced into exile, 'scattered all over the world'.[122]

Notes

1 G. C. Williamson, 'The Lord Ronald Sutherland-Gower: A Memorial Tribute', *Khaki* (1916), p. 267.
2 Mrs B. Lowndes, *The Merry Wives of Westminster* (London: Macmillan and Co. Ltd, 1946), pp. 207–8.
3 Williamson, 'The Lord Ronald Sutherland-Gower', p. 268.
4 M. A. B, 'Lord Ronald Gower: Sculptor, Author and Dilettante'. *English Illustrated Magazine*, no. 13 (April–September 1895), p. 119.
5 Lord R. Gower, *Last Days of Marie Antoinette: An Historical Sketch* (London: Kegan Paul, Trench and Co., 1885), p. 1.
6 M. Camille, 'Editor's Introduction', *Art History Special Issue on Queer Collecting*, vol. 24, no. 2 (April 2001), p. 163.
7 N. Bartlett, *Who Was That Man? A Present for Mr. Oscar Wilde* (London: Serpent's Tail, 1989), p. 178.
8 G. Dawson, *Soldier Heroes: British Adventure, Empire, and the Imagining of Masculinities* (New York and London: Routledge, 1994), pp. 1–2.
9 See for example C. Gere, *Nineteenth-Century Decoration: The Art of the Interior* (New York, H. N. Abrams, 1989); W. Davis, 'Lord Ronald Gower and the Offending Adam', in David J. Getsey (ed.), *Sculpture and the Pursuit of a Modern Ideal in Britain, c. 1880–1930* (Aldershot: Ashgate Publishing Limited, 2004).
10 For more on the decorative schemes of Stafford House see J. Helland, 'Translating textiles: "private palaces" and the Celtic fringe, 1890–1910', in J. Potvin and A. Myzelev (eds.), *Fashion, Interior Design and the Contours of Modern Identity* (Aldershot and Burlington: Ashgate, 2010).
11 Lord R. Gower, *Bric À Brac or Some Photoprints Illustrating Art Objects at Gower Lodge, Windsor* (London: Kegan Paul, Trench and Co., 1888), p. viii.
12 *Ibid.*
13 *Ibid.*
14 *Ibid.*, p. x–xi.
15 'The Art of Furnishing', *Cornhill Magazine* (January–June 1875), p. 537.
16 Williamson, 'The Lord Ronald Sutherland-Gower', p. 272.
17 J. G. Wilson, 'About Bric-à-Brac', *The Art Journal*, vol. 46 (1878), p. 314.
18 J. Loftie, *A Plea for Art in the House: With Special Reference to the Economy of Collecting Works of Art, and the Importance of Taste in Education and Morals* (London: Macmillan and Co., 1876), p. 11
19 See T. Veblen, *The Theory of Leisure Class: An Economic Study of Institutions* (New York: The Modern Library, 1934 [1899]).
20 Loftie, *A Plea for Art in the House*, p. 12.
21 C. Cook, *The House Beautiful Essays on Beds and Tables, Stools and Candlesticks* (New York: Scribner, Armstrong and Company, 1878), p. 103.
22 Wilson, 'About Bric-à-Brac', p. 314.
23 Loftie, *A Plea for Art in the House*, pp. 20–1.
24 Gower, *Bric À Brac*, p. xi.
25 *Ibid.*, p. xii.

26 Loftie, *A Plea for Art in the House*, p. 7.
27 *Ibid.*, p. 8.
28 Lowndes, *The Merry Wives of Westminster*, p. 208.
29 *Ibid.*, p. 208.
30 Gower, *Bric À Brac*, p. 2.
31 *Ibid.*, p. 8.
32 *Ibid.*, p. 6.
33 R. Saisselin, *The Bourgeois and the Bibelot* (New Brunswick: Rutgers University Press, 1984), p. xv.
34 Gower, *Last Days of Marie Antoinette*, p. 10.
35 Lowndes, *The Merry Wives of Westminster*, p. 209.
36 'The Art of Furnishing', p. 538.
37 *Ibid.*, p. 535.
38 In R. W. Belk and M. Wallendorf, 'Of Mice and Men: Gender Identity in Collecting', in Susan M. Pearce (ed.), *Interpreting Objects and Collections* (London and New York: Routledge, 1994), p. 2.
39 *Ibid.*, pp. 23–4.
40 J. Potvin and A. Myzelev (eds.), *Material Cultures, 1740–1920: The Meanings and Pleasures of Collecting* (Aldershot and Burlington: Ashgate, 2009), p. 2.
41 S. M. Pearce, *On Collecting: An Investigation into Collecting in the European Tradition* (London and New York: Routledge, 1995), p. 27.
42 In A. Anderson, 'Lost Treasures, Lost Histories, Lost Memories: Reconstructing the Interiors of Lord Frederic Leighton's Studio-House', *Interiors*, vol. 2, issue 1 (2011), p. 70.
43 W. H. Hunt, 'Aestheticism', in *Pre-Raphaelitism and the Pre-Raphaelite Brotherhood*, vol. ii (London: Macmillan, 1913), p. 295.
44 In A. Anderson, 'The "New Old School": Furnishing with Antiques in the Modern Interior–Frederic, Lord Leighton's Studio-House and Its Collections', *Journal of Design History*, vol. 24, no. 4 (2011), p. 2.
45 *Ibid.*, p. 2.
46 C. Kingsley, *Two Years Ago* (London: Macmillan, 1881), p. 140.
47 E. de Goncourt, *La Maison d'un artiste*, vol. 1 (Paris: G. Charpentier, 1881).
48 P. Bourget, *Nouveaux essais de psychologie contemporaine* (Paris: Lemerre, 1888), p. 149.
49 *Le Decadent* (1886) in D. Pick, *Faces of Degeneration: A European Disorder* (Cambridge: Cambridge University Press, 1989), pp. 41–2.
50 M. Nordau, *Degeneration* (New York: D. Appleton and Company, 1905), p. 27.
51 In N. Cooper, *The Opulent Eye: Late Victorian and Edwardian Taste in Interior Design* (London: The Architectural Press Ltd, 1976), p. 10.
52 D. Cohen, *Households Gods: The British and Their Possessions* (New Haven and London: Yale University Press, 2006), p. 93.
53 Cooper, *The Opulent Eye*, p. 8.
54 For a more detailed and complete analysis of the merging and developing intersections between health, hygiene and interior architecture see: A. Adams, *Architecture in*

the *Family Way: Doctors, Houses, and Women, 1870–1900* (Montreal: McGill-Queen's University Press, 1996).

55 H. J. C., *The Art of Furnishing on Rational and Aesthetic Principles* (London: Henry S. King and Co., 1876), p. 105.

56 In Cohen, *Households Gods*, p. 100.

57 H. Heynen, 'Modernity and Domesticity: Tensions and Contradictions', in Hilde Heynen and Gülsüm Baydar (eds.), *Negotiating Domesticity* (New York: Routledge, 2005), p. 3.

58 *Ibid.*, p. 1.

59 W. Hamilton, *The Aesthetic Movement in England* (London: Reeves and Turner, 1882), p. 99.

60 Rt Rev. Sir D. H. Blair, *In Victorian Days and Other Papers* (Freeport: Books for Libraries Press, 1969), p. 118.

61 *Ibid.*, p. 120.

62 N. McKenna, *The Secret Life of Oscar Wilde* (New York: Basic Books, 2005), pp. 15–16.

63 M. Girouard, 'Chelsea's Bohemian Studio Houses', *Country Life*, 152 (23 November 1972), pp. 393–4.

64 O. Wilde, *Essays and Lectures by Oscar Wilde* (London: Methuen and Co., 1908), p. 2.

65 *Lillie Langtry* by Edward Poynter was shown at the Royal Academy in 1878. Gere, *Nineteenth-Century Decoration*, p. 25.

66 Lord R. Gower, *My Reminiscences*, vol. ii (London: Kegan Paul, Trench, Trübner, and Co. Ltd, 1883), p. 153.

67 McKenna, *The Secret Life of Oscar Wilde*, pp. 15–16.

68 Gower, *My Reminiscences*, vol. ii, p. 134.

69 C. Gere with L. Hoskins, *The House Beautiful: Oscar Wilde and the Aesthetic Interior* (Aldershot: Lund Humphries, 2000), p. 13.

70 McKenna, *The Secret Life of Oscar Wilde*, p. 16.

71 Blair, *In Victorian Days and Other Papers*, p. 131.

72 *Ibid.*, pp. 131–2.

73 In P. Grosskurth, *The Woeful Victorians: A Biography of John Addington Symonds* (New York: Random House 1964), p. 277.

74 J. A. Symonds, *The Letters of John Addington Symonds*, Herbert M. Schueller and Robert L. Peters (eds.), vol. 3, 1885–1893 (Detroit: Wayne State University Press, 1969), p. 606, letter dated 18 September 1891.

75 *Ibid.*, p. 650, letter dated 15 January 1892.

76 *The Times*, 13 January 1879.

77 See A. Henkinson, *Man of Wars: William Howard Russell of The Times* (London: Heinemann, 1982), pp. 240–1.

78 P. Ward-Jackson, 'Lord Ronald Gower, Gustave Doré and the Genesis of the Shakespeare Memorial at Stratford-on-Avon', *Journal of the Warburg and Courtauld Institute*, vol. 50 (1987), p. 167. Over the years, Wilde praised Gower's *Marie Antoinette* as well as his famed *Old Guard*. In 1888 Wilde made one of a number of speeches on the occasion when Gower's Shakespeare Memorial was unveiled in Stratford-upon-Avon.

79 Gower, *My Reminiscences*, vol. ii, p. 103.

80 W. Davis, 'Lord Ronald Gower and the Offending Adam', in David J. Getsey (ed.), *Sculpture and the Pursuit of a Modern Ideal in Britain, c. 1880–1930* (Aldershot: Ashgate Publishing Limited, 2004), p. 86.

81 J. Baudrillard, 'The System of Collecting', in J. Elsner and R. Cardinal (eds.), *The Cultures of Collecting* (London: Reaktion Books Ltd, 1994), p. 7.

82 Camille, 'Editor's Introduction', p. 165.

83 Baudrillard, 'The System of Collecting', p. 9.

84 R. C. Bleys, *The Geographies of Perversion: Male-to-Male Sexual Behaviour Outside the West and the Ethnographic Imagination, 1750–1918* (New York: New York University Press, 1995), p. 18.

85 W. Koestenbaum, *The Queen's Throat: Opera, Homosexuality and the Mystery of Desire* (New York: Da Capo Press, 1993), p. 84.

86 Camille, 'Editor's Introduction', pp. 163–4.

87 Anderson, 'The "New Old School"', p. 9.

88 Camille, 'Editor's Introduction', p. 164.

89 W. Benjamin, *The Arcades Project* (Cambridge, MA, and London: The Belknap Press of Harvard University, 1999), p. 211.

90 Lowndes, *The Merry Wives of Westminster*, pp. 209–10.

91 M. A. B., 'Lord Ronald Gower', p. 123.

92 Gower, *My Reminiscences*, vol. ii, p. 112. In the nineteenth and twentieth centuries Marie Antoinette also served as a lesbian icon. See T. Castle, *The Apparitional Lesbian: Female Homosexuality and Modern Culture* (New York: Columbia University Press, 1993).

93 *Ibid.*, p. 118.

94 Gower, *Last Days of Marie Antoinette*, p. 157.

95 Gower, *My Reminiscences*, vol. i, p. 127.

96 Williamson, 'The Lord Ronald Sutherland-Gower', p. 267.

97 T. Schaffer, *Forgotten Female Aesthetes: Literary Culture in Late Victorian Britain* (Charlottesville and London: University Press of Virginia, 2000), p. 81.

98 Williamson, 'The Lord Ronald Sutherland-Gower', p. 270.

99 M. A. B., 'Lord Ronald Gower', p. 122.

100 Gower, *Last Days of Marie Antoinette*, p. vi.

101 *Ibid.*, p. 71.

102 *Ibid.*, p. 71.

103 Koestenbaum, *The Queen's Throat*, p. 85.

104 Gower, *My Reminiscences*, vol. ii, p. 103.

105 In S. M. Pearce (ed.), *Interpreting Objects and Collections* (London: Routledge, 1994), p. 256.

106 Koestenbaum, *The Queen's Throat*, p. 104.

107 S. Marcus, *Apartment Stories: City and Home in Nineteenth-Century Paris and London* (Berkeley, Los Angeles and London: University of California Press, 1999), p. 64.

108 J. Halberstam, *In a Queer Time and Place: Transgender Bodies, Subcultural Lives* (New York and London: New York University Press, 2005), p. 5.

109 H. M. Hyde, *The Trials of Oscar Wilde* (London: William Hodge and Company, 1948), p. 156.

110 Williamson, 'The Lord Ronald Sutherland-Gower', p. 276.

111 It is important to note, however, that adoption was not legalized in the UK until 1926.

112 Here I borrow the term from L. Berlant and M. Warner, 'Sex in Public', *Critical Inquiry*, vol. 24, no. 2 (winter 1998) from their more contemporary focused study.

113 Benjamin, *The Arcades Project*.

114 H. de Balzac, *Le Cousin Pons* (Paris: Garnier, 1962), p. 19.

115 *Ibid.*, p. 14.

116 Wilde in Hamilton, *The Aesthetic Movement in England*, p. 100.

117 In R. Ellmann, *Oscar Wilde* (London: Penguin, 1988), p. 45.

118 In Anderson, '"She weaves by night and day, a magic web with colours gay": Trapped in the *Gesamtkunstwerk* of the Dangers of Unifying Dress and Interiors', in J. Potvin and A. Myzelev (eds.), *Fashion, Interior Design and the Contours of Modern Identity* (Aldershot and Burlington: Ashgate, 2010), p. 51.

119 J. Elsner and R. Cardinal (eds.), *The Cultures of Collecting* (London: Reaktion Books Ltd, 1994), p. 1.

120 Although it is not entirely clear how the two men came into contact, it is believed it was through an amorous relationship; likely Sheckelton feigned an attraction to Gower to cheat him out of his money.

121 Williamson, 'The Lord Ronald Sutherland-Gower', p. 271.

122 Lowndes, *The Merry Wives of Westminster*, p. 211.

3 ❖ Vale(d) decadence: Charles Ricketts, Charles Shannon and the Wilde factor

*Nowadays all the married men live like bachelors
and all the bachelors live like married men.*
The Picture of Dorian Gray, Oscar Wilde

IN 2003 Canadian playwright Michael Lewis MacLennan wrote, published and staged *Last Romantics*, a play devoted to the lives of the aesthetes Charles de Sousy Ricketts (1866–1931) and Charles Hazelwood Shannon (1863–1937). Inspired by a visit the playwright paid to the National Portrait Gallery (London) in 1994, the play revolves around the two historical figures and their circle of intimates.[1] As the play theatricalizes, theirs was a domestic life premised on art, partnership and community. Not unlike MacLennan's own inspired visit, on my first and subsequent visits to the National Portrait Gallery I have been continuously struck by the now famous pendant portraits of Ricketts and Shannon (both painted by Shannon in 1898 and 1897 respectively) which hang in a room devoted to portraits of late nineteenth-century British artists. I am still, at times, taken aback, amused and even left uneasy by the way we are meant to walk through the doorway which separates these portraits; there they hang, staring, as if longingly and knowingly, at each other, but always from a respectable distance. And while this is my subjective, ahistorical experiential reading, I appreciate the exercise the gallery has initiated as a way to awaken a viewer's visual and spatial consciousness, while at the same time teasing us to ponder these two men's partnership and spatial intimacy.

The Victorian collective understanding of domesticity as an ideal worth striving for on the one hand and the emergence of the avant-garde and notions of modernity on the other were competing forces in the construction of masculine artistic identity. While the bourgeois domestic ideal revolved around stability and the family as a cohesive

3.1 Charles Hazelwood Shannon. *Self-Portrait*, 1897. Oil on canvas.

union, the avant-garde propelled the self as a creative, independent genius devoid of ties of filiation, interdependence and more significantly intimacy. Historian John Tosh, in a rare example of scholarship exploring the fraught relationship Victorian men had with the domestic sphere, has beautifully shown how by the end of the nineteenth century domesticity was an increasingly antagonistic sphere of influence to foster proper English masculinity. With the emergence of free-market capitalism, men were afforded greater access to the pleasures of the city and same-sex unions (sexual or otherwise). Art and cultural critic John Ruskin was amongst those who advocated sexual difference as inherent to the separate spheres, positing that it was a woman's role to 'secure its order, comfort, and loveliness'.[2] Progressively, men turned to alternative spaces to articulate their identities and sought out venues in which homosociability was welcomed, celebrated and even expected.

Vale(d) decadence 83

3.2 Charles Hazelwood Shannon. *Charles de Sousy Ricketts*, 1898. Oil on canvas.

In the last quarter of the nineteenth century, with increasingly expensive costs associated with marriage and setting up house and home coupled with greater access to flats for independent (bachelor) living, many Victorian middle- and working-class men managed to stave off companionate marriage either permanently or at least temporarily. Others celebrated performances of domesticity by devising environments as alternative settings for public encounters and private interactions, havens of safety and pleasure not only for themselves, but also for others. Separate from and as a response to these various ostensibly competing forces, painter Shannon and illustrator Ricketts provided a more creative response to the cult of domesticity by way of a threshold to a profound sense of community and rarefied alternative aesthetic. Charlotte Gere concludes that when Wilde 'died in Paris, in November 1900, ostracised and disgraced, the [Aesthetic] Movement soon died with him'.[3] This chapter sets the record straight by showing that, long

3.3 George Charles Beresford. *Charles Ricketts and Charles Shannon at Yeoman's Row, Brompton Road, London*, October 1903.

after Wilde's demise, Aestheticism did live on in the decadent homes of two of the movement's most astute acolytes.

The impact of Ricketts and Shannon's numerous homes together is made tangible in both the contemporary and posthumous accounts of the theorists, painters, critics and poets whose lives were touched by these two formidable aesthetes.[4] In the case of Ricketts and Shannon collecting as a vital extension of the rituals and performances of subjectivity was not an isolated thread or separated from the auratic experience their domestic interiors conjured for their guests and friends. Interior design and collected, precious objects worked together and were inseparable to the conceptualization of the lived-in space of their bourgeois domestic interiors. The overall sensations and visual impact the couple's rooms conjured for their visitors guide my approach to their domestic interiors, rather than cataloguing specific objects or any subsequent connoisseurial interests in provenance and authenticity. Objects and people move through and alter spaces, no matter how controlled and controlling are the custodians of these interiors. The photographs and recollections, memories and reminiscences I turn to as a means to contextualize the lives and collections of these men are either purposefully staged 'events' or subjective phenomenological expressions and thus necessarily limit any reading to mere shadows of the life and identity of these long since passed spaces.

Robert Edis, Mrs H. R. Haweis and Fred Miller were amongst those who published books on proper interior décor, domestic architecture and the Aesthetic home destined for the middle-class English reader. Premised on concerns for physical and moral hygiene, the Aesthetic home in these texts is not one characterized as debauched by perverse pleasures and decadent design, but rather stands as an ideal representation burdened by values, codes and mores.[5] Rather than an environment divorced from familial bonds and healthy social circles, a true Aesthetic interior and its decoration embodied these ideals. In his attempt to draw out connections between these interiors and homosexuality, Michael Hatt argues that an aesthete's domestic space was not merely a stage for performance or refuge from the homophobic threat of the streets, but rather 'spaces where private desire and public self are integrated; where all one's experiences can be invoked and unified'.[6] In this way domestic space, as at once both private and public environments for work and leisure, is marked as a series of differing sites for the interpolation of the aesthetic (queer) subject, made tangible in the highly social nature of the design, collection and phenomenological exchanges facilitated (between objects and people) within these rooms.

Ricketts and Shannon's collection was less a personal and private enterprise than it was a collective and embracing ideal. It was an extension of the couple's identity as aesthetes; a queer intimacy materialized. Whilst the aesthetic interiors created by these lifelong companions were couched in and buttressed by heteronormative middle-class bourgeois domestic ideals, their case highlights the, at times, precarious and opaque relationships between sexuality/domesticity, aesthetics/masculinity and collecting/consuming. By extending the discussions established in the previous chapter on Lord Gower around the fraught and vital expressions and experiences of collecting, this chapter seeks to uncover the material traces of identity by que(e)rying how the perception and performances of masculinity intersects with domesticity at a time when the two were said to be incompatible. The chapter also continues the exploration of Wilde as a shadow figure in the lives of these two men at a particularly fraught and ultimately decisive moment in the Irish poet and playwright's life. Wilde's role as a consummate urban tourist, moving between and betwixt spaces of ill-repute and honour threatened the threshold of hearth and home. By including Wilde in the discussion, I seek to problematize the relationship between Aestheticism, the interior and sexuality as worked out through Ricketts's own tense and complicated relationship with Wilde.

Sexuality, biography, historiography

In the same year the two companions began living together in 1887, two of Shannon's pictures were displayed at the Grosvenor Gallery. The gallery, founded by Sir Coutts Lindsay and Lady Harriett Lindsay, had garnered an almost immediate reputation for displaying pictures at once edgy, controversial and deeply aesthetic. Soon after, Ricketts decided that Shannon would not exhibit until he 'appeared as the complete and undeniable master, upon whose princely income Ricketts then proposed to live in ease for the rest of his life'.[7] Until such time as Shannon's work was suitable for public consumption, it was exclusively Ricketts who had complete critical control over his work, and on whom the financial burden of maintaining their home fell. It was also Ricketts' keen critical eye that led the couple to amass one of the most envied and coveted art and craft collections of their generation.

In the post-Wilde era, Ricketts and Shannon turned their backs on the new art produced in London and Paris. While Shannon's art remained decidedly outside modernist developments, Ricketts was adamant about his disdain for the Post-Impressionist invasion of England as well as the public, masculinist ethos that went along with it. In an article on the movement written for the *Morning Post*, Ricketts spoke of his contempt for the avant-garde for novelty's sake as well as his own desire for stability:

> Novelty in itself is valueless. The spirit of beauty and power, of which art is the expression, has centuries behind it; it is as old as thought ... art has aimed at permanence, not at novelty, which is a laterday fiction ... All these 'experimentalists' are united in one fault, they are over-confident; they forget that the place for the experiment is the studio; it is not an aim but a means. I would also accuse them of lacking in tenderness towards their craft, and of a lack of humour, were these qualities not rare still in the apostles and advocates of the movement.[8]

Behind his attacks is a commingling of art with life, a symbiosis inspired by the Arts and Crafts Movement and which remained intact throughout the couple's life together.

Ricketts and Shannon are a curious and rich case not the least because of their artistic achievements and the homes they decorated, but also because of how they queered and problematized heteronormative long-term committed relationships while simultaneously blurring gendered prescriptions. The single-minded vision with which Ricketts simultaneously built up the couple's collection and ensured Shannon's success as a painter underlies the complexity of the couple's psycho-sexual and social dynamics beyond the predominating active/passive axis. To this day, the persona and character of Ricketts, 'with his pale and delicate features,

Vale(d) decadence 87

3.4 George Charles Beresford. *Charles Shannon*, 13 October 1903.

fair hair and pointed gold-red beard … quick mind and … rapid speech' both 'eloquent' and entertaining, overshadow Shannon. With his 'ruddy boyish face, like a countryman's, with blue eyes and fair lashes', Shannon was 'quiet', 'recessive' and 'inarticulate'. According to Wilde, who used the queer art of floriculture, Ricketts was an orchid whereas Shannon was a marigold.[9] While Ricketts dominated their relationship, he always used 'we' in his response to any question and when lending his opinion he invariably turned to the master painter Shannon 'as a reasonable wife'.[10] The intricate nature of their relationship, which will never fully reveal itself to the historian, speaks volumes to how the scholarship to date has consistently portrayed and consequently privileged Ricketts, obscuring to a significant degree Shannon's contributions to their relationship, their collection and the history of art. This fundamentally heteronormative trope is seen repeatedly in male–female artistic and intimate partnerships wherein the masculine assumes a definitive position of power over the feminine within the purportedly public realm of cultural production.

3.5 George Charles Beresford. *Charles Ricketts*, 13 October 1903.

I am not affixing an essentialist label to Shannon as necessarily more feminine and Ricketts as more masculine. On the contrary, I think their relationship, activities within the home and their domestic partnership clearly expose the fallacy of such gendered attributions. I wish, as result, to insert a warning. The imbalance often seen in the writing of history that pits absences against presences emphatically underlines how genius has been gendered along an active/passive continuum. Moreover, this continuum belies the ways artistic-intimate partnerships and collaboration have been betrayed and twisted by invested bystanders to conform to the steadfast heteronormative notion of domestic unions in which one figure must necessarily take centre-stage to the occlusion of the other.

The sexual economy of the domestic realm as well as the public domain codes gender performances as either active or passive, a facile binary repeatedly maintained that begs a concern for historiography. Ricketts is characterized as more active, despite the fact he is at once comptroller of the couple's finances and doting 'wife', working hard at 'hack jobs' to ensure that his 'husband' became the successful painter, who would in turn take care of him in his old age. Shannon, on the other hand, is portrayed as the (public) master painter, yet quiet, shy and reserved, the creative genius lurking in the shadows. Shannon left fewer records and letters in comparison to his companion, and so it should come as no surprise that to date no biography exists of Shannon, despite how Ricketts fostered his career as the great painter. Rather, it is the so-called 'dutiful wife' Ricketts who was to become the subject of a biography by Paul Delaney, in addition to several other studies. In large measure surely this imbalance speaks to how prolific and varied a career Ricketts enjoyed. For at once he was a painter, illustrator, art theorist and critic, essayist, jewellery maker, theatre costumier and set designer. The reserved and unassuming Shannon was first and foremost, and yet quite simply, a painter. However, this can only reveal part of the pitfalls of historiography, and I suggest, once again, that the answer lay in the way the narrative of their purported respective sexualities and life together was written, a process which has set to normalize as much as to dismiss the polymorphousness and polyvalence of sexual possibilities these two men might have entertained. There can be no doubt that Ricketts and Shannon's life together was complicated and varied throughout their many decades together. What is certain is that they indeed did share their lives together, well beyond the potentially confining limits of sex. The ambiguity and at times ambivalence of their domesticity is precisely the threat to which Michel Foucault alludes in his essay 'Friendship as a Way of Life', discussed in Chapter 1, and underlines the tendency to define and separate these men's true intimacy. It is worth quoting Delaney at length here to expose the concerns I raise. According to Delaney:

> It is almost universally assumed nowadays that they were lovers, but there is no conclusive evidence of this, no acknowledgement in diary, letter, or reported conversation that this was the case. Ricketts himself was secretive, and theirs was the discretion of an age which did not discuss such things. A close friend, Gordon Bottomley, observed that if Ricketts and Shannon had never met, Ricketts's life would have been substantially the same, but Shannon's would have been entirely different. Shannon would have married and had a family. His works show how sensitive he was to female beauty, and the recurrent themes of mother and child suggest a yearning for these ordinary joys that life with Ricketts denied him.[11]

Delaney's 'what if' reading of their relationship in addition to the absence of any recording of *the love which dare not speak its name* betrays the normalizing tendency of the heterosexual matrix. In Delaney's reading, Shannon, the ostensible straight genius, is somehow limited even to the point of victimization by his queer relationship with Ricketts whose grip on him and their domestic union is seemingly too strong to be released from. For Delaney it was only later in life that Shannon began to express his resentment toward Ricketts and began to flirt with the possibility of marriage in his affairs with women. This supposed and possible suppression of Shannon on the part of Ricketts, in my estimation, serves only to further silence his position. When Shannon entertained protracted relationships with women, such as with Hetty (Esther) Deacon in 1903 (there were plans to marry), Ricketts forbade it solely on the premise it would be impossible to divide their collection.[12] Here the enviable assortment of *objets d'art* they amassed is the key to their relationship and acts at once as a source of stability and control. In his writing Delaney seems all too eager to 'in' Shannon, and in the process inadvertently denies the artist any true psycho-sexual agency. That Shannon exhibited a sensitivity to 'female beauty' coupled with a purchase made by Ricketts of a female nude by Etty, 'a concession', according to Delaney, 'to C. H. Shannon's sex instincts',[13] tacitly exposes the way in which, I posit, objects reveal the life-cycles, desires and pleasures of the collectors well beyond typological identities and mere concessionary acts. Ricketts, when on a trip to Naples with Robbie Ross, wrote from Rome to Shannon that 'I had no scarlet adventures'.[14] Scarlet, an aesthetic metaphor to be sure, referred to the rough trade guardsmen provided homosexual patrons. Delaney suggests 'not only that Shannon was more prim than Ricketts but also [that] their relationship was not as openly sexual as all that'. In one letter from Rome, Ricketts not only refers to the pictures of phalluses he and Ross saw, but also made note of the 'good looking people in Naples',[15] revealing a sexual as a much as playful side to his character.

Delaney claims that the companions 'never saw themselves as a homosexual couple, never belonged to any homosexual circle or organization. Nor were they prepared to make any revelations'.[16] Ricketts's biographer is at great pains to desexualize these men, to strip them of any genital relationship, and in the process disallows for queer happenings and possibilities. It would seem that for Delaney membership holds the key to identity itself, even in a period when sexual identities were not as prescriptive as we originally thought or would wish them to be. In Delaney's text sex and sexuality are only ever mentioned in relation to these two men in entirely separate contexts and never really as part of their union together. In this way, he sanitizes their domesticity as well as their interiors, which had played host to countless queer luminaries from the period. When Ricketts himself was pressed about his sexuality by John Addington Symonds upon a visit to the couple's home, 'But you are aren't you? You do, don't you?', Ricketts defiantly refused to answer.[17] Ricketts and Shannon in their own ways thwarted the spatio-sexual dynamics enforced by a closet that identifies sexuality and identity in binary terms: in/out, private/public, disclosure/opacity, homo/heterosexual, genital sex/phenomenological pleasure. In many ways these binaries mark out the co-ordinates of shame, for to move in any wrong direction incites the stigma and trauma it necessarily engenders whether enforced at the personal or the social level. The incident between Symonds and Ricketts occurred on the threshold marking the public from the private, between the interior and the exterior of their domestic setting, and Ricketts's refusal speaks to his desire for privacy and control. That they had or did not have sexual relations together is not in evidence, nor is such evidence needed. After all, their homes and lifestyle were in and of themselves queer enough.

Companionship: Intimacy, art and collecting

Fascinated and somewhat bemused by how the two men shared their lives and held the collection in common, the painter Jacques-Émile Blanche (1861–1942) once famously declared: '*Mais c'est alors une existence idéale que vous menez tout pout l'Art*'.[18] Elisa Glick argues that the queer subject may best embody modernity itself given its 'retreat' away from politics and history in favour of a life based entirely on aesthetic concerns.[19] 'Tout pour l'art' – or all for art's sake – is a lifestyle more suggestive than scholars have originally supposed. The shift in the 1870s from the term 'art for art's sake' to 'Aestheticism' also elicited a gradual move away from an association with productive avant-garde high art to one implicated in an 'affection in dress, manners and interior design'.[20] Design reforms at the end of the nineteenth century sought to integrate more intimately all aspects of creative production, to form a complete unity of the arts. 'The new frame designs prominent in Wilde's time were part of a larger design philosophy that minimized the boundary between the frame and the work of art and, more broadly, between art and decoration'.[21] There is also another implication here, that of the relationship between life/style and art/ifice, the aesthetic pose and material reality, laying bare how ultimately collecting is 'inherently public rather than private'.[22] Additionally, as Thad Logan has astutely noted, 'homosexuality was being constructed at very nearly the same time as the discourse of "art at home"', with Wilde figuring 'prominently in both'.[23] In these terms, Blanche's comments tacitly and reflexively allude to the commingling of aesthetics and sexuality in the domestic arrangement of these men. So interwoven were their identities and lives, the companions used two interlocking Cs as their collector's mark. Friend and art critic Lewis Hind also recognized the synergy between art and lifestyle and the symbiosis between the two artists when he noted:

> They love together; they collect together; they work in adjoining studios, and in any account of the life, aims, and appreciations of Mr Shannon, the name of Mr Ricketts runs to the tongue as dutifully as that of Sullivan to Gilbert, or Fletcher to Beaumont. It is surprising, therefore, to find that the influence of one upon the creations of the other is almost imperceptible.[24]

Writing about Ricketts, protégé and close friend Cecil Lewis best described the two key relationships in his life when he noted that

> [b]etween Ricketts and Shannon existed the most marvellous human relationship that has ever come within my observation, and in their prime each was the other's complement, but neither easily indulged the other; their union was more bracing than comfortable. Emotion never eluded Ricketts, and I remember when he had given a really beautiful necklace to a lady and afterwards discovered that it was not appreciated, he said: 'Hence forward I make a rule never to give away anything I really care for'.[25]

Intimacy for Ricketts is revealed in two unique and imbricated relationships, that is, between himself and his companion, and between himself and the precious *objets d'art* he either produced himself or purchased for the couple's mutually sustaining collection.[26] However, the objects that meant the most for both were those collected and created by the artists for themselves and held in common.

In his writings on the nineteenth century Walter Benjamin made much of the world created by the collector within the private confines of his home. He wrote of the interior as

> the asylum where art takes refuge. The collector proves to be the true resident of the interior. He makes his concern the idealization of objects ... The collector delights in evoking a world that is not just distant and long gone but also better – a world in which, to be sure, human beings are no better provided with what they need than in the real world, but in which things are freed from the drudgery of being useful.[27]

Assumptions abound in regards to the purported nature of the collecting practices of the sexes. Traditionally it was believed that '[w]omen usually collect with decorative values or a definite decorative purpose in mind; men, for study from a technical or historical standpoint'.[28] Collecting, idealized as a masculine and hence a legitimate enterprise since the eighteenth century, supports the economic wheel by targeting objects whose exchange value has been altered as they enter into an entirely different contemporary economy of meaning, desire and pleasure and more significantly the domestic sphere. Russell Belk and Melanie Wallendorf have explained that 'collecting supports a consumer culture. It allows both genders to participate in the feminine world of consumption in a way that simultaneously supports the masculine world of production.'[29]

In the realm of Kantian aesthetic disinterest in which the subject is removed from the objects surrounding him or her, material and visual culture are usually divorced from the identity of the collector and yet it is precisely this collection that renders him or her worthy of mention to begin with and in turn reveals the desires, whims, pleasures, drives, impulses and thoughtfulness of its custodian. Ricketts and Shannon purposefully blur the gendered line of respectability, for their collecting, more often than not, was dictated by aesthetic pleasure and yet informed by connoisseurial investments in historical significance.

Ricketts's letters to Shannon reveal how the artist was so ensconced in their aesthetic programme that even on his travels he was always in search not only of art but also of aesthetic delights. Cities like Berlin were, according to Ricketts, those that 'had neither luxuries to purchase nor beautiful or well-dressed people: the place is still in a sense provincial. The small hotels are not awe inspiring monuments of luxury and pride like those of Paris and London, and I have not seen a rare or costly thing in a shop yet, or a well dressed woman.'[30] The quest for beauty, aesthetics itself, was not some passing fancy, but a life/style constantly beating in Ricketts's heart and pumping life through his veins. More often than not, Ricketts wrote in his letters of two primary preoccupations: first, connoisseurial quips and conclusions on pictures by Old Masters housed in Europe's most celebrated institutions and, second, the material culture of the cities he visited and the hotels where he lodged. In good English style, vacation spots operated as extensions of one's house and home, the ideals of which were to be translated with relative ease. In a letter dated 2 May 1903 to Shannon, Ricketts betrays not only his aesthetic identity, but his national identity as well:

> Having like a Britton [sic] shown myself dissatisfied with my old room, I have since been promoted to a very pleasant one, furnished with an inkstand, a chair and a balcony hence this letter, for the smoking room (where dwelt the inkstand) was always full of Germans and women, a combination which does not tend towards silence and contemplation.[31]

Here the public impinged on private needs. What surfaced in this site of tension was how a certain gender or nationality interrupted Ricketts's aesthetic, contemplative and material needs. What he required, in other words, was a 'room of his own'. National identity came to the foreground yet again in another letter from Florence dated 24 March 1906, in which Ricketts discussed continental perceptions of collectors. According to 'an interesting old dealer' whom he met on his numerous visits to commercial galleries, the English and American collectors concerned themselves with price and were 'artificial and without genuine insight or appreciation. The French collector [on the other hand] was the only genuine collector.'[32]

Ricketts travelled to the continent on several occasions and his journeys are recounted in his numerous and often daily letters to Shannon who was left to his own devices in London. In a letter from Vienna from August 1903 and sent from the Hotel Kaiserine Elizabeth, Ricketts wrote: 'I miss you not at meals, which are lengthy and luxurious and leave no room for roaming thoughts, but I miss you in the mornings when I start forth to scatter the museums'.[33] Here, in this of many short and sweet letters from Ricketts to Shannon, Ricketts betrays how longing occurs [in]between the experiences of luxury and the material culture of his environment. Space is filled, for Ricketts, by his thoughts of his companion still in England as much as the aesthetic culture of his surroundings.

It was his homes with Shannon first and foremost which occupied his thoughts, time and emotions. On one occasion Wilde commented to Ricketts: 'What a charming old house you have and what delightful Japanese prints ... and you have yellow walls, so have I ... yellow is the colour of joy'.[34] However, Stephen Calloway has noted how 'unlike Ricketts and Shannon, for example, Wilde seems never to have developed much of a connoisseur's eye for quality in these, or indeed in any other individual works of art ... Wilde's splendour, it seems clear, was a splendour of phrases not of visual effects; a richness of word-pictures rather than of objects.'[35] The practicality of the colour of the walls, while important, was nevertheless subjugated to the auratic beauty of the pictures hung overtop. The significance of pictures in contrast to the monotony and sobriety of monochromatic walls was in keeping with contemporary advice for healthy living. A writer for *The Artist*, for example, extolled the virtues of how '[w]hen a room is adorned with pictures we have not merely occupation, but delight, and those higher emotions that are only excited by the fine arts'.[36] Twenty years later, in a letter from 17 April 1905, Ricketts expressed a similar, if not a more all-encompassing view of beauty's impact on the soul of humankind when he wrote that the beautiful

> produces that exaltation within us which we associate with happiness. Beauty has been defined as the promise of happiness, it is not merely the promise but the fact in the course of its accomplishment. Art is not only strong in its immediate appeal to our richest and noblest emotions and faculties, it holds constantly, or, if you will, 'for ever', that element of appeal; the nearest approach possible to permanence is achieved by beautiful thoughts and beautiful things.[37]

Reading between the lines of Ricketts's claims, art was beyond the vagaries of fashion, outside of modernism's endless march of 'isms'. By the twentieth century the couple were considered to be out of step with contemporary art and hence were to be forgotten by critics and historians. Permanence also suggested the longevity of his relationship with Shannon made possible by their mutual aesthetic endeavours. In other words, an aesthetic life premised on companionship and intimacy led to a lifestyle outside of dominant notions of modern art and thus outside history itself.

The art for art's sake mantra by which Ricketts and Shannon flourished in the early years would later become antithetical to that expounded by the 'true' English modernist circle of Roger Fry and the Omega workshop which Ricketts detested. Shannon and Ricketts's modernity would for a long time remain firmly ensconced in the twilight years of the Aesthetic Movement, a generation of decadent aesthetes to be repressed by more avant-garde artists as varied as the Vorticists and the Bloomsbury Group, but which lived, nonetheless, beyond the demise of Wilde in 1895. Like many of their fashionable peers, it was also a life/style they seemed to have gradually shed, if only in part, by the time they moved into Lansdowne House in 1902, opting for a more 'neo-Georgian simplicity'.[38] Inspired by the Arts and Crafts ethos of keeping home and work under the same roof, men like Shannon and Ricketts devoted their entire lives to the reform of art and society, which they believed to have been debased by the encroachment of industrialization. Upon his frequent visits to the couple's home artist and writer Sir William Rothenstein (1872–1945) paid witness to the couple's work ethic and meticulous attention to detail, a work ethic tied to an aesthetic long since past its glory days. Rothenstein recalled how

> [b]oth he [Shannon] and Ricketts were then busy cutting woodblocks for their edition of *Daphnis and Chloe*, working late into the night, and rising late in the day. Bending over their blocks they looked like figures from a missal. I had never come into touch with the Morris movement, and this craftsman side was new to me. I was therefore the more impressed by their skill and patience. From them I heard countless stories of Rossetti, of Burne-Jones, Holman Hunt, Millais and Madox Brown; in fact, at the time, I thought they would carry on the Pre-Raphaelite tradition.[39]

For the disciples of both the Arts and Crafts and Aesthetic movements, modernity was one and the same with the domestic realm wherein work and life were performed, aesthetically, in tandem.

Blanche's words quoted earlier speak not simply to the partners' mutual sacrifices for acquiring works of art and living out their ideal, if at times uncomfortable, 'aesthetic' life, but also to the devotion with which Ricketts dedicated himself to facilitating Shannon's painting career and the contentment of his beloved companion. To highlight this significant yet misplaced component of their aesthetic life introduces intimacy into the mix, anathema to any discussion of art, notions of the bourgeois independent self, competition and bonding, as well as modernist male artistic identity. Within the confines of the home, objects constitute a 'material culture of love' and foreground the 'labour of intimacy'.[40] For Ricketts and Shannon the boundaries marking out and separating labour and collecting from intimacy are dissolved. The issue is not so much about every single object in its singularity, but about how each object together constructed a *sense* of space and place and how each object enlivened and activated narratological connections between it and others to disclose material pleasure and meaning in which identity and subjectivity are unavoidably caught in the crossfire. Not unlike in a gallery or museum, the spaces between each object and the overall visual and material meanings ascribed to each room at once are static, controlled by the author of the space, yet at the same remain fluid, full of possibility and endless promise for the awestruck visitor. I argue then for a simultaneous phenomenological and material culture approach to the study of interior design and spaces of these artists.

According to Ricketts, the art of the Old Masters forms an integral part of the life of any collector and the 'sensations' of their greatness is tangible and seemingly universal. The pre-eminent role art took in the many homes Shannon and Ricketts shared is evinced by the way their (more often than not) simple Georgian-styled furniture reflected the sacrifices they made, how Ricketts churned out endless second-rate illustrations as a means to support them both and how their collection became the envy of many. Among their most prized possessions were the Greek *lekythoi*, tanagrettes,[41] drawings by Hokusai, Rossetti, Rubens and Puvis de Chavannes; many of which were the pride and joy endemic to most aesthetic interiors. These in particular, in addition to all sorts of miniature objects of curiosity, had become usual cues in their homes over the decades. Together, they represented an eclectic style and remained at the heart of the austere luxury characteristic of each and every lodging since their early days together.

On 18 November 1898, Ricketts purchased seven books of drawings for Shannon: the most notable were the Japanese Suikoden Ukiyo-e designs. Interestingly, all that was Japanese, in keeping with the Aesthetic craze, reflected Shannon's own personal collecting choices and pleasures and not those of Ricketts. So impressive and integral was their collection of Japanese drawings and prints that it warranted an invitation for them to exhibit forty-three drawings by Hokusai and four by Hokei in June 1909 at Galeries L. and P. Rosenberg – *Tableaux Anciens et Modernes* in 18 Avenue de l'Opéra, Paris. All of these pictures were later bequeathed to the British Museum where they remain today.

Having suffered a concussion after a fall hanging a picture in 1929, Shannon would die eight years later, lovingly cared for by Ricketts until he could no longer manage it. It seems fitting and painfully ironic that the artist should die by an accident doing something the couple had built their collective reputation on, decorating their homes with a most impressive and comprehensive collection of objects and pictures. For the most part the integrity of the couple's collection remained intact with a few notable exceptions. Chief among these was on the occasion of Shannon's fall when Ricketts began to sell a few of the their prized pictures to pay for the mounting health bills. In 1931 at the time of Ricketts's death their collection was valued at a formidable £36,203.

Fay consumers

The most celebrated house the two artists leased together, in 1888, was a Regency house (No. 4) in The Vale, a cul-de-sac off the King's Road that had once accommodated one of James McNeill Whistler's (1834–1903) model/mistresses, Maud Franklin (1857–1941). The Vale had a smaller house attached to it that they rented out to friends. Given their paltry incomes, Shannon and Ricketts also invited Thomas Sturge Moore (1870–1944) and Thomas Sterling Lee (1856–1916) to join them at The Vale, where Ricketts and Shannon occupied the top floor.[42] In this home, the couple were never truly alone. Amongst The Vale's more famous, if infamous, visitors was Wilde, a close associate of the couple. Rothenstein, who was taken to The Vale by Wilde, was also quickly 'charmed' by both the men and 'their simple dwelling'. He recalled the 'primrose walls, apple-green skirting and shelves, the rooms hung with Shannon's lithographs, a fan-shaped water-colour by Whistler, and drawings by Hokusai – their first treasures, to be followed by so many others'.[43] While Rothenstein recalls key pieces of the collection, he was nevertheless struck by the overall aesthetic effect the rooms evoked. Part of the strategy to elicit a specific mood or feeling was in keeping with Ricketts's advice that colour helps to define and maintain 'the temper of each room. When a room hides from the sun, [for example,] provide it with colours and hangings that love the shade: the green of green shadows in the heart of a wood, blue of that blue haunting a grot, the colours found under the sea.'[44] While Ricketts and Shannon may have inherited their green and yellow walls from Whistler, in their study of sexual inversion Havelock Ellis and John Addington Symonds concluded that green seemed to predominate amongst homosexuals as a colour of choice not only for their walls but for their garments, to say nothing of the green carnation used as a sign of identification and recognition.[45]

The Vale and its ambient impressions were best described by the couple's close friends the poets Edith Cooper (1862–1913) and her niece Katherine Bradley (1846–1914) (who together were known under the pseudonym of Michael Field). According to them it was 'a muddy retreat

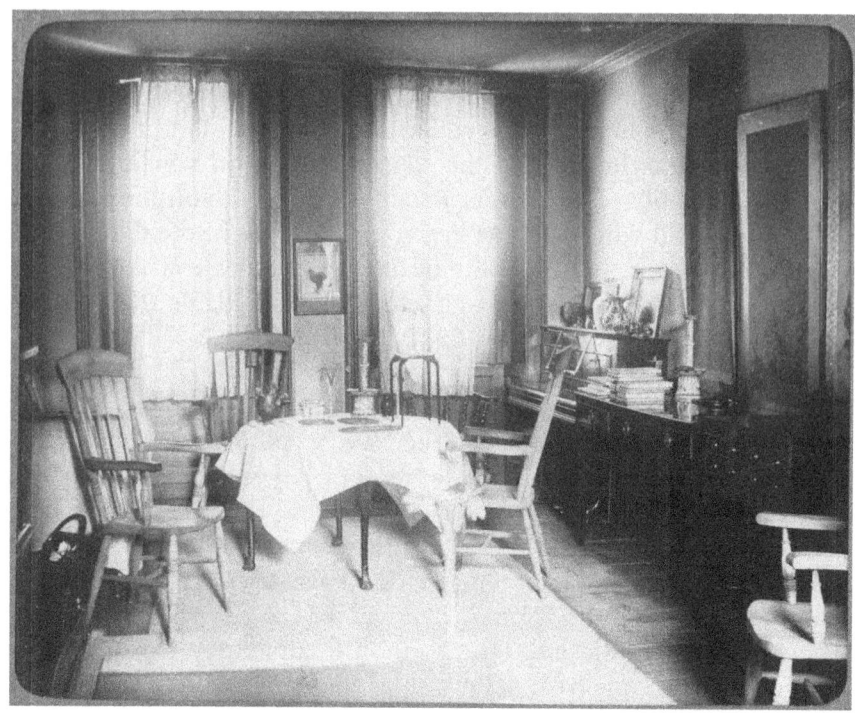

3.6 Dining room, The Vale.

from the highway, edged by gardens in which snowball-trees grow from the soil like wands that are full of sighing'.[46] Cooper and Bradley knew Ricketts and Shannon well, perhaps better than anyone else. So well, in fact, that, knowing of Ricketts's obsession for gossip, they nicknamed him 'Fay' and 'Fairyman'. Max Beerbohm, known for his satirical caricatures and parodies, also made light of the feminine nature of Ricketts and Shannon's domesticity when he christened them 'the ladies of the Vale'.[47] According to the poets, however, at the heart of The Vale's domestic sanctuary was the lively and formidable character of Ricketts, 'a decadent Christ' who 'talk[ed] fluently with a mere shrill of voice'. While Ricketts and Shannon did much to make their visitors feel at home and comfortable, Ricketts was adept at orchestrating aesthetic experiences as much as social control. So pervasive and powerful was Ricketts's influence over the aesthetic community which gathered together, The Vale, as a total environment – or *Gesamtkunstwerk* – necessitated, according to Cooper, that 'one be on one's rarest behaviour – for nothing ordinary is expected; a false tone might be an outrage'.[48] Control was always manoeuvred in the service of aesthetic perfection, an Aesthetic *Gesamtkunstwerk* wherein even the faintest hint of disharmony threatened to unhinge the atmosphere Ricketts worked tirelessly to hone and perfect. However, such perfectionism takes its toll, particularly on the nerves. Towards the noble end of creating a complete and total work of art out of any and all interior spaces, aesthetic exchange and sensual awareness were promoted and practised between the two couples. Years later Ricketts wrote to the poets to thank them for the ambergris they had sent him. His desire was to devote 'a separate drawer or a piece of furniture to a separate scent, and thereby having a pleasure house or palace of perfume with a chamber for each odour'.[49] In true Aesthetic style, sights, touch and smell commingle in the spaces Ricketts and Shannon created for themselves and their guests. The poets also knew well the power fragrance had, writing in their diary that by smearing ambergris on the doors of the home, it may 'appeal to all five senses'.[50]

Ricketts and Shannon likely met Wilde for the first time in 1889, after they sent him a copy of the first issue of their literary and artistic journal, *The Dial*, which they produced through their Arts and Crafts-inspired Vale Press. For this inaugural issue their mutual friend John Gray (the inspiration for Wilde's infamous character Dorian Gray) contributed a fairy tale, 'The Great Worm', itself inspired by Wilde and a short essay on 'Les Goncourt'. To a friend, Wilde also once commented: 'I am taking you to the one house in London where you will never be bored'.[51] Wilde frequently went calling on the artists at The Vale, of which he had much to say that was positive, if at times condescending. The auratic presence of the objects in the various rooms as well as the men themselves left an indelible impression on Rothenstein, for example. His memoirs remain one of the most complete and insightful descriptions of The Vale, and as such they are worth quoting at length:

> But in those early Chelsea days I was especially attracted by Ricketts and Shannon – they were so different from any artists I had met hitherto. Everything about them was refined and austere. Ricketts, with his pale, delicate features, fair hair and pointed gold-red beard, looked like a Clouet drawing. Half French, he had the quick mind and the rapid speech of a southerner. He was a fascinating talker. His knowledge of pictures and galleries astonished me; he had been nowhere except the Louvre, yet he seemed to know everything, to have been everywhere. And he knew the names of rare flowers, of shells and of precious stones ... Ricketts was a strong believer in tradition. He held that painters should learn their art by copying; that, through copying, the old masters had acquired all their knowledge. The most faithful of his disciples was Sturge Moore, who in his poetry and in his wood-cuts strove for a conscious beauty of form and content. Sturge Moore was one of the contributors to *The Dial*, the lovely quarto Ricketts and Shannon produced at their expense and risk, a work which has a powerful influence on contemporary drawing, engraving and printing, both in England and abroad. Another disciple was John Gray, for whose *Silverpoints*

> Ricketts has designed one of his exquisite bindings. John Gray was then a fastidious young poet and something of a dandy. He also wrote plays with André Raffalovitch, a wealthy friend of Ricketts.[52]

Rothenstein does not make mention of the fact that Raffalovitch and Gray would become lovers and that the four-act play they penned together, *The Blackmailers* (1894), was an apt title in a era of increased fears among homosexual men who were subjected to the Labouchere Amendment (commonly referred to as the 'blackmailer's charter'). Raffalovitch and Gray met in 1890 and the former was a strong advocate of homosexual rights and an apostle for an uneasy communion between Catholicism and homosexuality. The artistic community which formed primarily around Ricketts at the couple's Chelsea home also included Aubrey Beardsley and Laurence Housman, who 'looked to him as their leader', claimed Rothenstein. 'He was in fact the artistic Warwick of his age.'[53]

Lewis in particular, though he was not alone in his sentiments, recalled fondly how:

> He [Ricketts] opened the door to the world of Art for me. He gave me a sense of belonging, long before there was the least justification, to that curiously inchoate body of men, the 'artists' ... He apprenticed me to this world, inspired in me the desire to emulate, gave me the classic examples; suggested themes, subjects, situations; midwived my earliest efforts, advised, criticized.[54]

Ricketts was instrumental in initiating young and aspiring men like Lewis into a community of artists wherein bonding was performed outside of increasingly important spaces of aggregation, but within the domestic realm. Ricketts's knowledge and guidance were not only given freely to friends, but also led the National Gallery of Canada in 1927 to formalize its connection with the connoisseur as an adviser to the gallery's director Eric Brown. Artist, critic and director of the National Portrait Gallery (London) Sir Charles John Holmes also became a regular at their Friday night evenings. He too recalls how

> Ricketts and Shannon during the first few evenings at The Vale told me almost all about themselves which I was ever to know. Shannon, fresh, plump and curly-haired, was actually the senior of the two. At St. John's, Leatherhead, he had some repute as a footballer; then he became a teacher at the Croydon Art School, 'with heaps of friends until Ricketts quarrelled with them' ... Of his [Ricketts's] early days he said little, except that he had disappointed his father by not proving an athlete and a lover of field sports, and that much of his boyhood had been spent in France, his spiritual home. He and Shannon had become friends at Croydon, had started life together

in the Kennington Road, and were now settling down to an agreed programme, which had in it something of the heroic.[55]

Holmes offers a decidedly different vision of the heroic, one predicated on their domestic union wherein their work ethic flourished. According to him the two men were mostly to be found at home alone, and it was in these evenings that they introduced him to 'a literature and art very unlike the canonical classics of my schooldays ... These talks would last for hours. Then towards one in the morning, Shannon would disappear and return bearing a big tray with rolled tongue, bread and butter, quince jam (a speciality of these meals) and great cups of steaming cocoa'.[56] For these two men, domestic hospitality merged seamlessly with intellectual and aesthetic pursuits.

In 1899, Ricketts and Shannon moved to Richmond, where they lived in decadent simplicity and grand austerity, and one short year later, the couple found Bradley and Cooper a suitable small Georgian house, 1 Paragon, Richmond (now in the Petersham Road), where they lived out the rest of their lives. The artists functioned as their decorating consultants, as well as providing their friends with furniture and drawings made from their own hands to ensure their home conformed to true Aesthetic style, taste and comfort.[57] The move was a necessary one for the men, for it allowed them to remove themselves from the hubbub of society and concentrate more earnestly on their creative endeavours. In Richmond they spent four focused and successful years, with Shannon completing some twenty to thirty pictures, many of which were commissioned portraits. Shannon's family visited them at Richmond, and they, like many, were impressed by the balance between grandness and simplicity they managed to achieve with their satinwood tables and antique mantelpieces, well appointed in their roomy apartment.[58]

Phenomenological landscapes

Ricketts always had much to say about furniture, object placement and decoration and was always eager to share his thoughts with his friends. In cool rooms Ricketts advocated the placement of mirrors. Not unlike Narcissus who drowns in the pool of his own reflection, mirrors according to Ricketts were meant to 'listen to you [and] look like pools'.[59] Narcissist reflective surfaces and self-fashioning have long been associated with homosexuality.[60] However, their use by Ricketts helped to conjure the necessary spatial dynamic to elicit a conversation between objects as well as between objects and people. Precious objects as well as hand-made or hand-picked furniture were imbued with personalities all their own and as such formed an integral part of the artists' relationship to space, each other and their community. In Ricketts's own words 'rooms that love the sun ... mirrors should be allowed to *talk*. Provide them with subjects of conversation: carnations, roses, anemones, woodbine, rings on hands, fruit in a basket or on a silver dish, Chinese embroideries.'[61] Ricketts's eclectic dynamism was precisely what provided both appeal to the senses and intellectual intrigue. In their rooms the visual as much as the material vied equally for a guest's attention.

In his preface to *Self-Portrait: Taken from the Letters and Journals of Charles Ricketts, R.A.*, Lewis shares his recollections, fondness and the emotional attachments associated with objects once owned by men he admired so when he paid them a visit in the Fitzwilliam Museum (Cambridge):

> We go in. There, sure enough, is the sign 'To the Ricketts and Shannon Rooms'. Now the past comes crowding and I hurry down the corridor. There they all are, the things I have known for years! The noble Greek vases, the flying Tanagras, the bronze men (handles of an urn) arched neck like swallow divers, the wooden duck with sliding wings (rouge for an Egyptian queen), the ivory monkey, minus one leg, smaller than my finger; I can see it lying in the palm of his small hand – 'Look my dear boy, every hair.' Then the drawings: the Watteaus, the Fragonards, that superhuman Rubens head, that Angel by Tiepolo, the Rembrandt cartoon' ... Suddenly I don't want to look any more. These works of art brought together from every epoch with an eclectic and impeccable taste, displayed in the cool serenity of a Museum; it is like going to a cemetery, gazing at a mummy in a crystal coffin: the presence that once informed it all, the daily life which flowered among these things, the flow of conversation, of laughter, the sense of being in the intimate company of great art collected by a zealot, himself a genius, all that is gone, gone ... It is cold when we come out into the street again, and I am tired.[62]

Within a context of collecting decorative and applied art objects, the self takes on an added significance for '[o]rnament, décor, and ultimately decorum define the boundaries of the private space by emptying that space of any relevance other than that of the subject'.[63] Effectively, objects and the experiences of them have immense power over their owners and those fortunate enough to be in their presence. They activate memories of faces and places sublimated over time, often out of pain-induced practicality. Objects forming a collection amplify and are aggrandized by their owners, as was the case with Ricketts and his formidable personality. But for Ricketts, precious objects, those objects included in the companions' homes over the years, symbolized much sacrifice, vision, travels, memories and a joy shared with Shannon that it mustn't come as a surprise that the objects assume identities all their own. As if members of his aesthetic family, Shannon once referred to three delightful

3.7 Interior view of Lansdowne House, featuring cabinets of curiosity.

Sheffield jugs as 'Bullfinch', 'Swallow' and 'Fatty'.[64] Bradley also recorded how either Ricketts or Shannon once pronounced that '[o]ne ought to have very beautiful furniture and objects that are dear, calling a chair "Jennie" for instance'.[65] Objects populate a domestic landscape as much as humans do, and as such lend personality, attachment, sentiment and the presence of intimacy itself.

The domestic realm is such that objects in an interior and the interior as visual and material object itself develop into a sort of phenomenological cabinet of curiosity of constant visual delight and material pleasure. Ricketts and Shannon also used museum techniques such as the display cases in the sitting rooms to control and mediate the expression of touch and sight. A degree of control was important to the way they developed their spaces, whether it was the ascetic rigour they maintained in the more private spaces of their bedrooms and studios or the slightly more comfortable public spaces which proudly and prominently housed their *objets d'art*. Aside from this display technique, unlike a museum which places objects in a removed, static and distant past, objects, whether precious or not, remain amongst the living, activated by the safety, comfort and security offered up by the lived-in domestic sphere.

Spaces wherein the subject perceives and deciphers meaning through the senses, that is: '[p]henomenological space', according to Griselda Pollock, 'is not orchestrated for sight alone but by means of visual cues refers to other sensations and relations of bodies and objects in a lived world'.[66] Walter Pater observed that 'each object is loosed into a group of impressions – colour, odour, texture – in the mind of the observer … for that moment only'.[67] Indeed, even Max Nordau tapped into the phenomenological aspects of object and space when he noted that, towards distinctly differing ends,

> [e]verything in these houses aims at exciting the nerves and dazzling the senses. The disconnected and antithetical effects in all arrangements, the constant contradiction between form and purpose, the outlandishness of most objects, is intended to be bewildering … He who enters here must not doze, but be thrilled.[68]

Perception is fundamentally a seduction through the senses as much as a reduction to essences and it is these essences that inhabit objects and spaces. Michael Camille notes how 'pleasure – not as a passive and merely optical response but as an active, productive and shaping stimulation of all the senses – is the fundamental experience at the foundations of the act of collecting'.[69] Objects do not function as isolated entities, but work to conjure a feeling, sensation, memory, overall pleasure or delight within the domestic landscape, much in the same way Sir Kenneth Clark and Cecil Lewis recount their experiences and memories of Ricketts and Shannon's collections and interiors.

Each space, like each object, had its own personality awakened by the design and objects contained therein. The second to last house the Aesthetic companions shared together, in Holland Park, Lansdowne House, they acquired in 1902 and for which they paid £140 annually. It marked the beginning of a period that saw the couple's finances and social standing rise considerably. It was also a time when they were widely regarded as adept connoisseurs to be reckoned with. Lansdowne House was a newly built block of studio apartments commissioned by the couple's friend and patron, the South African millionaire Sir Edmond Davis (1861–1939), with whom, along with his wife, the artists shared a great friendship. Here the artists each had their own private studio. While Ricketts's studio was austere, Shannon's was in keeping with contemporary dictates for up-and-coming, promising young painters, which called for animal skins on the floor and oriental screens.[70]

In 1903 they inaugurated occasional 'tea-fights' to showcase Shannon's work. For the first of these sixty people attended including Roger Fry, Robbie Ross, the Fields; Ricketts was a disheartening force in the room, flitting about and making many guests nervous.[71] By 1914,

Vale(d) decadence

3.8 Charles Shannon in his private studio, Lansdowne House.

faced with the growing dilemma of an ever-increasing social circle and calendar, Shannon devised a plan to maintain the couple's social presence and importance by holding weekly late afternoon tea parties. Described by Ricketts as an event where '[q]uite interesting people turn up!', their inaugural tea-bash featured no fewer than seventy guests, coming from all sorts of cultural and social backgrounds.[72] Already by the 1890s, men taking tea in the afternoon was a symbolic ritual associated with effeminate aesthetes.[73] Ricketts and Shannon certainly took no notice of such claims and were so well respected that it was both a privilege and honour to be invited to such events. After the lease had run out on their flat at Lansdowne House in 1923, the pair sold a work by Puvis de Chavannes to purchase Townshend House, located near Regent's Park. Again Clark fondly remembered the company, the food, the laughs and the atmosphere the objects conjured from his visits to Townshend House

> where Ricketts and Shannon loved to be surrounded by what they would have called pretty things ... No anxiety about plastic values there: simply delight ... There was plenty of talk at Townshend House too, but one enjoyed it against a backdrop of visual delights. The dining table appeared to be one vast slab of lapis lazuli (I suppose it was made of several) at the end of which was a barrage of madonna lilies. I do not remember the food because by the end of the meal I was always tipsy, having had to swallow half a bottle of *orvieto secco,* and several glasses of revolting Italian liqueur which Ricketts drank because of its name, *strega.* No wonder that when

> Ricketts said 'Come and grub with me' one always said 'Yes', and put off any other engagement.[74]

In this, the last of the homes the two artists would share together, the rarefied realm that they staged was generated not only by Ricketts's aura and overpowering presence, but through the overall affect the spaces themselves engendered in visitors as well. Lewis vividly recalled how the eclecticism of their collection, dispersed variously throughout the house, worked mysteriously to form an unequalled aesthetic harmony:

> You would not think that Old Master drawings would be at home with a Chinese bird-cage; you would not think that red and green marble-topped tables could live in amity; you would fancy that Empire chairs might swear at Morris chintzes, French knives could not harmonize with Georgian silver, and a modern blue glass bowl could never stand at the feet of a Grecian statuette; the whole certainly could not be lit hard with clear bulbs hanging from sixpenny porcelain shades. Yet, strangely, all combined to give a sense of luxury and elegance that was incomparable.[75]

Every object's individual merit, according to Lewis, was sacrificed for the affect of an overall harmony: 'Each object, being in itself perfect, added its lustre to the whole, so that the room, which was, besides, winter and summer, filled with flowers, glowed with a radiant and compelling beauty'.[76]

Of course, the primary concern for Ricketts's putting his knowledge to best use was his own spaces for living and working as he was himself a self-declared 'grandee'. According to Ricketts the grandee's 'reception-room would be rich and luxurious, filled with noble and beautiful things, fit places in which to dispense hospitality and receive their peer; but the rooms in which they habitually passed their days would be almost poverty-stricken puritan in their simplicity'. This was precisely how Ricketts lived and allocated his spaces. Lewis's description is once again clear and vivid:

> He had no sense of comfort. The easy-chair, with its deep feather cushions into which you 'relax', was anathema to him. His 'easy' chairs cost 35s and were almost devoid of padding; his sofa was as uncomfortable as a waiting-room seat at a railway station. All were covered with blue cotton cloth at a shilling a yard, the stuff out of which butchers make their aprons. His ash-trays were saucers, his palette an old plate, his warmth a square black-leaded stove … All his life … he had skimped and saved on daily expenses in order to amass his magnificent collection.[77]

The term 'grandee' might surely be understood as an Aesthete in the queerest sense of the word. While his Spartan studio betrayed a lack of funds it also clearly delineated the spaces of work and dis/play. The parlour was where the so-called grandee entertained, elaborated his pretensions as aesthetic guru and consummate host. It was the space wherein the objects reflected, off their polished surfaces, the glow of brilliance emanating from their owners. However, in the rooms of reception, the rooms which facilitated a catholic taste of ideas, objects and people, Ricketts's middle-class Protestant austerity was never too far away, hinting at his bourgeois conformity, respectability and uncompromising work ethic.

The fact that the furnishings were not the focal point of sensorial delight forced the visitors to concentrate their attention and pleasure on the precious *objets d'art*. Collecting, rather than consuming for either luxury or consumption sake, was reinforced by way of the body's response to the environment. Following along from the Arts and Crafts Movement, Ricketts condemned the perceived rapid commercialism of the age. He argued that, beginning from within the home, the collector must begin and end with only those objects that delight, fascinate or conform to his/her own aesthetic:

> Our homes have been so invaded by an abject commercialism which counts pecuniary profit as the one thing necessary, that the craftsman is today always surrounded by hostile and depressing aspects. How can he free himself? I have one suggestion. Let him begin in the corner of one room or garret to order everything according to his tastes, to admit nothing into it that does not fascinate his gaze ... banishing whatever comes to offend him and replacing it by better.[78]

Works of art were inseparable from the material reality of these two artist-collectors in a concrete and tangible way; after all, the sale of one of their paintings provided the men with a way to move into a space of greater stability. In Townshend House 'great pictures and drawings hung over the red and green marble topped tables and Ricketts presided, his back to a Rembrandt, over a dining table made from slabs of real lapis lazuli'.[79]

Not unlike Lansdowne House, which boasted an ongoing conversation between luxury and austerity throughout the home, Townshend displayed both of the artists' bi-polar aesthetic inclinations. While Ricketts's studio may have been 'Spartan', visitors were not limited to such austerity but treated to rooms both 'princely' and pleasing. The parlour, or reception room, housed glass cases displaying Egyptian antiquities, Greek vases and various antique figurines while exotic beads and Chinese hair ornaments quietly rested in drawers below, living side by side with key furniture pieces like Adam sofas, Italian side-tables and an antique marble torso amongst their myriad pictures. These rooms of reception were simply that, spaces to carefully house

3.9 Dining room featuring the lapis lazuli tabletop dining table, Spring Terrace.

their collection, salons of display, marked as separate and removed from spaces of and for day-to-day living and working. These were spaces occupied and performed only in the presence of friends and colleagues. 'Yet [according to Lewis] it was not, like a museum, cold and detached ... but it was none the less a *room*, arranged in perfect taste.'[80] Increased funds in the 1920s meant that the companions embarked on a collecting frenzy of beautiful objects with no real rhyme or reason. The only selection criterion remained aesthetic beauty, just as Ricketts had long advocated.

In this house, Ricketts and Shannon claimed their own unique territory, using furniture from the mid-eighteenth century no longer in vogue. Gradually their Oriental *objets*, those most cherished by Shannon, began to disappear, as they ostensibly distanced themselves from the much-celebrated signs of self-conscious Aestheticism of decades since passed. Unlined Morris-patterned fabric with a dark background was used for the curtains, adding an overall lightness to the space. This same fabric was also transformed into co-ordinated cushions. The satinwood tables and 'Adam sofa' remained permanent fixtures resting on a few Persian rugs. Pictures reflected a heightened sophistication yet bourgeois palette with the staple Japanese prints from the Utamaro period, hanging side by side with oil paintings and sketches by European Old Masters, images long associated with their homes. Used to the best possible effect, this assortment of objects from various sources was premised on and expounded the universalizing 'principle that good things of all periods and cultures go together'.[81]

3.10 Charles Ricketts seated in front of part of his picture collection, Lansdowne House.

Is it a foregone conclusion that a nineteenth-century male artist is necessarily compelled to collect, obliged by technical concerns and interests? As Charlotte Gere has noted, artists were not simply producers but consumers in their own right.[82] This consumption, however, enabled and was part of a higher ideal, that of connoisseurial insight. In light of Ricketts's less than 'noble' birth, connoisseurship was a legitimate means to step up and move beyond the strictures of his middle working-class position, through the intellectual control of visual and material culture and the texts he published on the subject. It garnered for him greater access to the world of culture, an intellectual conduit by which to assert himself on the national and international art scene, while ensuring the success of his partner as a painter. However, for the nineteenth-century mind, collecting as well as consuming might prove to be a pathological condition rather than a diversion, pastime or source of legitimate pleasure. The aesthete has often been characterized as a commodity fetishist, a decadent degenerate. Jean Baudrillard has claimed that 'everything that cannot be invested in human relationships is invested in objects', a relationship overwhelmingly consonant in the aesthetic life of and relations between these two men.[83] However, I might highlight how the investment in objects and the investments in someone else, in the case of

3.11 Charles Ricketts at work amidst his treasures, Lansdowne House.

Ricketts and Shannon, informed the art for art's sake ethos by which they lived out their lives, rather than some sexual pathology which tarnishes Baudrillard's understanding of collecting. The sexual nature of collecting is not particular to postmodern thought, but harkens back to nineteenth-century men like Nordau who asserted that collecting was endemic to the decadence that characterized the end of the century. Nordau claimed that '[t]he present rage for collecting, the piling up of dwellings, of aimless *bric-à-brac* … has established an irresistible desire among degenerates to accumulate useless trifles'.[84] In Nordau's scheme degeneration and collecting went hand in hand and marked a serious gender trouble threatening normative sexual codes and performances. Nordau's position obliquely speaks to the manner in which modernist designers, theorists and artists pathologized Victorian interiors whose overabundance of objects reeked of feminine wiles, excess and decadence.

Painted and photographic pictures of Ricketts and Shannon, not together but separately holding a coveted object from their collection, reify and interpolate the men as collectors in the history of art rather than as consumers. Repeatedly representing Ricketts with an object in hand, or posing near one, not only reaffirmed his relationship to valuable objects of the past through his acquisitions, knowledge and discipline, but also the intimacy between the two artists. The man depicted in the picture is not simply a patron who commissioned the work, but the man responsible for the painter's own collection, shared together. Reinforcing Ricketts's connoisseurial talents in particular allows the duo's sanctity in the lineage of late Victorian art and culture to be

Vale(d) decadence

3.12 Charles Shannon. *Portrait of Ricketts / The Man with the Greek Vase*, 1916.

safeguarded. As part of the taxonomic ideal of collecting fine art and craft objects, they transformed their homes into museums that transcended both time and space.

One picture by Shannon, formally in the possession of Mrs Davis, is noteworthy for its representation of Ricketts as the pensive, thoughtful and astute collector that he was. In *The Man with the Greek Vase* (1916), Ricketts is displayed holding a Greek vase from their collection. An oil on canvas, it depicts Ricketts clothed in black sitting on a couch and set in relief against a gold abstract floral patterned screen [Figure 3.12]. Depicted as a man of culture and knowledge, Ricketts looks out at the viewer with a direct, preoccupied yet contemplative stare. In this picture Shannon immortalizes his lifelong companion as connoisseur and collector, aesthetic arbiter and mentor of a generation of modern artists, rather than necessarily an artist in his own right. The portrait also points to the link between Shannon and Ricketts as well as the type of man Ricketts was said to be: serious, driven and focused. It would seem that,

3.13 Charles Ricketts as the decadent Aesthete.

at least at first glance, his sexuality does not seep into the frame. As David Peters Corbett has noted of the significance of late nineteenth-century portraiture, 'it reenacts both the ideal of access to identity and the experience of its elusiveness, its blockage or deliberate withholding and dissembling'. He insists that while portraiture can be thought of as a representation of 'the social self, or as a fetish or ritual object', for the period 'the portrait promises to reveal precisely this reality or identity through a visual account of appearance'.[85] However, as we know, appearances are as much a product of performances and deception. For the aesthetes, which both Ricketts and Shannon remained well into the twentieth century, notions of personality and representation travelled into new and unchartered territory. Gradually, and certainly by the 1890s, the 'distinction between person and pose were worn away'. The more flamboyant Whistler could pass below the radar of acceptability for critics and the public precisely because the division between personality and labour could be maintained. Wilde, on the other hand, destroyed such illusions and proved indelibly that 'the pose was the person and the mask was the man'.[86]

Threat and the threshold

Wilde in shackles walking toward his new home predicated on hard labour was the outcome of a series of events and a number of trials that led jury and court to convict him under the proviso established under the Labouchere Amendment of 1885. In March 1893 Alfred Taylor introduced Wilde to Charles and William Parker, and the first alleged offence with Charles was said to have taken place at the illustrious and glamorous Savoy Hotel. Opened on the Strand in 1889, the hotel served both its well-heeled clientele and, after an extension in 1903–4, also offered small private flats with all the amenities one would expect of an establishment of its calibre.[87] As the site of Wilde's first so-called recorded offence as well as Britain's first luxury hotel, the Savoy Hotel is marked as a space of material excess and corporeal transience, with people coming and going, living and sleeping in close proximity. 'The assumption was that sex as a vice of *luxuria*, a vice that sprang up spontaneously among the rich, the privileged, the effete, who spread it, almost as a communicable disease, outwards into the commonality of the population' corrupting the lower classes.[88] The fear that excess, the deadliest of sins, was contagious was certainly borne out by the fact that Wilde, for example, 'was the center of a hideous circle of corruption, which forced young men into a world of decadence and prostitution'.[89] Other alleged offences were said to have taken place from October 1893 to March 1894 with Sidney Mavor and Charles Parker in rooms Wilde occupied at 10/11 St James's Place, spaces meant expressly for his work, away from the distracting mayhem of quotidian family life. However, at the trials it was Taylor's lodgings that preoccupied the prosecution. In the cross-examination, Wilde noted that 'Taylor was living at 13 Little College Street, and I have been there to tea parties on many occasions. They were all men at the parties, but not all young men.'[90]

Alfred Waterhouse Somerset Taylor was thirty years old when he met Wilde in the autumn of 1892. The son of a cocoa manufacturer, he was expelled from Marlborough having been caught in the lavatory with a much younger boy engaging in lewd acts. In 1883, when of age, he came into a handsome fortune of £45,000, but with weekly expenses ranging from £40 and £50 a week on rent boys, bankruptcy within a year was inevitable. Taylor was married, and his husband, Charles Spurrier Mason with whom he staged a mock wedding in 1893, was a twenty-five-year-old prostitute. Maurice Schwabe introduced Wilde to Taylor. Schwabe was both Taylor's former schoolmate and Bosie's lover, and was sent abroad to Australia by his family for fear he might be implicated in Wilde's queer network during the trials. Schwabe regularly invited gentlemen like Wilde to meet younger lads at tea parties hosted at Taylor's Little College Street flat, a social event, as we have seen, deemed suspect for men by the last quarter of the nineteenth century. It was soon after Wilde's now infamous and eloquent monologue on the 'love that dare not speak its name' that the lawyer for the prosecution, Mr C. F. Gill, turned his attention to Taylor's 'curious establishment' and the dubious relationship these two men seemed to have. Taylor's flat, for which he paid £3 in rent, occupied the upper part of a two-storey house and comprised a kitchen, bathroom, sitting room and bedroom. His daily domestic habits were even called into question when the prosecution asked whether he did his own cooking or opened his own door, given he did not keep a servant. Gill inquired whether Wilde 'saw nothing peculiar or suggestive in the arrangement of Taylor's rooms'. For Wilde they were at worst 'Bohemian'.[91] The prosecution fixated on the fact that one could not see in through the windows, disallowing the exposure of the private interior to the public domain. The relationship between the public and private realms and sexuality was, after all, at the heart of the amendment suggested by Labouchere.

After repeated questions concerning curtains being drawn and if daylight was permitted into the sitting room, Gill forced Wilde to answer whether he could 'declare specifically that any daylight was ever admitted into the room?' The fascination with and attention to the windows, the eyes into the soul of the interior, and the allowance of daylight into the space speaks of fears of artificiality, unnaturalness, vampiric decay and decadent opacity, all of which pointed to an inability to survey the spatio-sexual life of the domestic sphere. The window as metaphor of the revelation of health also spoke to broader late Victorian concerns for sexual health. It was believed that eyes were not merely the windows to the soul, but also the indicators of an individual's sexual health and conditions. 'Reddish, discoloured eyes [we]re a sure sign of "sexual impairments"'. Women were told to '[g]et a good look into their eyes', when attempting to find a husband. In a cultural context of surveillance, eyes and windows become thresholds to exposure.[92]

Not only was sight scrutinized, but so too were the other senses. Instigated by suggestions that incense and exotic perfumes were regularly burnt in Taylor's rooms, olfactory perception was called into question. Again, Gill wondered whether Wilde found the space 'peculiar'; Wilde *naturally* did not. For him, it 'was merely a bachelor's place'. When suggested that there 'was rather elaborate furniture in the room', Wilde concluded that the 'rooms were furnished in good taste'.[93] Yet, the good taste of the bachelor led the prosecution to conclude that Taylor's flat was 'a place where persons who had these filthy appetites might meet and gratify them'.[94] Swiftly and surely the court and subsequent media reportage conflated the figure of the bachelor, taste and queer sexual appetites.

Vale(d) decadence

3.14 Oscar Wilde relaxing on the (plush) divan during his lecture trip through America, 1882.

At this juncture it is worth underlining how fears of gross indecency precipitated a widening of the juridical purview, effectively enlarging the spatial parameters of indecency and deviance by decisively moving from public to private. Under the Labouchere Amendment, an act of indecency was ostensibly now simpler to define. Institutional, and by extension public, perception understood that immorality, degeneracy and sexual perversion could easily traverse the porous borders between the domestic and the public realms. What was it, exactly, that was understood to be at stake here? Was it public safety or the sanctity and preciousness of the domestic wherein normative masculinity was formed, codified and performed?

Perception and the illusion of domestic perfection at the end of the nineteenth century conjured spatial essences informing and informed by the identity of the occupants. Understood in polarized terms either as of luxury and excess or of ascetic self-denial, space was further complicated by how perceptions of sexuality impinged on the proper gendered uses of space. Meaning is prescribed by, through and as a result of the competing spatial narratives of perception. These infuse essences into spaces through sights, sounds and smells contained therein. It is the phenomenology, the materiality of a space, deemed in keeping with normative prescriptions that assures its inhabitants and tourists to pass through safely, seemingly absolved of any potential indecency. The

Evening News reported that the rooms Taylor rented were 'draped and furnished' in a 'remarkable manner' and 'curious way', 'perfumed and always lighted by artificial light'.[95] The unnatural way Taylor manipulated scents toward an exotic, decadent and erotic, though domestic, environment was in keeping with his contemporary Ricketts, who wrote that he 'long pondered ... devoting a separate drawer of a piece of furniture to a separate scent, and thereby having a pleasure house or palace of perfume with a chamber for each odour'.[96] One surely must ask what distinguishes, if anything, Ricketts and Shannon from Taylor, given that they were all queer aesthetes who constructed spaces separate from heteronormative, supposedly rational dictates? Despite Taylor's elite class position and the decidedly sexual nature of his domestic space, like Shannon and Ricketts, he too successfully constructed a well sought-out environment conducive to homosociability, painstakingly falling below the radar, sheltered by the auspices of hearth and home; at least until his trial. Unlike at Ricketts and Shannon's homes, the perfumed aura infused with artificial lighting at Taylor's home was seen to demonstrate the artifice by which he conducted his life, and proved apparently indexical of his character as suspect under the scrutinizing eye of the Labouchere Amendment, which forcibly threatened and exposed the veil that house and home once provided men like him. In Taylor's queer version of bourgeois domesticity, the cohesive economic union assumed by a family unit was tinged by *laissez-faire, laissez-passer* supply and demand. The 'indecent acts' performed in Taylor's apartment significantly defied the ever-increasing separation between work and home, at least outside of the context of artists' and Arts and Crafts houses. With the exchange of money, now deemed a public act, for sexual services, Taylor's domestic realm was perceived as sullied and polluted. Men's responsibility was to secure the safety of the home; however Ruskin's notion of the threshold, according to John O. Jordan, is at once 'barrier and point of access' engendering an important interplay between absences and presences, as 'it allows and perhaps invites transgression'.[97] Taylor was guilty of polluting the home and worse of sullying the threshold that demarcated home from the public. But wasn't Labouchere guilty of the same crime in his call to expose publicly, for all to see, the privacy of sexuality?

The myth of the middle-class home as a safe haven, and decidedly cleaner and better managed environment than those of the working classes, has been disproved by Annmarie Adams, who has convincingly shown that '[t]he house was not a safe, protective shelter, removed from a dangerous and unpredictable Victorian city. Between 1870 and 1900, middle-class houses were considered much more poisonous and dangerous than public spaces or working-class neighbourhoods, the subject of earlier reforms.'[98] Robert Edis, for example, who published a handbook on the interior on the occasion of the 1884 International Health Exposition, had already for some time warned against the dust, for example, that lurked in plush fabric and warned against excess and luxury, also seen as forms of dirt.[99] In tandem with the Labouchere Amendment, medical experts, social commentators, architects and moralists alike were heavily weighing in on the debates surrounding health, hygiene and the home, with some advocating 'healthy decoration in the home'. As they would become in the case against Taylor, windows were the starting point in the health and cleanliness of the home, design itself an index of sexuality. As one anonymous critic commented: 'We cannot have our windows cleaned too often. When they are dirty they not only exclude light and sunshine ... but are covered with thickened human exhalations and dust.'[100] The relationship of the window to the home was akin to the relationship of the eyes to the body; where the window operates as the eye into the domestic interior and its occupant, so too the eye is the window into the interiority of the body's occupant, the very soul of his identity. While the interior should comprise all things 'beautiful in form, elegantly simple, and all the colours harmonious and restrained; these great qualities seem to impart to us the feelings of self-restraint, dignity, and repose'.[101] Luxury, then, is not the goal of the proper, healthful home, its aesthetic goal is a moral one, in which the Protestant ideal of 'self-restraint, dignity, and repose' make up its foundational pillars.

In the 1889 Cleveland Street scandal illustrious clients like Lord Arthur Somerset and Prince Albert Victor (second-in-line to the British throne and only rumoured to have been a client) were charged with hiring young men at a homosexual male brothel in Cleveland Street, Fitzrovia. The scandal made it all too painfully obvious that degeneracy and urban decay were no longer contained to the city's exoticized East End, but dwelt and flourished at the edge of the London's fashionable Regent's Park. Taylor's flat also served as a frightening reminder of such precarious proximity, as Little College Street is a stone's throw away from the Houses of Parliament as well as Westminster Abbey. Undoubtedly this sense of proximity lent itself to fears of the excess and deviance that London hosted in its centre. In this consideration, we need look no further than to the English language itself, namely to the identical etymological origins of contact, contingent and contagion which share the same Latin root *contingere* meaning to have contact with, pollute, befall. This apt contiguity underpins how concerns for health and hygiene as well as the fear of dirt, disease and contagion were swiftly imbricated into the issues of domestic and social safety expounded by the amendment of 1885. In this era of surveillance, bodily health, domestic comfort and social control formed a united discursive formation neatly embodied in the figure of the homosexual.

Wilde, of course – that seemingly omnipresent, all-consuming aesthetic tourist and liminal figure – straddled these various worlds, whether the world of class, refinement and good manners as exemplified by his frequent and beloved visits to The Vale, or the demi-monde characterized by Taylor's apartment in Little College Street, wherein every desire and pleasure of the flesh was made available to those whose pockets were purportedly deeper than their morality. As Rothenstein once commented, if Wilde was at his 'best' when in attendance at The Vale, he was certainly at his 'worst', or most unfortunate, in Taylor's lodgings and at the Savoy Hotel. Ricketts himself also recalled how he knew of Wilde's 'love of luxury' and how it made him

> live in costly hotels and restaurants, paradises for the vulgar, and sometimes in strange company. Wilde had often smiled at the austerity of my habits … and would laughingly say 'Both you and Shannon are ascetics of art, you turn away from life and like most painters, you lack curiosity'.[102]

Ricketts quickly and morally counterposed his shared middle-class austerity with Wilde's easy love of luxury, the frequency with which he associated himself with ill-reputed places and faces, and the resulting abdication of his obligations to the safety and strength of hearth, home and hence the nation itself.

Wilde's reputation preceded him wherever he went, and once Rothenstein questioned whether Wilde knew just 'how gross, how soiled by the world he appeared, sitting in one of the white scrubbed kitchen chairs next to Ricketts and Shannon and Sturge Moore'.[103] The allusion to the whiteness of the kitchen furniture, the labour implicated in the fastidiously scrubbed cleanliness, rendered sanitary and pure in this inner sanctum of the domestic environment, is counterposed with, and is meant to conjure, the duplicitous nature of Wilde's character, sullied and dirtied by commodified sexual relations which threatened to adulterate sanctified thresholds. Advocates of clean homes maintained that '[d]irt, mud and debris come into the home to soil it'.[104] The threshold leading into the home stood foursquare as the boundary between contagion/ health, chaos/order and cleanliness/pollution. Encoded in Rothenstein's apt choice of words, the use of cleanliness, incidental to domestic purity and refinement, also acted to sidestep the potentially revealing nature of Ricketts and Shannon's intimacy. Ellis Hanson has argued that 'gay men are obliged to inhabit' a space which is 'unspeakable and unnameable, itself defined as orifice, as a "dark continent" men dare not penetrate'.[105] But Wilde did penetrate, and left his tainted mark on the spaces he travelled through. An orifice like a threshold marks an entrance to the other side; and, whether a body or domestic space, its contours must be maintained and contained at all costs. The question of sexual tourism or even the debris left behind by those who engage in such activity is fundamentally a heteronormative contest to police the threshold and maintain the integrity of what resides on the other side. Victoria Rosner contents that as a 'space that forms a bridge between two discrete rooms' the threshold 'figures as an unsettling intermediary in the otherwise black-and-white world of separated spheres'.[106] In its liminality marking out space as in between two distinct, unique rooms, a threshold establishes itself as transitional, intermediary and unstable. In queer terms, threshold also implies the inchoate, nebulous and ever-shifting co-ordinates of the closet and one's relationship to it. It is, then, an ideal metaphor for the queer sexualities of this book, men defined neither by one identity, role or room nor another, but somewhere or something in between. As Mary Douglas importantly claims '[d]anger lies in transitional states, simply because transition is neither one state nor the next, it is undefinable'.[107]

In her evocative essay on the homoeroticism in Bram Stoker's *Dracula*, published one short month after Wilde was imprisoned, Talia Schaffer argues that Stoker could speak of Wilde and express his conflicting emotions regarding his incarceration only through the characters of his ghastly novel and a constellation of allusions to the news reports that flooded the newspapers. What he offered through his writing, in other words, was a threshold that distanced any association with Wilde's unfortunate outcome and yet at the same time always threatened to expose hidden connections. Schaffer importantly posits that Wilde, 'the historical figure', was not so much *what* Stoker wrote about, but rather that he wrote of 'Wilde-as-threat'.[108] Here I wish to raise the issue of the omnipresence and the true threat Wilde's excess represented: crossing thresholds threatened the seeming bourgeois quietude of Ricketts and Shannon's homes, for example. Schaffer notes how the testimony at the Wilde trials surfaced in clear and direct allusions in *Dracula*, particularly the description of his and Taylor's flats. She references how, for example, in Chapter Three, which also marks the beginning of Jonathan Harker's journal, he writes: 'When I found that I was a sort of prisoner a wilde [sic] feeling came over me'. Schaffer, however, omits the next line from his text in her own discussion, simultaneously ignoring the important aspect of domestic interior endemic to his 'wilde feeling': 'I rushed down the stairs, trying every door and peering out of every window I could find; but after a little the conviction of my helplessness overpowered all feelings'.[109] Here, as in Taylor's flat, windows could not help to reveal anything. Interiors, identity and emotion cohere tragically in Stoker's tacit, though fictive, allusion to Wilde.

Christopher Reed has proposed the term 'immanent' to describe queer spaces that emerge as a result of a 'process of, literally, taking place, of claiming territory'.[110] I wish to extend Reed's notion of imminent queer spaces by suggesting that the experience and expression of appropriation and/or transformation of built environments by queer men must take into consideration the aesthetic value attached to these spaces. As we have seen in the case of Taylor, interiors that affronted public decency by removing the veil of ambiguity of intimate relations between men in the domestic realm were quickly and shrewdly vilified by society, the courts and the popular press, evidence of whose supposed degeneracy was provided through the aesthetic. That was because the interior spaces of ideal bourgeois domesticity served as a microcosm of a healthy English nation. Indeed, the Labouchere Amendment seems to echo the sentiments of Ruskin's famous lecture, 'Of Queens' Gardens' from twenty years earlier, while at the same time legalizing a remedy for the acute fears of many that the home was under siege by those who dared threaten the threshold of the separate sphere.

Shame, remorse and the time of deferral

Modern art is a flower of suffering.

Jean Paul Raymond and Charles Ricketts

Like Stoker's deferral of the core issues of the Wilde trials to his fantastically dark and morbid *Dracula*, Ricketts in an entirely different manner deferred his own deep-seeded feelings of remorse and alliance to Wilde when he published his memoires of *Oscar Wilde: Recollections* (1932). Written with his alter ego, Jean Paul Raymond, the essay provides the conduit through which Ricketts was able to defer his own feelings of remorse and shame. Born in Geneva to a French mother, Ricketts always maintained a deep link and fascination with France and its art and culture. Summoning his French alter ego, Ricketts not only exposed his own discomfort with sexual mores, as well as his own vacillation between the two cultures, deferred the discussion, at least in part, to a foreign and seemingly more permissive cultural frontier. Decades after Wilde's sentencing and death, shelter for Ricketts could be provided only through the deferral of his true beliefs and ideals to a French fictional character and not his English self. In the introductory notes to the essay, Thomas Lowinsky notes how by creating the fictional character of Raymond 'Ricketts created a sympathetic audience for his words of passionate indignation at the fate of his friend'.[111] Ricketts initially positioned Wilde as the misunderstood and unappreciated artist in a land of dilettantes (Britain) and concluded that '[t]o be witty is to be found out'.[112] To be found out was the perennial concern of the aesthete, that is, to be identified and labelled as queer in a cultural context that held artistic sensibility as suspicious. Near contemporary Irish poet and playwright W. B. Yeats corroborated Ricketts's claims when he asserted that '[t]he rage against Wilde was also complicated by the Britisher's jealousy of art and the artist, which is generally dormant but is called into activity when the artist has gone outside his field into publicity of an undesirable kind'.[113] For Yeats, distrust was bred through excess, a surplus of one's station and perceived static identity; any deviance through self-promotion or aggrandisement is met with suspicion. Class, celebrity and an overt aesthetic sensibility were deployed to queer Wilde well beyond any sexual act he might have performed. According to Ricketts, the 'fear of ideas [was] recent' and was the result of 'public school training' said to be sterilizing the country's men of any trace of intellect and replacing it with 'an inane worship of sport. Grown men, who would shrink at the statement of an idea, will discuss a game for hours.'[114] The verdict against Wilde, Raymond and Ricketts asserted, was a bias against 'art, artists, and even culture'.[115] The court's verdict and Wilde's demise led to the downfall of culture and art itself for the remainder of the decade.[116] Aesthetics (queer under Wilde's pen) and the national best interest, for Ricketts, were set on a collision course that would not only ruin the artistic culture of Britain, but would also implicate the aesthete in discussions of decadence and effeminacy.

Whether with Forster, Warren (as we will see) and Ricketts shame compelled them to handle queer subject matter as an (an)aesthetics of deferral, distancing it temporally by publishing queer tracts as memoirs after the fact or even posthumously. Throughout their friendship, Ricketts was always irritated by Wilde's flamboyance – I suspect a product of what we would today label internal homophobia and anti-feminine sentiment. Ricketts, however, was one of the very few who dared visit Wilde in his jail cell. Tinged with a sense of shame, part of queer time is, I wish to suggest and honour here, a writing after the fact, and is perhaps conceptually adjacent to the spatial metaphor of the proverbial closet. As we have seen in Chapter 1, Forster could only bear to publish and reveal the true source of inspiration for *Maurice* posthumously. As we will see in the chapter that follows, Edward Perry Warren's three-volume Uranian tract was partially published posthumously, and significantly behind its time. With *Oscar Wilde: Recollections*, Ricketts also performed the queer deferral of time, distanced and removed from the sting of Wilde's prison sentence, near the end of his own life, and yet not too distant from a generation all too aware of the sting's effect.

Graham Hammill contends that 'the aesthetic – broadly conceived – gives form to a history of sexuality in such a way that some changes are rendered significant while others go simply unrecognized. The question of sexuality, that is, urges the problem of historiography.'[117] Institutional bodies such as medicine and the law, for example, have structured and veiled the threshold into queer history for many generations. For a significant portion of our history, queerness has appeared almost exclusively through the auspices of court and medical reports. Ricketts and Shannon managed to pass unnoticed, forging a domestic environment that was perceived as respectable and admirable by friends, colleagues and society at large, in which no illicit transactions were perceived as having occurred; emphatically reiterated many decades later in Delaney's biography on Ricketts. Respectable bourgeois domesticity, even if queer, is easily silenced by history whereas scandal, especially of a sexual nature, guarantees a position of continued visibility throughout history. Friends, colleagues and historians were never quick to vilify or obliterate Ricketts and Shannon from public memory, as was the case for Wilde soon after his demise. Not subjected to legal prosecution, Ricketts and Shannon were not repressed by their peers in the way that Wilde and Taylor were, because of the way the latter blurred the boundaries between sexuality and commerce within the domestic sphere. By virtue of their apparent bourgeois domesticity, however, Ricketts and Shannon were subsequently forgotten by a first-generation of masculinist modernism, which valorized heteronormative avant-garde genius whose ideal subjectivity remained undefined by and antithetical to the domestic.

Audiences flocked to see the detailed sets of Wilde's comedies, which Ricketts called 'modern drawing-room plays with pink lampshades'.[118] Ricketts's allusion to frivolous and decorative interior design is a revealing one as it exposed his own thoughts of Wilde's association with the feminine and frivolous, to say nothing of the obvious irony of his choice of colour, which later in the twentieth century would become associated with gay men. It is also consonant with a jury and court that found him guilty exclusively through objects of interior design. Luxury and consumption feminized men like Taylor and Wilde, while Ricketts and Shannon obliquely reaffirmed the gendered culture of domesticity. Thus, perception and spatial narratives provided the evidence as to why some cultural producers passed unnoticed (then as much as now) whilst others were vilified. For Wilde and Taylor, the court case single-handedly exposed the mask by which these men initially passed unnoticed by society, how domestic pleasures could be made painfully public, how the boundaries of the domestic were not secure and, finally, how the artifice by which all men performed their public lives threatened to reveal sublimated desires directed away from and yet toward the domestic. Ricketts and Shannon remained collectors in the queerest understanding of the term, freed from the constraining and pejorative label of consumers of luxury vilified by the press in the wake of the Wilde trials. I wish to posit that the degree of luxury and comfort of same-sex domesticity directly impacted the perception and sense of its spaces and the relationships of those men who occupied them. Comfort, denied in the interest of loftier goals such as connoisseurship and aesthetic ideals, coupled with a English sense of purity and morality, meant that Ricketts and Shannon passed below the radar despite their intimate relationship.

I wish to conclude by suggesting that while domestic spaces may have undergone a transformation and appropriation by artists such as Shannon and Ricketts in the later nineteenth and early twentieth centuries, they did not, in any way, threaten thresholds, especially those demarcating commodity from sexuality. In naming, identifying and defining queerness in a culture, perception is tantamount, and what these artists skilfully and honestly projected was the semblance of maintaining, with an artistic flair, the integrity of the middle-class values of safety, order, cleanliness and peace attributed to the domestic realm. Wilde's and Taylor's crime was not that they simply affronted public decency or even that they performed lewd sex acts, but that they had directly, queerly, threatened the fictional spatial narrative which ensured gender and sexual continuity, precariously kept in check through the complexities of encoding the public/private axis. Neither spiritual nor intellectual, Taylor's activities in the home, and by extension Wilde's, were doubly vilified because interior design was perceived as in the service of bodily excess, luxury and commerce; a decadence not tolerated by Victoria's loyal subjects.

Notes

1 First presented by the Necessary Angel Theatre Company and The National Arts Centre, the play, ironically, premiered at the Berkeley Street Theatre (Toronto) just down the street from my own flat, though a decade before my arrival in the neighbourhood.

2 J. Ruskin, *Sesame and Lilies* (New Haven and London: Yale University Press, 2002 [1865]), p. 99.

3 C. Gere with L. Hoskins, *The House Beautiful: Oscar Wilde and the Aesthetic Interior* (Aldershot: Lund Humphries, 2000), p. 11.

4 Ricketts and Shannon lived in numerous homes together over the years. These included: 12a Edith Terrace, Edith Grove Chelsea, 1887–88; 2 The Vale, King's Road, Chelsea, 1888–94; 31 Beaufort Street, Chelsea, 1894–98; 8 Spring Terrace, Richmond, Surrey, 1899–1902; Lansdowne House, Holland Park, 1902–23; Townshend House, Regent's Park, 1923–31; Chilham Keep, Kent, 1919–28.

5 See M. Hatt, 'Space, Surface, Self: Homosexuality and the Aesthetic Interior', *Visual Culture in Britain*, vol. 8, no. 1 (summer 2007).

6 Ibid., p. 105.
7 J. Darracott, *The World of Charles Ricketts* (London: Eyre Methuen, 1980), pp. 26–7.
8 *Morning Post*, 9 November 1910.
9 Sir W. Rothenstein, *Men and Memories: Recollections of William Rothenstein, 1900–1922* (London: Faber & Faber Limited, 1932), p. 173.
10 Kenneth Clark, introduction to S. Calloway, *Charles Ricketts: Subtle and Fantastic Decorator* (London: Thames and Hudson, 1979), p. 7.
11 P. J. G. Delaney, *Charles Ricketts: A Biography* (Oxford and New York: Oxford University Press, 1990), p. 22.
12 Ibid., p. 160.
13 Ricketts in Delaney, *Charles Ricketts*, p. 24.
14 Letter to Shannon 20 March 1906, BL (British Library).
15 Delaney, *Charles Ricketts*, pp. 203–4.
16 Ibid., p. 24. For an important discussion of kinship, domesticity and community in the case of Ricketts and Shannon see M. Cook, 'Domestic Passions: Unpacking the Homes of Charles Shannon and Charles Ricketts', *Journal of British Studies*, vol. 51, no. 3, June 2012.
17 In *ibid.*, p. 25.
18 S. Calloway and P. Delaney, Charles Ricketts and Charles Shannon (Orleans: Galley Twickenham, 1979), p. 5.
19 E. Glick, 'The Dialectics of Dandyism', *Cultural Critique*, vol. 48 (spring 2001), p. 131.
20 E. Prettejohn (ed.), *After the Pre-Raphaelites: Art and Aestheticism in Victorian England* (New Brunswick: Rutgers University Press, 1999), p. 4.
21 V. Rosner, *Modernism and the Architecture of Private Life* (New York: Columbia University Press, 2005), p. 22.
22 M. Camille, 'Editor's Introduction', *Art History Special Issue on Queer Collecting*, vol. 24, no. 2 (April 2001), p. 167.
23 T. Logan, *The Victorian Parlour* (Cambridge: Cambridge University Press, 2001), p. 234.
24 M. Birnbaum, *Introductions: Painters, Sculptors and Graphic Artists* (New York: Frederic Fairchild Sherman, 1919), p. 25.
25 C. Lewis (ed.), *Self-Portrait: Taken from the Letters and Journals of Charles Ricketts, R.A.*, collected and compiled by T. Sturge Moore (London: Peter Davis, 1939), p. 17.
26 Charles Ricketts was a noted jewellery designer in addition to illustrator and theatrical set designer.
27 W. Benjamin, *The Arcades Project* (Cambridge, MA, and London: The Belknap Press of Harvard University, 1999), p. 19.
28 Louis Hertz in R. W. Belk and M. Wallendorf, 'Of Mice and Men: Gender Identity in Collecting', in Susan M. Pearce (ed.), *Interpreting Objects and Collections* (London and New York: Routledge, 1994), p. 12.
29 Ibid., p. 12.
30 Letter dated August 1903, BL.
31 Ricketts letter to Shannon 2 May 1903, BL.
32 Ricketts letter 24 March 1906, BL.

33 Ricketts letter to Shannon August 1903, BL.
34 J. P. Raymond and C. Ricketts, *Oscar Wilde: Recollections* (London: The Nonesuch Press, 1932), p. 28.
35 S. Calloway, 'Wilde and the Dandyism of the Senses', in Peter Raby (ed.), *The Cambridge Companion to Oscar Wilde* (Cambridge: Cambridge University Press, 1997), pp. 49–50.
36 'Art in the Home: Healthy Decoration in the Home', *The Artist*, 1 August 1884.
37 P. J. G. Delaney (ed.), *Some Letters from Charles Ricketts and Charles Shannon to 'Michael Field' (1894–1902)* (Edinburgh: The Tragara Press, 1979), p. 120.
38 S. Calloway, 'Tout pour l'art: Ricketts, Charles Shannon and the Arrangement of a Collection', *Journal of the Decorative Art Society*, 81 (1984), p. 25.
39 Rothenstein, *Men and Memories*, pp. 173–4.
40 G. Noble, 'Accumulating Being', *International Journal of Cultural Studies*, vol. 7, no. 2 (2004), p. 253.
41 Tanagras were charming little ancient Greek terracotta figurines named after the town where they were first found in 1874, and were much sought after by collectors by the end of the century.
42 C. Hussey, 'The Keep of Chilham Castle Kent: A Residence of Mr. Charles Shannon, R.A. and Charles Ricketts A.R.A', *Country Life*, vol. 55 (21 June 1924), p. 40.
43 Rothenstein, *Men and Memories*, p. 167.
44 Ricketts letter to Michael Fields 26 February 1899 in Delaney (ed.), *Some Letters from Charles Ricketts and Charles Shannon to 'Michael Field'*.
45 See J. A. Symonds and H. Ellis, *Sexual Inversion* (Basingstoke and New York: Palgrave Macmillan, 2008).
46 Together the two women collectively wrote their poetry under the pseudonym Michael Field.
47 N. McKenna, *The Secret Life of Oscar Wilde* (New York: Basic Books, 2005), p. 115.
48 Recorded in Calloway, *Charles Ricketts*, p. 12.
49 Ricketts letter dated 18 February 1904, BL.
50 10 February 1904, BL.
51 Rothenstein, *Men and Memories*, p. 16.
52 *Ibid.*, pp. 175–6.
53 *Ibid.*, p. 176.
54 Lewis (ed.), *Self-Portrait*, p. viii.
55 C. J. Holmes, *Self & Partners (Mostly Self)*, (London and Toronto: Constable and Co., 1936), p. 163.
56 *Ibid.*, p. 165.
57 Delaney (ed.), *Some Letters from Charles Ricketts and Charles Shannon to 'Michael Field'*, p. 6.
58 Darracott, *The World of Charles Ricketts*, p. 56.
59 Ricketts letter, 26 February 1899, BL.
60 For a more in-depth discussion of this relationship in the period under discussion here see for example M. Hatt, 'Space, Surface, Self: Homosexuality and the Aesthetic Interior', *Visual Cuture in Britain*, Vol. 8, no.1 (summer 2007).

61 Ricketts letter to Michael Field, 26 February 1899, in Delaney (ed.), *Some Letters from Charles Ricketts and Charles Shannon to 'Michael Field'*.

62 Lewis (ed.), *Self-Portrait*, pp. v–vi.

63 S. Stewart, *On Longing: Narratives of the Miniature, the Gigantic, the Souvenir, the Collection* (Baltimore and London: The Johns Hopkins University Press, 1984), p. 157.

64 Shannon letter January 1899, BL.

65 S. Moore (ed.), *Works and Days, From the Journal of Michael Field* (London: J. Murray, 1933), p. 16.

66 G. Pollock, *Vision and Difference: Femininity, Feminism and the Histories of Art* (London and New York: Routledge, 1988), p. 65.

67 According to Pater, 'experience itself, is the end', encouraging us to 'grasp at any exquisite passion' or 'any stirring of the senses, strange dyes, strange colours and curious odours' that will 'set the spirit free for a moment'. W. Pater, *Marius the Epicurean* (New York: Penguin Books, Ltd, 1985), p. 152.

68 M. Nordau, *Degeneration* (New York: D. Appleton and Company, 1905), p. 11.

69 Camille, 'Editor's Introduction', p. 164.

70 Calloway, 'Tout pour l'art', p. 24.

71 Delaney, *Charles Ricketts*, p. 186.

72 Darracott, *The World of Charles Ricketts*, p. 78.

73 J. Tosh, *A Man's Place: Masculinity and the Middle-Class Home in Victorian England* (New Haven and London: Yale University Press, 1999), p. 181.

74 See Clark's Introduction to Calloway, *Charles Ricketts*, p. 7.

75 Lewis (ed.), *Self-Portrait*, p. x.

76 *Ibid.*, p. x.

77 *Ibid.*, pp. viii–ix.

78 *Ibid.*, pp. 82–3.

79 Calloway, 'Tout pour l'art', p. 27.

80 Lewis (ed.), *Self-Portrait*, p. x.

81 Calloway, 'Tout pour l'art', p. 27.

82 C. Gere with L. Hoskins, *The House Beautiful: Oscar Wilde and the Aesthetic Interior* (Aldershot: Lund Humphries, 2000), pp. 55–75.

83 J. Baudrillard, *The System of Objects* (London: Verso, 1996), p. 90.

84 Nordau, *Degeneration*, p. 27.

85 D. P. Corbett, *The World in Paint* (Philadelphia: Penn State University Press, 2004), p. 144.

86 S. K. Tillyard, *The Impact of Modernism, 1900–1920: Early Modernism and the Arts and Crafts Movement in Edwardian England* (London and New York: Routledge, 1988), pp. 56–7.

87 S. Perks, *Residential Flats of All Classes Including Artisan's Dwellings: A Practical Treatise on the Planning and Arrangement* (London: B. T. Batsford, 1905), p. 55.

88 McKenna, *The Secret Life of Oscar Wilde*, p. 154.

89 *Westminster Gazette*, 27 May 1895.

90 In H. M. Hyde *The Trials of Oscar Wilde* (London: William Hodge and Company, 1948), p. 134.

91 *Ibid.*, p. 239.

92 *Eye and Ear Memory: The Memory and Thought Series* (Harrisburg and New York: James P. Downs Publisher, 1891), p. 208.

93 *Ibid.*, p. 240; M. Cook also comments on similar aspects of the case: see *London and the Culture of Homosexuality, 1885–1914* (Cambridge: Cambridge University Press, 2003), pp. 56–8.

94 *Ibid.*, p. 248.

95 *Evening News*, 6 April 1895.

96 Here both men appear to be referring to Huysmans's *A rebours* and Wilde's *The Picture of Dorian Gray*, in which each author devotes a chapter to perfume's aesthetic and effects. See Delaney (ed.), *Some Letters from Charles Ricketts and Charles Shannon to 'Michael Field'*, p. 14.

97 J. O. Jordan, 'Domestic Servants and the Victorian Home', in Murray Baumgarten and H. M. Daleski (eds.), *Homes and Homelessness in the Victorian Imagination* (New York: AMS Press 1998), p. 80.

98 A. Adams, *Architecture in the Family Way: Doctors, Houses, and Women, 1870–1900* (Montreal: McGill-Queen's University Press, 1996), p. 164.

99 See R. Edis, *Decoration and Furniture of Town Houses* (London: Kegan Paul, 1881).

100 'Art in the Home', p. 253.

101 *Ibid.*, p. 254.

102 Raymond and Ricketts, *Oscar Wilde: Recollections*, p. 40.

103 Rothenstein, *Men and Memories*, p. 174.

104 'Art in the Home', p. 253.

105 E. Hanson, 'Undead', in Diana Fuss (ed.), *Inside/Out, Lesbian Theories, Gay Theories* (New York: Routledge, 1991), p. 325.

106 Rosner, *Modernism and the Architecture of Private Life*, p. 62.

107 M. Douglas, *Purity and Danger: An Analysis of the Concepts of Pollution and Taboo* (London: Routledge, 1966), p. 97.

108 T. Schaffer, '"A Wilde Desire Took Hold of Me": The Homoerotic History of *Dracula*', in Nina Auerbach and David J. Skal (eds.), *Dracula* (New York and London: W. W. Norton, Inc., 1997), p. 472.

109 B. Stoker, *Dracula*, N. Auerbach and D. J. Skal (eds.), (New York and London: W. W. Norton, Inc., 1997), p. 32.

110 C. Reed, 'Immanent Domain: Queer Space in the Built Environment', *Art Journal*, vol. 55, no. 4 (winter 1996), p. 64

111 In Raymond and Ricketts, *Oscar Wilde: Recollections*, n.p.

112 *Ibid.*, p. 9.

113 Hyde, *The Trials of Oscar Wilde*, p. 69.

114 Raymond and Ricketts, *Oscar Wilde: Recollections*, p. 10.

115 *Ibid.*, p. 11.

116 *Ibid.*, p. 44.

117 G. L. Hammill, *Sexuality and Form: Caravaggio, Marlowe and Bacon* (Chicago and London: University of Chicago Press, 2000), p. 2.

118 Raymond and Ricketts, *Oscar Wilde: Recollections*, p. 38.

II ✧ Country living

4 ✧ Askesis and the Greek ideal: Edward Perry Warren and Lewes House

COMMISSIONED FROM Greek craftsmen in 1-20 CE by a Roman client, the infamous so-called Warren Cup is a rare silver Roman *skyphos* (drinking cup) depicting explicit sex acts. Purchased by the British Museum for £1.8 million in 1999, the cup acquired its name from its first modern owner, Bostonian collector, antiquarian and Uranian writer Edward Perry Warren (commonly and affectionately nicknamed Ned) (1860–1928) who likely acquired the crowning glory of his collection around 1911. Included amongst the cup's five sections are depictions of two different scenes in low relief that expose two male couples engaged in various sexual acts. On one side, the viewer can see a slightly older, bearded man, whom we might identify within the sexual economy of same-sex activity as the active participant – or *erastēs* – penetrating his clearly younger, clean-shaven companion (the passive participant, or *erōmenos*) who lowers himself on to his partner with the help of a leather strap attached to the ceiling. Meanwhile, in the same scene a boy opens the door, an act that helps to domesticate the activity, and enforces the scopophilic dimension the cup itself possesses. On the other side, the second scene displays a greater age difference with the younger of the two men, once again, being penetrated by the older *erastēs*. In this instance, the activity occurs on a clearly articulated bed. Two things are notable in these scenes, at least for our purposes here. First, there is a clear attention to and delineation of age and status. Second, and ignored by scholars to date, in both scenes space is heavily accessorized and mapped out through domestic design: doors and frames, heavy drapery suspended from fictive walls, furniture, cushions and beds draped in linens. Although the cup itself is not the focus of the present study, the contents of the aforementioned scenes serve nonetheless as a visual analogy to the fundamental concerns I wish to tackle here, that of the spatial and more explicitly the domestic nature of the ideal of Greek love espoused by Warren and his community of young men at

Lewes House, East Sussex, which he acquired in 1913 (for £3,750), after having leased it since 1899.[1] Much has been made of how middle- and upper-class gentlemen have attempted to recreate and deploy classical Greek notions of pederastic love and same-sex desire as a model for sexual and civic virtue.[2] To date very little scholarship exists on queer experiences of the domestic and even less on the spatialized dimension of askesis and the domesticated aesthetic programme of ideal Greek love.

Askesis refers to an ascetic lifestyle maintained at a distance from worldly and material pleasures in favour of actions leading toward a moral or spiritual code of conduct. Inspired by classical Greece, and unlike a Christian understanding of the term which advocates a complete denial and discipline of the self, the conditioning involved in this rigorous practice of the self, according to Michel Foucault, takes on many forms from 'training, meditation, tests of thinking [and] examination of conscience' to the 'control of representations'.[3] Lewes House was characterized by a Spartan simplicity of interior design and furnishings and a strictly homosocial membership (save for a few maids), ideally suited to Warren's Uranian-inspired programme of askesis. In the 1880s and 1890s men began to carve out lives based on all-male society or just postponed marriage altogether, and 'the characteristically Victorian culture of domesticity can be said to have entered a new phase'.[4] In the wake of the Wilde trials of 1895, Lewes House provided an alternative queer domesticity to that represented by the case and subsequent press coverage. I do not read Lewes House and Warren's domesticity as a closet, that is, a sanctuary for safety and retreat from the homophobia of the period. Rather, I see Warren as having fashioned a queer space by keeping within the codes of askesis and as a result controlling the representation of Lewes House in terms of both the actual and perceived spatio-sexual life of the estate. Warren also engendered a queer time in his Uranian text, a treatise out of step with contemporary early twentieth-century sexual politics. By exploring the 'cognitive maps'[5] the spaces of Lewes House enabled as well as the apologetic writings found in *A Defence of Uranian Love*, this chapter opens up to a discussion of how Uranian bachelors might have used the domestic realm as the site for the performance of a modern identity made possible through the practices of askesis. A slightly open-ended definition of queer proves useful when exploring the Uranian appropriation of the notional domestic sphere inherited from the Victorians and brought into the twentieth century; an ideal further inflected by Wilde's and Taylor's convictions. As David Halperin suggests, queer marks itself as a 'horizon of possibility whose precise extent and heterogeneous scope cannot in principle be delimited in advance'.[6] In this way queer spaces are necessarily always *in* formation.

The biography of a home

Warren was one of six children born to a wealthy Bostonian paper manufacturer. Life growing up for Warren was less than ideal, the subject of much bullying; he was nicknamed Tassels, a biting pun on his interest in the decorative and the collecting he began at an early age. Warren himself recalled how his 'statuettes and photos must have made [him] seem different from the other boys, as also [his] efforts to convert them'; his zeal for conversion was a symptom of his early ambition to become a missionary, predicated on his secret desire to tame the naked 'Indians'.[7] As is often the case for many men, collecting began in earnest as a young child, inspired by his mother. Warren recounts the 'private life' his china collection took, and the clandestine and titillating thrills it offered. He recalled:

> I took favourite pieces to my room and put them by my bed at night. If I breakfasted in bed I used to direct that the whole breakfast set should be brought up and further specify the cups to be used. In the afternoon I would hunt in the antique shops to buy. Mamma used to buy them for me sometimes. I remember her giving what she thought a foolish price for a cracked Lowestoft cup because I wanted it. I had my little shelves of china in my bedroom (on the same floor as Mamma's room), and used to stay up late arranging them to the best advantage, getting a little nervous and excited over the work because I knew I ought to be in bed.[8]

Later in life Warren was well aware of the negative stereotypes attributed to the collector, the worldly connoisseur who flitted about the world in search of his next prized conquest. 'A collector', he noted, 'is thought to be a dreamer of days gone by, a loafer in idle lands, who culls a vase from a shelf or chooses many objects in a shop. By many he is supposed to live a life of disinterested and luxurious nonchalance, gloating over beautiful things, free of his time, lavish in his expenditure, a leisurely grandee.' However, he made clear to assert that '[t]his impression is a mistake'.[9] For him, the collector facilitated intellectual pursuit and knowledge itself, distinct from and yet not unlike the university researcher for whom he had profound respect and admiration.

At Harvard (B.A. 1883) and then at New College, Oxford (M.A. 1888), Warren's college days were marked by a balance of passing and blending on the one hand and standing out, on the other, through various marks of distinction such as his interest in both music and beautiful things. His dress was, for the most part, save for his fashionable boots and unique ties, in keeping with the mainstay of contemporary men's sartorial codes befitting an elite Ivy League student, later transplanted to English soil. His initial, though reluctant biographers, friends and associates Osbert Burdett and E. H. Goddard, described their subject's physique while at Oxford as 'shortish, stocky, with a pair of heavy shoulders and a torso that seemed too bulky for the waist'. Most revealing is how the pair at once feminize and queer Warren when they note that his 'toddling gait added an incongruously feminine touch to his bodily movement' while 'the square and heavy fingers' would pick up, touch and handle the myriad precious *objets d'art* of his fine collection 'with a queer gentleness' comparable to an elephant in an antiquarian shop.[10] Despite his feminized appearance and queer touch, at Oxford Warren made every effort to blend in with his fellow classmates, avoiding calling attention to his wealth and sexual inclinations. Students often mistook him as socially and economically their equal. Warren's wealth would not become visible until he professionally took up one of his primary life obsessions, that of collecting.

It was while at Oxford that Warren met the man who not only would become his 'alter ego', but would help him amass one of the USA's most impressive and celebrated private collections of antiquities. At Oxford he developed his passion for all things Greek, and began his friendship with John Marshall, who was to become his secretary, lover and longtime companion.[11] Companionship and collecting antiquities were conjoined as Marshall persuaded Warren to foray into this field. It was with his help and guidance that Warren built up an enviable collection of rare antiquities, decorative objects and art for both Lewes House and the Museum of Fine Arts, Boston. The American expatriate always viewed the USA as Boston, and for him Boston stood as unquestionably provincial. His acquisitions for and substantial donation of Greek antiquities to the museum was an oblique and subversive way for the expatriate to challenge what he perceived to be the conservative and moribund uppercrust Bostonian ethos that dominated that city's cultural life. Warren created a queer space distinctly away from and in contradistinction to his native environment, with differing domestic protocols, landscapes and choreographies.

It was soon after his arrival at Lewes House that Marshall replaced his own obsession with Greek texts with one for art and antiquities. While collecting remained the couple's joint passion and trade, their decisions were not always unanimous and gradually it became a source of frustration, especially for Marshall. While at Oxford Warren wrote in a letter dated September 1890 of the two guiding principles underlining his and Marshall's collecting practices that would help to fill their 'shared' home: '1) furnish with things of lasting value; 2) take advantage of extraordinary chances … This is the standard I shall want applied.'[12] The objects, chosen to furnish the home and provide for their ascetic lifestyle, were mostly collected by the end of 1890. The following year they began concerted and focused trips to the continent to locate and purchase

4.1 Edward (Ned) Perry Warren (*left*) and John Marshall with their dogs, c. 1890s.

antiquities, and, in 1894, Marshall took a lease on an apartment in Rome to remain at the heart of the antiques trade.

The death of Warren's father in August 1888 meant a handsome inheritance of £10,000 per annum for the young man. As a result of the bequest, he set out to locate a residence to benefit his growing collection and station, and in October 1899 wrote to Marshall claiming to have found such a place. Despite incessant queries on behalf of Warren, in his letters Marshall carefully steered away from any discussions or references to the future house they would eventually occupy together. Warren guaranteed Marshall's salary of £200 a year, excluding expenses. In Marshall, however, Warren not only found a secretary, but importantly a companion with whom to conquer the antiques market; someone who was to become his intimate 'other'. Warren described Marshall as '[s]ometimes inappreciative of others who did not strike his own fancy, a better judge of art than of people, but unpretentious and very touching in his affections'.[13] When he finally accepted to become his secretary Marshall revealingly wrote to Warren: 'You were to me at first a quality, then a collection of qualities … now everything you say and do seems inseparable from you and my love for you'.[14] Whether purposeful or not, Marshall's use of 'collection' is remarkable and reveals how collecting and subjectivity quickly became mutually sustaining aspects of their joint venture and reciprocal feelings. Not unlike Warren, Marshall was short, broad-shouldered, but 'more nervous and lively in movement'. He was more delicate than his partner, with hands slender, fingers long and slight. His constant need for activity, amusement and challenges made for an ideal companion for Warren, whose lofty ambitions required someone at once 'witty, amusing, changeable, jolly and talkative'.[15] Their relationship began neither quickly nor easily; Warren spent much time and energy attempting to woo Marshall who finally succumbed. Apart from the numerous acquisition trips either took, the two were inseparable to the point that they began to look so much alike that people usually mistook them. In a photograph of the two with one of six of their St Bernards, their features and sartorial choices reinforce their similarities and clear bond [Figure 4.2]. Again, in a less than complimentary fashion, Burdett and Goddard compared the pair, 'so alike in girth', to 'twin Punchinellos, and when they were pacing arm-in-arm the lawn at Lewes House they presented a pair of indistinguishable backs, so that one could hardly tell one from the other. Warren's shuffling toddle of a walk, and Marshall's slightly more staccato shamble, completed this likeness as of Tweedledum to Tweedledee'.[16] Despite their slight condescension, the biographers do, nonetheless, underscore the intimacy and reciprocity involved in their relationship to the point of corporeal similitude. Their mutual affection and admiration was also made clear in their choice of mutual nickname, 'Puppy'; the couple were often photographed with their domestic pets in the grounds of Lewes House [see for example Figure 4.1].

While collecting remained the companions' joint passion and trade it also gradually became a source of frustration, particularly for Marshall. Living alone in Rome, Marshall felt isolated and too dependent on Warren's erratic choices and directions, stating in a letter dated 20 March 1893: 'I feel so weak here; I am rather down – I can do nothing. I go round and round seeing worthless things … I am sick of being alone and Puppy dear, it is bad for me. I would do anything but live alone. Do, therefore, if you can, hurry up the business here. I am a bit unhappy'.[17] Collecting was clearly not the only source of Marshall's mounting frustration and fears, but so too did domestic isolation and detachment creep into their union. However, Warren, as was often the case, was indifferent and ungrateful to Marshall's needs and feelings in his responses, which would, in part, prove to be detrimental to the relationship. Warren's single-mindedness forced Marshall to continue the high-paced collecting they had established, not realizing or choosing to ignore Marshall's loneliness. Departing Rome Marshall met up with Warren in Greece where, in the fashion of the 1890s, they purchased a number of Greek tanagras.

Askesis and the Greek ideal

4.2 Edward (Ned) Perry Warren, John Marshall and St. Bernard, c. 1890s.

Given their popularity at the time, these small Greek figurines were being heavily copied: the copies were passed off as originals, making victims out of the most adept collectors; even connoisseurs like Charles Ricketts fell victim to the forgeries trade early on in his career.

In 25 April 1890 Warren received the assignment of the lease for Lewes House, a foreboding and large building, which an extant plan of the estate reveals occupied the grounds as far back as 1624.[18] The house itself was of blue brick with a porch of cream stucco. Its façade was unremarkable, its only seeming purpose to clearly demarcate a barrier for the activity and ideal culture engendered inside, distinct from the mundane irrelevance of the outside world. Warren described the building as 'huge, old, and not cheap. It has only three or four sunny rooms ... It is the centre of Lewes and yet has a quiet garden, a paddock, greenhouse, and stables *ad lib*. Downs accessible and green woody country as well. I am much inclined to it.'[19] Of the number of men comprising the so-called Lewes House brotherhood, Harold Parsons, who took up collecting antiquities later in life, characterized Lewes House in the following way:

> the back of the house is a perfect Queen Anne structure with large rooms, flagstone entrance hall, a noble staircase, the windows giving onto an

> immensely long garden with tapis-vert walled lawn like a billiard table and walls down the sides with shallow garden beds; the walls vine-covered and with best figs I have ever eaten ... The great South Downs rolled away to Brighton, and when we rode our horses up there, on a fine day you could see the Channel glistening in the distance like a great silver shield.[20]

The gardens and the grounds of the estate covered two and half acres. However, it was neither the building nor the grounds themselves which fascinated or proved particularly compelling. Warren furnished the house with fifteenth- to eighteenth-century furniture, Old English continental and Oriental china and porcelain, over 900 ounces of silver, embroideries and brocades, Grecian columns and ivories. He also owned fourteen different dinner services from Worcester, Minton, Capo di Monte and Wedgwood amongst others. In the dinning-room would eventually appear a picture by Lucas Cranach, *Adam and Eve* (1526). The apple in the picture was precisely, according to Warren, what made it appropriate to the room.

According to Burdett and Goddard:

> It was to be a house of bachelors and scholars, and the 'good life' was to include much fun and good fellowship, with horses to keep the men fit and good wine and food to complete their well-being. Warren differed from many scholars in not being, primarily, a man of books ... scholarship to him was not an end but a means. The end was the good life as described by Aristotle and Plato, and scholarship was chiefly valuable in preserving the theory, for in the absence of the theory the 'good life' itself would break down.[21]

In the coach house Warren kept his most prized example of modern art, a version of August Rodin's famed sculpture *Le Baiser* (1899) that he specially commissioned the artist to create for him.[22] It was here, in the coach house, where he built his private study affectionately christened 'Thebes', suggestive of its reclusive nature, devoid of the communal hubbub of the house itself. The choice of name for this special and removed space suggestively harkens back to the Ancient Greek Sacred Band of Thebes from the fourth century BCE. This specially picked band of Thebian elite soldiers comprised 150 same-sex couples (each consisting of one older and one younger man) who were housed and trained by the city-state. The warriors garnered their name from Plato's *Symposium* in which Phaedrus famously extolled the virtues of same-sex love in the defence of their beloved, communal polis.

> And if there were only some way of contriving that a state or an army should be made up of lovers and their beloved, they would be the very best

governors of their own city, abstaining from all dishonour, and emulating one another in honour; and when fighting at each other's side, although a mere handful, they would overcome the world. For what lover would not choose rather to be seen by all mankind than by his beloved, either when abandoning his post or throwing away his arms? He would be ready to die a thousand deaths rather than endure this. Or who would desert his beloved or fail him in the hour of danger?[23]

Here in Thebes, same-sex love, honour and a defence of the communal good were at the heart of the domesticity Warren instilled in the imbricated landscapes of home and work. The key to Thebes was worn around Warren's neck on a gold chain. The study was half panelled in oak, above which the wall was painted jade-green and decorated with a single Elizabethan group portrait of mother and child and two carved corbels, while the floor was covered in red linoleum. Two 'emergency' bedrooms were also included in Thebes, whose regular occupants were books, documents, papers and other scholarly materials. Connecting the various rooms were oak cupboards, themselves the dwellings of additional books, ancient Greek vases, jewellery and a tin box referred to as 'the Will box'. Warren's working room bore his emblematic Spartan ideal. A centre-table at which Warren wrote also hosted a Greek marble group. The only colour, sobering though it was, was to be found in the Elizabethan group portrait. As an environment dedicated to work, Thebes was the hallowed inner sanctum of Lewes House, removed and yet a crucial part of the space and culture of the community that gathered and thrived there. Although electric bulbs lit the staircase and other passageways, Warren reportedly responded '[f]or fear it might be used', when asked why electric lighting was not used also in the sitting rooms.[24] Lit by candles, Thebes was not only marked as a space of intellectual work, but also importantly served as a venue for interesting and lively conversation.

Warren's preferred daily ritual at Lewes House began with him rising at five o'clock to read Greek until the first meal of the day. Breakfast was usually taken at eight o'clock, though he often was alone as many of the household's ever-revolving members were never on time. He then went back to bed until eleven after which he dealt with correspondence and matters brought forward by his secretaries. Riding would follow lunch, after which tea was taken. The household would assemble in the so-called Red Room following dinner until the evening ended around ten or so. Worth quoting at length, friend, artist and writer Sir William Rothenstein recounted how the house was

> a monkish establishment, where women were not welcomed. But Warren, who believed that scholars should live nobly, kept ample table and a well-stocked wine-cellar; in the stables were mettlesome horses, for the Downs

> were close at hand, and he rode daily with his friends, for the body must be as well exercised as the mind. Meals were served at a great oaken table dark and polished, on which stood splendid old silver. The rooms were full of handsome antique furniture, and of Greek bronzes and marbles in place of usual ornaments ... There was much mystery about the provenance of the treasures at Lewes house. This secrecy seemed to permeate the rooms and corridors, to exhaust the air of the house. The social relations, too, were often strained, and [John] Fothergill [later to become Warren's secretary after Marshall's departure] longed for a franker, for a less cloistered life.[25]

As the centre of a community based on intellectually and sexually likeminded men rather than premised on the hierarchy implicated in a familial structure and hegemonic, compulsory heterosexuality, Lewes House saw pass through it important queer and artistic figures like George Santayana, Oscar Browning, Robbie Ross, Auguste Rodin, Sir William Rothenstein and Roger Fry; the first three of these were proponents of the pederastic ideal. When Warren occupied Lewes House, it was referred to as the one owned by the 'mad millionaire'. It was rare that the inhabitants were ever seen in public, save on horseback, in canoes or at the public baths. The house 'resemble[d] a tiny German court'.[26] 'The effect', according to Burdett and Goddard, 'was to make the household seem a society apart, an isolated community. The outside world shrank to a memory'.[27] Clothes, accessories and even personal articles such as towels and bath sponges were communal, without any bourgeois sense of property or propriety. The bathroom was also a highly communal space, and, despite the fact it could only fit two bodies easily, it was not uncommon after riding sessions or sporting activities to find the room overcrowded with several men. On the departure of any man from the house, he was usually bid farewell with the following: 'We shall miss you from the bathroom'.[28] The house was busy with varied activities and various people, which for Warren was the true ideal of domestic perfection.

The atmosphere at Lewes House coupled with Warren's generosity towards the townspeople was such that their activities, however odd or out of sorts, were noted by the locals, but not decried or questioned, maintaining a unique though tense equilibrium between the two seemingly distinct groups. Servants in Warren's employ were exceptionally respectful and tight-lipped about the communal life lived out at the house. When she entered Warren's employ, Mrs Kathleen Arnold Warner, a former kitchen maid, was told by her aunt, Martha Sheperd, then head cook, that 'anything heard within the walls of Lewes House must remain within the walls of Lewes House'.[29] Warren's staff remained faithful until the end and were amongst the very few who attended his funeral, with the majority of his friends having moved on or forsaken the eccentric millionaire. As for Warren's sexual identity, Mrs Warner recalled how she never once heard any disparaging comments or 'anything derogatory about his lifestyle'.[30]

In 1900 Warren wrote *The Prince Who Did Not Exist*, a quirky fairy tale published privately and interestingly dedicated to Warren's cousin, Mary Bliss[31] who was to marry his beloved Marshall. With years of loneliness, coupled with growing interests in pursuing numerous other side projects, Marshall believed Mary to be an ideal and fit companion. For her part, Bliss believed that her marriage to Marshall would bring him and Warren closer together; she even courted both men at one point. By her own admission, Bliss might be seen as a normalizing force similar to Eve Kosofsky Sedgwick's notion of the triangulation of desire between two men and a woman, a trope commonly seen in nineteenth-century literature. In her queer formulation the woman is used as a surrogate and displacement for the desire, love and even intimacy between the two men. Sedgwick has provocatively exposed how 'in erotic rivalry, the bond that links the two rivals is as intense and potent as the bond that links either of the rivals to the beloved: that the bonds of "rivalry" and "love", differently as they are experienced, are equally powerful and in many senses equivalent'.[32] It was not a rivalry inspired by the two men per se, but rather the actions initiated by Bliss that prove to be a provocative variation on what Sedgwick has witnessed and theorized. Bliss proved to be an ideal consort for Marshall's collecting enterprises, especially when he took up a position for the Metropolitan Museum of Art (New York), charged with acquiring European *objets d'art*. Following Marshall's marriage to Bliss, Warren turned his attention away from collecting and dived headlong into his writing and Uranian philosophy, which culminated in the controversial if long ignored three-volume treatise *A Defence of Uranian Love*.

Home is where Uranian heart is

Printed privately in 1928 and written under the pseudonym of Arthur Lyon Raile, *A Defence of Uranian Love* was published by Warren as a three-volume tract. The first volume was released soon before his death in 1928, with the last published posthumously in 1930. Partially biographical, hopeful and difficult, the treatise must be read through Warren's own cultural and domestic ethics. Overt and blatant in its defence of a queer lifestyle, the tract was even vilified by his close friends and associates, many fearing what repercussions might befall them by association. For the most part, however, his friends simply dismissed it and avoided discussing it altogether when at Lewes House. However, the house was precisely where Warren endeavoured to enact the theories and dreams he wrote about in *A Defence*. Burdett and Goddard dismiss *A Defence* as the 'lonely monument of a lonely man'.[33] While this may hold some degree of truth, it is nevertheless a rather limited view of what was a culminating point in his life that revolved almost exclusively around the Hellenic ideal. His biographers' and peers' dismissal of the treatise has had the long-term effect of closeting the document, and in its wake denying any relevance it might possess.

While Lewes House was always busy and full, Warren was ultimately alone in his fulfilment of the Greek-inspired Uranian ideal and lifestyle. Committed to his cause, Warren was not dissuaded and singularly attempted to recreate Ancient Greek ethics through a preferred Uranian domesticity which advocated first and foremost askesis, through his writing (always performed within the confines of in the inner sanctum of Thebes) and finally through his ongoing and fervent association with his idealistic vision of Oxford. As a larger social yet private space, the university for Warren remained the only place in the modern world where the Greek master and pupil coupling and the domesticated ideals of an all-male society was manifest, despite women's gradual admittance into its hallowed halls.

Originally coined by German sexologist Karl Heinrich Ulrichs (1825–1895) as *Urning* in 1862, the Uranian was a direct allusion to Plato's discussion of *Eros* in his *Symposium*. In Ulrichs's modern appropriation of the term, the figure referred to a woman's soul trapped in a man's body. The ancient myth tells of Cronus avenging his father Uranus by severing and throwing his genitals into the sea from whence Aphrodite (Venus), the goddess of love, was born. While Ulrichs's elucidation of the term certainly had a significant impact in continental Europe, perhaps the only element that his theories shared with his British cohorts was the idea of a sexual otherness which resided outside the conventional, normative blueprints of family and procreative matrimony. In Britain, apologists, or what we might today label queer activists, like John Addington Symonds and Edward Carpenter took up the term towards emancipatory ends. Carpenter, for example, saw the Uranian figure as 'fine, healthy specimens of [its] sex, muscular and well-developed in body, of powerful brain, high standard of conduct, and with nothing abnormal or morbid of any kind'.[34] Symonds maintained that in both medieval Europe and Ancient Greece, 'both paiderastia and chivalry ignored the family, while the latter even set the matrimonial tie at nought'.[35] He also, significantly, noted how '[m]orality for the Greeks … was aesthetic'.[36]

In Part I of *A Defence*, entitled *Uranian Love*, Warren theorized the development of and blueprint for a Uranian code of ethics, identity and lifestyle. The autobiographical permeates this first volume and the author recalls how he was 'brought up mostly at home';[37] home, specifically Lewes House, and not the public domain, would form the locus for the expression of masculine identity. While caution must be exercised here, avoiding essentialization of gender and sexual identities, this opening remark nonetheless, I suggest, prompts his reader to think about the significance of the domestic realm in the formation and formulation of Uranian identity. Further on, in a chapter simply yet aptly titled 'Gentleness', a clear allusion is made to the gendered nature of an ideal domesticity he desired for Lewes House:

> Rough and careless he may be in the things about which women are particular; reckless of flummery and fuss; hater of ceremonies and needless courtesies [the Uranian's] home-life has a different colour from that of most homes which women control, but it is, none the less, a home-life and even, in one respect more intimate.[38]

He also suggests that men who remove themselves from mainstream culture as well as their own society become adept in the arts traditionally ascribed to women.[39] Noteworthy is how Warren sets up a significant opposition to the heteronormative Victorian domesticity emblematized in such theories as those advanced by art and cultural critic John Ruskin who advocated a clear-cut gendered understanding of the ideal divide between public and private, the latter dominated by the feminine and women. It is important to recognize that this gendered separation of spheres was maintained and naturalized well into the twentieth century. Ruskin's articulation of a preferred spatial and cultural understanding of bourgeois domesticity served as a microcosm of a healthy English nation in which it was, according to Ruskin's powerful and paradigmatic *Sesame and Lilies* (1865), a *woman's* role to 'secure its order, comfort, and loveliness'.[40] Indeed in his essay, 'Of Queens' Gardens', Ruskin made clear the distinctions and performances necessary to gain cultural capital within the economy of Victorian sexual politics. As 'the place of Peace', the home provided a clearly articulated spatio-sexual blueprint for the performance of gender and identity. According to Ruskin:

> man's power is active, progressive, defensive. He is eminently the doer, the creator, the discoverer, the defender. His intellect is for speculation and invention; his energy for adventure, for war, and for conquest, wherever conquest necessary … The man, in his rough work in open world, must encounter all peril and trial; – to him, therefore, must be the failure, the offence, the inevitable error; often he must be wounded or subdued; often misled; and always hardened.[41]

In 1883 Congregational minister James Baldwin Brown weighed in on the notion of the ideal home in his final book, *The Home: In Its Relation to Man and to Society*. Residing at the core of a true home were 'self-control, self-denial, self-sacrifice', ideals clearly subsumed within a Christian understanding of askesis.[42] Love, according to the minister, was not simply the heart of the home but comprised its very foundation. As a foundational element of the domestic blueprint, love was linked to salvation itself. Brown preached that

> [i]t was the redemption of the home when Christ's redeeming love to the world was made the pattern of its love. It had fallen in utter contempt and shame – how utter let Roman satirists and historians tell; Christ redeemed it by associating it with His life, and it began to be re-sanctified from that hour.[43]

Within the sacred enclosure of the domestic realm, love can be made intelligible only when gender and sexual identity remain steadfast in the service of a Christian cross-sex union, rather than within the confines of a same-sex homosocial community. Importantly it is also worth noting how by the 1870s in Britain domesticity was deemed 'unglamorous, unfulfilling and ultimately – unmasculine'.[44] This view of masculine domesticity continued well into the interwar period and it is for this reason that men like Warren stood foursquare as a threat to the sanctity of the domestic sphere and the sexual division of space itself.

Warren also attacked the normalizing ethos of the domestic realm when he argued for an aesthetic stripped of the artificial: 'He [the Uranian] reaches home in that which is furthest removed from the modern woman's ideal of home ... He would really live only where she would think it impossible to live, – in the bare simplicities. This is *his* contempt of the world.'[45] Warren relegated the perceived superficiality of the Rococo to the waste bin, a style he advocated to be symptomatic of decadence and feminine frivolity.[46] The material expression of this ideal in Lewes House ensured that nothing about its design and interiors made it particularly homely or welcoming, 'nothing in it that a woman, or for that matter men, could call comfortable'.[47] Despite the impressive collection of antiquities and works of art, the spaces of Lewes House were Spartan, cold and bleak, with hard, uncomfortable armchairs, few carpets and drapes, beds fit more for monks than a millionaire and his friends and lovers. In two separate pictures of the study of Lewes House, the room is restrained in its decoration. Objects are limited to Greek vases and bowls on the mantel and desk, statuettes of classical Greek male nudes. In one picture a print of a portrait of young Greek man hangs on the wall [see Figures 4.3 and 4.4]. Ideally suited to the intellectual pursuits the study portends, these objects reinforce the ascetic training and inspiration implied in the domesticated all-male askesis Warren attempted to fashion. Passions ran deep for both the men as well as the objects he collected, both filling the rooms of Lewes House; one might

Askesis and the Greek ideal 145

4.3 One of Lewes House's studios.

suggest, rightfully so, that the men were the real decorative and atmospheric gems of the space. Warren was well known for taking care of any young man with whom he might come in contact, regardless of his past affiliations or future promise.

Spiked with a discernable misogyny, Warren's queer reconceptualization of the domestic ideal left little room outside the bonds of male friendship and the particular relationship between master and his pupil; for him 'love should be ranked below friendship as the female below the male'.[48] In his investigation of the various historical and gendered expressions of homosexuality, Halperin has underscored how the codes and performances of 'pederasty and friendship are both traditionally masculinising, insofar as they express the male subject's virility and imply a thoroughgoing rejection of everything that is feminine'.[49] In a series of poems penned between 1881 and 1882, and another entitled "If Some of You Were Living" from 1887, Warren expresses his sense of queer time through a deep discontent with the contemporary view of traditional forms of male friendship 'so little understood in the modern world'.[50] For Warren this comes down to a question of pedagogy as '[t]here is no education like that which a lover can give'.[51] This communion was the means through which man could live better, a more perfected state of being-in-the-world. Further, Halperin contends that sexual love

4.4 One of Lewes House's studios.

(*eros*) is a question of positionality inasmuch as it suggests a subject's dynamic within the economy of penetration. 'Friendship, by contrast', he asserts, 'is all about sameness: sameness of rank and status,サメness of sentiment, sameness of identity. It is this very emphasis on identity, similarity, and mutuality that distances the friendship tradition, in its original social and discursive context, from the world of sexual love.'[52] At the root of the expressions and traditions of homosocial friendship, Warren thought, education had devolved into a random series of largely inconsequential facts, devoid entirely of experiential knowledge. The key to a new pedagogical model, he proposed, was a return to the dynamic and essential relationship between masterful teacher and youthful pupil elaborated by the Ancient Greeks.⁵³ What exactly comprised this ideal way of life, this queer pedagogical exchange? What constituted the identities of the actors involved? Self-control was the guiding principle underpinning this youthful education, an education that necessarily entailed a space set apart from mainstream society. Warren's pedagogical ideal was also meant to offer a alternative experience of the cycles of life: the one-time young, unmarried Uranian student would grow up and rightfully assume the role of Uranian master-teacher further ensuring a queer lineage, posterity and continuity. Master and pupil enter into a period of 'training' – or askesis – in which all that is unnecessary and frivolous is stripped bare; the body renewed and perfected. This is not to be confused with 'Christian "ascetic" mortification. There is no function of the human being which is to be atrophied.' Youthful beauty requires the guidance of the elder who must 'give without return' in his guidance. While love is the ultimate goal, this love is achieved through the prism of Philosophical Eros embodied in a 'masculine ideal' difficult to locate but found in 'conduct, art and thought'.⁵⁴ The Christian formulation of askesis implies a decided removal from the world of materiality (of things) and a denial of the flesh (of corporeality) in its potential toward the higher ideal. At its root, I posit, askesis is a form of practical training that can happen only within a specific and equally ideal type of environment.

Warren claimed that 'Our boy-lover, when a boy, learnt to love the masculine; the man was to be privileged as an ideal in himself; he possessed the highest beauty'.⁵⁵ Uranian aesthetics, ethics and the expressions of love bestowed on the idealized figure of youthful masculinity offered a rapprochement between the higher Platonic and Homeric ideals. Amongst those apologists who advocated such a return was John Addington Symonds, who argued that, within the chivalric code, Greek love was marked by 'a passionate and enthusiastic attachment subsisting between man and youth, recognized by society and protected by opinion, which [while it] was not free from sensuality, did not degenerate into mere licentiousness'.⁵⁶ While the relationship straddled the fine line marking sensuality from sexuality, within the sexual and cultural economy of Ancient Greece, the older male lover, or active partner (*erastēs*), desired the sensual companionship of the passive partner (*erōmenos*) who derived his identity from the past participle of the verb *eramai* (love; desire; the object of this love and/or desire). The Greek antecedent clearly informed perhaps one of the most important and widely cited homosexual apologias of the late nineteenth century written by Charles Kains Jackson (1857–1933). In 'The New Chivalry' (1894), Jackson asserted that 'intimacy of constant companionship, of physical and personal knowledge is also a power of help and aid which cannot be put into words ... tenderness'. Jackson was a member of the queer brotherhood and secret society of the Order of Chaeronea founded by George Ives in 1897.[57] The choice of name is a significant historical and geographical allusion to the location of the final battle of the Sacred Band of Thebes of 338 BCE, when they were eradicated entirely. In his apologia Jackson alludes to the love 'of the elder for younger, of one who has endured for him that has yet to endure, of the strong for the weak, the developed for the developing, is retained in all fullness, while these other things are added, is perhaps not that which gives its highest value to the New Chivalry'.[58] Within the continuum expressed by Jackson the younger object of love and affection, the ephebe, occupied a liminal position, on the threshold of adult manhood, not yet ready to assume his civic role and duties and marked by his domesticated relationship with his older mentor, purposefully removed from mainstream society. It is noteworthy that Jackson published his infamous Uranian apologia in *The Artist and the Journal of Home Culture* for which he was the editor (1888–94). Through the lenses of Social Darwinism and Platonism, the essay propounded the merits of same-sex moral, social and erotic bonds, relationships that could redirect and better the conditions of society. Through his stewardship, home, art and activism played themselves out side-by-side on the pages of the journal. Here, I wish again to simply underscore the political dimension of aesthetics and design in the lives of men like Jackson and those whose lives and homes fill the pages of this book.

In Athens, the *ephebia* were those young men at the 'threshold of adult life' generally between the ages of eighteen and twenty, who spent two years devoted to military education and physical perfection.[59] The term was derived from the combination of *epi* meaning near to or on the periphery and *hēbē*, the term which designated the early stage or threshold of manhood. The pederastic union espoused by Jackson and Warren suggested the vital relationship between master and pupil in the development of civic virtue and a future social position, an education to take place within the company of an all-male society, much like the one Warren attempted to enact at Lewes House. In this vein, Warren saw the role of the master as a pedagogue, whose only danger was that 'of becoming a mystagogue'.[60] Yet a mystagogue was more aptly suited to Warren's desires for the Lewes House brotherhood, for at once the term designates the pursuit of the mystical (in this instance the Hellenic ideal of Greek love) and the codes and styles of a fraternity, a close and closed community of like-minded men, spatially set apart, domestically distinct. Together these men occupied a liminal state. In his extensive research on ritual and cultural performance Victor Turner demonstrates how those on the indeterminate space of the threshold are singled out through their placelessness, their position outside the laws of the dominant and the normative.⁶¹ In its liminality, thresholds and those who inhabit them are accounted for as 'dangerous, inauspicious, or polluting to persons, objects, events, and relationships that have not been ritually incorporated into the liminal context'. Turner insists that this hostility is the result of a societal desire to control and maintain power over its social structure and subjects. According to Turner, what is to follow this liminal stage is a complete reintegration into mainstream society.⁶² With Uranian theorists like Jackson and Warren, however, when the young male completes his formative education he does not enter the world anew to assume its restrictive roles and fulfil its normalizing structures through reintegration and aggregation. Rather, he enters it to fulfil an alternative queer civic mandate, forever limiting himself to the placelessness of liminality.

Beau idéal

The like-mindedness of homosociality coupled with the single-mindedness by which the eccentric collector and antiquarian fashioned his lifestyle revolved around the aesthetic experience of the *beau idéal* to be found, naturally, in the male body, more expressly embodied in Greek sculpture (to be collected) and the younger boy-love (to be educated) for which he provided shelter. For Warren, the pursuit of beauty, by which all friends must be judged, was akin to 'the conception of a gentleman'. It is within an all-male community, then, that the Uranian 'can feel free only in such a place: it is the only roomy ground where the seed of love, sown in the corruptible, can be raised in incorruption. [And w]here the gentleman is paramount the pederastic lust, which exists universally, will have a change to become love.'⁶³ The gentleman to which Warren referred harkens back to Jackson's earlier formulation of a new chivalry. While I have already noted how Warren's and Marshall's collecting praxis focused on Grecian objects and youthful male nude sculptures and how these were variously housed in the studies of Lewes House, the ideals underpinning his collection were identical to, if not interchangeable with, his Uranian writings and same-sex relationships. In his study of homoerotic art collecting between 1750 to 1920 Whitney Davis argues that the period was characterized by a symbiotic interplay between on the one hand 'aesthetic idealism' and on the other what he refers to as 'erotic historicism'. Homoerotic aesthetic judgement, he contends, was characterized as 'an on-going universalization of the judgment of beauty, *from* work to work in the whole array and *by* viewer to viewer, such that an emergent male *sensus communis* could recognize itself to be aesthetically beautiful and erotically desirable to itself, or discovered its aesthetic subjectivity to be same-sex loving'.⁶⁴ In regard to classical art and culture

Warren contended that '[t]he simplicity which we admire in the Greeks is due to the acceptance of a canonical interpretation of manhood, a common standard ... But this collective unity and simplicity would not have been noble, if the noble had not been traditional'.[65] Here Davis's notion of the *sensus communis* or a collective aesthetic programme is resonant and in keeping with other queers who sought to forge a distinct community through the *beau idéal*.

As late as 1933, physician, psychologist and social reformer Havelock Ellis commented on how many homosexual men were drawn to the 'study of antiquity'.[66] These ideals, however, did not simply emerge in the last quarter of the nineteenth century, but were already forcefully advocated in the previous century through the historically significant and ground-breaking writings of the German classicist and art historian Johann Joachim Winckelmann (1717–1768). In *Thoughts on the Imitation of Greek Works in Painting and Sculpture* (1755) Winckelmann's focus was on the sculptural unit of *Laocoön and His Sons* (c. 200 BCE) which embodied par excellence 'noble simplicity and calm grandeur' of soul. For Winckelmann the Greek male nude at once both exposed sexual fantasies and embodied 'the ideal of subjective and political freedom with which it [the male nude] came to be so closely identified'.[67] In this way, the male nude was at once 'an object of desire and an ideal with which to identify'.[68] The tension set up by Winckelmann between sexuality and gracefulness on the one hand and austerity and purity on the other not only plays itself out in his writings on the *Laocoön* in particular,[69] but also permeates Warren's own musings on the ideal (Uranian) male.

In his 1763 'Essay on the Beautiful in Art', Winckelmann boldly claims: 'I have observed that those who are only aware of beauty in the female sex and are hardly or not at all affected by beauty in our sex, have little innate feeling for beauty in art in general and vital sense. The same people have an inadequate response to the art of the Greeks, since their greatest beauties are more of our sex that the other'.[70] Winckelmann's focus on Greek society and culture through the material documentation of sculpture was premised on a close reading of the male body's physicality, its seeming perfection rendered in marble and stone. At the centre of his aesthetic theories and readings of Greek sculpture and civilization was the youthful nubile male body, which stood as the ultimate expression of his unabashedly sensuous homoerotic reading of the nude. Winckelmann provided an important language through which to elevate the bonds of male friendship, and in turn inadvertently assisted in the creation of an archaeological lineage of art historical writings that allowed men like Warren a meaningful space to theorize the commingling of sensual aesthetics with a queer materialism. Here, then, in vivid realization we see the tendency of Winckelmann to escape from abstract theory moving toward intuition, that is, to the sensory experiences offered by sight and touch. In large measure Winckelmann could get away with such a strategy given that he lived within a prescribed homosocial arena in which male privilege was taken for granted and male aggregation expected. Robert Aldrich has underscored the theorist's 'aesthetic sensibilities and his missionary zeal for the classical mode'.[71] Askesis, as I underline here, required a necessary and healthy dose of narcissism for the training required of both mind and body to achieve the necessary fitness, understood as intellectual as much as physical. As George Mosse comments: 'Winckelmann himself has written about the Greek gymnasium where gymnastic exercises demonstrate the manly contours and sublime beauty of the naked male body'.[72] Following from Winckelmann, Warren too recognized the centrality of the masculine ideal in Ancient Greek culture and art, which set themselves apart from other races and periods as a result of this achievement. It was on the shoulders of the male form that civilization itself rested its hopes, dreams and aspirations.[73]

At the heart of what constituted the *beau idéal* for Warren was a sort of masculine minimalism, a decidedly ascetic antidote to the perceived frivolity of the feminine and the degeneracy warned against following the Wilde trials. The Uranian 'despises the pretty, the unnecessary, the superficial, the artificial, the accessories of decoration and manners, which she [a woman] is apt to import. But he goes further than most men, because the instinct for the beauty of the masculine drives him on'.[74] With its unadorned façade and cold, uncomfortable furnishings Lewes House materialized the moral blueprint of askesis. The house personified how the sublime simplicity of the masculine form through the codes of askesis sought to pare back the superfluous and frivolous in favour of a controlled representation through rigorous simplicity and vigorous aesthetics, one which inadvertently offered a threshold between Victorian nostalgia and modernist heroism. Here strength and beauty are coeval in the symbolic and semiotic struggle for the Ideal. The Uranian, Warren asserted, 'wishes to remove that which distracts the mind from the study of noblest beauty, most strict in itself, most free from accessories; and distractions become to him profane; it is just this refinement which it is the merit of Greek art of lack'.[75]

The supposed lack of colour of Greek sculpture, its reduction to the bare essentials reinvested aesthetic and cultural meaning to the all-male domestic haven Warren established, and could easily be translated to the modern Uranian male body and the interior design of Lewes House. His is a modernity inspired by – and whose ideals transferred, through the aesthetic – the moral blueprint provided by the Ancient Greeks and the freedom and democracy it purportedly offered its (male) citizens. For

Warren the body of the lover was not merely an abstracted intellectual ideal, adjacent to a Christian denial of self. Rather, his was an identity rooted in the sensuous, phenomenal, perceptual world of things and bodies. He wrote:

> [r]eaction from the spiritual is toward the sensual, less dreaded by the Greeks than by the philosophers. But among those in whom philosophy superseded life, whose life consisted in the contemplation of beauty and in a visual relation to virtue, the reaction lay toward an aesthetic, not an athletic, sensuality, in a nature weakened by music. In this bodiless worship there existed a danger of loss of virtue of the body, its health, potency and efficiency, which demand action, if not as an end, at least as if it were an end ... a valuation of manhood by deeds and not by beauty which is a fitness for deeds.[76]

This material corporeality is, in itself, enough. In his second volume of *A Defence*, *The Uranian Eros*, Warren refers to the Greek ideal as an ultimately masculine ideal on which hung all civic, national, social and sensual hopes. Christian sublimity and pagan nobility formed the dialectical ideals that governed Warren's quotidian praxis reconciled in his scholarship, art collecting and all-male community. Art collected for the home it might be said, rather than any esoteric or metaphysical goals, was where these opposites were best and most beautifully reconciled. Warren 'was always for the solid, the concrete, the masculine, against the airy, abstract, the feminine'.[77] This idiosyncratic gendering of his reconciliation was somewhat at odds with a cultural ethos that privileged the abstract rather than the concrete as a decidedly male prerogative, emblematized in Kantian aesthetic disinterest.

In Walter Pater's (1839–1894) essay 'Winckelmann', the German classicist is honoured as the forebearer of the *fin-de-siècle* obsession with Hellenic ideals and principles. Originally published in 1867 in the *Westminster Review*, it was reprinted with some changes in Pater's now famous and much-cited *Studies in the History of the Renaissance* (1873). What stands out is how, through the historical character and writings of Winckelmann, Pater importantly collapsed the sensual into the aesthetic. Pater began the essay thus: '*Et ergo in arcadia fui*' ('I too was in Arcadia'). Introducing the essay in this fashion, Alex Potts contends, Pater inferred a 'recreation of a lost utopian world, the whole youthful world of the ancient Greeks'.[78]

The Oxford fellow's famous proclamation of and much-celebrated 'House Beautiful' is worth a brief mention here, especially given Warren's own deep admiration of the aesthete, academic and Hellenic scholar. For Pater and subsequent acolytes (like Wilde) the term designated a space at once removed from the vagaries and tumults of the public realm and coded as the harmonious experience of and expression for 'sensuous beauty'. Although Pater delighted in that which sparkled, glittered and shone brightly, unlike Warren, what is crucial about and can be extracted from Pater, as Michael Hatt importantly asserts, is that Greek sculpture in particular 'is about an active imbrication of self and world; it is about the experience of space'.[79] For Pater subjectivity was comprised of three defining features: it was embodied, devoid of any mind–body split; it was temporal; and finally it was social, in that it depended on the 'other' to understand itself as being-in-the-world.[80] In Pater's various books and essays, notably 'The Child in the House' (1878), *Gaston de Latour* (1896) and *Marius the Epicurean* (1892), it is neither luxury nor excess which characterizes the main characters or their environments, but rather understatement and self-restraint. Pater was a firm advocate of the idea that a child's development, mental evolution more generally, was predicated on its interaction with its environment, an ideal he shared with numerous contemporary psychologists, most notably James Sully.[81] In these terms a nascent Uranian boy (or Uranian ideal) was best developed in a proper Uranian, understated environment. Emphasizing sensation as the starting point for development, Maureen Moran has also noted how for Pater '[t]he association of the aesthetic interior with unconscious impressions that shape intellectual priorities also endows the aesthetic personality with moral "safety," implying its foundation in an attractive domesticity of order, purity and moderation'.[82]

For Warren domestic space was never compromised by a love of luxury, but adhered to the structures of Spartan rigour and an abundance of members of a community that shared in common a practice premised on aesthetic rigour and intellectual discipline. For Pater and his kind, 'these aesthetic interiors embed discriminating habits of mind because they maximize pleasure through moderation and understatement, rather than through luxury and excess'.[83] While Pater's important musings on Winckelmann are far from revealing a queer identity and emancipation, they nonetheless show how sexuality is an important constituent of identity-formation and subjectivity itself.[84] Warren, like Pater, invested much in the phenomenological expression of, in this case, Uranian identity and the expression of corporeality arguing for the supremacy of the sense of touch as a particularity of this ideal. Uranians 'touch more closely', according to him. 'It is, indeed, characteristic of Uranians, whether metaphorically or physically, that they are sensitive to touch and prone to touch: their touch has the peculiar gentleness, warmth, and firmness of sympathy. Love is love.'[85]

Closeting Warren
Contemporary, friend and fellow pederast George Santayana (1863–1952)[86] was direct in his criticism of Warren's obsessive Hellenism,

stating it had become an embarrassment and threatened his credibility and reputation.[87] As an act of closeting and shaming on his part, Santayana's use nevertheless of the term Uranian significantly marked an important historical moment in the queer politics of appropriation. In *The Sense of Beauty Being the Outlines of Aesthetic Theory*, Santayana concludes that 'beauty also can be a cause and a factor of happiness. Yet the happiness of beauty is either too sensuous to be stable, or else too ultimate, too sacramental, to be accounted as happiness by the worldly mind.'[88] Victorian Hellenism and its early twentieth-century remnants embodied fears surrounding degeneration and effeminacy, perceived as an 'empty or negative symbol of civic enfeeblement and ... monstrous self-absorption' threatening the cultural and political welfare of the nation;[89] a far cry from the way Winckelmann theorized a commingling of homoerotic desire and political freedom in the eighteenth century. The transformation of Hellenism within the cultural and political landscape, according to Linda Dowling in her extensive study of homosexuality and Hellenism at Oxford University, was embodied in Wilde's ennobled defence of same-sex love and must be seen as a shift in the perception of Hellenism as a discursive site for cultural renewal.[90] As Dowling argues, Hellenism, particularly within the intellectual confines of Oxford University, 'could cast a veil of respectability over even a hitherto unmentionable vice or crime. The "love that dare not speak its name" could be spoken of, to those who knew their ancient history, as *paiderastia*, Greek love.'[91] However, associations with this decidedly Victorian form of Hellenism, or any other overt expression of Uranian ideology, suggested guilt, even decades after Wilde's trials. Santayana's dismissal and the abandonment of Warren by many young men he had financially and intellectually supported and provided shelter for, through various tacit and effective forms of shame, erected a new closet in which to place Warren and his seemingly idiosyncratic philosophy and domestic praxis. Ultimately Warren's taste for Uranian love, which elevated collective male bonds through the spaces of the domestic, would forever remain an unattainable utopian, alternative ideal in a period that continuously reinforced the gendered separation of the spheres. It should then come as no surprise that *A Defence of Uranian Love* was written near the end of Warren's life, a final defiant queer pedagogical act of providing another or ideally several future generations with an aesthetic and domestic ideal worth striving for.

There exists a long and proud lineage of queer scholars and writers who have consistently turned their back on the present in favour of the past. Winckelmann, Pater, Jackson and Warren in their thinly veiled escapes to the past performed their temporal reality in a queer manner. In *On the Imitation of the Greeks* Winckelmann's focus on the *Laocoön's* 'noble simplicity and calm grandeur' of soul was what made the antique both morally and aesthetically superior to the modern – contemporary – period. As Pater wrote of Winckelmann, he was 'like a relic of classical antiquity laid open to accident, to our alien, modern atmosphere'.[92] For Pater the German classicist did not simply copy but, given 'his own nature', imitated the Greeks, which he achieved through a 'constant handling of the antique'.[93] Furthermore, his passion for the Greeks was embodied in his relationships with younger men.[94] Winckelmann's mimetic impulse surely influenced the Uranian ideal in which art and by extension life gave way not merely to imitation but to sensual, material embodiment itself.

Warren's antiquated views, predicated on a Uranian ideal long since past, heavily influenced by Pater, marks his work and domestic lifestyle as a sort of queer temporality and lent a degree of suspicion even amongst his queer peers, like Santayana, whose naturalism was very much predicated on contemporaneity. Warren did not live in the modern times of the early twentieth century, but stood at its threshold, with one foot firmly rooted in a past that never really existed in the nineteenth century either. Like Pater, Warren saw no place for himself in the contemporary moment and experiences. In its etymological origins from the Greek, 'Ou', meaning not, and 'topos', meaning place, utopia simply designates 'no place', or perhaps more aptly placelessness. However, feminist and queer theorist Elizabeth Grosz underscores the ironic interplay at work within the term. 'Ou' also has a parallel association with 'Eu', meaning well, good and fortune. The pun suggests a good place as no place, no place as a good place.[95] Utopias, Uranian or otherwise, constitute 'pure phantasmagorical projections of desire – otherwordly', of another time and space. 'Because utopias cannot be "built" in the conventional sense of the term, what is created is a spatialization of a purported personal and communal memory through the projection of fantasy; an architecture, which controls not only the environment (read space), but time and bodies'.[96] As a form of nostalgia, Warren's Uranian utopia was 'also a romance, with one's own fantasy. Nostalgic love can only survive in a long-distance relationship',[97] a fundamental mode of resistance to contemporary modes of heteronormative bonding and aggregation, forever residing in the placelessness of liminality. Like Winckelmann, Jackson and other advocates of Uranian love and homosociability, Warren differed his queer leanings to another (queer) place and time, removing it from the present space and condition, making it less threatening and yet at the same time using a classical language easily understood by a university educated man.

In the pictures of Lewes House the stark simplicity and absence of any material luxury coded the space as decidedly not feminine, a way to stave off any pejorative connotations often associated with both the putative effeminacy of the domestic realm and queer bachelorhood. Warren also circumvented the widely held view that bachelors craved luxury and turned their backs on the normative, masculine virtues of thrift and self-restraint.[98] Stefano Evangelista has concluded that the 'appeal to Plato also serves to distance homosexual practice from the connotations of vulgarity prevalent at the time: this process is best captured in Wilde's attempt during the trials to shift the setting of modern homosexuality from the brothels and seedy hotel rooms invoked by the prosecution to the high-cultural and noble rhetoric that Platonism carries with it'.[99] It is important, however, to consider that Wilde's appeal to Platonic virtues was overturned and remained in the realm of vice, the residues of which are evident in Warren's own time, decades after the trials. Even for Warren, despite his best efforts to distance himself from these sullied and dirty connotations, he was compelled to opt for a pseudonym for the publication of his Uranian tract. As seen in the Wilde trials, effeminacy and artifice were contrived to vilify not simply the men themselves but the domesticity they performed and inhabited. After all, domesticity and the formation and formulation of identity went hand in hand. The Lewes House brotherhood as it would be known, on the other hand, managed to straddle the domestic (with all its feminizing inferences) and the privatized public spaces men began to forge for themselves away from the domestic by way of the notions of control and training implicit in askesis yet distinct from the contemporaneity and heroism associated with British and continental modernism of the 1920s.

Warren's life and prose provided an intellectual and historical space in which to elevate the bonds of male friendship, celebrated within the domestic realm, in a culture that repressed same-sex sexual acts as much as the private sphere. By advocating the enjoyment of the male body in all its ideal bodily perfection Warren allowed, through all male friendships (homosocial bonds), the sensual and even the sexual to seep in. The sense of struggle, conflict and tension also reflected Warren's (not unlike Winckelmann's although in a clearly less overt manner) desire to see in and promote Ancient Greek sculpture as the embodiment of freedom, for it was clearly informed by a life marked by a struggle to be recognized and respected as an independent writer and scholar of antiquity, rather than a mere fanatical dilatant. By his own admission, Warren's protest against modernity and advocacy for the ties that bind, that is, his queer resistance to the shaming that modernity and modernism can inspire, was achieved through his collections and writings. He defiantly asserted:

I like to think of my life as a fight for friendship, against modern ideas – my protests are the collection of Greek antiquities and my writings, and against domesticity when it tends to be hostile. I was faithful to my friends, the married and the unmarried; I put them before my people at home.[100]

Friendship, then, was indeed a way of life, perhaps not entirely unfamiliar to Foucault when he himself wrote of his own longing to find a new way of being-in-the-(modern)-world. In this way, the bond of friendship is transformed into an act of resistance, a form of activism, one that boasts a long, complicated, rich if much neglected past.

Notes

1 For complete and thoughtful analyses of the Warren Cup see J. R. Clarke, 'The Warren Cup of the Contexts for the Representations of Male-to-Male Lovemaking in Augustan and early Julio-Claudian Art', *The Art Bulletin*, vol. 73, no. 2 (June 1993); J. Polloni, 'The Warren Cup: Homoerotic Love and Symposial Rhetoric in Silver', *Art Bulletin*, vol. 81, no. 1 (March 1999).

2 R. Aldrich, *The Seduction of the Mediterranean: Writing, Art and Homosexual Fantasy* (New York and London: Routledge, 1993); D. M. Halperin, *One Hundred Years of Homosexuality and Other Essays on Greek Love* (New York and London: Routledge, 1990); L. Dowling, *Hellenism and Homo-sexuality in Victorian Oxford* (Ithaca and London: Cornell University Press, 1994); M. Foucault, *History of Sexuality, Volume 2: The Uses of Pleasure* (New York: Vintage Books, 1990).

3 Foucault, *History of Sexuality*, p. 74.

4 J. Tosh, *A Man's Place: Masculinity and the Middle-Class Home in Victorian England* (New Haven and London: Yale University Press, 1999), p. 146.

5 R. Shields (ed.), *Places on the Margin: Alternative Geographies of Modernity* (London and New York: Routledge, 1991), p. 25.

6 D. M. Halperin, *Saint Foucault: Towards a Gay Hagiography* (Oxford and New York: Oxford University Press, 1995), p. 62.

7 O. Burdett and E. H. Goddard, *Edward Perry Warren: The Biography of a Connoisseur* (London: Christopher's, 1941), p. 10, 9.

8 *Ibid.*, p. 13.

9 *Ibid.*, pp. 338–9.

10 *Ibid.*, pp. 86–7.

11 Two biographies exist on Warren. The first, published in 1941, was a co-operative endeavour inaugurated by Osbert Burdett, who was the collector's literary editor and whom Warren had commissioned to write his biography after his death. Burdett however died in 1936 before completing the project and the task of finishing it was reluctantly assumed by E. H. Goddard, his associate. This biography remains, nevertheless, an important text and provides evidence of the life led at Lewes House. While David Sox, Warren's second and more recent biographer, refers back to the limited correspondence and notes left behind by Warren at the Ashmolean archives, he too relies heavily on Burdett and Goddard's biography. Despite the apparent limitations of these two biographies as concerns queer expressions of domesticity, aesthetics and community, I rely on

both biographies simply when and where they reveal contemporary opinions, personal accounts, anecdotes and exceptional facts.

12 In Burdett and Goddard, *Edward Perry Warren*, p. 133.
13 In D. Sox, *Bachelors of Art: Edward Perry Warren and the Lewes House Brotherhood* (London: Fourth Estate, 1991), p. 42.
14 *Ibid.*, pp. 44–5.
15 Burdett and Goddard, *Edward Perry Warren*, p. 100.
16 *Ibid.*, p. 101.
17 In Sox, *Bachelors of Art*, pp. 64–5.
18 In 1913 he would purchase the Lewes House estate outright for £3,750. Warren also had Few Acres estate, a summer home at Westbrook, Maine; however, it impacted neither Warren's life nor his Uranian pursuits or ideals.
19 In Sox, *Bachelors of Art*, p. 44.
20 *Ibid.*, p. 45.
21 Burdett and Goddard, *Edward Perry Warren*, p. 131.
22 The sculpture was given to the Lewes council, which displayed it for two years, then returned it, claiming it was unsuitable for public consumption.
23 Plato, *Symposium* (Indianapolis: Bobbs-Merrill, 1956), p. 178.
24 In Burdett and Goddard, *Edward Perry Warren*, p. 130.
25 Sir W. Rothenstein, *Men and Memories: Recollections of William Rothenstein, 1900–1922* (London: Faber & Faber Limited, 1932), p. 343.
26 Burdett and Goddard, *Edward Perry Warren*, p. 143.
27 *Ibid.*, p. 144.
28 In Burdett and Goddard, *Edward Perry Warren*, p. 144.
29 In Sox, *Bachelors of Art*, p. 46.
30 *Ibid.*, p. 47.
31 Note the irony of her name and the heteronormative implications of it, that is, marital bliss, which Marshall's marriage to her was to assume.
32 E. K. Sedgwick, *Between Men: English Literature and Male Homosocial Desire* (New York: Columbia University Press, 1985), p. 21.
33 Burdett and Goddard, *Edward Perry Warren*, p. 302.
34 E. Carpenter, *Homogenic Love and Its Place in a Free Society* (London: Redundancy Press, 1895), p. 13.
35 J. A. Symonds, *A Problem in Greek Ethics Being an Inquiry into the Phenomenon of Sexual Inversion* (London: The Apeonatitita Society, 1908), p. 64.
36 *Ibid.*, p. 69.
37 E. P. Warren, *A Defence of Uranian Love*, part i, privately printed (1928), p. 3.
38 *Ibid.*, part i, p. 53.
39 *Ibid.*, part i, p. 54.
40 J. Ruskin, *Sesame and Lilies* (New Haven and London: Yale University Press, 2002 [1865]), p. 99.
41 *Ibid.*, p. 77.

Askesis and the Greek ideal

42 J. B. Brown, *The Home: In Its Relation to Man and to Society* (London: James Clarke and Co., 1883), p. 25.

43 *Ibid.*, pp. 23–4.

44 Tosh, *A Man's Place*, p. 6.

45 Warren, *A Defence*, part i, pp. 169–70.

46 *Ibid.*, part I, p. 68.

47 Burdett and Goddard, *Edward Perry Warren*, p. 130.

48 Warren, *A Defence*, part i, p. 22.

49 D. M. Halperin, 'How to Do the History of Male Homosexuality', *GLQ: The Journal of Lesbian and Gay Studies*, vol. 6, no. 1, (2000), p. 102.

50 In Burdett and Goddard, *Edward Perry Warren*, p. 279.

51 Warren, *A Defence*, part i, p. 158.

52 Halperin, 'How to Do the History of Male Homosexuality', p. 101.

53 Burdett and Goddard, *Edward Perry Warren*, p. 386.

54 Warren, *A Defence*, part i, p. 59.

55 *Ibid.*, part i, p. 19.

56 Symonds, *A Problem in Greek Ethics*, p. 36.

57 For a thorough and important discussion of Ives's later years see M. Cook, 'Families of Choice? George Ives, Queer Lives and the Family', *Gender and History*, no. 22 (April 2010).

58 C. K. Jackson, 'New Chivalry', *Artist* (2 April 1894), p. 104.

59 See P. Vidal-Naquet, *The Black Hunter: Forms of Thought and Forms of Society in the Greek World* (Baltimore and London: The Johns Hopkins University Press, 1981), p. 6.

60 Warren, *A Defence*, part i, p. 195.

61 V. Turner, *The Ritual Process: Structure and Anti-Structure* (New York: Aldine de Gruyter, 1995), pp. 94–5.

62 *Ibid.*, p. 109.

63 Warren, *A Defence*, part i, p. 21.

64 W. Davis, 'Homoerotic Art Collection from 1750 to 1920', *Art History*, vol. 24, no. 2 (April 2001), p. 250.

65 Warren, *A Defence*, part ii, pp. 149–50.

66 H. Ellis, *Studies in the Psychology of Sex* (New York: Random House, 1942 [1933]), pp. 27–8, 35.

67 A. Potts, *Flesh and the Ideal: Winckelmann and the Origins of Art History* (New Haven and London: Yale University Press, 1994), p. 4.

68 *Ibid.*, p. 5.

69 *Ibid.*, p. 7.

70 In Aldrich, *The Seduction of the Mediterranean*, p. 53.

71 *Ibid.*, p. 50.

72 G. L. Mosse, *The Images of Man: The Creation of Modern Masculinity* (Oxford and New York: Oxford University Press, 1996), p. 40.

73 Warren, *A Defence*, part i, p. 11.

74 *Ibid.*, part i, p. 67.
75 *Ibid.*, part i, p. 68.
76 *Ibid.*, part ii, pp. 113–14.
77 Burdett and Goddard, *Edward Perry Warren*, p. 132.
78 Potts, *Flesh and the Ideal*, p. 239.
79 M. Hatt, 'Space, Surface, Self: Homosexuality and the Aesthetic Interior', *Visual Culture in Britain*, vol. 8, no. 1 (summer 2007), p. 114.
80 *Ibid.*, p. 116.
81 M. Moran, 'Walter Pater's House Beautiful and the Psychology of Self-Culture', *English Literature in Transition, 1880–1920*, vol. 50, no. 3 (2007), p. 295.
82 Moran, 'Walter Pater's House Beautiful', p. 299.
83 *Ibid.*, p. 296.
84 Potts, *Flesh and the Ideal*, p. 240.
85 Warren, *A Defence*, part i, p. 52.
86 Santayana held a rather ambiguous and ambivalent attitude toward his own (homo)sexuality which largely explained his irritation towards Warren's Uranian programme. For more on Santayana see: J. McCormick, *George Santayana: A Biography* (New Brunswick: Transaction Publishers, 2003).
87 G. Holzberger and J. Saatkamp (eds.), *Persons and Places: Fragments of an Autobiography* (Cambridge, MA: MIT Press, 1986), p. 81.
88 G. Santayana, *The Sense of Beauty Being the Outlines of Aesthetic Theory* (London: Adam and Charles Black, 1896), pp. 64–5.
89 Dowling, *Hellenism and Homo-sexuality*, p. 8.
90 *Ibid.*, pp. 3–5.
91 *Ibid.*, p. 28.
92 W. Pater, *The Renaissance, Studies in Art and Poetry* (Oxford and New York: Oxford University Press, 1990), p. 175.
93 *Ibid.*, pp. 175–6, 145.
94 *Ibid.*, p. 152.
95 E. Grosz, *Architecture from the Outside: Essays in Virtual and Real Space* (Cambridge, MA, and London: MIT Press, 2001), p. 135.
96 J. Potvin, 'Perversely Mystical: Towards a Queer Semiology of Breton Male Bodies', *Genders*, issue 41 (spring 2005), n.p.
97 S. Boym, *The Future of Nostalgia* (New York: Basic Books, 2001), p. xviii.
98 K. V. Synder, *Bachelors, Manhood, and the Novel* (Cambridge: Cambridge University Press, 1999), p. 31.
99 S. Evangelista, '"Lovers and Philosophers at Once": Aesthetic Platonism in the Victorian "Fin de Siècle"', *The Yearbook of English Studies*, vol. 36, no. 2 (2006), p. 244.
100 Burdett and Goddard, *Edward Perry Warren*, p. 279.

5 ✧ Of art and irises: Cedric Morris, Arthur Lett-Haines and the decorative ideal

ONE OF three children, Sir Cedric Morris (1889–1982) was born in Skety, Swansea, to the industrialist George Lockwood Morris[1] and Wilhelmina (née Cory) who had not only studied painting but was widely recognized for her highly accomplished needlework. Less academically inclined, at the age of seventeen Morris set sail for Canada where he took on odd labour jobs to support himself. The prospects of a singing education and potential future career brought him back to London, but were quickly abandoned for painting. The young Morris moved to Paris where, in 1914, he attended the Academie Delacluse located in the centre of bohemian life in Montparnasse. There he studied until war broke out when in vain he attempted to join the Artists Rifles, which declared him medically unsuitable for active duty. He spent the war working as a trainer at Lord Rosslyn's stables at Theale, Berkshire, but was discharged when the Remounts took over the stables in 1917. Morris moved to Cornwall in south-west England where he became fast friends with painter Frances Hodgkins (1869–1947). It was also in Cornwall that he developed his other lifelong study and passion, floriculture. On one of his frequent visits to London in November 1918 Morris attended celebrations of the Armistice hosted by Arthur Lett-Haines (known to all as Lett) (1894–1978) at his house at 2 Carlyle Square, Chelsea; a meeting that would forever change the course of his life. Not unlike Charles Ricketts and Charles Shannon, in many ways the two were opposites: 'Cedric was quiet, intuitive, impractical in administrative matters, and absolutely single-minded in the practice of painting and in his involvement with the world of plants, animals and with the country, Lett was complex and roundabout in thought and behaviour, ostentatious and oracular in manner, at home in the city, and perpetually deflected from pursuing his vocation as an artist by schemes of one kind and another to help others and the cause of art in general'.[2] The son of Charles Lett and Frances Laura Esme, the young painter and sculptor served in the army and soon married his second wife Gertrude Aimee Lincoln. Former student and fellow artist Joan Warburton (1920–1996) described Lett as an 'intellectual, cosmopolitan, sophisticate with an immediate perception of peoples' character and weaknesses ... Cedric remained always close to the earth, gentle but firm, giggling happily at the latest scandal and always did exactly what he wanted to do, his garden and painting came first'.[3] In so many ways the two men could not have been more different, so 'different in temperament' in fact, that artist Glyn Morgan (b. 1926) thought 'it seemed impossible that they should live in the same building'.[4]

In spite of Gertrude, Lett and Morris fell in love immediately. Morris moved in with the couple and in 1919 the trio planned a journey to the USA. However, Gertrude left on her own, leaving the two men to set up house and home in the small fishing port of Newlyn in Cornwall while they continued to sublease Hodgkins's studio in Kensington. In Newlyn they converted a series of terraced cottages into a single, larger house they christened The Bowgie, made conspicuous to the outside community by their home's unconventional style. Hodgkins described it as 'Futuristic abode', offering a hint of the impression held by local residents of the couple's avant-garde and decidedly odd home.[5] Many years later, writer and editor Ronald Blythe (b. 1922) recalled how when the couple lived in Newlyn

> there was a feeling of Cornwall in the colour of the house and a definite whiff of the Mediterranean in the food and wine. The atmosphere was one of intellectual freedom. Everything was discussed. It was Bohemian in the best sense. Lett and Cedric were open about their homosexuality at a time when it was illegal to have such a relationship and they also conducted a fight against the philistinism of their day. The whole atmosphere was exiting and liberating.[6]

Their bohemian lifestyle at once infused the admiration many held for the couple while fuelling regional gossip. Throughout the area, Morris was commonly referred to as the 'Cézanne of Newlyn', alluding to the clearly non-English, decidedly continental bohemianism of his personality and style. The Bowgie served as their home until December 1920, when they set off for Paris, abandoning only temporarily the rustic simplicity of the countryside.

In as much as I am able, given the paucity of extant records of their interiors and domestic culture, in this chapter I explore Morris's unique and divergent modernism, which began while in Paris; a modernism that cavorted with abandon with the decorative, long held as anathema to the manly heroism modernist critics and historians have honoured and privileged and continue to do. Aware of the potential of his partner's career, with total devotion and love Lett set his career as a (surrealist) painter and sculptor aside to aid in the development of Morris's success, a domestic partnership not dissimilar to what we have seen with Ricketts and Shannon. Lett believed firmly in Morris's abilities and declared 'that next to Matisse, Cedric was the finest colourist' of the twentieth century.[7] Unlike Ricketts, Lett was neither a theorist nor a critic. Life for him was simpler and far more communal, especially by 1937 when the two men founded the East Anglian School of Painting and Drawing (EASPD) at Dedham, Essex. As a result of their domestic arrangement, I will turn to Morris as a source towards understanding the decorative as a true and shameful sin attributed to the modern/ist bachelor. The highly domestic and decorative nature of Morris's art in addition to the domesticated art education they provided to an entire generation of successful and highly acclaimed artists such as Lucian Freud, dwells at the heart of their absence from the records of modern art in Britain.

The art education and domestic topography these two men developed over the decades and in several homes did not favour one over the other as did their collective creative output. Their chorography reveals much about the way time does not always soften or deepen love, but rather draws to light the sometime inevitable cleavages, differences and power struggles that exist in long-time companionship. As a result, this chapter is concerned with the distance (both emotional and physical) that develops, rather than simply and only the proximity that flourishes in a sustained intimate relationship. More often than not we tend to romanticize relationships set against the backdrop of history, those storied love affairs that have withstood tests of life and time itself. Rather, here, I want to suggest that there are other sides to relationships, ones that can teach us much, perhaps even more about the material and visual cultures of *bachelors of a different sort*.

Further, we often tend to focus on the domesticity as a series of interior spaces and private corporeal choreographies. In this chapter, however, I spend some time, as did Morris, Lett and their students, outside the home itself, in the fecund spaces of the garden that Morris, in large measure, would be better known for in his later years and following his death. Ironically, numerous photographs remain of their famous gardens, while sadly no image recaptures any of the spaces of their so-called bohemian interiors. Morris's avid connoisseurship, interest in and renown in the domain of floriculture was both a source of profound inspiration for his modern decorative painting practice and a useful subject in his pedagogical programme, while proving to be the basis of deep frustration and jealousy on the part of Lett. Over time, the garden as an extension of the domestic interior landscape and its colourful inhabitants would gradually determine the domesticated choreography the coupled performed.

5.1 Cedric Morris (*left*) and Arthur Lett-Haines with Rubio the parrot, c. 1930–36.

These men who lived together for sixty years are certainly an evocative example of the vagaries of aesthetic life and the trials of domestic bliss. Their lives as aesthetic mentors have touched and affected the lives of many who witnessed, lived with and learnt from them along those many years until Lett's death in 1978. So much so that in 2002 numerous were those who came together to immortalize their memories and experiences in *Benton End Remembered*. This collection of amassed memories and reminiscences has proved helpful to reconstruct a domestic and aesthetic life largely gone unrecognized. The collection also serves an important function when faced with a man like Morris who decried the necessity of auto/biography, going to such lengths as to destroy many of his own drawings, works and writings, leaving ultimately very little despite the over five thousand items contained in their collective archives at The Tate (London). In a letter dated 21 May 1977 to Dr William Mason (a researcher hoping to gain access to the couple's archives and lives) Lett warned how: 'My partner Sir Cedric is very much opposed to biography, autobiography, and profiles etc. and regards them as an impertinence … On the other hand I personally do not see how history can come to be written without such things.'[8] Indeed, I wonder how Sir Cedric would view my interest in the design of their domestic lives. Likely, I presume, with a degree of suspicion, yet certainly peppered with a great sense of humour.

Beginnings and bohemia

If little material of the domestic and personal life remains of these two men, even less has been made available from their early years together in Paris. Lett found an artist's studio initially in Rue Lepic and from 1924 they rented a studio from Mr J. Borel on the first floor at 39 rue Liancourt at a cost of 1,600Fr per annum, paid in four instalments. By 1921 Morris had begun his informal artistic education, studying at the Academies Moderne, Suédoise, La Grande Chaumiere and Atelier Colarossi, which by then no longer adhered to the strict salon system they once sustained throughout the nineteenth century. Among his most notable instructors were André Lhote, Othon Friesz and Fernard Léger. Life in the City of Lights was rich and textured for the couple, who quickly integrated themselves into a bohemian, expatriate community that included friends like Juan Gris, Nancy Cunard, Man Ray, Marcel Duchamp, Peggy Guggenheim, Djuna Barnes, Iris Tree, Berenice Abbott, Mary Butts and Ernest Hemingway, amongst others. It was also, importantly, whilst in Paris that the couple met writer and fellow artist Kathleen Hale (1898–2000), with whom Lett would have a long-standing affair. They were also good friends with Lady Tuff Twyseden, who served as the model for Lady Brett Ashley in Hemingway's *The Sun Also Rises* (1927). In the less than flattering novel, Lady Ashley is accompanied by a group of young men, among whom are the 'tall, dark one' named Lett as well as 'the wavy blond one' who is both unworthy and inconsequential to be given a name (a clear allusion to Morris's distinctive golden curls). Characters like these, American and British expatriates who populated the cityscape of the novel, were part of the decadent so-called 'lost generation'. Lady Ashley's male companions were offensive precisely because of their homosexuality, especially to the story's protagonist, Jake Barnes, whose own gendered and sexual identity was questionable at best.[9] In another report, Lett is the guide to the underworld, initiating one reporter into the sultry and seedy nightclubs he and his set frequented; a portrayal not dissimilar to the one provided by Hemmingway. The reporter's description of the interior space and atmosphere lend an rich impression of these environments at the time:

> The air is damp and smoke-laden, with the smoke of millions of cigarettes and cheap cigars, in the packed rooms there are many men of the lower world of Paris, mostly with high necked sweaters under old jackets, and caps drawn down over one eye, and there are a few artists from the nearby Montparnasse quarter who are in company with their models, or friends interested in the real life of the great city ... The long song continues, and Lett-Haines, who took me to see the place, whispered: 'There won't be anything else, there never is, except once in a while so often a fight, when someone gets shot, or a knife thrust, and someone else crushed in the rush to get out before the police arrive ... I'm no good with a knife so cover your pearls'.[10]

Lett's bohemian, if slightly clichéd, Paris is represented as tough, shady and resolutely dangerous.

The couple were also renowned for the parties they threw (especially in their London days), but which they stopped throwing in 1939. As one reporter noted, Morris 'soon became a popular figure in artistic circles, and gave some memorable parties in his Bloomsbury studio' in Great Ormond Street into which they moved in 1927.[11] In this studio Morris proudly displayed his collection of exotic cacti, specimens brought back from their travels to Algeria and which appeared frequently as subjects in pictures from the period.[12] During the 1920s they travelled extensively throughout Europe and North Africa and took numerous photographs either of rare botanical specimens or of themselves and their friends, sometimes posing naked on the beach in awkward expressive modernist poses as their archives still lays bare. So infamous and 'memorable' were their parties that Fox Studios requested to photograph the costumes at a planned party at Great Ormond Street on 4 June 1930.[13] Dress code for their fancy dress parties, arguably 'some of the best of private entertainments' in all of London, was strictly imposed on the men they invited, leaving women, already better equipped for such events, to fend for themselves. As one reporter noted: 'Women are usually far keener on wearing fancy dress at a party than men. It is a little surprising, therefore, to read on the invitation to the party Mr Cedric Morris is giving on Saturday to celebrate the opening of his new exhibition at the Leicester Galleries, that fancy dress is for men only. Men are told firmly on the invitation that they must appear in fancy dress; the women are instructed to wear whatever becomes them most.'[14]

Of art and irises

One critic characterized Morris as 'not at all typical of those London "Bohemians" … nor does he, like so many modern artists, try to look like a successful businessman. His weather-beaten face is clean shaven, his hair is close-cut, and his lean form is clad in a perfectly ordinary lounge suit. You would probably take him for a gentleman-farmer enjoying a day in town. He will discuss horses and dogs far more readily than he will talk about art.'[15] *The Paris Times*, on the other hand, described Morris as a sartorial trendsetter: 'The Prince of Wales may be responsible for the tremendous vogue of blue collars, but I believe that Cedric Morris instigated the fashion of wearing Faroe Island sweaters. This Welsh artist is famous for his swaggerly disreputable attire. Life is just one art show after another for Cedric.'[16] Morris was often seen throughout his life wearing an old single-breasted suit or thick Aran sweaters and Welsh flannel shirts paired with corduroy trousers in the winter months. He often wore a brown leather jacket coupled with corduroy trousers and a neckerchief fastened with a toggle. Despite his supposed uncharacteristically non-artistic demeanour and style, his work was quickly taken up and reproduced in such varied periodicals as British *Vogue*, *Transatlantic Review* and *Gargoyle*.

5.2 Cedric Morris, the image of the bohemian artist in Paris, c. 1920s.

Between painting and decoration

While in Paris both men's artistic interests took on decidedly different trajectories. Lett was influenced by Surrealism and Cubism, and noted Picasso's inspiration on his work. In London their associations with members of Wyndham Lewis's Group X and others affected Lett's work more profoundly, while Morris remained indifferent to the vagaries of the avant-garde. Throughout the 1920s Lett exhibited his work at the Casa d'Arte Braglia, Rome (through Fillipo Tommaso Marinetti) and in New York under the auspices of *The Little Review* and the Société Anonyme, for example. Morris also held highly successful exhibitions in London in 1924 and later in 1926 when they settled back in Britain. He also showed at the Venice Biennale in 1928 and 1932 as well as the Carnegie International in Pittsburgh in 1931. The reporter from the *South Wales Daily News* noted that Morris's pictures 'are being greatly admired for their beauty of texture and harmony ... Morris is one of the most original modern painters. He is very independent and does not follow any school ... He is also entirely self-taught, but his work has been acclaimed at the exhibitions he has given in Paris, New York, Manchester, Liverpool, and Edinburgh.'[17] Apart from the primitivizing undertone and somewhat misleading comments concerning Morris's artistic education, the reporter noted the increasing awareness of Morris's art as well as how the artist and his pictures remained outside of modernist styles current at the time. Success was further guaranteed in London when Morris became a member of the London Artists Association and was proposed admittance by Winifred and Ben Nicholson into the Seven and Five Society, short-lived though his associations with these societies would be. In 1926 it was clear to Lett that Morris's career would guarantee their stability and income, when they permanently resettled in London. Lett then subordinated his career to care for the couple's affairs and the business of his partner's budding success.

Three definitive, yet interwoven, motifs emerge in the numerous reviews of Morris's work from the 1920s and 1930s, the period of his greatest success and notoriety. Critics observed his inability to move his pictures into the three-dimensional, the definitive decorative nature of his work and, finally, his odd and striking bohemian appearance that in turn inflected the pictures with an aura of queer bohemia. Here I wish to focus on the criticism of his work and how it anticipated a new domestic ideal. I also wish to posit that it is precisely the decorative and domesticated aspect of his pictures that would lead art historians and critics to write Morris and his companion out of the canon of British modern art. This flagrant omission cannot entirely come as a surprise. After all, art historians such as Thomas Crow, for example, have fiercely disputed any relationship between fashion, commerce and painting.

5.3 Sir Cedric Morris. *Self-Portrait*, 1930.

Fashion and finance, Crow claims, are antithetical and antagonistic forces to avant-garde modernist art.[18] To his detriment, Morris was not merely financially successful but decidedly 'in' fashion in the interwar period, associating himself with The Picture Hire, Limited, at 56 Brook Street, London, for example. The Picture Hire was a unique venue where people purchased and rented art works for the sole purpose of decorating their homes. Morris regularly and proudly displayed pictures there, work seen through the supposedly polarizing prism of the decorative on the one hand and the conventions of naturalism on the other.[19] Even British *Vogue* weighed in on the debate, reinforcing the decidedly gendered aspect of the decorative. In an article from 1929, 'Picasso as Decorator', a writer for *Vogue* remarked that genius (citing Picasso as *the* examplary model) was distinct from female practices of decoration for the home. The author contended that

> [p]urely decorative arrangements can be achieved by any woman of taste in the disposition of flowers in a bowl, in the choice of colours in her boudoir, in the nice adjustment of a jewelled buckle. But for an artist like Picasso such processes of arrangment are without significance unless they symbolise relationships of universal form.[20]

Floral arrangements, jewel boxes and colour choice are no match to the universal laws evinced in a work of male genius. We would do well to remember, as Lisa Tickner reminds us, that the Baudelairian notions of the fleeting, the contingent and the ephemeral, the very heart of modernity and the avant-garde aesthetic, were indelibly linked to mass consumption and important developments in technology in the latter half of the nineteenth century.[21] However, as Christopher Reed convincingly shows, 'in the arts the linkage of domesticity and modernism has been obscured by another conceptual invention of the nineteenth century: the idea of the "avant-garde" ... Ultimately, in the eyes of the avant-garde being undomestic came to serve as a guarantee of being art.'[22] He contends that the divergence between modernism and domesticity occurred when Baudelaire's notion of the *flâneur* was coupled with a defence of Impressionism and its artists' depiction of the countryside and the city, the great outdoors of public culture. In this restrictive formulation, the home was no longer given space, decisively emptying it of any cultural meaning or currency.

The 1920s, however, marked the first period in which modernity and modernism were no longer the purview of a select elite from the cultural and artistic avant-garde, but a reality that had reached the masses. While modernist developments promulgated on the continent would not reach Britain's conservative shores well until the early to mid-1930s, by the interwar period modernity had became itself *the* commodity, no longer the handmaiden to intellectual bohemianism.²³ Walter Benjamin claimed that the bourgeois, the antithesis of avant-garde modernity, exploited textiles and comfortable furniture as a point of resistance to the armature and harsh steel cladding of modernity.²⁴ Within the fraught territory of the modern interior, art could be made to secure its homeliness and comfort.

Morris's domesticated pictures fall uneasily, for many critics, betwixt the decorative of domestic avant-gardism on the one hand and artistic conservativism on the other, a space far too fraught and not admitted to in conservative modernist re/visions of modern art's supposed singular and univocal history. Richard Morphet has correctly suggested that '[i]n a context dominated by styles, a major factor which for decades militated against recognition of Morris was the exceptional primacy in his paintings of preoccupation with *the subject*'.²⁵ To say, however, that Morris was not admired by interwar critics would, however, do him a great injustice. The domestic nature of his work more often than not held appeal for a number of critics. Nonetheless, it is fair to say they had an equivocal relationship with his pictorial work, though indifference would likely have been Morris's response. As early as 1920 the *Daily Express* commented how *Birds of the Barbary Coast* stood out because of its colour scheme and 'would make an admirable decoration for a modern room'.²⁶ In his early days in Paris his work was praised precisely because of its 'highly original and extraordinarily decorative' nature.²⁷ The *American Review* also gave Morris a backhanded compliment when its critic stated that his work 'is modern without being exaggeratedly so, and while he paints the same flowers that others paint, his are real, and the other men and women only succeed in executing a painting'.²⁸ While the *New York Herald* also praised his pictures of gardens and birds 'for their decorative possibilities' its critic noted the 'sensitive appreciation of their inherent qualities'.²⁹ Morris took inspiration from the French, most notably Paul Gauguin's Post-Impressionist work and its tendency to lend a harsh, dark contour to objects, the effect of which was a flattening of the picture plane. This insistence on the two-dimensional rather than three-dimensionality left Morris's art 'flat and decorative', which according to the *South Wales News*, risked slipping 'into flimsiness',³⁰ rather than achieving the 'relationships of universal form' Picasso was adept at symbolizing. Referring to pictures he had presented in the London Artists Association exhibition of 1927, British *Vogue* dismissed his work outright as 'not expression but decoration. The slight and very clever modifications of these bird-forms remind of a Japanese screen rather than a picture by Cézanne. Let us hope that this good painter, now that he is become one of a group of pre-eminently serious and plastic artists, will recover his own seriousness and sense of plasticity.'[31] Another critic, despite his faint praise for the artist, went so far as to boldly claim that he 'has not the stuff that makes a major artist. His success will be more fashionable than enduring, for he has none of the major artist's seriousness, passion for form, severity, and strength of draughtsmanship.'[32] Yet another critic called upon Morris to 'lose his love of eccentricity, exemplified in the ridiculous group of cacti (nice enough in themselves)'.[33] Here, I might remind my reader that in early twentieth-century Britain such allusions to art's potential ability to be fashionable were meant as condescending and derisive.

Morris's focus on surface, flatness and the decorative would continue to inform the conceptual thrust of his paintings well into the 1930s and 1940s. *The Studio*, which had long advocated an important synergy between painting and decorative design and had reported on the new developments of Impressionism, Cubism and even Futurism, valued Morris as 'indubitably one of our most interesting landscape painters'.[34] The magazine's critic remarked on the 'command' of the tactile nature of his bird pictures, while his landscapes show 'a remarkable response to the English "spirit of place"', emphasizing the Englishness of his work.[35] Two salient features of the review stand out more than any others. The first is how the critic praised Tooth for its 'heroic step in introducing Bond Street to modernity, and were lucky in choosing Mr. Morris as their banner, for he is not only a painter as good as, technically speaking, one could expect any French painter to be, but essentially voices his work in the spirit of the real England'.[36] Nationalism and heroism commingled uneasily in the critic's reception of Morris's pictures, lending to his modernity important regional credibility in deference to ever-encroaching French currents. Morris's decorative modernism, however, was itself a way to bridge the continental influences of his training in Paris in the early 1920s while at the same time responding to distinctive British taste not yet attuned to continental aesthetics. The second point to highlight is the final remark made by the critic who buttressed his praise through an analogy of a home's architectural structure. 'Mr. Morris's work, on the other hand, is based always on a firm composition, an elemental basis of sound design, without which a picture leaves the unsatisfying impression of a house without a staircase.'[37] While the analogy should not be read exclusively through the prism of the home, it nevertheless underscores how both painting and the domestic insinuate a national ethos, for clearly English art in the English home perform a distinct and important national function.

The art of the decorative domestic

He is a young painter whose work is of that decorative quality which so well finds its place in the modern home.
The Science Christian Monitor (7 July 1924)

Morris's pictures for the home were important, so much so that their inclusion in the homes of people of note was reported on regularly and positively in the press. One particular example stands out, if for no other reason than the number of reviews it garnered, that of his painting destined for the Adam flat in Adelphi, London, of South Cardiff labour politician Major Dr Graham Pole. It was remarked that his pale, neutral cream walls were perfectly suitable backdrops to Morris's abstract floral cacophony, 'riot of colour'. Here the juxtaposition is important, and draws attention to the monochromatic wall coupled with a solitary picture, a decided affront to the former Victorian ethos of plenty. It was commented that these were the sorts of pictures women were increasingly turning to, when decorating their modern interiors.[38] In one review of this 'Queer New Kind of Art', Morris was himself characterized, 'as one would expect from his pictures, an unusual personality'. The critic also noted that it had become 'quite fashionable to have a Cedric Morris picture let into the wall of one's room as a panel. They certainly add a decorative note to the prevailing style of furnishing.'[39]

The art of collecting modern art was the subject of an article in *The Observer* by well-known art critic P. G. Konody. In his article 'Pictures for Collectors' Konody initiated his discussion by posing the question of what characterized a collector of pictures and whether he was akin to other sorts of collectors who might collect, for example, such things as postage stamps, coins or prints. He contended that '[p]aintings are', after all, 'pre-eminently destined for interior decoration, and lose much of their charm if they do not fulfil a decorative function on the wall. Overcrowding is obviously detrimental to that decorative function. Therefore the real connoisseur, who buys pictures to enjoy not their possession but their aesthetic appeal, is scarcely ever a collector in the true sense of the word.'[40] For Konody aesthetic enjoyment and appreciation negated financial considerations, a marked formal distance away from nineteenth-century concerns for the economic value of *bric-à-brac* and *objets d'art* destined for the English home. The critic singled out the work of Morris as a good aesthetic investment, one that confirmed the times and thus reinforced his being in fashion; perhaps, and likely, an oblique suggestion of a feminine, rather than heroic, attribution to his pictorial work. Other critics took a more practical position regarding what constituted good collecting practices for the modern home. A critic for *The*

Star advocated cohesion between dress and interiors. In fact, the critic maintained the belief that the dilemma of cohering body with art with interior was best resolved by women.

The problem of what pictures to buy for the home was best resolved at Mrs Wetheim's Burlington Gardens gallery where she furnished the space 'exactly like a comfortable modern drawing-room'. Here the walls were painted in a 'soft creamy yellow [while] the furniture is Queen Anne walnut'. The 'comfortable sofas and armchairs everywhere' were ideally appointed not only to view portfolios of pictures, but also to experience an entire wall devoted to a series of pictures by Morris including one of his famed bird paintings and another of an Essex church. In the same gallery another wall was devoted to the work of one of his closest friends, Hodgkins, whose work was also 'treated in the same way'. This novel formulation should, according to the critic, 'simplify the business of picture selection'.[41] On the other side of the Atlantic a similar approach had been taken up in the exhibitions of the Société Anonyme and its influential patroness and marketer Katherine Dreier. In this context, Richard Meyer has cogently concluded that the history of modernism is 'not only of artists objects, and movements, but also of exhibitions, collections, and institutional framings, which is to say in part, as a history of rooms'.[42] Notably, in the 1920s Dreier sought to show how modern art was best viewed in an 'intimate, nearly domestic surrounding that would enhance the personal experience of viewing. This experience should induce the viewer to treat art as part of everyday life, not merely as a temporary exhibition.'[43] In fact, between 1920 and 1924 the Société Annonyme held regular exhibitions of modern art in two rooms of a Mid-Town Manhattan brownstone it had acquired. In the two separate instances of Mrs Wetheim's Burlington Gardens gallery and the Société Annonyme, the needs and developments of modern art were served by women towards clearly and decisively domestic ends. It is precisely at the point when high art merges with the decorative that this uneasy relationship opens itself up to the free market and allows itself to be consumed as any other commodity, a domain long held as antagonistic to the purported creative independence of the modern genius.[44]

Despite the significant exhibitions that Roger Fry, who admired Morris's work, had curated in 1910 and 1912 featuring the work of the Impressionists and Post-Impressionists, modernist tendencies in art and especially interior decoration remained decidedly conservative and insular. Fry tirelessly challenged the rampant division between pictorial art and domestic decoration. He argued that '[u]ntold harm has been done to art by the rigid distinction between picture making and applied art. This distinction has grown up since the days of the Renaissance, and until our own time has been continually increasing ... The question arises whether the artist might not compete, and compete successfully, with the house painter.'[45] Inspired by the Arts and Crafts zeal for the social and political transformative potential of art and design, Fry's formalist modernism underscored how 'objects of daily life reveal and perpetuate the social and moral conditions of their creation'.[46] His Omega workshop was associated with the styles and ideals of the French avant-garde, foreign in origin. He and his Bloomsbury compatriots domesticated pictures while furniture became decorative and interiors were painterly. As he stated, if an artist possesses 'a subtle sense of proportion and of colour harmony which will enable him to make a definite work of creative art out of an interior', as a result he will then be able to 'transform a room completely, giving it a new feeling of space or dignity or richness'.[47] On the other side of things, Wyndham Lewis's manifestos heavily and unabashedly championed the division between the heroism of modern art and the decorative decay of the domestic. 'Prettiness', he extolled, remained the purview of artists hailing from Bloomsbury amongst others, whose 'greenery-yallery' pallor reeked of the mid-Victorian. Not only was Lewis referring to Gilbert and Sullivan's parody of Wilde, *Patience*, but so too was he explicitly commenting on the new (queer) aesthetes of modern art who were seemingly incapable of handling the new 'rough and masculine work of art'.[48]

In the early to mid-1930s writings on and criticism of art and interiors were galvanized and polarized in their concerns for nationalism, protectionism and at times down right hostility to so-called foreign incursions, particularly those emerging from the continent set to disrupt the traditions of Britain. Referring to Morris's contributions to the Exhibition of Contemporary British Art at the Anglo-German Club, one critic praised it as 'especially notable, for he is the only English artist who shows not the slightest Continental influence'. This exhibition and its artists should 'kill the Continental fancy'.[49] The critic's nationalism emerges precisely at the moment when modernist tendencies were making inroads into domestic and interior architecture in Britain. The critic's use of 'fancy' diminishes French art as decorative and fashionable, and hence fleeting. Foreign incursions into British art, design and culture were also laced with fears of feminization a direct consequence of the impact of the decorative. The 'widespread fear in the early decades of the century that British culture was being somehow feminized, infected by a "feminine" sensibility', as Cheryl Buckley has stressed, was vilified as decisively 'domestic, insular and essentially decorative'.[50]

In an unidentified press clipping titled 'Sane Art and Lunatic Art', its anonymous author set out to attack modernist influences infecting

British art. So rampant was this tendency in Britain, according to the critic, that even '[t]he Board of Education encouraged it. The B.B.C. gave it the advantage of their interest. It paid to write and lecture and teach something utterly opposed to tradition.' The author reminded his reader that '[m]odernistic pioneers were weak-minded Frenchmen – nearly all died insane – who had ambition to become painters but neither skill nor the mentality to attain the skill. They were cleverly exploited by an art-dealer ... Keep clear of modernistic art as you would of the plague ... There is no more room for anarchy in art than for anarchy in our social system.'[51] Modern art was swiftly and crudely conflated with anarchy, the embodiment of lawlessness itself. While it is easy to dismiss these words as the ramblings of an extreme traditionalist or alarmist, it nevertheless betrays a pervasive undercurrent in the criticism from the period. As Deborah Cohen has shown, '[e]ndowed with sentiment and personality, the British house was not easily transformed into Le Corbusier's machine for living ... One critic', she notes, 'complained that it gave ordinary life "the atmosphere of a perpetual cocktail party". Few among the middle classes were willing to forsake ornament.'[52] Britain in the 1920s and 1930s created 'an Englishness at once less Imperial and more inward looking, more domestic and more private, and, in terms of pre-war standards, more feminine'.[53] Nikolaus Pevsner, who immigrated to England in 1933 and studied the country's architecture and industrial design, also advocated the industrial over the domestic, abstraction over the decorative.

In his influential *Room and Book* (1932) Paul Nash set out to establish the parameters of what constituted proper English interior design, which he saw as beginning with the Adam brothers in the eighteen century. They were the first to conjure a distinct and complete aesthetic according to Nash. Their merits and uniqueness pertained less to concerns for originality than their ability to extract from 'foreign material an essence with which they founded a style, not only personal but national'.[54] Design in England for Nash had become the victim of numerous foreign incursions. Modernism was the current design phenomenon causing England's anxiety and identity crisis, one rooted in questioning how to participate and yet retain its distinct national aesthetic character. Such a dilemma is to be resolved from within England's borders, however.[55] For him the Victorians represented 'a century of fantastic chaos where it may be amusing to explore but hardly profitable'.[56] The Victorian parlour after all was nothing more than 'a demented parish bazaar'.[57] He claimed that the work of the Omega workshop and the 1925 exhibition of the work of Fry, Bell and Grant marked a 'great period of the artist renovator and the beginning of the Interior Decorator who has since captured the field'.[58] Nash, however, was keen to veer away from the Bloomsbury versions of the decorative, with their propensity toward the floral. Nash's own unique brand of the decorative, a response to encroaching continental whitewashed interior architecture, was to provide an important and needed corollary in objects but ones that never flirted with excess or degraded decorative ornamentation. Frills, thrills and the feminine were never admissible within the new, modern domestic framework he espoused and heavily circulated in his numerous publications and reviews for *Architectural Review* and *The Listener*, amongst others. Andrew Causey has argued that 'Nash believed that the plainness of modern architecture required, in ancillary areas such as curtain and carpet design, a degree of visual complexity and controlled depth of design to arrest and interest the eye and relieve the bareness of architecture, but that interest had to be created without a collapse into ornamentation, décor, or excess'.[59] Modernity was conceived as inner truth, a sort of interiority, while the decorative in its excessiveness was the surface or superficial exterior. English painters and decorators were forced to walk a precariously thin, if not altogether invisible, line.

Unlike Nash, in their book *The New Interior Decoration* from 1929 Dorothy Todd and Raymond Mortimer were at great pains to demonstrate and honour modernist currents in art and their effect on modern domestic interiors and posited the importance of the decorative in both. They stated that '[t]he qualities that distinguish a good carpet or bowl from a bad one are purely *formal*, qualities that is to say of design and texture'. These formal qualities brought Todd back to Clive Bell's notion of 'significant form',[60] evoking feelings and sensations all viewers are equally privy to. Modernist to the end, they asserted that there was not a single 'good' work of art produced under Queen Victoria's reign. However, for them, English modern art slowly had begun to produce works influenced directly by France, citing Cézanne in particular as single-handedly altering the 'face of contemporary art'.[61] Their criterion for 'good' art was that it 'must be in a sense decorative'.[62] Modern art was such that it 'has made a renaissance of interior decoration possible. The virtue of a good picture is the same order as the virtue of a good carpet.'[63] For modernists like Todd and Mortimer modern painting and modern decoration entered into an important symbiosis, and were not, as they would become, diametrically oppositional or antagonistic forces within contemporary culture. While Reed is correct to signal the 'schizophrenic' nature of Todd and Mortimer's text,[64] it nevertheless eminently speaks to the contradictory, overlapping, competing, parallel and imbricated modernism(s) that emerged in Britain in the 1920s and to a fuller extent in the 1930s.

Irises, a cockatoo and art in the garden

> *Vigorous, eccentric, serious and amused, the pictures are a bold record of a life well lived in an oasis of decency outside the system.*
> Country Life (16 April 1984)

In 1929 Morris and Lett took up the lease of The Pound Farm, in Higham, Suffolk. Having found an ideal home, they retired for good to the country, giving up their London studio in 1930, purposefully moving away from the mayhem of the city and its art critics. Life was never dull at The Pound however, for the couple's infamous and much celebrated parties continued to rage on well into the 1930s. The Pound was owned by a former student who bequeathed the estate to Morris when he died in 1932, allowing the couple to establish more permanent roots and begin thinking about formalizing the education they were already giving local students. Morris was of the opinion that painting could not be taught, and his students learnt by trial and error, and certainly by example. Although Morris continued to exhibit and sell his art, by the Second World War and more acutely after its end his teaching, rather than his creative production, became the source of his quiet fame. With the formal inauguration of the EASPD in 1937 the couple's aesthetic, cultural and social efforts were expressly channelled into a new generation of artists. These efforts would help pave the way for students like Maggi Hambling, Lucian Freud and Millie Hayes to achieve the stature they enjoyed long after Morris's and Lett's deaths. By the late 1930s, Morris had also become a victim of his own success, clearly identifying a particular style he stuck with for the remainder of his career. Once fashionable, his steadfast idiosyncratic style was precisely what caused him to become one of fashion's many victims by war's end. He also purposely, we must recall, removed himself from public view, out of site/sight of those who mattered, the gatekeepers of modern art. While Lett thrived on the social mayhem that their artistic communities in London provided them, Morris always felt like an outsider. Morris was also deeply committed to teaching in Wales, where unemployment had crippled many communities.[65]

One approached The Pound and its farm through a tunnel of trees, a 'surprising place to come upon in the quiet English scenery of East Suffolk'. According to one reporter it was owned by 'an unusual person … the painter whose bird and flower pictures are much sought after by connoisseurs of modern art'.[66] The house and garden were, for many, 'a paradise'.[67] Inside the Tudor house were 'dozens of very covetable modern paintings (many of them by Frances Hodgkins, one of the best women artists), and decorative objects of such varying character as a blue and red Welsh quilt slung over a settee, and glass balls … netted together with rope and

Of art and irises

5.4 The Pound at Higham with sculpture by John Skeaping in foreground, c. 1940–50.

suspended from the wall'.[68] In the front and back yards were large-scale sculptures by John Skeaping. Morris continued to grow his beloved cacti and various flowers in a greenhouse, and the sloped back garden faced south and boasted its own pond. The garden with its numerous flowerbeds also housed Morris's studio where he spent hours painting his beloved and famed irises amongst numerous other favoured flowers. Warburton, who provides one of the most accurate and vivid recollections of life at The Pound, remembers how the irises 'were all round him, stuck in bottles, and I remember so well their scent. Later he became well known as an iris breeder and I have never seen such beautiful colours as he created by cross-pollination.' She recalled how the characters who filled the spaces of these gardens and the rooms of their home 'made a deep impression on' her and how '[t]o work with Cedric in his garden was a delight and made one feel in tune with all around, it was also an education, and they were happy days'.[69] Entering into the circle of characters at The Pound 'was to enter a complete world, as if stepping into a novel … No less apparent was the extreme seriousness with which art itself was taken by all who were part of this circle. This blended quite naturally with their sense of fun and of extreme curiosity about individual behaviour. It would be difficult to imagine a circle in which art was more inextricable from its central subject, life'.[70]

Lett was not unlike Ricketts in that he was a dominating personality

5.5 Group shot of students with Cedric Morris: 'Belton, Boo, Jan, Self, Mildred, Cedric' c. 1930–1936.

and yet put his professional life almost entirely on hold to manage and take care of Morris's career. Morris was utterly inept as much as he was indifferent to mundane practicalities. Lett took great care of these things as well as protecting his companion from any 'unwelcome visitors or those who were considered bores'.[71] Initially the couple always hired a manservant who attended to the cooking and serving.[72] It was not until war broke out that Lett took charge of the cooking, for which he became renowned. The people and flowers were not the only living creatures that filled the various spaces. There was also the menagerie of animals that Morris lovingly tended to as well.[73] Animals had always played a significant role in Morris's domestic life and public image. In the late 1920s reporters often photographed Morris with Maria Marten the couple's rabbit, of which the press made much. One could usually find Ptolemy the peacock strutting about, while Cockey the yellow-chested cockatoo and Rubio the scarlet, green and blue macaw were free to roam all quarters of the house. While Muscovy the mallard inhabited the garden, parrots also flew about the garden and in and out of the house. Unlike Cockey whose vocabulary was limited to 'Five, five, five ... hallo', Rubio possessed a slightly richer vocabulary, the result of his time with a sailor in Jamaica, brought over to England by Stella Hamilton (one of Lett's first of many female lovers).

Warburton began to take art lessons from Morris and Lett three days a week in 1937, the year the EASPD took official shape in a building in Dedham three to four miles away from where they lived at The Pound. The EASPD was staffed by Morris (who taught painting), Lett and Ian Brinkworth; the latter two taught drawing. Margery Sisson, who lived with her husband, an architect in Dedham, served as the accommodation secretary. When the number of students exceeded the rooms available she found them accommodations in cottages and pubs in the local village, which were also called upon to house life models brought in from London. During the summer months life classes were held in the back garden, where students also learnt how to prepare their own canvases. While painting in the gardens or at the nearby river, Morris would visit each student and at the end of every day both he and Lett would provide much-needed and generally appreciated criticism of their work. As with their personalities, their approach to instruction differed vastly. Lett had a 'splendidly authoritative voice that he used to advantage with his very original wit, sometimes to the discomfort of others'.[74] He was also a good draughtsman, while Morris was decidedly more instinctive and as a result more laid back in his comments. The students' space also played host to exhibitions of their work. Warburton reported how one exhibition in December 1937 brought in nearly two hundred visitors over the two days of its opening and several of the forty students represented sold art. Various rooms provided special showcases for drawing, textiles and oil painting.[75] Other exhibitions followed and were usually accompanied by fancy dress balls largely prepared by Lett. The goal of the EASPD was to allow a space in which amateurs and professionals alike could work side by side in a free and unrestrictive (near domestic) environment. This allowed students to create the most sincere work, helping them to find their own style, aesthetic and personal identity. At The Pound life and art commingled freely and loosely and extended into the famous dinner-table gatherings. The school burnt down on 26 July 1939, destroying many of their papers and numerous pictures including work by their good friends Christopher Wood, Frank Dobson and Frances Hodgkins. When news of the fire reached the local community, artist and future president (1944–49) of the Royal Academy Sir Alfred Munnings could be seen driving around his car cheering the death of modern art in the region. Munnings was a staunch conservative whose acerbic and vitriolic attacks of continental modernism were often channelled towards compatriots like Morris and Lett.

5.6 Sir Cedric Morris, c. 1920.

The chorography of the separate spheres

> *The greatest crime at Benton End was to be boring!*
> Ronald Blythe

Despite the fire, life got back to normal rather quickly for Morris and Lett and by the end of 1939, they had purchased Benton End (for £1,000). Located on nearly four acres of land, the large sixteenth-century Georgian-fronted Elizabethan house overlooked the Brett valley, near Hadleigh, and had been left abandoned for nearly fifteen years. The house was large enough to accommodate eight live-in students and countless day students. Here, the cult of the home took on layers of additional meaning. At Benton End, for the first time in their history, the couple lived and taught under the same roof. As at The Pound, the residents of Hadleigh regarded the residents of Benton End with a degree of suspicion. It was here within the couple's home that they taught modern art, a tradition premised entirely on priding itself as being anti-domestic, virile and indifferent to sentimental bonds. These dictates were not

5.7 Benton End, n.d.

only challenged with indifference and impunity, but were thrown out altogether. After all, the goal of the school was to continue to provide students with 'an oasis of decency for artists outside the system'.[76] Another aim of the EASPD was 'to decrease the division that has grown up between the creative artist and the general public'.[77] Indeed, one and all, were welcome, even students who could ill afford the fees. Morris and Lett provided a queer space not entirely unlike Edward Perry Warren. Although decidedly wealthier, Warren saw to it, like the couple, that the home was opened up to all those who sought out knowledge and community, regardless of class and finance.

With Morris and Lett, however, women were always treated as equal to men, shown neither favour nor condescension. Women were regarded as equal participants in the life and culture of what Lett and Morris constructed. In his analysis of the life at Benton End, Morphet compares it to the Bloomsbury Group's Charleston, the Sussex home of Vanessa Bell and Duncan Grant. He writes how

> [b]oth were many-roomed, centuries old houses, not too far from London and with walled gardens, which provided constant motifs for the two artists who lived there. In each house art, food and the way of life had strong connections with the Mediterranean world, as well as with that of Paris and Bloomsbury in the 1920s, so that the great majority of the remarkably varied range of people who visited both homes felt they had learned there something valuable about life. Finally both flourished in economic and social conditions, which were destined not to last.[78]

Morris felt increasingly alienated from English and artistic societies and when they moved to Benton End it seemed that London was now officially a distant land and part of the past. This was certainly fuelled by his love of Wales, his Labour Party sympathies and his sexuality.[79]

Benton End had large rooms on the ground level, on the first storey there was a large studio, and not surprisingly many cats came to inhabit their new home. Then a young and impressionable Welsh artist, Glyn Morgan recalled his first night in the house and the imprint its interior and objects inscribed on him:

> A large scarred and studded zinc-covered table stood on the uneven brick floor. On the table an enormous pot of irises echoed a painting (now in Tate Britain) of the same subject on the wall; the air was heavy with the pungent scent of the flowers and the room roared with conversation and laughter. To a young man from the Welsh valleys the whole place was exotic and exciting.[80]

Although The Pound offered its inhabitants, students and visitors a paradise, Benton End seemed to take this wish-fulfilment to a whole new level of accomplishment. For some it was not another life or alternative reality, it was reality itself, while the world outside its gardens was merely a 'shadow world'. It became a sanctuary and even an addiction for some. Morgan 'never left without tears in [his] eyes'. For him '[i]t was difficult to convey the magic of such a place in words, but I think it stemmed essentially from Cedric's personality. Why was he so much loved by so many people? I think mainly because he possessed a freedom of spirit that few achieve and this enabled him to give out unstintingly, expecting nothing in return but good manners and a commitment to work. His sense of humour was simple but robust.'[81] For Ellis Carpenter, '[g]oing through the gates of Benton End was like arriving in France. There was a bohemian atmosphere – the wine, the food and the marvellous conversation.'[82] These visitors were equally important to these men, and Lett honoured their presence by giving them their own nickname and immortalized them within the interior by pasting their name with cut-out newsprint script on the walls of the downstairs lavatory. Again, not unlike with Lewes House, the space of the lavatory, long associated with homosexuals, begs signification of a queer kind, an index as a sort of decorative memorialization that forever bound together community, interior space and presence.

The dinning room at Benton End was part of a massive space at whose centre was a grand refectory table. Drying herbs coupled with ropes of garlic hung together on the kitchen door, as if warding off evil intruders from Lett's inner sanctum. Coloured glass, vases and an assortment of objects were placed side by side on shelves, the debris of their numerous travels to distant lands. Overall the kitchen was chaotic, lacking any decorum, hygiene or order, decidedly contrary to English or rational dictates. Some called the kitchen downright 'primitive'.[83] Washing-up following dinners was the responsibility of students, who had to navigate the piles of bills, books, papers and supplies that made every surface their permanent residence. Floors were also barely discernible through the mounds of bottles and saucers for the numerous house pets as well as the ancient Aga long past its glory days.[84] One could equally find 'woollen underwear steeping in bowls'.[85] Despite the chaos the kitchen presented, Benton End had 'an overall feeling of Spartan grandeur'.[86]

Dinner conversations orchestrated by Lett were meant to scandalize, shock, entertain and sometimes even inform the community gathered. To many of the students Lett was 'intimidating', even 'malicious', and yet 'warm-hearted'. He always managed to supply one and all with two tremendous meals a day, which, without exception, were accompanied with wine as well as 'loud and eloquent complaints and scurrilous comments on everyone he could think of … The conversation was unusually free and sometimes bawdy' and Gwyneth Reynolds confessed to being so 'naïve [that] it often went above [her] head'.[87] Humour and camp were also never too far away from Morris's own repertoire of entertainment. Sometimes he would walk around 'with a wilting, wincing step but could laugh at "screaming queens" … He was outrageous, he was fun.'[88] During dinners at which Morris held court, Lett was always sure to draw attention away from his partner, leaving the room after serving the food nonchalantly quipping, 'Do you know that camels copulate backwards?', arresting Morris in his conversation with the others.[89] After dinner was served, however, Lett would immediately retire to his room, while Morris would often be found 'curled up in a flowerbed'.[90] Many years later Warburton noted how on her several visits to Benton End, having long left it behind, Lett would often be found 'upstairs sipping gin, smoking cigars, making obscene "toys" out of *objets-trouvé* [sic], and painting slowly'.[91] Recurring in countless recollections and fond reminiscences by students was the couple's own queer articulation of the separate spheres which was informed by a chorography of separation, independence and perhaps even at times indifference. The elaborate topography of Benton End was acutely premised on the logic of circulation and exchange, between the spaces of the interior and the gardens, through which communication, bodily interaction and spatial dynamics were played out. Gardens grand, rich and expansive as those of Benton End were necessarily an important extensive of the domestic landscape. What they constructed for themselves was a new and unique articulation of separate spheres within the domestic landscape. For Morris the garden at Benton End took on its most complete and perfect articulation, and for many it served as a unique 'collector's cabinet'.[92]

Morris and Lett possessed what Diana Fuss has discussed in another context, a 'confounding a sense of security with a fear of isolation, or a promise of seclusion with a threat of suffocation'.[93] Cedric's domain was the garden, while Lett presided over the house. 'Lett made his presence felt all over the house, even when lurking in his room. It was widely accepted that he listened in to telephone conversations on the extension in his bedroom'.[94] The choreography at once of both distant intimacy and separate togetherness within the landscape of their home meant that students had to negotiate between the various, at times, highly distinct and volatile spaces, adhering to codes unique to each. Separate spheres were then not only erected between inside and out, but within the home itself. The result was a division of space – the separate spheres – which was premised in and outside the house rather than along the public/private axis; as within the myriad spaces of Benton End no such division could be entertained, where work and home life were indistinguishable. The school, and by extension the domestic landscape itself, was dominated by tensions and power struggles between Lett and Morris, given how the former liked to create little dramas and tended towards gossip. Carpenter, for example, remarked how the two 'were like an old married couple arguing gently. Lett would tease Cedric and Cedric would get annoyed, put his head on one side and his hands on his hips and say "well, we will have to agree to disagree"'.[95] Students could sometimes 'detect a certain rift between [Morris] and Lett', noting how 'Lett never appears at meal table with Cedric and guests; Cedric never ventures into the kitchen' and how 'they have separate rooms and studios'.[96] Some students became painfully aware of the role each had to play within physical as much as emotional topography; all were conscious of the time they were compelled to spend separately with Lett upstairs and Morris in his studio or garden. In this way, I want to highlight how students' experiences, whether during their education or long after on visits to the couple's estate, were compelled to secure, confirm and perform a queer space and time. Despite their complicity and companionship, the couple fundamentally 'led a bachelor lifestyle with no comforts, not even easy chairs or proper heating, and through the winter the house was locked up and Cedric and Lett went their separate ways abroad'.[97]

Their relationship was never easy from the outset, despite their falling madly in love from the moment they laid eyes on each other. Lett dated the beginning of their ongoing troubles of joyful highs and unbearable lows to December 1923. In letters to each other from the period, mention is made of other intimacies and infatuations, which seem to have taken their toll on the couple. In a letter from Morris to Lett,

Of art and irises

5.8 Arthur Lett-Haines takes some sun, c. 1930–36.

their infidelities are candidly mentioned, a writing culture of openness not easily discerned in the previous generation with men like Shannon and Ricketts.[98] In another follow-up letter dated 14 March 1925 from Morris to Lett, the tone is strained and overwrought with discussions of Morris leaving with Paul Odo Cross for a month in Bordeaux, France. It was clearly only an infatuation, one whose 'obvious' remedy was to see 'too much of each other', at least according to Morris.[99] This situation, while on the surface free from social constraints, was not without anxiety and fear. Not having heard from Lett for some time, Morris was clearly nervous their relationship might have proved to be more than mere infatuation. He ends the letter: 'P.S. I don't want you to stay away from me unless you want to!', leaving room to let Lett back into his intimate life.[100] In a final letter regarding this amorous trist, Morris concluded:

> I have not telegraphed because this is too complicated for that – Now for the truth as near as possible. Of course I want you to come here as soon as

possible. Now about Paul – The infatuation I think with both of us is much better ... but I have not finished with him or he with me – I can't cut him altogether out of my life for he loves me.[101]

The seemingly obsessive love for each other did end, however, and this relationship was one of a number both men entertained throughout the years; Lett primarily with women, Morris with men. Amongst Lett's long-term and most notable affairs was one with artist and member of their community Kathleen Hale. She described her former lover years later in the following manner:

> Lett was six feet tall, with a fine physique, and regular features saved from being conventionally good-looking by his slightly satanic eyebrows, piercing grey eyes (which I teased him by likening to pieces of splintered glass), and a mouth he described as resembling a split liver. He went bald in his early twenties, but was inspired to keep his whole head shaved like a Tibetan monk, giving him a distinguished but sometimes sinister air. His personality was composed of many warring factors. He was sophisticated, but could reveal sudden glimpses of child-like innocence. Mischievous and sometimes wicked, he liked to dramatise situations, and delighted in stirring up scandals. He was exceptionally patient and unself-serving, but, though fundamentally affectionate and gentle, his razor-sharp perception of the strengths and weaknesses of the human race made him an adept manipulator, able to detect people's most sensitive areas and then wound them.[102]

While these liaisons certainly took their toll for various and sundry reasons, it was perhaps the garden that took on one of the most acute forms of distance between the two men. While it served as inspiration to Morris and countless students of art and floriculture, it also grew into a source of contention and hostility on the part of Lett, jealous of how it took up more time than their relationship did. Beth Chatto remembers her time with Morris, the gardener, at Benton End with fond nostalgia, but notes that '[i]t was not always dream-like. Meal times could be electrified by sudden squalls and conflicts, but the roof never fell in. We sat and waited, suffering with our idols, seeing them, as human beings, our bonds of shyness shattered by the storm.'[103] Already by the war, Lett was beginning to complain that Morris was 'a contrary and stubborn dreamer who won't help a bit about the place, whereas he himself would love to paint but his time is spent in endless cooking and washing-up'.[104] By the 1960s Lett was complaining that Benton End was less an artists' retreat and home for the couple than a commercial nursery. It is fair to say that Morris became an avid collector and producer of numerous award-winning hybrid irises of his own, many of which are regarded today as the finest in the world.

Morris started to breed irises in 1936, and John Banting and Daphne

Bousfield could be seen at their place working about in his gardens. He was the first person in the country to produce a pink iris, so admired by the Queen Mother that she allowed it to be named after her own home, Strathmore.[105] This was an unusual name, given Benton was included in the names of his most prized hybrid irises: Benton Ophelia, Benton Fandango and Benton Demote, for example. Each summer Morris usually grew a thousand new iris seedlings. Many of the varieties he cultivated were given names of those close to him or who held a special place in his life. Benton Cordelia was named after the wife of sculptor Frank Dobson, while Benton Rubio was named after his menacing brightly coloured macaw, which would often silently nip female students' ankles while they painted outside in the gardens. In her queer readings of American artist John Singer Sargent, art historian Alison Syme shows how since the nineteenth century 'invert artists ... mobilized the idea of cross-fertilization and the hermaphroditic sexuality of flowers to "naturalize" sexual inversion'.[106] Des Esseintes, in Huysmans's celebrated decadent novel *A rebours*, declared that 'man is able to bring about in a few years a range of choice that slothful Nature can only produce after several centuries; unquestionably, as matters stand today the only artists, the real artists, are the horticulturalists'.[107] Indeed within Des Esseintes's artificial world, man creates his own built environment and aesthetic lifestyle. Morris was a modernist descendant of the same aesthetic ideal as both decorative painter and cross-pollinator, creating hybrid species using nature and defying it at the same time and always within the extended confines of the domestic realm. While most of the Benton irises were given female names, what they all shared in common was Benton, the home of their birth and the flourishing of a community. The space of Morris's garden is a hybrid one, one always in the process of fecundity and growth, natural and artificial, but always first and foremost decorative.

'Concerning Flower Painting': death and the closet

> A personality like his does not easily leave a house ... The summer after he died I stayed again at Benton End to paint ... The next year I called once more. The house was just a house, the rooms seemed half the size. Cedric had finally gone.
>
> Glyn Morgan

Morris's lifelong love affair with flowers and irises in particular also held a definitive aesthetic position for him in regards to the history of British art. In an article he penned for *The Studio*, 'Concerning Flower Painting', in May 1942, the artist noted that there is a difference to be made between 'flower painting and a good painting of flowers', and

5.9 Sir Cedric Morris. *Iris Seedlings*, 1943.

that unfortunately the 'English love of flowers has found a nasty mate in English lack of taste'.[108] However, for Morris the most important aspect of creative production was a direct relationship with the subject matter. Indeed, in regards to flower painting, no one could have possibly held more of a deep relationship than he with his subject matter. Long have flowers held a hidden and privileged position in queer culture, often operating as an index for sexuality itself, whether it was Wilde's decadent floriculture he devised with the help of Frank Miles or Robert Hichens in his *The Green Carnation* from 1894, in which the flower itself became an identifying sign amongst homosexuals in an urban environment fraught with danger and surveillance.[109] Floriculture and the hothouse, however, also became identified as a symbol for the decadence of the past faced with the heroism of modern architecture and the new virility that architects were advocating. Le Corbusier was amongst the most vociferous detractors of feminine domesticity in its competition with masculinist modern architecture. In *Toward a New Architecture*, Le Corbusier attacked his 'enemies', who were '[a]rchitects, emerging from the Schools, those hot-houses where blue hortensias and green chrysanthemums are forced, and where unclean orchids are cultivated'.[110] Here floriculture is equated with a negative and aberrant form of architecture, that is, the decorative domestic that modern architecture was meant to weed out. What Le Corbusier and others advanced was the home as a 'machine for living', a mechanical, rather than organic, spatial regime.

Reed contends that 'Bloomsbury's exclusion from the modernist mainstream', and I would importantly add The Pound and later Benton End, 'was part of broader trends as, around 1930, the multiplicity of self-styled modernist movements was narrowed to the few that could be sequenced to culminate in the International Style'.[111] By the 1930s national concerns surrounding gender and sexuality made Bloomsbury's long-held concern for the domestic all the more a palpable reason it was 'pushed ever further toward the margins of the modern'.[112] Peter Wollen has challenged the separation of high art and the decorative in the early decades of the twentieth century by exploring the work of Henri Matisse, Leon Bakst and Paul Poiret.[113] According to Wollen, these artists were 'the first modernists. They broke with the official art by which they were formed, but without embracing functionalism or rejecting the body and the decorative.'[114] However, the subsequent discourse around them and their respective disciplines has been purposefully deployed as a means to eradicate any notion of excess or decorative sensuality to the work of these men. In this way, one might perversely argue that the decorative is itself the site of modernist excess, not only that which falls outside of modernism, but that which also marks itself out as perverse, effeminate and degenerate. As Isobel Frank argues, the 'story of Modernism is the story of the dismemberment of the concept of decorative art'.[115] It is also, significantly, the story of the dismemberment of otherness, deferring this difference to its margins. Nancy Troy also queries the disavowal of decoration in modern art when she states:

> In view of the fact that for most of the twentieth century most modernist discourse has consistently maintained a distinction between high art and the decorative arts, embracing the former while keeping the latter at a distance, one might well ask what it is about the decorative arts that has made them so unacceptable to both practitioners and historians of modern art.[116]

Theorists and historians alike have ensured that the decorative remains 'modernism's other', to borrow from Tag Gronberg.[117] In the postwar era, those days of openness and celebration of life and art that Morris, Lett and their friends conjured seemed long gone. During the Second World War and in its aftermath, arch-conservative critics like Clement Greenberg along with avant-garde artists pitted masculine heroism against domesticity. They exhorted that their art 'must insult anyone who is spiritually attuned to interior decoration; pictures for the home; pictures for over the mantel'.[118] He famously and staunchly advocated: '[d]ecoration is the spectre that haunts modernist painting, and part of the latter's formal mission is to find ways of using the decorative against itself'.[119] Greenberg's zealous view of the decorative and its supposed parasitic relationship to modern art would not only come to inflect itself on contemporary criticism, but was also subsequently deployed to revisit the art of the past, a retrospective attempt to sever forever the indelible symbiosis modern art enjoyed with the decorative. This left little room for modernists like Morris whose work unabashedly cavorted with the pale walls of modern interiors. However, their exclusion from the canons of modernism and modern art is not merely academic and fought on the fields of art's wars, but fought also in the trenches of sexual equality and emancipation. Upon examination of Charles Harrison's heavily circulated expansive text *English Art and Modernisn, 1900–1939*, as but one example of this disavowal or amnesia of modernism, Morris is conspicuously absent from discussions of what constitutes truly English modern art. Morris's omission from the canon is not entirely surprising given how Greenberg famously declared that when the artist turned away from abstraction, 'he became an interior decorator'.[120] The history of British modern art has yet to be written with a view toward the study of the interior, despite how it has informed the developments of British modernism itself. The domestic, after all, provided the Englishman refuge against continental incursions on to domestic soil.

In *The Times* obituary for Sir Cedric Morris from 1982, no mention of Arthur Lett-Haines, the man with whom he shared, lived and loved for sixty years, is ever made. Rather, the final and solitary sentence of the obituary read: 'He was unmarried'.[121] Within a modernist ethos that has dominated Western academic, political and cultural life, the cult of the domestic, sexual difference and the decorative beauty of flowers still seem to stand in as the enemy, even as late as the 1980s. *The Times* shamed the couple's intimacy and life by obscuring *the love that (still) dare not speak its name*. Perhaps the solution, then, is simply, as Morris himself might have suggested, to stop and smell the irises.

Notes

1. In 1947 Morris succeeded his father as the Ninth Baronet.
2. R. Morphet, *Cedric Morris* (London: Tate Gallery, 1984), pp. 19–20.
3. J. Warburton, *A Painter's Progress, Part of a Life, 1920–1987*, unpublished manuscript, Tate tga 986.2.29.
4. Morgan in B. Tufnell et al., *Cedric Morris and Let-Haines: Teaching and Life* (Norwich and Cardiff: Norfolk Museums and Archaeology, 2003), p. 5.
5. In B. Tufnell et al., *Cedric Morris and Let Haines*, p. 6.
6. Ronald Blythe in G. Reynolds and D. Grace, *Benton End Remembered: Cedric Morris, Arthur Lett-Haines and the East Anglian School of Painting and Drawing* (London: Unicorn Press, 2002), p. 146.
7. Mollie Russell-Smith in Reynolds and Grace, *Benton End Remembered*, p. 30.
8. Morphet, *Cedric Morris*, p. 14.
9. E. Hemingway, *The Sun Also Rises* (New York: Scribner, 2006 [1926]), p. 28.
10. *The American Review*, January 1925.
11. No identification is given for this press clipping. Tate archive file no. 8317-8-1.
12. *Daily Chronicle*, 28 February 1927.
13. Tate archive file no. 8317.1.1.1120.
14. *The Star*, 8 April 1931.
15. Tate archive file no. 8317-13–2.
16. *The Paris Times*, 9 September 1924.
17. *South Wales Daily News*, 18 December 1925.
18. T. Crow, *Modern Art in the Common Culture* (New Haven and London: Yale University Press, 1996), p. 4.
19. *The Times*, 10 October 1935.
20. British *Vogue*, 17 April 1929.
21. L. Tickner, *Modern Life and Modern Subjects: British Art in the Early Twentieth Century* (New Haven and London: Yale University Press, 2000), p. 190.
22. C. Reed (ed.), *Not at Home: The Suppression of Domesticity in Modern Art and Architecture* (London: Thames and Hudson, 1996), p. 7.
23. See D. Slater, *Consumer Culture and Modernity* (Cambridge: Polity Press, 1997), pp. 13–14.
24. See W. Benjamin, *The Arcades Project* (Cambridge and London: The Belknap Press of Harvard University, 1999); F. Hartzell, 'The Velvet Touch: Fashion, Furniture and the Fabric of the Interior', *Fashion Theory*, vol. 13 no. 1 (2009); J. Potvin, 'The Velvet Masquerade: Fashion, Interior Design and the Furnished Body', in John Potvin and Alla Myzelev (eds.), *Fashion, Interior Design and the Contours of Modern Identity* (Aldershot and Burlington: Ashgate, 2010).
25. Morphet, *Cedric Morris*, p. 11.
26. *Daily Express*, 11 February 1920.
27. *The Paris Times*, 9 September 1924
28. *The American Review*, November 1924.
29. *New York Herald*, 12 October 1924.

30 Unidentified press clipping: *South Wales News*, 'Welsh Painters: Development of the Impressionism'.
31 British *Vogue*, March 1927.
32 *Scotsman*, 11 April 1931.
33 *Connoisseur*, June 1929.
34 T. W. Earp, 'Cedric Morris' *The Studio*, vol. xcvi, no. 427 (October 1928), p. 242.
35 *Ibid.*, p. 242.
36 *Ibid.*, p. 241.
37 *Ibid.*, p. 245.
38 See *Western Mail*, 9 February 1926; *The Evening News*, 5 February 1926.
39 *The Leeds Mercury*, 9 February 1926.
40 *The Observer*, 24 January 1931.
41 *The Star*, 11 October 1935.
42 R. Meyer, 'Big, Middle-Class Modernism', *October*, no. 131 (winter 2010), p. 79.
43 *Ibid.*
44 N. Troy, *Modernism and the Decorative Arts in France: Art Nouveau to Le Corbusier* (London and New Haven: Yale University Press, 1991), pp. 1–2.
45 R. Fry, 'The Artist as Decorator', in Christopher Reed (ed.), *A Roger Fry Reader* (Chicago and London: University of Chicago Press, 1996 [1917]), p. 207.
46 C. Reed, *A Roger Fry Reader* (Chicago and London: University of Chicago Press, 1996c), p. 169.
47 Fry, 'The Artist as Decorator', p. 208.
48 Lewis in C. Reed, *Bloomsbury Rooms: Modernism, Subculture, and Domesticity* (New York: Yale University Press, 2004), p. 4.
49 *Yorkshire Post*, 23 December 1933.
50 C. Buckley, 'The Decorated Object: Gender, Modernism and the Design of Industrial Ceramics in Britain in the 1930s', in Bridget Elliott and Janice Helland (eds.), *Women Artists and the Decorative Arts 1880–1935: The Gender of Ornament* (Aldershot and Burlington: Ashgate, 2002), p. 54.
51 Tate archive file no. 8317.7.1.8.
52 D. Cohen, *Households Gods: The British and Their Possessions* (New Haven and London: Yale University Press, 2006), p. 172.
53 A. Light, *Forever England: Femininity, Literature and Conservativism between the Wars* (London: Routledge, 1991), p. 8.
54 P. Nash, *Room and Book* (London and New York: Soncino Press and Charles Scribner's Sons, 1932), p. 4.
55 *Ibid.*, pp. 7–8.
56 *Ibid.*, p. 16.
57 *Ibid.*, p. 18.
58 *Ibid.*, p. 26.
59 A. Causey, 'Paul Nash as Designer', in J. Peto and D. Loveday (eds.), *Modern Britain 1929–1939* (London: Design Museum, 1999), p. 112.
60 D. Todd and R. Mortimer, *The New Interior Decoration* (London: B. T. Batsford, 1929), p. 9.

61 *Ibid.*, p. 10. It is worth noting that Morris was himself referred to, in the 1920s, as the Cézanne of Newlyn.
62 *Ibid.*, p. 11.
63 *Ibid.*, p. 12.
64 Reed, *Bloomsbury Rooms*, p. 1.
65 For example, he taught courses in design and handicraft in 1939.
66 *Daily Mail*, 14 February 1933.
67 See for example Warburton, *A Painter's Progress*, Tate tga 968.2.20.
68 *Daily Mail*, 14 February 1933.
69 Warburton, *A Painter's Progress*, Tate tga 968.2.20.
70 Morphet, *Cedric Morris*, pp. 11–13.
71 Warburton, *A Painter's Progress*, Tate tga 968.2.20.
72 These were, not surprisingly, equally eccentric characters. One servant named Bob was known for making inappropriate comments to special guests when serving in his white jacket.
73 At Benton End they would also own a goat, Little Billy, who eventually had to be eaten during the lean years of the Second World War.
74 Warburton, *A Painter's Progress*, Tate tga 968.2.20.
75 *Ibid.*
76 Morphet, *Cedric Morris*, p. 73.
77 Morphet in Reynolds and Grace, *Benton End Remembered*, pp. 11–12.
78 Morphet, *Cedric Morris*, p. 74.
79 *Ibid.*, p. 61.
80 In Reynolds and Grace, *Benton End Remembered*, p. 17.
81 *Ibid.*, p. 20.
82 *Ibid.*, p. 49.
83 Gwyneth Reynolds in Reynolds and Grace, *Benton End Remembered*, p. 43.
84 *Ibid.*, p. 19.
85 *Ibid.*, p. 43.
86 R. Blythe, 'Sir Cedric Morris', in Susan Hill (ed.), *People, Essays and Poems* (London: Hogarth Press, 1983), p. 27.
87 In Reynolds and Grace, *Benton End Remembered*, p. 42.
88 Glyn Morgan in *ibid.*, p. 20.
89 Elizabeth Wright in *ibid.*, p. 146.
90 Glyn Morgan in *ibid.*, p. 17.
91 Warburton diary entry for 19 March 1973, Tate tga 968.2.
92 *Country Life*, 17 May 1979.
93 D. Fuss, *A Sense of an Interior: Four Writers and the Rooms that Shaped Them* (New York and London: Routledge, 2004), p. 14.
94 Glyn Morgan in Reynolds and Grace, *Benton End Remembered*, p. 19.
95 In *ibid.*, p. 51.

96 Bernard Reynolds in *ibid.*, pp. 37–8.
97 Gwyneth Reynolds in *ibid.*, p. 44.
98 Letter dated 8 March 1925, Tate archive file no. 8317.1.4.2.
99 Letter dated 14 March 1925, Tate archive file no. 8317.1.4.7.
100 Letter dated 2 April 1925, Tate archive file no. 8317.1.4.5.
101 Undated letter, Tate archive file no. 8317.1.4.10.
102 In Grace and Reynolds, *Benton End Remembered*, p. 55.
103 B. Chatto, 'Sir Cedric Morris, Artist-Gardener', in David Wheeler (ed.), *Hortus Revisited: A Twenty-First Birthday Anthology* (London: Frances Lincoln Limited, 2008), p. 20.
104 Bernard Reynolds in Grace and Reynolds, *Benton End Remembered*, p. 34.
105 Chatto, 'Sir Cedric Morris, Artist-Gardener', p. 18.
106 A. Syme, *A Touch of Blossom: John Singer Sargent and the Queer Flora of Fin-de-Siècle Art* (University Park: Pennsylvania State University Press, 2010), p. 12.
107 J. K. Huysmans, *Against Nature* (Oxford: Oxford World's Classics, 1998 [1884]). J., F. B., 'When a Man Entertains: What a Bachelor Should Do in the Position of Host', *Homes and Gardens* (June 1926), p. 79.
108 Morris C., 'Concerning Flower Painting', *The Studio* (May 1942), pp. 124, 130.
109 See G. Chauncey Jr, *Gay New York: Gender, Urban Culture and the Making of the Gay Male World. 1890–1940* (New York: Basic Books, 1994), pp. 77–80.
110 Le Corbusier, *Toward a New Architecture* (London: Architectural Press, 1927 [1923]), p. 20.
111 Reed, *Bloomsbury Rooms*, p. 2.
112 *Ibid.*, p. 272.
113 See P. Wollen, *Raiding the Icebox: Reflections on Twentieth-Century Culture* (Bloomington and Indianapolis: Indiana University Press, 1993).
114 *Ibid.*, pp. 17–18.
115 I. Frank (ed.), *The Theory of European Decorative Art: An Anthology of European and American Writings, 1750–1940* (New Haven and London: Yale University Press, 2000), p. 1.
116 N. J. Troy, *Modernism and the Decorative Arts in France: Art Nouveau to Le Corbusier* (London and New Haven: Yale University Press, 1991), p. 1.
117 T. Gronberg, 'Décoration: Modernism's Other', *Art History*, vol. 15, no. 4 (December 1992), p. 547.
118 E. H. Johnson (ed.), *American Artists on Art: From 1940 to 1980* (Boulder: Westview Press, 1982), pp. 10–11.
119 C. Greenberg, 'Milton Avery', *Arts Magazine*, no. 32 (December 1957), p. 41.
120 C. Greenberg, 'Review of Exhibitions of Joan Miro, Fernand Léger, and Wassily Kandinsky', in John O'Brian (ed.), *The Collected Essays and Criticisms: Volume 1, Perceptions and Judgements, 1939–1944* (Chicago and London: University of Chicago Press, 1986), p. 64.
121 *The Times*, 10 February 1982.

III ✧ Stage design for living

6 ✧ Coward in the room: interwar glamour and the performances of a queer modernity

> *I cannot remember*
> *I cannot remember*
> *The house where I was born*
> *But I know it was Waldegrave Road*
> *Teddington, Middlesex*
> *Not far from the border of Surrey*
> *An unpretentious abode*
> *While, I believe,*
> *Economy forced us to leave*
> *In rather a hurry.*
> Noël Coward

FOR NOËL Coward (1899–1973) all that comes to mind of the first home he grew up in, perhaps the most emotive for a child, was the family's inability to pay the rent, forcing them to flee. Transformed into verse, Coward's recollection weds trauma, loss and memory with the modern interior, experiences at once autobiographical as much as aesthetic. Despite these humble experiences of domestic flight and financial malaise, Coward would spend the rest of his life overcoming his economic and social limitations to forge a visual and material culture that would help define an entire generation. Coward's rise to celebrity was achieved through sheer grit and wit. He began his career as an actor and playwright living in the attic of the family's 111 Ebury Street, London, house where they also rented out rooms to lodgers. In 1919 he was offered $500 for a year's option on *The Last Trick* by Gilbert Miller in New York. He accepted and immediately took himself to a tailor to indulge in a shopping spree, bought a second-hand grand piano and paid off the rent of the family's Ebury Street home. Coward established himself quickly as an arbiter of style. Throughout his life the actor-playwright embodied the power that visual and material culture can bestow; a life and oeuvre that tangibly chronicle social mobility and accrued cultural cachet. Queer author, friend, fellow playwright and noted journalist Beverley Nichols confessed to finding Coward 'not only the most entertaining figure of the decade [1920s] but also, in a sense which few critics would admit, the most significant and enduring'. Neither Coward nor Nichols came from economic or social privilege, and both suffered at the hands of what Nichols defiantly identified as 'the hearty, muscular, hair-on-the-chest type of critics … At the time when Noël's first success was being slanged as morbid and degenerate, my own first novel – a little school story called *Parade* – was being attacked as epicene and decadent.'[1]

Nichols and Coward worked and played in deeply conservative times. The 1920s witnessed numerous British artists and writers (including Sir Cedric Morris and Arthur Lett-Haines) fleeing London to the more liberating bohemian enclaves of Paris and Berlin. King George V famously proclaimed: 'I thought men like that shot themselves', in reference to a queer aristocrat who also fled Britain amidst scandal and shame.[2] The roaring twenties were provocatively ushered into Britain when in early 1918 right-wing Member of Parliament Noël Pemberton Billing published a scathing article, 'The Cult of the Clitoris', in which he accused Robbie Ross, Oscar Wilde's former consort, of membership in a network of 47,000 homosexual traitors who were aiding and abetting the Germans. It was through Ross that Coward entered into the social world of queers and actors, having attended a party at his home. This was the only encounter the two enjoyed as Ross died two short days after meeting Coward on 5 October 1918, after suffering a heart attack brought on by the scandal. Ross's former friend Bosie (Lord Alfred Douglas) testified against him in the trial, outing him as the supposed 'leader of all the sodomites in London'.[3] Scapegoating and witch-hunts like this one took on operatic proportions and unfortunately were not uncommon in the culture of shame and blackmail the Labouchere Amendment had unleashed. It is within this environment that Coward first encountered his sexual identity, which he always preferred to keep private, hidden from public view. However, as we have seen, the Labouchere Amendment made no distinction between public and private in its policing of the borders of space and sexuality.

As a *bachelor of a different sort* who continued to live with his family in different ways well into adult life, Coward acted out his role as narrator of a queer sort of modernity through his scripts, characters and stages. Thad Logan points out how '[d]escriptive detail' in classical narratives is seen as a filler between moments of narratological importance and as a result 'must be subordinate to the whole work: ornament, innately inferior, must be disciplined, must serve rather than dominate'.[4] Although the dismissal of detail and anecdote as mere ornament (read: the decorative) was the call to arms for modernists to purge the superfluous, the extraneous and the excessive, an analogy between narrative and the interior is a powerful one in the case of Coward. After all, the playwright deployed detail through design, words, objects and spaces to stage a queer modernity. Thus far we have seen how queer men placed a considerable value on the objects they collected and the spaces they transformed to accommodate themselves and their communities. The descriptive interior, whether the purposefully fashioned stages for various plays or Coward's own accommodations, did not limit itself as banal or incidental detail within the narratives of identity, but rather functioned as an important facilitator of narratological development, as I hope to show. It is, in other words, the so-called excessive or ornamental elements of the interior that at once complicate meaning and facilitates the interpolation of the queer subject into the narrative of the modern interior. As a result, they cannot be ignored, for through their silent charm they reveal and celebrate Coward's true expression of modernity.

Since the nineteenth century, the interior as conceptual force and spatial reality referred not simply to the 'inside of a building or room, especially in reference to the artistic effect' or the 'picture or representation of the inside of a building or room', it also designated 'a "set" consisting of the inside of a building or room' of a theatre.[5] In its modern usage the interior functioned at once as a space both artistic and theatrical in its effect, public as much as private, personal as much as collective. Each section of this chapter necessarily moves back and forth between life and design on and off the stage; after all, interiors from the 1920s and 1930s constructed a 'stage-set modernism',[6] suggesting that spatial divisions between reality and fiction were blurred while the borders marking private from public were collapsed. In the theatrical space of the home and home as stage for modernism, Coward advertised modern design as much as he played out modern sexualities; what he staged, in other words, was modern living itself. Certainly, by the time he produced his successful and highly acclaimed *Private Lives* (1930) and *Design for Living* (1933) Coward's scripts for sexuality were heavily informed by and suffused with a Jazz Age notion of glamour and a distinctly modern international style.

Placed side by side, Coward's oeuvre, private persona and public life betray a fundamental tension between modernity, sexuality and the art of performing the self that can truly be understood only, I posit, when we also take into consideration his interiors, the designs he commissioned and material culture he fashioned. Not without contradiction and a heavy dose of shame, Coward's modernity was akin to a new generation of continental architects who viewed homosexuality as deviant and dirty, best set in relief and exposed against the whitewashed walls of modern interiors. Set against this background Coward nevertheless provided his generation with a decidedly queer display of glamour, a quality more often than not associated with the feminine. And yet, for Coward, it was effeminate masculinity (best embodied, he believed, in the long-lost figure of Wilde) that he shunned and loathed most. In Coward's hands, glamour attracted as much as it was meant to repulse; after all, the efficaciousness of modern glamour is that it always keeps its admirers – as much as its detractors – at a distance for fear of revealing that which it is meant to obscure. Elizabeth Wilson posits that '[i]n periods when sexual preferences and behaviour were less openly discussed than they are today this glamour of mystery created an aura of danger, and dangerous fascination'.[7] It was the site/sight, scene/seen of a modern performance of glamour that precariously teetered on the edge between masculinist modernism/modern perversions; homophobia/effeminacy; public/private; and stage set/domestic interior. Forty years after the Labouchere Amendment was enacted, forever blurring the boundaries between public and private at least as it concerned sexuality, Coward's queer aesthetics vacillated between exposure, display and revelation on the one hand and secrecy, privacy and interiority on the other.

In the vortex of gender

The Vortex was Coward's first critically acclaimed and financially successful production and was staged simultaneously in both London (1924–25) and New York (1924–26). In *The Vortex*, as with all of Coward's major plays, 'one gets carried away by glamour, and personality, and magnetism' as soon as the curtain rises.[8] Coward's good friend, one of many lesbians who formed his immediate circle, Gladys Calthrop (1894–1980) was commissioned to design the costumes and set for the play. This first collaboration launched her career in the theatre and was only one of a number of fruitful experiences her partnership with Coward provided for.

The play recounts the uncommon story of an over-sexed socialite Florence Lancaster (played by Lilian Braithwaite) and her son Nicky (Coward), a cocaine-addicted musical composer. 'In Coward's world first impressions count',[9] and the twenty-nine-year-old Nicky is obsessed with fashion and image. Our first encounter with him is upon his return from Paris, well attired in travelling clothes. His mother enjoys numerous extramarital affairs with significantly younger men while he, on the other hand, has proposed to his sweetheart Bunty. The fraught relationship between mother and son progressively deteriorates throughout the play as Nicky continues to fall victim to his addiction, Florence to hers. The two central characters embody the perceived decadence of the period, providing profiles of moral depravity. We must also not forget the elderly

6.1 Howard Coster. Noël Coward in front of the window in the sitting room of his 17 Gerald Road, Belgravia, home, 1939.

Pawnie, fastidious in the decoration of his home, a clichéd side character who helps to signify, even if only obliquely, the excess and ornament of the play. In many ways, Pawnie provides an embodied presence to what Logan describes as 'decorative detail', mere ornament that nonetheless helps to buttress the degenerate nature of the main characters and the play itself. After all, it was 'through the conjunction of homophobia and misogyny that the category of the camp male decorator continues to circulate as a type'.[10] Coward's biographer Philip Hoare states it best when he described the utter modernity of the play: 'The Vortex is more than a nod at this culture; it defined it. Even the title of the play asserts Twenties modernity, evoking the Vorticists, stylised interiors and Art Deco; or, more intellectually, but equally fashionable, Freudian theory and psychoanalysis.'[11] The hidden realities of the person lurking below the surface, sexual identities emancipating themselves, even if only, subtly coupled with a modern and dynamic design programme, became fodder for arch-conservatives. It was only when Coward went to see the Lord Chamberlain, Lord Cromer, that The Vortex was given approval and opened on 25 November 1924. When King George V was shown the play's script, he declared it 'disgusting' but could find no official reason to ban it from production.[12] Coward asserted that the drug culture he so blatantly represented was a moral tract, an indictment of addiction.

Hoare was not alone in claiming that Nicky's cocaine addiction was a cloaked index of the character's homosexuality, a white angelic powder hidden away from public view in a small snuffbox. Decades later Derek Jarman wrote that 'Coward put his sexuality in a little silver box and sniffed it', and the play's style was 'confession as innuendo'.[13] Homosexuality or any of its cognates were strictly forbidden in plays until as late as 1958, importantly, less than a year after the Wolfenden Report was tabled. Plays were, nevertheless, still subject to restrictive and at times draconian censorship laws under the Lord Chamberlain's office (which granted a play's licence to be performed in public) until 1968.[14] Duplicity as much as subtlety became hallmarks of a particular sexual as much as aesthetic style performed on the London stage. Allusion and allegory were covert and convenient contrivances at once to make available a hidden subtext to those in the know, while circumnavigating mainstream taste and social decorum. As Nichols commented of the period, even the term 'homosexual' was not yet known 'by the man-in-the-street ... But in the twenties it was taboo, and I think it is correct to say that the first time it began to come into general circulation was during the case of *The Well of Loneliness* (1928), by Radclyffe Hall.'[15] Following its publication, Hall became the subject of an obscenity trial that began in 9 November 1928. The novel was deemed corrupt and depraved, to be destroyed by orders of the judge. The *Daily Express* called for it to be banned and burned. On the heels of Billing's inflammatory article on the co-called 'Cult of the Clitoris', homosexual identity became current to many on the streets of England and subsequently subject to intense scrutiny and surveillance. Punitive measures against *the love that dare not speak its name*, as a crime in England in the 1920s and 1930s, were well enforced. Incidents of 'unnatural offences' were reported to have risen by 185 per cent between 1919 and 1938, while the number of cases of indecency also rose by 155 per cent in the same period.[16]

Despite the King's disapproval, Coward became a household name and enjoyed great success. With the triumph of his new hit play, he redesigned his interior and altered his sartorial look altogether, a look with which he would become forever identified. It was with *The Vortex* that Coward became, along with screen legend and British heart-throb Ivor Novello, the most popular and most photographed actor of his time. He soon stood as the embodiment of decadence, exuberance, luxury and, above all, the glamour of the Jazz Age. Coward himself noted: 'I was seldom mentioned in the press without allusions to cocktails, decadence and post-war hysteria'.[17] When the play moved from the Everyman Theatre, Hampstead, to the West End at the Royalty on 16 December 1924, Coward's understudy John Gielgud recalled how his 'room looked very glittering, with large bottles of eau-de-cologne on the wash-stand and an array of dressing-gowns hanging in the wardrobe'. 'Noël', according to the young actor, 'was charming'.[18] During this period, another admirer would grace the threshold of his dressing room. According to Coward, he 'walked nervously, and with slightly overdone truculence into my life'. The man was the American John ('Jack') Chapman Wilson whose charm – equal to that of Coward's – proved to be his greatest asset and perhaps eventually Coward's greatest annoyance. Cole Lesley, whom Coward employed after Lorn Loraine in the mid-1930s as his personal secretary, described how Wilson, in addition to his 'film-star looks', also had 'an immense amount of charm, and with his sharp wit he could be so funny that one forgave, or didn't even notice the mocking irony' of his words.[19] Nonetheless, Wilson would become Coward's companion and primary lover.

Wilson soon gave up his job as a stockbroker and assumed the position of Coward's personal manager. Coward was unsure how Wilson could fit in with and be received by his close-knit London-based family, in which everyone was given a pet name by Coward. Jack was the youngest member of the so-called family, and was appropriately called 'Bay-Bay', while Coward was known as 'Pop'. Personal secretary Lorn Loraine was the playwright's right hand, and was soon nicknamed 'Mother Hen' and even at times 'Girl Friday'. Loraine was not only an efficient and highly prized asset and member of Coward's family, but was often creative in the execution of her daily work. She and Coward would regularly leave letters to each other in the different rooms of his house in the form of pithy little poems:

6.2 Noël Coward reclined on an Art Deco sofa in the newly decorated 111 Ebury Street flat, London, 1 September 1927.

> Now, master dear, when next you do your packing
> And you and Cole in solemn conclave sit
> Please see that no essential thing is lacking
> That should be in your luggage, gear or kit.
> Please pack your pepper wash, your solo denture,
> Your ointment, just in case of you know what,
> And thus be sure before you start your venture
> That all the things you're going to want you've got.[20]

Even the mundane aspects of daily life precipitated dramatic flourishes. Stability and ritual were important to and expected by Coward.

With the success of *The Vortex* the house at 111 Ebury Street was sold, though Coward continued to rent a suite on the first two floors until he purchased his own home at 17 Gerald Road in 1930. The move from the upstairs attic with its cramped quarters to more roomy and suitable spaces was a domestic migration and spatial signifier of his success, which Coward commented on himself: 'As I moved up in the world, I moved down in the world'.[21] For Coward success necessitated not simply new or refashioned spaces, but movement as well. At the Ebury Street house he refurbished a sitting room in chintz and bold deco patterned fabric and Art Deco furniture [Figure 6.2], while the bedroom was painted scarlet;

6.3 Noël Coward working in bed in his by then standard Chinese silk robe. *The Sketch*, 29 April 1925.

for this Calthrop also provided erotic murals of pink nudes placed over the fireplace devised from her own imaginings. In this bedroom, Coward was famously and, by his own account, unwisely photographed working in his bed in a Chinese dressing gown 'and an expression of advanced degeneracy. This last was accidental and was caused by blinking at the flashlight, but it emblazoned my unquestionable decadence firmly on to the minds of all who saw it' [see Figure 6.3].[22] Architect Adolf Loos made a clear connection between the degenerate and interior architecture in his polemical text of 1908, 'Crime and Ornament', in which he claimed that a man who gives way to his inner urges in the decoration of his home is either 'criminal' or a 'degenerate'.[23] Harsh words to be sure; however, over the following two decades when Coward reached his greatest successes, the severity by which the modern interior and identity were scrutinized and linked attained epic proportions largely aided by the popular press and the vehicles of mass consumption.

Coward did indeed begin his day's work in bed when Loraine would bring in his breakfast. After the performance of his *levée*, he would move into a second room designed as his office. That infamous dressing gown he was photographed wearing would symbolize the glamour of the Jazz Age and its luxurious insouciance. The loose-fitting gown was a practical measure according to Coward and not a symbol of loose living with which it would soon become associated. He also wore coloured jersey turtlenecks, so unique and daring that it started a craze. Cecil Beaton famously remarked that

> [i]n affecting anything other than the normal mode of masculine dress, Noël was opening himself to criticism. Those who knew about such matters whispered about his sexuality; those who did not, excused it as a garb of theatrical folk, who were 'different'. To the homosexual enclave within the theatre (and without), Noël became an icon. But his influence was not confined to those who shared his sexual tastes.

Beaton also recalled how 'Coward's influence spread even to the outposts of Rickmansworth and Poona. Hearty naval commanders or jolly colonels acquired the "camp" manners of calling everything from Joan of Arc to Merlin "lots of fun", and the adjective "terribly" peppered every sentence. All sorts of men suddenly wanted to look like Noël Coward – sleek and satiny, clipped and well groomed, with a cigarette, a telephone, or a cocktail at hand.'[24] With his newfound success Coward 'immediately' indulged 'a long-suppressed desire for silk shirts, pyjamas and underclothes [opening] up accounts at various shops, happy to be able to charge things without that inward fear that [he] might never be able to pay for them'. Coward asserted that the vast sums of money he spent in the days, weeks and months during and after the success of his first hit play were well worth it; decadence without shame or regret, a true expression of modern glamour.[25] As soon as his fame increased so too did his representation. As he noted: 'I was photographed in every conceivable position. Not only was *I* photographed, but also my dressing room was photographed, my car was photographed, my rooms at Ebury Street were photographed. It was only by an over-sight, I am sure, that our lodgers escaped the camera.'[26] He soon realized the sartorial and cultural effect he was having on the young men of London, a realization that came to him after seeing numerous men wearing turtlenecks like he did. He noted modestly: 'I was informed by my evening paper that I had started a fashion. I believe that to a certain extent this was really true; at any rate, during the ensuing months I noticed more and more of our seedier West End boys parading about London.'[27] *The Evening Standard* went so far as to call him *the* new fashionable trend setter.[28] His good looks and tailored body were widely disseminated within the media and popular culture, and as Hoare asserts, 'for the first time since Oscar Wilde, a writer's appearance seemed as important as what he wrote'.[29]

Coward engendered a whole new performative, sartorial style through

6.4 Radclyffe Hall influenced by Noël Coward's manner of dress with Lady Una Troubridge (cut off), undated.

which to articulate one's queer identity. Hall was particularly 'in advance of the Coward vogue'.[30] Nichols was himself embarrassed by Hall, when out in public. 'But she [Hall] was embarrassing to meet in public. She used to attend many first nights wearing a black millinery cape, with a high stiff collar and a man's stock. Her grey hair was cut and parted like a man's. Her entry into the theatre always caused a minor sensation, and whenever I saw her striding towards me I used to be near a rapid retreat into the one place where, ironically enough, she was unable to follow me.'[31] The 1920s witnessed this vogue of gender bending in which men fashioned themselves to look more feminine and women more masculine. This new 'come what may' generation was deftly attuned to the vagaries of life and turned to new pursuits of leisure and luxury, weary of the devastation the war had wrought, a war waged by their fathers and grandfathers.[32] When asked whether he believed those who experienced the gay days of the 1920s were indeed happy, Coward responded: 'On the whole I think most of us were but we tried to hide it by appearing to be as *blasé*, world-weary and "jagged with sophistication" as we possibly could. Naturally we had a lot of fun in the processes.'[33]

Public lives, private queers

> [T]he interior is dying ... life threatens to become public ...
> Edmond de Goncourt
> One's real inside self is a private place, and should always stay like that.
> Noël Coward

As the quotes above suggest, 'real' identity as much as the interior is a private affair; both are marked as a place removed from public view, sheltered by the safety that comfort and control portend. However, if the Wilde trials, under the increasingly panoptic gaze of the Labouchere Amendment, taught queers anything, it was that performances of privacy and the supposed privacy of sexual identity were just as dangerous as were the spaces of publicity. D. A. Miller has outlined how the 'open secrete' of homosexuality functions along a private/public axis which sequesters subjectivity from public view. Within this spatial and metaphorical dyad, the figure of the homosexual teeters on the edge between private and public, only a door – a threshold – away from complete exposure and public disturbance.[34] Moreover, Michael Brown offers perhaps one of the most complete and insightful explorations of the history, mechanics and confines of the closet by arguing for its importance as a spatial modality. He notes how, for example, Eve Kosofsky Sedgwick's seminal readings of the closet occupy a purely textual analytical realm and occlude spatial dynamics even when discussing the 'materiality of the home'.[35] If the act of asserting oneself out of the closet is ultimately constituent of a performative act, then the closet itself becomes exclusively a product of language and avoids materializing it in any other (concrete) form.[36] What can we make then of the closet if seen through the prism of a spatial metaphor? As a sort of resolution to the question of space and sexuality, perhaps we might think along the line of a queer phenomenology in which people and things orient themselves towards something or someone in a specific place and time. Space is itself, after all, a form of orientation and Brown suggests it as *the* dimension through which power and knowledge are materialized. He cogently asserts that '[s]pace does not just represent power; it materialises it'.[37] We know this to be true if we simply turn our attention back to the Wilde and Taylor trials whose focus on the latter's interiors powerfully provided the very materiality by which to prove their culpability and perverse identity. Since 1869 when the homosexual was 'called into being', the power relations through which these cases against homosexuals were tried were often adjudicated through the material cultures of space (i.e.: drapes, clothes, furnishings). This initial discursive and performative act of naming on the part of sexologists, doctors and judges set in motion a spatial regime in which the homosexual became the sight of surveillance and site of deviance.

As Sedgwick argues, the closet was *the* defining structure of sexual and gender oppression deployed throughout the long twenty century.[38] The closet elicits performances that are not defined or confined by discursivity alone, but are situated corporeal, sartorial and spatial acts that at once both occlude and betray its own co-ordinates within the ever-changing interior and externalized landscape of identity. Despite becoming a trend setter in the mid-1920s, Coward would also become increasingly self-conscious about his own corporeal performance and publicity. Much later, on one occasion when with Marlene Dietrich, Coward famously asked: 'Marlenah! I must not appear effeminate in any way. Do be a dear – watch out for anything that could be considered less than "butch", if you see me at all "queer", tell me immediately.'[39] While Coward's sexuality was an open secret, the fear here was less of homosexuality, but of an effeminate masculinity. Coward's words signify a larger and ongoing programme of enforced self-scrutiny that was meant to ensure proper gender performances as much as a way to secure the closet within the public domain.

Coward's fear and misapprehension of his own effeminacy was also an important part of a larger modernist programme he orchestrated in which Wilde stood as totemic of effeminate enfeeblement. In his three-act operetta *Bitter Sweet* (1930), the story suggestively moves backwards through time. In the third and final act, Coward's song 'We All Wore a Green Carnation' (the title already an allusion to Wilde and his coterie), draws a clear impression of Coward's thoughts on the subject.

> 'We feel we're rather Grecian'.
> Pretty boys, witty boys, you may sneer
> At our disintegration,
> Haughty boys, naughty boys, dear, dear dear!
> Swooning with affectation.
> Our figures sleek and willowy,
> Our lips incarnadine,
> May worry the majority a bit.
> But matrons rich and billowy,
> Invite us out to dine, And revel in our phosphorescent wit.
> Faded boys, jaded boys, come what may,
> Art is our inspiration,
> And as we [are] the reason for the 'Nineties' being gay,
> We all wear a green carnation.

The aesthetes who wore green carnations and paraded around with young pretty boys serve as the epitome of a sexual aesthetics of the past, one premised on the Ancient Greeks. Coward's modernity was premised entirely on the fleeting and volatile vagaries of contemporary life, in all its luxurious abandon. Logan posits how it was 'only after Wilde's sensational appearance on the Victorian horizon that we find a strong conflation of the effeminate and the aesthetic'.[40] Alan Sinfield is more specific when he points out that the identity of the homosexual, for at least the first half of the twentieth century, was dominated by an image of Wilde at trial, understood to embody 'effeminacy, leisure, idleness, immorality, luxury, insouciance, decadence and aestheticism'.[41] It is precisely this image that Coward rails against and which impels his performances of dissemblance. Wilde's outcome left tangible scares inscribed on the deep surface of the bodies of British men, particularly for Coward who lived off the quick wit of one-liners and turns of phrases, the very same currency that propelled Wilde to celebrity. Coward's queer time and place were firmly rooted in the present, a whitewashed surface meant to obscure any (left over) filth or debris of times long past. Wilde is expunged from Coward's cultural repertoire from which to glean inspiration or with whom to form a lineage and as such fulfils the modernist drive to destroy that which came before. In Coward's hands it is an aesthetic destruction as much as one predicated on sexual liberation (from the past). Sexual perversity per se, was the source of fear less of how effeminacy would betray his secret, than of a truly queer masculinity. As David Halperin importantly claims, 'effeminacy deserves to be treated independently because it was for a long time defined as a symptom of an excess of what we would call *heterosexual* as well as homosexual desire. It is therefore a category unto itself.'[42] Coward thought that '[t]he trouble with him [Wilde] was that he was a "beauty-lover"'.[43] Ironic is this statement from a man who was a grand arbiter of contemporary taste and style, who set in motion the sartorial codes of modern masculinity and male glamour in an era when women wore suits and ephebic men relished the label 'glamour boys'. Referring to Coward and the film heart-throb Novello, Stephen Gundle notes how they both wore 'highly aestheticized exteriors [as] part of the disguise, although there was always a risk, as Coward's best photograph showed, that an ill-judged pose might give the game away', that is, ruin the disguise of his sexuality.[44] It is precisely at the points where sexuality and aesthetics converge that interiority, privacy and the interior internalize homophobic shame and where public display and private self are uncomfortably but ultimately blurred for Coward.

Glamour boy

The *Oxford English Dictionary* defines glamour, with its Scottish origins, as: '1) magic, enchantment, spell, especially in the phrase to cast glamour over someone, 2a) a magical or fictitious beauty attaching to any person or object, a delusive or alluring charm, 2b) charm; attractiveness; physical allure, especially feminine[45] beauty'. In these definitions Coward's affect is laid bare, but we also see within the latter definition the feminine associations of glamour. Coward's glamour was the result of much self-scrutiny; every movement, gesture and even the gait of his walk was regulated and controlled. His was a purposefully studied glamour, one that many men nevertheless sought to emulate precisely because Coward managed to walk the precarious line between the feminine and the masculine, the private and the public. Coward singlehandedly constructed his own glamour, a protean aesthetic devised on such a widespread level of publicity through the theatre, periodicals and photographs. Yet, the camp nature of many of his characters, especially those of the 1930s, would provide for an expression of his effeminate masculinity through the guise of glamour that had gained considerable currency in the period. Glamour 'cast[s] a sheen, that is to say dazzling or blinding the spectator, and this led to it having the additional meaning of having a shiny and a hard surface'.[46] The mask of glamour as a hard and seemingly impenetrable surface becomes a talismanic tool to ward off revealing what lurks below the surface, or in Coward's own words 'one's real inside self'. 'The appearance of glamour resides, though, or is created in combination with dress, hair, scent, and even *mise en scène*. Its end result is the sheen, the mask of perfection, the untouchability and numinous power of the *icon*.'[47] This notion of perfection is indelibly bound up with the experience and expression of shame; the constant quest of staging a different public persona, the (mis)recognition of the image in the mirror, the unattainable phantasmagoric ideal that glamour portends within the heterosexual matrix of mass and popular entertainment.

As a conceptual and aesthetic force, glamour entered into popular and visual vocabulary in the 1930s when large Hollywood studios, as with Broadway, designed character types easily identifiable on the silver screen aided greatly by a capitalist impulse. The strategy was a purposeful exercise in the standardization and abstraction of an incitement to desire.[48] Postwar recovery, as Gundle has shown, was greatly assisted by the USA as a way to replace politically motivated narratives with capitalist, consumer-based ones.[49] Don Slater has also claimed that '[c]onsumer culture is about continuous self-creation through the accessibility of things'.[50] One was compelled to buy into the ideals of capitalist glamour, rather than political ideology, a perfect blueprint for Coward's own success and those of his devastatingly glamorous characters. The industrial doyens of popular culture in the 1930s 'created a star system in which dozens of young men and women were groomed and moulded into glittering, ideal types whose fortune, beauty, spending power, and exciting lives dazzled the film-going public'. Writing in 1939 about American film stars, Margaret Thorp defined glamour as 'sex appeal plus luxury plus elegance plus romance'.[51] It was this film-inspired consumer-based aesthetic that set the stage for Coward's own designs of glamour, an aesthetic he had become all too familiar with on his numerous travels to, and in his productions in, the USA. Glamour 'emerges with the modernist attention to aesthetic form and subsequently becomes visible, even most familiar, in, the worlds of entertainment and mass culture'.[52] Glamour, it must be said, is indelibly imbricated in the aesthetic culture of modernism. It 'has its own recognizable aesthetic that finds its ideal conditions in the clean (synthetic, cold, abstract) lines of high modernism and provides a way of reading the modern cultural landscape'.[53] In this way, interwar glamour, I argue, was not simply a product of entertainment, but equally one of design, or perhaps more appropriately of a design for modern living. Coward also became part of the jet set that vacationed in Deauville and Saint-Tropez and returned to gleaming new apartments in Paris, London and New York. This decidedly international cosmopolitanism resided at the heart of the whimsy and nonchalance of his most celebrated play, *Private Lives* (1930), in which spouses are exchanged as easily as travel was easy between the South of France and Paris, the capital of modernity itself. Coward naturally embodied this carefree lifestyle, retreating often to the South of France, staying with Nichols, for example, at Syrie Maugham's famed modernist haven at Le Touquet. This was the life/style Coward advertised on, as much as off, stage and was one sought out by consumer-hungry theatregoers.

In 1932 *Vogue* published a two-page glam shot and exposé, 'Glamour and the Lunts', in which Lynn Fontanne was pictured 'dazzling' in a Lanvin rose-and-blue crêpe tea gown, while her husband Alfred Lunt lay elegantly on a velvet settee, cigarette poised at the ready near his lips. Fontanne and Lunt were Coward's closest and best friends in the USA, with whom he first charted out their collective rise to fame, stardom and celebrity. As *Vogue* quipped, glamour was 'an overworked word'; however, the fashion magazine assured its readers that the couple 'seems to have captured it and held it as a personal possession', a tacit hint at the material and yet elusive nature of this most coveted of all star qualities. Together the couple fulfilled the criteria set out by Thorp as late as 1939: 'their flying trips to exciting spots where the smart world gathers – the Riviera, London, Paris, their own home out in Wisconsin, which they are now doing over enthusiastically in modern Swedish style'. The 'strong individuality' of Fontanne's choice of fashion was listed as a significant factor in her success as an icon. The tea gown she is pictured wearing, for example, offers an ideal 'costume for keeping glamour in the home. It's exactly right for intimate home dinners – and it couldn't be more flattering'.[54] Glamour resides in the domestic realm, the stage for stylish dinner parties and gay soirées. By the end of the 1930s glamour and the quest for its attainment had expanded its discursive proportions. By 1937 'glam' was incorporated into the language, as was pizzazz, while in 1939, clearly influenced by stage and movie stars like Valentino, Novello and Coward, 'glamour boy' made its debut as a slang term to designate 'a young man who possesses glamour', a feminized affectation to be sure.[55] By the end of the decade the need to specifically define male glamour became a crucial and clear by-product of the period's consumer-driven culture, set in relief to ongoing stark deprivation. As Beaton recalls, Coward's plays 'caught the sophistication of the age', and theatre was one of the most important venues through which a 'whole new spirit of affectation and frivolity' was advertised.[56] Beaton went further and concluded that Coward embodied 'the glamour of success'.[57]

The playwright had a number of lesbian and bisexual female friends and appeared in countless double portraits with them, including Gertrude Lawrence and Calthrop displaying himself as part of a 'creative duo' [see figure 6.5].[58] In these conventional and yet non-normative pictures, '[s]exual differences, including power differences, seem to be blurred or undone; masculinity and femininity lose their emotional outlines. Men and women meet on the same plane, as affectionate comrades or androgynous reflections'.[59] This staging of perverse double-portraits served as

> a manifestation of '20s and '30s sexual style, which so often turned upon an implicitly 'homosexual' confounding of traditional sex roles. Unlike more conventional double portraiture, such as the standard heterosexual marriage portrait in which the husband stands behind his seated or otherwise visually subordinated spouse, the binary portrait emphasizes the sameness and equality of the two individuals portrayed.[60]

Wilson importantly underlines how, in its Celtic origins, glamour designated a 'corruption of "grammar"'.[61] If in the modern use of the term, glamour was bound up within the language of capitalism, then the 'corruption of grammar' within our context must certainly refer to Coward's staging of a visuality and materiality that adulterated that culture. The numerous double portraits of the playwright and (often lesbian) women visualize a sinful corruption of the traditional grammar of cross-sex images meant to designate not only heteronormative formulations of companionate marriage, but the hegemonic privilege of normative masculinity as well.

6.5 Maurice Beck and MacGregor. Double portrait of Noël Coward and friend and set designer Gladys Calthrop, c. 1924.

Background: living by design

As part of his increasing fame and fortune Coward decided to assume the lease of a country house (for £50 a year), which he purchased in 1927, to set up house and home for himself, his parents, aunt Vida and Wilson. The Goldenhurst farm in Romney Marsh, Kent, was located in a region of England replete with queers living idly in the countryside; even Hall had a country home near by. There were two houses on the premises, one for the family and a converted guesthouse where he and Wilson lived with a semblance of privacy. The main house 'was poky, with dark corridors and small rooms, and has a "lop-sided ... Victorian Air", partly the result of an extension, "a square edifice wearing perkily a pink corrugated tin roof and looking as though it had just dropped on the way to the races"'.[62] The property accommodated a barn, two ponds, an orchard and poplars on six grand acres of land. It remained Coward's country home until 1956 when he was forced to sell it owing to a mounting tax burden. When he committed to purchase it 'at a ridiculously small price',[63] Coward called upon the professional expertise of interior decorator Syrie Maugham (1879–1955) to refurnish it. Maugham combed the numerous antique shops that peppered the region. She managed to purchase a seventeenth-century tin 'Winged Allegory' and a Grinling Gibbons woodcarving from an auction at the neighbouring Herstmonceaux Castle, which she proceeded to bleach. Maugham was renowned for taking seventeenth- and eighteenth-century furnishings and whitewashing them to conform to modernist dictates and her rigidly anaemic aesthetic. The house was 'personalized' with Coward's song sheets pasted along the corridor that led to the Big Room where Coward's two grand pianos were housed and which was the stage of many performances, parties and the usual location of his collaborative efforts with Calthrop. Here, wood beams were exposed, walls were white and plastered and open fireplaces made for a congenial environment for modern living. *Bric-à-brac* was sequestered to family bedrooms. Katharine Hepburn once remarked how her stay at Goldenhurst 'was nice, but it was Noël in the country, you know. He wasn't interested in the country. It was just like the city, only the temperature was different.'[64]

In 1930 Coward sought out an additional address, though this time in London, which he located at 17 Gerald Road, near the stylish Eaton Square.[65] The house was a converted eighteenth-century coach house, formerly owned at various points by Chester Studios, Victorian artist Henrietta Mary Ward and dancer Frankie Leverson who refitted it in a Spanish style. The house was in keeping with the new and fashionable studio homes that Calthrop, for example, had taken a few blocks away in Spencer Street. These flats featured large windows and expansive spaces, the antithesis of the darkly lit, over-populated rooms of their Edwardian and Victorian forebearers. The house in Gerald Road was accessed through a high gate that led into a dark tunnel. Inside was one very large room, thirty-three by twenty-five feet with a twenty-five-foot vaulted ceiling and exposed oak crossbeams. A raised dias made for a small stage, and a gallery above gave the sense of a theatrical box overlooking the spectacle of the main floor living area. The upper part of the house was soon baptized 'The Studio'. *Vogue* commented that the parties held there were 'enlightened [and] all very white and witty'.[66] Maugham was called in again to help Wilson and Coward with the redesign. She converted the studio space in her classic signature style. Maugham deployed Louis quinze-styled chairs, zebra-patterned cushions, geometric-patterned rugs and frosted Lalique glass to lend a homely, yet sophisticated allure to the environment. As a nod to indulgence a mirror was placed on the ceiling over the bathtub. Maugham had decorated the homes of Coward's closest friends including Gertrude Lawrence who was photographed by Beaton in the designer's London store languishing on a trademark Maugham bed replete with white satin sheets. She also decorated the homes of the Lunts and Edward Molyneux, the French couturier whom Coward called upon to design the exquisite white dress sported by Lawrence in *Private Lives*. No matter where Coward travelled, visited or lived, Maugham's modern(ist) imprint asserted its omnipresence.

The interior shots of his home were not unlike the artists' studios and homes reproduced in numerous art and cultural magazines since the nineteenth century; the cult of celebrity took on new and exciting proportions in the interwar period and were infused with a heavy dose of jet-set glamour. In the nineteenth century, artists' homes and studios were held up as unique specimens whose interiors became emblematic of ideal aesthetic living. By the 1920s and 1930s glamorous homes included those of actors like Coward and society couples like the Lunts. Coward was rather private about having reporters feature his homes in magazines or newspapers after the infamous picture of him as a Chinese-robed, decadent working from bed was taken. On one occasion he permitted Joan Woollcombe from *Homes and Gardens* to feature his Belgravia home in the magazine's February 1937 issue, many years after having bought it [see Figures 6.6-6.9]. Interesting is how no mention is made of Maugham in the article, a hint to how by 1934 her monochromatic schemes had spiralled out of fashion. Woollcombe commented how 'the gateway on the pavement gives no idea of the amazing little house behind'.[67] 'For it appears that Noel Coward had no preconceived ideas about his own decorative "design for living," other than knowing what he did or did not like when he actually saw it. It is his friend and partner, John C. Wilson, whose real genius for interior decoration as a sideline to his main work, found this background for him, and who is best qualified to explain it.'[68] Woollcombe noted that 'neither of Noel Coward's homes is "mannered," nor is either self-conscious in the carrying out of a special style or period. As the story goes, Coward was indifferent to the design and location. The final outcome, a space perfectly appointed to his work and entertaining, fit this house "like a glove"'.[69] As soon as one enters the oasis located on the other side of the gate, London is forgotten, for the environment conjured 'a courtyard of the Paris of, say the rue St. Anne of the better sections of Montparnasse, Luxembourg Gardens – a type of courtyard home that must inevitably disappear'.[70]

The entrance opened to a small hallway, giving way to a turning staircase of pickled pine. The various spaces were decorated with selected *objets d'art* assembled from his numerous travels abroad. The studio, according to Woollcombe, was successful precisely because it 'ha[d] none of the dreadful defects of the deliberately "Bohemian" dwelling'.[71] Coward was admired for the 'catholicity and non-rigidity of his tastes'.[72] The spaces and objects Woollcombe highlighted provided what she suggestively described as the "background' to Coward.[73] Background implies at once

HOMES and GARDENS

HOUSES FURNITURE AND EQUIPMENT GARDENS

NOEL COWARD'S "COTTAGE INTERIOR"

As we might expect, this is something quite out of the ordinary.

GERALD ROAD is definitely rather a prim back street in Belgravia ; and demure among the many doorways and gateways is the studded gate and small wicket entrance of No. 17. This is the London home of Noel Coward ; and the gateway on the pavement gives no idea of the amazing little house behind.

It is best to have no preconceived ideas based upon any theory that as a general rule the successful man will select personally and with some care the "background" from which the observant can glean something of his tastes and character. For it appears that Noel Coward had no preconceived ideas about his own decorative "design for living," other than knowing what he did or did not like when he actually saw it. It is his friend and partner, John C. Wilson, whose real genius for interior decoration as a sideline to his main work, found this background for him, and who is best qualified to explain it. It was he who took the writer round one afternoon when the best thing in that house seemed the immense log fire that defied the climate outside.

It is worth remembering that neither of Noel Coward's homes is "mannered," nor is either self-conscious in the carrying out of a special style or period. Actually the pleasures of planning (delight to the real decorator) appear

The panelled hallway leading to the studio ; and Noel Coward with a figure he recently brought back from Bali, Dutch East Indies.

to mean nothing to him ; but he is by no means immune to dislikes, and rounds upon "preciousness" or absurdities. Mr. Wilson remembers Coward, faced by some perfect and careful "Georgian" decoration, and his vivid reaction with "*What on earth is all this ?*"

Did he plan this house, his London home ? Apparently he "hardly noticed it when he first saw it"—he just walked in

Photo : *Dallison-Leadley*.

6.6 First page of an article by Joan Woollcombe in *Homes and Gardens's* feature of Noël Coward's 17 Gerald Road home. *Homes and Gardens*, February 1937, p. 313.

a scenic backdrop and lineage or narrative leading to a present condition or circumstance. The author's use of 'background', in this context, points to two interdependent meanings. The first is the backdrop that helps to set in relief the personality or character of the home's owner, that is, the stage on which his modern identity is performed. The implication is not

This most unusual room has three uses—a sitting-room, dining-room and music-room—and over a portion of it two bed-rooms have been formed.

The shuttered windows are those of the bed-rooms; notice, on the left, the corner doorway and the "prompter's box" above.

—looked round and sat down and started to work. Actually he and his work, his friends and his entertaining, fit this house "like a glove"—his habits of work most certainly; and (to stretch the metaphor) rather like the steel hand in the velvet glove.

Come through the wicket gate from the street. Almost immediately you are conscious of being not in London, but in Paris: in a courtyard of the Paris of, say, the rue St. Anne or the better sections of Montparnasse, Luxembourg Gardens—a type of courtyard home that must inevitably disappear.

Across the courtyard the doorway of No. 17 opens straight into a tiny hallway from which the stairs rise and turn; small, with a general aspect of pickled pine in colour and that peculiar freshness the wood gives. A sharp turn of the stairs brings you into the narrow foyer, rather dark, that leads to the studio. Mr. Coward's travels have

6.7 Views of Noël Coward's 17 Gerald Road home. *Homes and Gardens*, February 1937, p. 314.

one of private space then, but of a publicity facilitated through interior design and material culture. The second exposes how the various *objets d'art* as a whole provide a material index, that is, a narrative – or history – of the man himself. For the author the domestic interior serves a teleological function in the narration of the self. Through space and objects,

HOMES AND GARDENS, *February*, 1937

At the back end of the studio the floor has been raised as a platform for two grand pianos.

supplied him with unusually cleverly selected "trophies"—an example to collectors. This foyer has a Chinese mandarin picture in a rich deep red-gold effect that defies description but does exactly what is required of it in this quiet dark hallway.

In the studio the ingenuity of the architect is only matched by the skill of the decorator, and yet, fortunately, it has none of the dreadful defects of the deliberately " Bohemian " dwelling. It is, in fact, an enormous room that contains, to all intents and purposes, a complete small cottage overlooking it on one side.

Under the balcony recess is the dining-room. The illustrations show clearly how the "cottage" windows overhang this and overlook the rest of the room; one vast window, simply curtained, is immediately opposite, and below it is a dais with twin grand pianos, twin mirrors and twin lights. Central circular steps lead down to the " main floor " of this room, which has, as focus point, a large moulded stone fireplace with its rather flat-toned heraldic picture and three Bali ornaments brought back by Noel Coward. The decorations and arrangement of the smaller objects is flexible. Mr. Coward is highly intelligent in the catholicity and non-rigidity of his tastes. On the day when the accompanying photographs were taken the picture to the right of the fireplace was relatively a newcomer; but, as Mr. Coward has only once before allowed a photographer within his gates, there is no record for checking just how often the minor details of the home change.

Main colours? The tall window curtains are a natural-coloured tapestry with dull red borders, and pickled pine dominates the general impression; rugs echoing this rather pleasant " oatmeal " tone. The textiles do not disturb this general impression. They have a rough neutral-coloured canvas surface, and are tailored to fit with floor valances that redeem them from plainness.

The dining-room

This part of the studio is used as the dining-room, the sideboard serving to cut it off from the sitting-room portion.

6.8 Views of Noël Coward's 17 Gerald Road home. *Homes and Gardens*, February 1937, p. 315.

identity is not only performed, but also clearly – or unclearly as the case may be – exposed.

Through an unassuming door the studio gave way to another building at 1 Burton Mews used as Loraine's personal office. 'The whole effect is of an adaptable, almost flexible background *for work*, as well as an ideal

recess has also a side table that serves as a bar: Noel Coward drinks very little indeed, but smokes an enormous amount, says Mr. Wilson. The actual small size of this recess is almost entirely camouflaged by the strips of mirror on the far wall, and the sideboard of solid blocks of crystal and dull brass with its bronze head of the master of the house set against the mirror that also reflects crystal candlesticks.

The ceiling of the recess is, in effect, rather lowered by the heavy beams that not only appear to, but actually do support the floor above; in the same way, the three shuttered windows of this interior cottage really do open and shut.

It is true that Noel Coward writes in bed. His room "upstairs" has beside it the "prompter's box," that is a miniature minstrels' gallery to the studio. His bed has its coverlet of fur, and the inevitable telephones beside it. The general colouring is of brown, green and yellow, with curtains of an amusing green-and-yellow printed cotton. There is a fitted wardrobe and a polished walnut tallboy.

The spare room has cream walls, dark polished furniture, and a strangely shaped bed; the pottery decoration and the stately porcelain cat on the hearth are other details to notice;

Immediately above is Noel Coward's own bedroom; below is a view of the guest-room, with its porcelain cat and amusing chair cover; and on the left is a detail of the main room, by the entrance, showing an interesting grouping of furniture and pictures.

(*Photographs: Copyright, Joan Woollcombe.*)

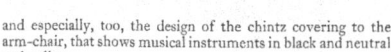

and especially, too, the design of the chintz covering to the arm-chair, that shows musical instruments in black and neutral and yellow.

This, in some detail, is the "background" to Noel Coward: not forgetting the all-white bathroom. The home itself is run by his secretary, Lorn Loraine—and very efficiently and unobtrusively, too. It is she who tells me of the rather obscure pedigree of the place; explaining that the door on the right of the fireplace leads eventually through to the rest of Mr. Coward's small estate, 1 Burton Mews, which backs on to 17 Gerald Road. It is only a surmise, but it is reasonable to assume that, before the woman artist who was one of Mr. Coward's predecessors here had the place, it was some kind of a vast storehouse to the Burton Mews section of the whole. Its various owners since then have developed its potentialities very intelligently.

The whole effect is of an adaptable, almost flexible background *for work*, as well as an ideal stage for entertaining; of no special "period" and completely unpretentious; embodying fitness for purpose without the priggishness generally associated with too much of that phrase. In fact, it seems characteristic of Noel Coward that he should, in his own machinery for working, "debunk" a Bohemian legend once and for all as regards successful writers. JOAN WOOLLCOMBE.

6.9 Views of Noël Coward's 17 Gerald Road home. *Homes and Gardens*, February 1937, p. 316.

stage for entertaining ... it seems characteristic of Noel Coward that he should, in his own machinery for working, "debunk" a Bohemian legend once and for all as regards successful writers.'[74] The effects of virile, continental aesthetics have clearly gripped the image of Coward, and more importantly have helped to remove any 'bohemian' association, which the machine for living (and working) desired to eradicate with its white walls and techno-functionalist aesthetics. Undoubtedly, Woollcombe would have cringed at the chaotic bohemianism of Cedric Morris and Arthur Lett-Haines's various homes of the same period.

Hiring Maugham to redecorate both his London and country homes was part of the cultural expectations comprising the social set Coward formed. However, the playwright's commission of a female decorator conformed to contemporary dictates as much as providing a pose through which he could be seen as 'indifferent to the design and location'. Hiring a decorator of Maugham's stature as one of the best and most fashionable designers provided for a necessary sense of masculine detachment. 'The domestic, perpetually invoked in order to be denied, remains throughout the course of modernism a crucial site of anxiety and subversion'.[75] Before the First World War decorators were mostly male, as were reformers, moralists and upholsters. By the 1920s interior design was no longer a heterosexual man's domain, but almost exclusively the purview of women, and gay men.[76] Moreover, as women gained more professional credibility, success and independence, objects for the home and the spaces that housed them became decidedly more masculine.[77] While hiring the right decorator lent cultural credibility and social cachet, for Coward, however, glamour was achieved in the sheen and gloss of indifference, a masculine pose that allowed him to ward off and yet call attention to his own performances of masculinity and effeminacy simultaneously.

At the precise moment when decorating gained professional credibility, men were rarely called upon to choose the objects filling their homes. Men who became professional decorators were quickly assumed to be homosexual. An opposing image was disseminated by men's magazines of the period that also began to compete as arbiters of design. However these equipped men with information and guidance on the proper outfitting of a bachelor flat. In 'A House Built for a Bachelor' published in *The Ideal Home*, the quintessential living room 'dear to the heart of a bachelor' was a 'bright sunny apartment furnished for masculine tastes ... furnished according to the canons of masculine comfort'.[78] In the 1930s, *Esquire* in particular managed to corral various aspects of male consumption into 'a coherent representation of a modern masculine ideal'.[79] The so-christened bachelor pad helped to consolidate a deeply heterosexual space for men in a period bracketed by two world wars; a style of living and a term that gained considerable currency in the immediate aftermath of the Second World War. *Playboy*, for example, featured interior designs both 'chic and elegant, but also carefully incorporated an iconography of status and power to underline the masculine and heterosexual integrity of the archetypal "bachelor pad"'.[80]

The openness achieved by way of large-scale windows and the linear architecture of modern homes was born out of a desire for exposure and revelation, leaving little in the way of spaces in which to hide. For Le Corbusier the issue of architecture was indelibly linked to issues around health, a concern said to be on the brink of a 'moral crisis'.[81] As Penny Sparke argues, '[t]he idea of bodily cleansing becomes a metaphor for cultural cleansing within modernist architecture and it found its most obvious aesthetic expression in the dominance of the colour white'.[82] For the French architect whitewashing walls was a 'manifestation of high morality, the sign of a great people'.[83] The modern architecture advocated by men like Loos and Le Corbusier 'strips off the old clothing of the nineteenth century to show off its new body, a fit body made available by the new culture of mechanization'.[84] Leading up to the heroic modernism best embodied in the design blueprints advanced in Le Corbusier's writings of the mid-1920s, the decorative was already seen before the war as a sign or concealment of 'impotence', antithetical to the 'bachelor pad'.[85] By war's end, subject to severe loss and devastation, virile masculinity was forever severed from the comforting, plush interior of bourgeois domesticity embodied in feminine trifles. In the mid-1920s Le Corbusier, for example, 'presented the unornamented, whitewashed building and its industrially designed contents as embodiments of his anti-decorative stance'.[86] In his *The Decorative Art of Today* Le Corbusier referred to the 'bourgeois king' and his '*bric-à-brac* mind', the feeble occupant of the bourgeois interior.[87] The *bric-à-brac* bourgeoisie so maligned by Le Corbusier, amongst others, were perceived as provincial, moribund Victorians whose notions of aesthetics and sexuality could no longer hold sway in the new world that followed the First World War.

In 1928, Robert Stanley writing in *Homes and Gardens* noted how continental modernism had yet to make inroads into Britain. According to Stanley: 'The leaders of this movement have been men of talent and originality, and their efforts have met with wide appreciation and approval … in England,' he contended, 'very little evidence of this movement is yet seen, but there are many who think that it is only a question of time, and that as soon as out innate conservativism is overcome, houses designed and furnished in this new manner will be carried out on a larger scale … The movement is provocative.'[88] Among the 'outstanding features these homes possess', according to Stanley, was how they provide 'plenty of light – both natural and artificial', while neutral-toned walls are best to showcase the brilliant fabrics, especially those influenced by Parisian artists.[89] Windows could expose the precarious interface between public and private, wherein the home itself became a public venue through magazine features, parties recorded by social columnists. Le Corbusier maintained a 'primordial ideal of the house', for him it was 'a shelter, an enclosed space, which affords protection against cold, heat *and outside observation*'.⁹⁰ Yet it is precisely these windows, which help to expose the ills of contemporary culture and interiors. Along with Beatriz Colomina, I wish to argue that Loos's and Le Corbusier's notion of degeneration becomes clearly identified as homosexuality. Loos's 'raid against ornament is not only gender-loaded but openly homophobic'.⁹¹

In his reminiscences of the 1920s, Nichols, once lover to Syrie's first husband the celebrated writer W. Somerset Maugham, recalled the importance of white in the decade's overall aesthetics: 'It did not dominate, but it provided many delightful passages … largely thanks to Syrie Maugham. She used it in the prettiest ways, with huge armchairs in white leather and carpets made out of clipped sheep-skin and white pots of china camellias in the hall'.⁹² Maugham even threw an infamous 'all white' ball at which servants wore white, with lilies set against a backdrop of white screens. Following the Renaissance, colour has been deemed irrational and intuitive, in contradistinction to drawing, understood as the by-product of masculine design.⁹³ In this way, Maugham's all-white spaces might serve to distance her interiors from frivolous and irrational feminine spaces, often attributed to female decorators. Rather, she created rational, streamlined and simplified interiors, if loaded with multi-historical objects and meanings. In Britain detractors of modernism, vocal and numerous, believed the new style 'represented nothing

6.10 Howard Coster. Noël Coward with personal secretary Lorn Loraine in the sitting room of his 17 Gerald Road home, 1939.

less than an attack upon British national character. "Modern tendencies" summoned' up images of cocktail parties, jazz and the motor car: 'a menacing combination of American hedonism and Teutonic conformity. Such purely functional interiors were alien to British sensibilities'.[94] Mark Wigley asserts that '[n]ot only can fashion never cut off from modern architecture, modern architecture emerges from the very economy of fashion that it so loudly condemns'.[95] Undecorated white walls personified masculinist, modernist discourse in its attempt to remove the decorative, the feminine and the vagaries and perceived fleeting frivolities of fashion from architecture. However, as Wigley shows, the white walls were themselves subjected to the very surface readings they were meant to avoid. In other words, the modern white walls announced themselves as the very height of fashion.

Despite the French influence of her lifestyle and work coupled with the jet-set pace she kept along with her clients, Maugham's styled interiors were an ideal compromise for British sensibilities. Sparke argues that in the modern era women acted 'as guardians of the past, maintaining a sense of continuity by keeping one foot in the pre-industrial past',[96] a balancing act that was particularly British in its acceptance of the continental modernist impulse that arrived on its shores in the early part of the 1930s. Maugham's interiors embodied at once the distinctly conservative British design influences that embraced traditional motifs and objects as well as the modernist minimalist dictum that stripped them of the burden of any historical affiliation, providing her clients with a blank 'background'. Modern design was as much, or perhaps even more, to do with producing new or redesigned subjects and bodies as it was about redesigning space.[97] Maugham's unique stripping, pickling and bleaching were, I contend, a hybrid product that sat uneasily at the margins of modernist dictates that championed objects bearing universalized and unintelligible pasts and yet could still be 'identified' by her English clients. In effect, she provided Coward with a queer time and place, one that simultaneously thwarted critics and theorists on either side of the Channel. Maugham appropriated the purity of non-colour to lend a sense of modernist glamour. Even as late as 1936, *Homes and Gardens* was advocating the importance of hybrid spaces similar to those conjured by Maugham herself. In a nod to modernist rigour the periodical advocated first and foremost to 'eliminate, eliminate' for the 'hybrid room', a room which ostensibly served multiple purposes for living and aesthetics, the old must blend with the new.[98]

Despite Maugham's impact, we must not haste to dismiss the importance of Art Deco – or the moderne style – in Coward's aesthetic programme. Whether used for the cover design of his first autobiography *Present Indicative*, the refurnished rooms in the last years when he rented a flat at 111 Ebury Street or the sets for *The Vortex*, *Private Lives* and *Design for Living*, Coward aided by the women in his life fashioned his spaces replete with Art Deco references and furnishings; a style that often borrowed the white wall aesthetic to best set in relief the luxury of its furnishings. The style was indelibly linked to the emergence of mass consumption as well as the New Woman, a refutation of the excesses and limitations of the Victorians. Mark Winokur states that 'Deco was accessible – in a way the various other modernisms were not. In fact, the value of Art Deco … resided in its ability to be avant-garde while circumventing completely the difficult-to-watch wrenching of reality that were intrinsic to expressionism, surrealism, or cubism.'[99] Art Deco was the first truly populist aesthetic programme tied to consumer culture rather than an exclusive and elusive art system directed by manly modernists. In the USA, Art Deco was seen as a style more open to all. In an article in *The New York Times* from 1926, 'Luxury Is Democratized', the author claimed that with the new French style beauty could be obtained by 'all the classes'; it was, after all, a truly international style propagated by the glamorous jet set and advertised through the networks of mass media.[100] The 1920s distinguished itself as the first moment in history that witnessed an entire and widespread 'ideology of affluence. Above all, it promoted a powerful link between everyday consumption and modernization. From the 1920s, the world was to be modernized partly *through* consumption; consumer culture itself was dominated by the idea that everyday life could and should be *modern*, and that to a great extent it already was.'[101] Theatre and films were ideal vehicles of dissemination. The moderne style was not only new, it was highly visible and public in its representation. Hotels, beauty shops, boutiques amongst other public spaces of consumption and leisure were, in the 1920s and 1930s, sporting this fresh new simplified look that defined the golden age of glamour. However, many decried the perceived logic of the populist movement. In 1937 Leslie Martin wrote of the moderne aesthetic as 'the appeal to surface decoration; yet another manifestation of that passion for "surface" which dragged out its life through the nineteenth century'.[102] Surface, as it always tends to point to, pejoratively denotes the decorative and connotes the superficial. The moderne (or Art Deco) celebrated consumption and new identities, some of which hung off the traditions, styles and ideas of the past, while others appeared to be mere poses, masks (as surface implies) or feigned gestures of decadent identities.

Identity, design, publicity

Private Lives opened at the new Phoenix Theatre on 8 September 1930 and ran for 101 performances and in 1931 opened on Broadway. Its demise in London was due in large part to Coward himself, who wanted to play the role of Elyot for only three months. Coward wrote *Private Lives* laid up in Shanghai at the Cathay Hotel, the result of a terrible bout of influenza. To this day, the hotel retains a lush 'Coward Room', replete with decadent glamour and luxurious splendour. According to Coward, the idea and images for the play came to him the first night of his illness; 'the moment I switched out the lights, Gertie appeared in a white Molyneux dress on a terrace in the South of France and refused to go again until four a.m., by which time *Private Lives*, the title and all had constructed itself'.[103] The play tells the story of two honeymooning couples, Elyot (Coward) and Sybil Chase (Adrianne Allen) and Victor (Laurence Olivier) and Amanda Prynne (Gertrude Lawrence). Vacationing in the fashionable Deauville, by happenstance the couples are lodged in the same hotel, rooms side by side. By the end of Act I we realize that Elyot and Amanda were previously married for three tumultuous years. Both beg their respective spouses to leave the hotel; they refuse and dine by themselves, where they, again by happenstance, meet each other. Elyot and Amanda soon realize they are still in love and flee together to Amanda's Paris flat in Avenue Montaigne [Figure 6.11]. Act II takes place in the interior of Amanda's flat, established by Coward in his stage directions as

> charmingly furnished, its principal feature being a Steinway Grand on the left, facing slightly up stage. Downstage centre, a very large comfortable sofa, behind which is a small table. There is also another sofa somewhere about, and one or two small tables, and a gramophone.[104]

In Amanda's flat one witnesses the volatility and chaos of the couple's relationship. It is also in this act that the tragic and at times melodramatic exchange of jealousy and passion is played out back and forth between the piano and the couch. In Act III, Sybil and Victor catch up with the two lovers. However, along the journey to Paris the two have formed an unusual relationship and are themselves stuck in a progressively destructive pattern of bickering. Realizing their former spouses' new situation, all is forgiven, and Amanda and Elyot sneak out of her apartment to leave the two to play out the drama of their own unhealthy relationship. Despite the cross-sex couplings, the play does not provide any inkling of normative gender role play or sexual codes. Moreover, Coward publicly displays the usually private experiences of separation and divorce centre stage, while also refusing reconciliation within the heterosexual contest.[105] Harmony is never restored, normativity never ensured. Here private lives are displayed openly, staged through the publicity of theatre. Coward dares to play with what are ultimately artificial

6.11 Vandamm Studio. Gertrude Lawrence and Noël Coward on sofa in *Private Lives*, Times Square Theatre, New York, 1931.

boundaries between private and public, using the semi-domestic space of the hotel and its balconies where the former lovers reconnect with each other. Early in the play, Amanda claims: 'I think very few people are completely normal really, deep down in their private lives'. Normativity is set along the public/private axis and proves itself to be nothing more than a spatial masquerade. Marriage, for Amanda, is given publicity, for, as she describes it, it is like being 'clamped together publicly'. Can we assume then, marriage, given its location within the public domain, to be contrary to the privacy of true identity, the interiority of subjectivity to which Coward so faithfully clutched? As David Innes remarks, '[d]isplay is also self-exposure; and while promoting the star images, in which glamour serves as a survival strategy, Coward's plays question the inherent self-obsession of stardom. At the same time, living up to this image imposed strategies that make his own comments on the significance of his plays particularly deceptive.'[106] These diversions away from normative and compulsory companionate marriage are a measure of Coward's desire to play with social norms and sexual rules. Penny Farfan goes so far as to suggest that '[t]he impossibility of marriage for the apparently straight primary characters in *Private Lives* is suggestive of the historical fact of the legal impossibility of marriage for homosexual partners, for whom Amanda and Elyot may function as queer stand-ins'.[107] While Farfan tacitly alludes to a commonly held belief that queer men are unable to script believable female characters, she does nevertheless intimate the instability by which Coward's characters' gender and sexual identities teeter precariously between the public and the private.

If *Private Lives* exposed the precariousness of the stability and inseparability of compulsory heterosexuality and companionate marriage, then surely things come to a dramatic head in *Design for Living* (1933), a play so decadent according to official censors that Coward was forced to place its debut in New York. Indeed the play was *too* modern for London,[108] in terms of both its content and its design. It opened at the Ethel Barrymore Theatre on 24 January 1933, and became an instant success. *Design for Living* was meant to be an unabashed vehicle for the star power of Alfred Lunt, Lynn Fontanne and Coward himself who together plotted to become famous when they became fast friends in 1921. The three acts of the play are each set in a different metropolis, Paris, London and New York, and recount the sorted triangulated relationship between Otto (Lunt), Leo (Coward) and Gilda (Fontanne). In Act I we find the three in Otto's dilapidated bohemian Paris studio in 1932. Gilda, an interior designer, lives with him and was once attached to his best friend Leo, a writer. Gilda is paid a visit from a friend of theirs, the art collector Ernest Freidman eager to show them his latest acquisition, a painting by Henri Matisse, *the* quintessential modernist painter. Gilda lies to Ernest, claiming Otto has been taken ill to bed. Ernest informs her that Leo (like Coward) has become a great success as a playwright in New York and has returned to Paris. However, Otto comes home only to reveal her lie. Ernest and Otto leave to fetch Leo at the George V hotel where he is supposedly staying only to return to find out he has already spent the night with Gilda. Enraged, Otto abandons them both.

In Act II the story moves to London, eighteen months later, when Leo and Gilda are living together. While Leo is away Otto turns up at their home, announcing that he too has become wildly successful as a painter. Gilda and he dine together which quickly leads to them rekindling their romance. While Otto is sleeping Ernest, once again, calls on Gilda to whom she announces she is leaving Leo. She runs off with the art collector and leaves Otto and Leo a letter. Leo is furious not the least because Otto confesses to having slept with Gilda. They become overwrought with the prospect she has left them both and drown their pitiful sorrows in sherry and brandy and embrace, sobbing. In Act III, two years have gone by and we find our trio in New York. Gilda, now a highly successful interior decorator, has married Ernest. While her husband is away Gilda hosts an important party which Otto and Leo crash in their pursuit to recover the missing link in their unusual and highly sorted relationship. In the final scene, Ernest returns home only to find Otto and Leo wearing his pyjamas [Figure 6.12]. Gilda, on the other hand, has spent the night at a hotel, allowing herself space to think. When she returns she witnesses Otto and Leo explaining that his formal, public, status as her husband has no consequence to them. Ernest is repulsed and calls their relationship a 'disgusting three-sided erotic hotch-potch' at which Leo, Gilda and Otto famously fall down on the couch and have a hearty laugh about it all, engendering one of the most iconic stills of Coward's illustrious career [Figure 6.13].

Design for Living catapults the complications of *bachelors of a different sort* on to the stage. Coward, however, importantly adds a third character, that of the modern decorator, a female character who functions, within Sedgwick's formulation of a Victorian literary trope, as the embodied host or surrogate for the bond and desire shared between Otto and Leo, not entirely or exclusively for the woman, but for each other. Sedgwick provocatively asserts that 'in erotic rivalry, the bond that links the two rivals is as intense and potent as the bond that links either of the rivals to the beloved: that the bonds of "rivalry" and "love", differently as they are experienced, are equally powerful and in many senses equivalent'.[109] The homosocial bond between Otto and Leo is clear throughout; however, the headstrong interior decorator Gilda also provokes further the gender trouble that Coward presented in his plays. The profession of interior decoration allowed women, usually of the middle and upper classes, an entry into the workforce at a time when women were meant to remain economically dependent on either their fathers or their husbands.[110] In Coward's sorted triangulation we see a new contest of gender, in which men and women are equal players, desiring participants and active agents of their own decidedly modern destinies.

Star power coupled with rumour and the affects of plays like *Private Lives* and *Design for Living* left Coward vulnerable to journalists' scrutiny. Upon his arrival back in New York in September 1937 reporters probed him about his personal life and rumours of him marrying, to which he replied: 'People just cannot bear to see me being a happy and unmolested bachelor'.[111] These questions were not entirely surprising given how Lunt was bisexual and Coward a homosexual, the open secret that is always on the edge of exposure or publicity. Sedgwick asserts that '[t]o draw the "homosocial" back into the orbit of "desire", of the potentially erotic, then, is to hypothesize the potential unbrokenness of a continuum between homosocial and homosexual – a continuum whose visibility, for me, in our society is radically disrupted'.[112] That Coward emancipates the woman in the triangulation of *Design for Living* is one thing, that he also provides a vehicle for queer desire and feelings between the men is

6.12 Lynn Fontane, Alfred Lunt and Noël Coward in *Design for Living*, Ethel Barrymore Theatre, New York, 1934.

an altogether different and equally provocative move. In his equation, all three are ambiguously and ambivalently complicit in the deceits of desire and pleasure. In the 1920s and 1930s, in a post-Wildean era, when sexologists and psychoanalysts had purposefully conjured a typological template of the male and female homosexual, Coward allowed for a fluidity and ambivalence in the identities of his equally strong characters. While playing off the idiomatic images of the effete dandy and the mannish woman of the period, on stage Coward celebrates fluidity and openness to the possibilities that exist within the landscapes of sexuality. Although the interiors and material culture more broadly Coward fashioned on and off stage were pungent with cultural signification, at home the man himself kept the feminine realm of decorating at bay through the act of commissioning an acclaimed female decorator. In the play, through the character of Gilda, he could channel strong female characters who populated his own life, characters who were more often than not associated in some way with interiors and design, a realm no longer open to men, without the stereotype being applied to himself, one Coward would never have tolerated.

6.13 Lynn Fontane, Alfred Lunt and Noël Coward in *Design for Living*, Ethel Barrymore Theatre, New York, 1934.

Whether in photographs of his private life or in stills of plays, the various iterations (read: performative in every sense of the term) of Coward represent him seated in two important types of 'scenes'. The first, and by far the most obvious, was at the piano, the instrument of his vocation as entertainer and celebrated songwriter. The second, less obvious, is reclined on a couch. By the 1920s, couches had become wider than their Victorian and Edwardian predecessors, ideal spaces to lounge more comfortably and idle the time away in languid abandon. Within the visual culture of Coward, couches serve at once as the location of action (rather than passivity), the publicity of modernity and modern identity itself. The Freudian couch on which the scrutinized subject reveals its secrets and private passions is also transformed in Coward's staging and made public and decidedly more fashionable and glamorous. As always, modern identity teeters precariously on the edge between privacy and publicity; Coward never fully exposes the parameters of either, allowing fact and fiction to cavort joyfully on deco couches.

The couch also furnished moments of languid repose (ornamented pauses), rather than a place of work, and as such this decorative element became an important material signifier for the jet-set class he portrayed and embodied as much as integral to narratological development and the play's characters' personalities and perceived identities. With Coward, the couch furnishes a performative staging of a queer masculine glamour, as Beaton conceptualized it years later in *The Glass of Fashion*. Numerous images of Coward display him reclining on a couch, including the one reproduced here in his deco-styled redesign of 111 Ebury Street. Beaton also drew a sketch of the playwright in the early 1930s, again reclined fully outstretched on a sofa. The couch helps to materialize a picture of elongated and attenuated male glamour, premised on the languid, ephebic deco silhouette [see for example Figure 6.11]. In the plays it is the site of dramatic poses and utterances, as well as comedy and exasperation. The couch in Coward's plays and in pictures of him spatialize excess, through the image of idle life and decadent, unhealthy relationships. The bed, on the other hand, provided a slightly different image, one of work, bedside telephone at the ready, though still tinged with a soupçon of decadence. Erving Goffman characterizes the various spaces within the home in theatrical terms in which the space undergoes a 'symbolic manipulation … creating "staged", "front spaces" (e.g. the salon, living room, etc.) and relaxed, less-strictly regulated "back spaces" (e.g. the kitchen or "family room")'.[113] Coward, on the other hand, reverses the domestic order, challenging the public/private associations of spatial use.

Perhaps the most spectacular and one of the most reproduced images of Coward's long career remains the one in which *Design for Living*'s three main characters fall on to the couch in complicit abandon. Here the gender and sexual continuum is visually blurred. The couch frames the decadence and sexual ambiguity, where arms, legs, bodies interfold: Coward's Leo gaily in the centre, naturally, held on either side by Gilda and Lunt's Otto, the cross-sex couple's heads connecting while Otto holds Leo. Here Coward is framed by the two and by the couch itself, while the decadence of their lives and actions is set in sharp relief to the white wall of the background and the by then fashionable white, solid modernist grand staircase, exposing the vice and unhealthy nature of their communion [Figure 6.13]. The white wall coupled with the decadent, ambiguous *ménage-à-trois* pays tribute to the queer spaces Maugham designed, which I described earlier, which employ modernist dictates while at the same time reversing them to stage an alternative terrain. The two themes come together at the point where the white wall, which exposes all degeneration and polluting impulses, exposes the decadence taking place on the couch. Colomina has shown how the modern interior was a product of a mass image, more than any specific physical reality. In *Privacy and Publicity: Modern Architecture as Mass Media*, she notes that architecture was less a site than a sight to behold through cinema, periodicals, photographs, theatre and important exhibitions. Walls themselves became less important, unlike the representations of homes. Here, whether consciously or not, Coward deploys the 'background' (read interior wall and character's identity) made common in the modern metropolises of Paris, London and New York and turns its health-obsessed origins on its head. Through the modern and liberating space of New York, where the final act and scene take place, Coward used the very visual and material vocabulary used to hunt and decry homosexuals and exposed it publically and played up the queer nature of modern glamour. Colomina contends that 'modern architecture only becomes modern with its engagement with the media'.[114] In this way, Coward truly services modern interior design. However, his is a perverse modernity, a queer play with space that allows for the ills Le Corbusier and the exponents of the International Style saw in more recent historical and contemporary specimens of domestic architecture.

'Modernity, then, coincides with the publicity of the private.'[115] At one point in the play Leo states: 'It's all a question of masks, really, brittle, painted masks. We all wear them as a form of protection; modern life forces us to.' For Corward modern identity, modernity itself, is always on the cusp of exposure, hence the need for masks. By the 1920s and 1930s, psychoanalysis had made significant inroads into popular culture, precisely at a time when gender roles were being questioned and challenged. Leo's words point not only to Coward's own purported desire for privacy of those aspects of a person deemed to be the 'real inside self', but underscores the performative nature of gender and identity. In her much-cited essay 'Womanliness as Masquerade' published only four years before *Design for Living* was staged, British psychoanalyst Joan Riviere posited that womanliness was simply a façade, or more precisely a mask donned by professional women in certain circumstances in which she was made to perform in front of male colleagues. Interestingly, in her Freudian analysis, Riviere was particularly fascinated with the liberated mannish women who obliquely suggested the lesbian subset Coward was an integral part of.[116] Long before Butler's important work, Riviere concluded that gender – identity itself – was nothing more than a mask we don, a performance we enact in myriad different circumstances. If identity is performative, where does privacy begin and publicity end?

On the edge: between privacy and publicity
While Coward was performing on a Broadway stage, in London the most significant exhibition of the decade took place in Dorland Hall, Lower Regent Street, London. The Exhibition of British Industrial Arts in the Home was the official and sanctioned vehicle for design reform, an

6.14 Vandamm Studio. The set for the original Broadway production of Noël Coward's *Design for Living*, Ethel Barrymore Theatre, New York, 1933.

answer to encroaching continental modernism [Figure 6.15]. It importantly sought to reform industrial design in Britain and did so by tacitly acknowledging Le Corbusier's core tenet of the home as a machine for living and by positioning social reformation through technology and industry. The fundamental goal was 'to improve the taste and quality of manufacture through exhibitions of industrial art'. Arranged by Oliver Hill, it showcased arch-modernist design that displayed either 'functional efficiency' or the 'exotic'.[117] Everything from rugs and textiles to lighting to silverware was displayed side by side to demonstrate the new equipment of the modern family home. In the process it also condemned the Great Exhibition of 1851, the very exhibition that helped to propel the design and core tenets of the Industrial Revolution. John Betjeman, for example, concluded that the Great Exhibition 'was conceived by Royalty, it was a risk and a poetic dream. Manufacturing was still largely in the hands of the enlightened, or rather there was still an aristocracy of class, which laid claim to an authority in taste. Commerce was still a splendid new pet which had not grown dangerous.'[118] Amongst the extensive architectural work exhibited, the Canadian expatriate Wells Coates (1895–1958) showcased a mock-up of one of his 'minimum flats' he had been working on since 1931 [Figure 6.16]. In it he emphasized reinforced concrete, white walls and built-in furniture for domestic architecture, features which had yet to be attempted in Britain, but had become more common on the continent. As much as his interiors, his exteriors had a streamlined aesthetic, reminiscent of steam liners. In an article published in 1932 in *The Architectural Review*, Coates spoke of the interior as a 'dwelling-scene', a concept that merged notions of the home as domestic landscape with ideas of public staging. He wrote how '[t]he natural starting-place for this new service must be the scene in

6.15 Moderne-styled advertisement for the Exhibition of British Industrial Art in the Home London, 1933, *Homes and Gardens*, July 1933, p. xviii.

which the daily drama of personal life takes place; the interior of the dwelling – the PLAN – and its living-equipment, the furniture'.[119] Coates also captured a crucial aspect of early twentieth-century domestic architecture and the new patterns of living, that is, its transience. Since the First World War, young professionals en masse had become less attached to a specific 'dwelling-scene' and moved around more frequently then they had ever in history. As a result, interiors mimicked this lifestyle shift. As with Otto, Gilda and Leo, modernity, fluidity and migration became hallmarks of modern living: 'The "home" was no longer a permanent place from one generation to another. The old phrase about a man's "appointed place" meant a real territorial limit.'[120] Through modern aesthetics, Coates and Coward, on the other side of the Atlantic, along with the exhibition shared in common a desire to bring a new interior to the people of Britain, an interior fit for new identities. In short, they offered a new *design for living*.

While Coates was best known for his exhibition displays for modern living, he also produced important interiors for leading social figures. In 1933 he completed the design of a home for actors Elsa Lanchester and Charles Laughton in Gordon Square, Bloomsbury, where the bohemian couple lived before moving permanently to Hollywood in 1939. Coates managed to 'translate their desire for "new scenes", in which the daily drama of their lives could be enacted, into a new spatial and formal language'.[121] According to Lanchester, the couple wanted interior spaces both 'airy and white'.[122] According to Elizabeth Darling, Lanchester's 'bohemian practices could not be accommodated within a conventional interior'; so she, Laughton and other like-minded bohemians 'made new ones [that embodied] a sense of freedom, the lack of responsibility'.[123] Indeed, this new freedom that the postwar generation sought was not simply spatial, but also represented a new sexual freedom as well; Laughton was bisexual and the couple had an open marriage that allowed both to fulfil their insatiable need for various companions. This fluid and free sexuality required to be accommodated in a modern interior, a space not unlike those advocated by Loos, Le Corbusier and others. However, unlike them, morality was not a part of the white walls Coates designed for them. The dramas they performed against white and open spaces allowed new scenes indeed, scenes that countered the generation's perceptions of the moribund sexual mores of their Victorian and Edwardian forefathers.

White walls became ideal surfaces on to which to project and picture modern identities, modern living. The home as private domain become a decidedly public one, one that exposed the identities of its inhabitants, the effect of which was a realignment of the experiential terrain of the domestic interior. The modern home 'is a space of the media, of

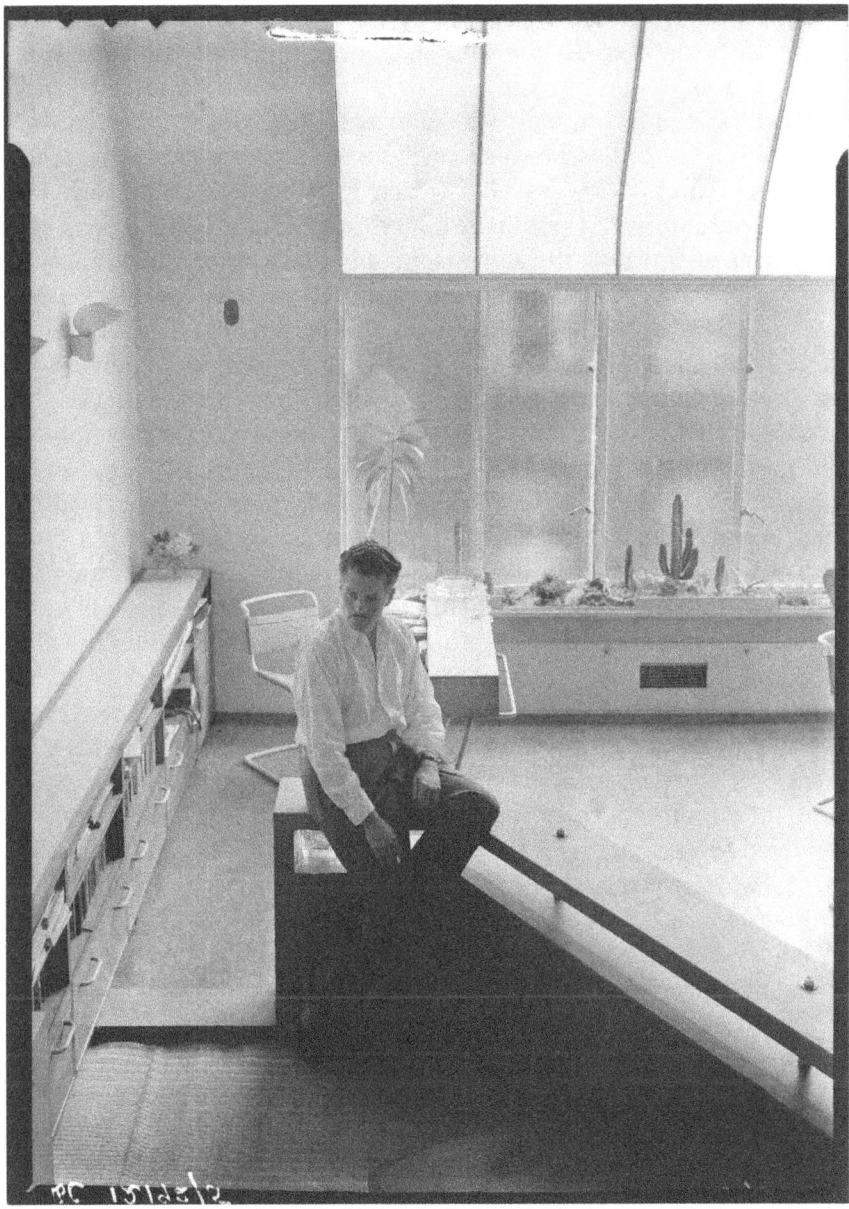

6.16 Howard Coster. Wells Wintemute Coates, 1937.

publicity. To be "inside" this space is only to see. To be "outside" is to be *in* the image, to be seen whether in the press photograph, a magazine, the movie, on television, or at your window.'[124] Within this visual structure the image we see is one of Coward reclined on a sofa, idling away time, a decidedly un-masculine, one could even say effeminate, thing to do, especially given it is performed in the purportedly unmasculine spaces of the domestic; a queer publicity of glamorous living to be sure.

Design for Living precariously teeters on the edge between fiction and autobiography through style and so-called substance. As such it flirts with the borders between inside and outside of the closet, for, as Sinfield notes, Coward always managed 'to hold homosexuality poised at the brink of public visibility'.[125] Visibility is made possible, however, only through the advertising of modern sexualities set against the 'background' of modern interiors, as both become complicit in the dynamics of the closet as spatial metaphor cum reality. The white wall purposefully and self-consciously exposes the very modern perversions they were meant to expose, shame and vilify. Coward's ongoing staging of modern living was perceived as contrary, however, to the effeminacy and past tense associated with Wilde and his (Victorian) kind. Wigley contends that: 'The white surface is the antifashion look, both in the sense of the "look" of the tabula rosa, with every excess cleared away, and in the sense of an active look, a surveillance device scanning the very spaces it has defined for the intrusions of fashion. The white wall is at once a camera and a monitor, a sensitive surface and a sensor.'[126] A camera implies the capturing of an image for longevity while surveillance reinforces the desire of modernist architects to eradicate decadence and degeneration from within the spaces of the modern interior. The so-called *tabula rasa* that modernity was said to provide for was a blank background against which Coward performed a new sexual and gendered subjectivity, with the Wildean excess of the past cleaned away. In this way, glamour is at once a performance of internalized shame and mode (read: fashion) of resistance. After all, modern architecture, as Wigley has convincingly shown, is fashion itself. Languid shapes, attenuated cigarettes, slicked-back, jet-black hair and razzmatazz tunes were the very stuff of modern/ist glamour. This chapter hopes to have shown the affect of glamour on the relationship between identity and the interior through the auspices of theatre and lived spaces. Modern identity is itself a visual product that, at the time, could be showcased to its fullest potential only on Broadway in an era of heightened and unbridled glamour. For Coward the networks between Paris and New York channelled the modernity he ultimately sought, away from the restrictive and moribund censorship of the Lord Chamberlain, ironic for a man who was constantly performing the choreographies of self-scrutiny. The Paris–New York axis, excluding London, also importantly became the network for the International Style that dominated the image of interior aesthetics. Modernity and advertising went hand in hand; economic and political realities demanded it, mass consumption fulfilled it. In this climate, Coward staged modernity as much as he staged the performances of identities, commodities bought and sold as easily as characters to be performed.

Notes

1 B. Nichols, *The Sweet and Twenties* (New York: British Book Centre, 1958), p. 37.
2 In *ibid.*, p. 101.
3 P. Hoare, *Noël Coward: A Biography* (New York: Simon & Schuster, 1995), p. 72.
4 T. Logan, *The Victorian Parlour* (Cambridge: Cambridge University Press, 2001), p. 202.
5 *Oxford English Dictionary*.
6 D. Cohen, *Households Gods: The British and Their Possessions* (New Haven and London: Yale University Press, 2006), p. 178.
7 E. Wilson, 'A Note on Glamour', *Fashion Theory*, vol. 11, no. 1 (2007), p. 100.
8 C. Innes, *Modern British Drama: The Twentieth Century* (Cambridge: Cambridge University Press, 2002), p. 265.
9 Hoare, *Noël Coward*, p. 129.
10 P. McNeil, 'Designing Women: Gender, Sexuality and the Interior Decorator, c. 1890–1940', *Art History*, vol. 17, no. 4 (December 1990), p. 38.
11 Hoare, *Noël Coward*, p. 130.
12 N. de Jongh, *Not in Front of the Audience: Homosexuality on Stage* (London and New York: Routledge, 1992), p. 19.
13 In Hoare, *Noël Coward*, p. 112.
14 A. Sinfield, 'Private Lives/Public Theater: Noël Coward and the Politics of Homosexuality', *Representations*, no. 36 (autumn 1991), p. 44.
15 Nichols, *The Sweet and Twenties*, p. 102.
16 F. Tamagne, *A History of Homosexuality in Europe: Berlin, London, Paris 1919–1939*, vol. ii (New York: Algora Publishing, 2004), p. 136
17 C. Lesley, G. Payne and S. Morley, *Noël Coward and His Friends* (New York: William Morrow, 1979), p. 63.
18 In Hoare, *Noël Coward*, p. 138.
19 In B. Day (ed.), *The Letters of Noël Coward* (London: Methuen Drama, 2007), pp. 88–9.
20 Reproduced in *ibid.*, p. 105.
21 Coward in *ibid.*, p. 153.
22 N. Coward, *Present Indicative* (Garden City and New York: Doubleday and Company, Inc., 1937), p. 203.
23 See A. Loos, 'Crime and Ornament', in Melony Ward and Bernie Miller (eds.), *Crime and Ornament: The Arts and Popular Culture in the Shadow of Adolf Loos* (Toronto: YYZ Books, 2002 [1908]).
24 C. Beaton, *The Glass of Fashion* (London: Weidenfeld and Nicolson, 1954), p. 153.
25 Coward, *Present Indicative*, p. 204.
26 *Ibid.*, p. 198.
27 *Ibid.*, p. 198.
28 *The Evening Standard*, 2 February 1923.

29 Hoare, *Noël Coward*, p. 140.

30 T. Castle, *Noël Coward and Radclyffe Hall: Kindred Spirits* (New York: Columbia University Press, 1996), p. 33.

31 Nichols, *The Sweet and Twenties*, pp. 104–5.

32 Tamagne, *A History of Homosexuality in Europe*, p. 69.

33 Coward in Day (ed.), *The Letters of Noël Coward*, p. 165.

34 In Sinfield, 'Private Lives/Public Theater', p. 50.

35 M. P. Brown, *Closet Space: Geographies of Metaphor from the Body to the Globe* (London and New York: Routledge, 2000), p. 15.

36 *Ibid.*, pp. 28–9.

37 *Ibid.*, p. 3.

38 E. K. Sedgwick, *Epistemology of the Closet* (Berkeley: University of California Press, 1990), p. 71.

39 In Hoare, *Noël Coward*, p. 268.

40 Logan, *The Victorian Parlour*, p. 235.

41 A. Sinfield, *The Wilde Century: Effeminacy, Oscar Wilde and the Queer Moment* (New York: Columbia University Press, 1994), p. 12.

42 D. M. Halperin, 'How to Do the History of Male Homosexuality', *GLQ: The Journal of Lesbian and Gay Studies*, vol. 6, no. 1 (2000), p. 92.

43 In Hoare, *Noël Coward*, p. 290.

44 S. Gundle, *Glamour: A History* (Oxford and New York: Oxford University Press, 2008), p. 169.

45 For a different and important analysis of Coward's queer identity and subversive use of effeminacy see S. Gilbert *Noël Coward and the Queer Feminine* (Toronto: University of Toronto, 2006).

46 Wilson, 'A Note on Glamour', p. 96.

47 *Ibid.*, p. 105.

48 S. Gundle, 'Hollywood Galmour and Mass Consumption in Postwar Italy', *Journal of Cold War Studies*, vol. 4, no. 3 (summer 2002), p. 98.

49 *Ibid.*, p. 99.

50 D. Slater, *Consumer Culture and Modernity* (Cambridge: Polity Press, 1997), p. 10.

51 In Gundle, 'Hollywood Glamour', pp. 96–7.

52 J. Brown, *Glamour in Six Dimensions* (Ithaca and London: Cornell University Press, 2009), p. 8.

53 *Ibid.*, p. 1.

54 *Vogue*, December 1932.

55 *Oxford English Dictionary*.

56 Beaton, *The Glass of Fashion*, pp. 153–4.

57 Beaton in Gundle, *Glamour: A History*, p. 167.

58 Castle, *Noël Coward and Radclyffe Hall*, p. 25.

59 *Ibid.*, p. 27.

60 P. Farfan, 'Noël Coward and Sexual Modernism: *Private Lives* as Queer Comedy', *Modern Drama*, vol. 48, no. 5 (winter 2005), p. 681.

61 Wilson, 'A Note on Glamour', p. 95.

62 Hoare, *Noël Coward*, p. 167.

63 Coward in Day (ed.), *The Letters of Noël Coward*, p. 139.

64 In Hoare, *Noël Coward*, p. 182.

65 17 Gerald Road remained Coward's London home until 1956. The house also served as the blueprint for Garry Essendine's flat in the semi-autobiograhical *Present Laughter* (1939).

66 See *The New York Times*, 14 September 1980.

67 J. Woollcombe, 'Noël Coward's "Cottage Interior"', *Homes and Gardens* (February 1937), p. 313.

68 *Ibid.*, p. 313.

69 *Ibid.*, p. 314.

70 *Ibid.*, p. 314.

71 *Ibid.*, p. 315.

72 *Ibid.*, p. 315.

73 *Ibid.*, p. 316.

74 *Ibid.*, p. 316.

75 C. Reed (ed.), *Not at Home: The Suppression of Domesticity in Modern Art and Architecture* (London: Thames and Hudson, 1996), p. 16.

76 See McNeil, 'Designing Women', and Cohen, *Households Gods*.

77 P. Sparke, *As Long as It's Pink: The Sexual Politics of Taste* (London and San Francisco: Pandora, 1994), p. 9.

78 'A House Built for a Bachelor', *The Ideal Home* (October 1928), p. 273.

79 Tom Pendergast in B. Osgerby, 'The Bachelor Pad as Cultural Icon: Masculinity, Consumption and Interior Design in American Men's Magazines, 1930–65', Journal of Design History, vol. 18, no. 1 (spring 2005), p. 101.

80 *Ibid.*, p. 100.

81 Le Corbusier, *Decorative Art Today* (Cambridge, MA: The MIT Press, 1987 [1925]), p. 271.

82 Sparke, *As Long as It's Pink*, p. 116.

83 Le Corbusier, *Decorative Art Today*, p. 192.

84 M. Wigley, *White Walls, Designer Dresses: The Fashioning of Modern Architecture* (Cambridge, MA, and London: The MIT Press, 2001), p. xviii.

85 See C. Reed, *Bloomsbury Rooms: Modernism, Subculture, and Domesticity* (New York: Yale University Press, 2004), p. 3.

86 N. Troy, *Modernism and the Decorative Arts in France: Art Nouveau to Le Corbusier* (London and New Haven: Yale University Press, 1991), p. 159.

87 In Sparke, *As Long as It's Pink*, p. 104.

88 R. Stanley, 'Houses of the Future? Machines to Live in', *Homes and Gardens* (February 1928), p. 315.

89 *Ibid.*, p. 316.

90 In B. Colomina, *Sexuality and Space* (New York: Princeton Architectural Press, 1992), p. 6.

91 B. Colomina, *Privacy and Publicity: Modern Architecture as Mass Media* (Cambridge: Cambridge University Press, 1994), p. 10.

92 Nichols, *The Sweet and Twenties*, p. 112.

93 McNeil, 'Designing Women', p. 643.

94 Cohen, *Households Gods*, p. 179.

95 M. Wigley, 'White Out: Fashioning the Modern', in Deborah Fausch et al. (eds). *Architecture in Fashion* (Princeton: Princeton Architectural Press, 1994), p. 242.

96 Sparke, *As Long as It's Pink*, p. 5.

97 See for example J. Rault, *Eileen Gray and the Design of Sapphic Modernity: Staying In* (Burlington and Aldershot: Ashgate, 2011), pp. 27–55.

98 M. Speyer, 'The Hybrid Home: Mixing the Old with the New', *Homes and Gardens* (January 1936), p. 318.

99 In L. Fischer, *Designing Women: Cinema, Art Deco and the Female Form* (New York: Columbia University Press, 2003), p. 170.

100 *The New York Times*, 26 February 1926.

101 Slater, *Consumer Culture and Modernity*, p. 12.

102 In J. Leslie, B. Nicholson and N. Gabo (eds.), *Circle: International Survey of Constructivist Art* (London: Faber and Faber, 1937), p. 125.

103 Coward in Day (ed.), *The Letters of Noël Coward*, p. 1667.

104 N. Coward, 'Private Lives', in *Three Plays* (New York: Vintage, 1999 [1930]), p. 214.

105 Farfan, 'Noël Coward and Sexual Modernism', p. 681.

106 Innes, *Modern British Drama*, p. 263.

107 Farfan, 'Noël Coward and Sexual Modernism', p. 681.

108 The play was later performed in London at the Haymarket Theatre in 1939.

109 E. K. Sedgwick, *Between Men: English Literature and Male Homosocial Desire* (New York: Columbia University Press, 1985), p. 21.

110 McNeil, 'Designing Women', p. 631.

111 *New York News*, 7 September 1937.

112 Sedgwick, *Between Men*, p. 2.

113 In R. Shields (ed.), *Places on the Margin: Alternative Geographies of Modernity* (London and New York; Routledge, 1991), p. 36.

114 Colomina, *Privacy and Publicity*, p. 14.

115 *Ibid.*, p. 9.

116 See J. Riviere, 'Womanliness as Masquerade', in Victor Burgin, James Donald and Cora Kaplan (eds.), *Formations of Fantasy* (New York: Routledge, 1986 [1929]).

117 D. Jeremiah, *Architecture and Design for the Family in Britain, 1900–1970* (Manchester and New York: Manchester University Press, 2000), p. 92.

118 In N. Kuzmanovic, *John Paul Cooper: Designer and Craftsman of the Arts and Crafts Movement* (Phoenix Hill and New York: Sutton, 1999), p. 150.

119 W. Coates, 'Furniture Today – Furniture Tomorrow', *The Architectural Review*, vol. lxxii, no. 428 (July 1932), p. 31.

120 *Ibid.*, p. 32.
121 E. Darling, '"The scene in which the daily drama of personal life takes place": Towards the Modern Interior in Early 1930s Britain', in Penny Sparke et al. (eds.), *Designing the Modern Interior: From the Victorians to Today* (Oxford and New York: Berg, 2009), p. 97.
122 In *ibid.*, p. 102.
123 *Ibid.*, p. 97.
124 Colomina, *Privacy and Publicity*, p. 6.
125 Sinfield, 'Private Lives/Public Theater', p. 58.
126 M. Wigley, 'White-Out: Fashioning the Modern [Part 2]', *Assemblage*, no. 22 (December 1993), p. 8.

7 ✧ Cecil Beaton: artifice as resistance

I would like to live in scenery.
Cecil Beaton

CELEBRATED PHOTOGRAPHER, diarist and stage and costume designer Cecil Beaton (1904–1980) was consumed by other peoples' interiors, the way they lived and the manner through which they staged the spaces of their notoriety and creative work. Unlike most of the subjects of this book, in which friends, colleagues and even at times foes provided the evidence of the descriptive interiors, Beaton often reversed the order entirely, describing at length the domestic spaces of influential figures of the early twentieth century. Beaton's descriptions of Paris's luminaries, for example, were particularly redolent with descriptive language only a photographer and stage designer could conjure. The vivid image he painted, while brief, of Jean Cocteau's opium-laced interior evoked an atmosphere steeped in decadence and near decay. He observed that '[i]f a stranger looks at the objects in the room, he will perhaps guess Jean's unhappy side – the great disasters, the personal tragedy of being abandoned by lovers. There is a lurking sentimentality in the crimson wools, a death-like aura about the life masks of his head and hands, a secretly depressing claustrophobia in this atmosphere redolent of the seminal smell of opium.'[1] For Beaton objects of decadence and decay betrayed the interior's occupant's identity and history. Beaton was not alone in his perceptions of the true function of the interior. As Deborah Cohen has shown, from the 1890s to the First World War, interior design took on a decidedly new and important mandate, that of paying witness to and highlighting 'the individual' through unique and idiosyncratic decorative schemes.[2] Like fashion, personality, class affiliation and cultural aspirations could best be expressed through one's interiors and decorative flourishes, which together formed a composite impression of the inhabitant. However, this ideal, I wish to extend, did not stop with the war, but continued to flourish within the consumer-driven ethos that dominated the West in the interwar period.

In this respect Beaton's descriptions of the lived-in interiors of Paris's most prominent same-sex couple, Gertrude Stein and Alice B. Toklas, are perhaps all the more revealing. In the summer of 1935 Beaton paid the couple a visit in their new flat in the rue Christine. 'Oddly', he recalled, 'I had never imagined Miss Stein's apartment would be so impressive, though there was no reason to believe otherwise: whenever we met, I'd always been particularly struck with her sense of taste. Here now was the expression of a *goût impeccable*. Tall ceilings, panelled walls and high windows delighted the eye. Each piece of furniture seemed solid and beautiful in design. There was no *chichi* or vulgarity anywhere. The Misses Stein and Toklas live like Biblical royalty: simply, yet in complete luxury.' High-polished furniture and pictures by Picasso and Cézanne occupied each room, displayed alongside a select assortment of 'unique objects'. According to Beaton's account, '[f]uss, bother and discomfort seemed eliminated from an apartment whose great strength resides in its uniformity'.[3] On this visit he set out to photograph Toklas, the mistress of taste of the couple's domestic union. That afternoon Toklas was '[d]etermined not to talk' and was busying herself quietly with her sewing. In response to his solicitation to take her photograph she acknowledged him simply, though provocatively, by responding: 'Interior'.[4] In this performative utterance, identity, interior and image cohere seamlessly; the embodiment of a queer design. Beaton returned to visit the couple again in the summer of 1939, this time at their summer home in Bilignin, Bellay, Ain. There, according to him, they designed

> the most ideal environment in which to work, creating an atmosphere that every artist must respond to ... Colours, sounds and smells combine to produce an impression of complete simplicity and harmony. Here everything necessary is at hand, nothing more ... Each room is as satisfying as the solution of a mathematical problem. Throughout the house, there are few objects. But each object is of merit. There is nothing to offend the eye. A polished perfection dominates this rusticity. The cakes of soap in the bathroom are placed in rigid, sharp-edged precision. The food is the best food, for Alice has not only a cordon bleu but watches her cook with a rapid eye. The plates and goblets are bold and beautiful.[5]

For Beaton even Toklas's cut floral arrangements were at once 'esoteric still-lifes' and possessed 'an 'architectural quality'.[6] Thanks to her fastidious touch, the couple lived out their exemplary aesthetic life in interiors contrived through artifice. In its Old French origins, artifice came from the Latin *artificium*, a combination of *ars* (art) and *facere* (to make). Artificiality, the debauched cousin of artifice with whom it shares its etymological origin, is often easily subsumed in conceptualizations and perceptions of the origins of the latter term as both are used as signs of shame. Artificiality marks a sign of affectation, occupying the dubious realm of the unnatural, while artifice acts as a mode of deception. Artificiality, artifice and affectation infected in varied ways Beaton's fascination with the interior, principally produced within him through the sheer joy and genuine appreciation of thoughtful workmanship and the art and refinement of taste. However, even Beaton himself later warned against overstepping the boundaries of artifice when writing on women's fashion in *Vogue* in 1959 that the 'correct use depends upon instinct. But when properly invoked, it is not merely an illusion: rather, it makes the observer see what he should see'.[7] Although Beaton was extolling the virtues of enhancing the uniqueness with which nature endows each woman, his comments are equally pertinent when discussing the interior as both a product of instinct and a revelation of identity as much as a mode of directing the observer's gaze. Here, stage and interior designer meets photographer.

While Beaton's rich descriptions betray his love of artifice and the workmanship of designed space, it is easy to perceive and rest on the by-now standard image of Beaton: the author of countless memorable portraits of his era's greatest luminaries, the creator of iconic *Vogue* images, the wizard of *My Fair Lady*. While artifice, affect and creativity were the sources of Beaton's fame and fortune, these would also provide innumerable ambivalent experiences of shame. And while this shame spurred greater creativity and a sense of self, it nonetheless must bear properly in the narrative of the man who staged the defining impressions of an entire generation. After all, as Eve Kosofsky Sedgwick questions, is shame not itself 'a form of communication'?[8] It also takes on a double movement, one might suggest, an orientation 'toward painful individuation, toward uncontrollable relationality … shame effaces itself; shame points and projects; shame turns itself skin side out; shame and pride, shame and dignity, shame and self-display, shame and exhibitionism are different interlinings of the same glove'.[9] The metaphor of the glove is not only a fashionable accessory but also points to the tightness, the protective and yet restrictive space it provides its wearer. The affective language of artifice for the queer practitioner inevitably brings with it a contest between pleasure and shame, a coupling not entirely unlike the workmanship and unnaturalness that artifice implies. Shame has long been an important part of queer identity, often indelibly imbricated within its very formation, seeping into the very fibres of our clothes and the walls of our homes. It is this contest between joyful artifice and the affect of shame that I seek to understand Beaton's personal landscape of the modern interior.

7.1 Peter North. Cecil Beaton, c. 1920s.

Following the Second World War, artifice, gay identity and the modern interior became so indelibly linked that it engendered a stereotype that still holds currency in the English-speaking world today. As Penny Sparke asserts, '[f]or almost three decades the idea of bourgeois taste, linked with that of display, and, by implication, the aesthetic of feminine domesticity, provided an image against which modernist architects could react'.[10] Through the culturally burdened notion of taste, men like Beaton threatened the modernizing zeal of the new century. In the exercise of their taste in objects and interiors, queer men reinforced, even if unwittingly, stereotypes they were burdened with, stereotypes loaded with fear and loathing. Perhaps no other cultural document best embodies the contest over the moral health of the modern interior than Mardaunt Shairp's play *The Green Bay Tree* from 1933. The largely forgotten play helps, nevertheless, to situate the cultural links between interior space, artifice and queer identity in the interwar years. As we shall see, the play's central protagonist, Dulcimer, suffers an untimely and unfortunate death entirely because of his unhealthy love with the artifice by which he constructs and controls both his interiors and adopted son.

Like Dulcimer, Beaton resisted dominant cultural perceptions associated with a purportedly exaggerated mode of display (read: feminine), the embodiment of artifice itself, through the workmanship of the interior. Both theatrical and historical characters embodied, by default, the prototypical figure of the 'gay decorator'; who along with women had come to dominate the professional identity of the interior designer since the 1920s. Unlike with Coward, as we saw in the previous chapter, the pose of aesthetic indifference was not assumed by Beaton, but fantastically rejected with abandon. I wish to make clear from the outset that Beaton was not a victim of the myriad and nefarious techniques of shame, but rather that his cultural significance lay in his ability to bridle an unholy relationship between shame and artifice as a creative and productive means of resistance which he staged in domestic performances and interior designs.

Bright Young Things

The so-called Bright Young Things of the carefree and rebellious 1920s were characterized by their flamboyance and Wildean dandyism. In 1909 *The Modern Man* decried the modern 'effeminate' dandy and attempted to define this creature. According to the periodical, while the dandy pays considerable attention to his dress and appearance, 'he should not be confused with the fop. The fop', it noted, 'is a man who pays an inordinate amount of attention to his attire, which is a different matter from being particular.' What, however, constituted their differences? The dandy was 'seldom' if ever 'eccentric or extravagant in his attire' as was the fop. Clearly it was the fop who cut an unmasculine silhouette. There were admittedly, according to the author, 'effeminate dandies', however, these he concluded 'are generally more correctly to be described as fops'. The dandy per se is clearly not the problem for the modern man, as the numerous 'successful businessmen have been and are dandies, and the value of a good appearance, as a business asset is well known'; the problem is the effeminate one, the very type Coward was at pains to avert.[11] As Stephen Gundle has argued: 'Their [Bright Young Things] love of fancy dress was a refusal of the regular world … They were widely despised for the antics and their careless display of privilege without responsibility'.[12]

The modern aesthete, the lover of artifice, was the subject of numerous attacks long after Wilde's death in Paris. Even in the supposed glory days of the 1920s, the queer figure of the aesthete was held as a degenerate sort lurking the halls of hallowed British universities like Oxford and Cambridge, the latter attended by Beaton and which he left without a degree in 1925. In his detailed and lengthy analysis of *Degenerate Oxford: A Critical Study of Modern University Life*, published on the cusp of the

7.2 Attributed to Cecil Beaton. Self-Portrait, 1927.

1930s, Terence Greenbridge was at great pains to describe the realities, conditions and true nature of the aesthete, the decidedly intellectual sort who turned his back on the 'prevalent' athleticism of the day.[13] In his introduction to the subject, Greenbridge argued that the press unfairly misrepresented the aesthete in praise of the athlete, 'a sturdy, plus-four-wearing beer-drinking Englishman, the kind of fellow who throws agitators into horse-troughs and then goes out hunting. And we hear the [aesthete] stigmatised as untidy, lank, pale, decadent, degenerate, the kind of man who produces doubtful Elizabethan plays under the name of Art.'[14] A particular feature of the modern aesthete, in contradistinction, was 'his keen individualism'; a remarkable feature given it owed much to Liberal philosophers of the 1890s, a clear allusion to Wilde and his sort. However, the insinuation of the past, a particular past burdened by trauma and shame, was not always appreciated by the aesthete of the 1920s (best embodied as we have seen in the public figure of Coward), who, as a true modernist to the core, 'never lik[ed] to think of himself as in any way nineteenth century'.[15] The effeminacy these young bright aesthetes performed was meant to be seen as a rupture from the past, free of guilt and association.

As 'types' in the grand tradition of the Enlightenment Project, the athlete and the aesthete as antagonistic cultural figures had long been reported on in the popular press. In 1883, for example, *The Illustrated London News* published a cartoon aptly titled 'Aesthetics versus Athletics' in which the sullen-cheeked, hunched-back black-wearing degenerates are juxtaposed with robust masculine athletes placed in the immediate foreground, pictured in form-fitting sporting attire and accompanied by two enamoured Victorian maidens [Figure 7.3]. By the turn of the century the two male types, within the contest of national wellbeing and imperial vigour, were indelibly linked to fears of sexual health. Bernarr Aldophus Macfadden, an exponent of physique culture, surmised in 1900 that the source of nervous energy implicated in athleticism was the 'same power that controlled his sexual instinct'. In fact, sexual impotence, concluded Macfadden, suggested weakness in every domain of intellectual and bodily endeavour.[16] Greenbridge also made note how terms such as 'decadence' and 'degeneracy' were often deployed in journalists' descriptions of the aesthete. These terms designated 'a pallid, indoor creature, that he is given to morbid brooding about his own soul, that he is fond of obscenity for the sake of obscenity, even though he delights to call it Art, and that homosexuality attracts him'. However, for Greenbridge, they avoided using 'crude words' like 'effeminate' and 'unmanly' while these necessarily were 'in reality synonyms'.[17] Indeed the effeminate aesthete was seen to possess too high a fondness for the domestic sphere, a space to idle his time away and to divine a life-world of his own imagination and fantasy.

What brings the aesthete together with the athlete, however, is a more anodyne Romanticism, a term developed by Greenbridge to designate at once romantic friendship and homosexuality, the latter not favoured by the author. 'For the law of the attraction of the opposite

7.3 'Aesthetics versus Athletics', *Illustrated London News*, 17 March 1883.

holds quite as strongly in exotic Oxford as it does in the more normal world. The object of the Aesthete's admiration is frequently the Athlete, and often the Athlete feels a counter-admiration for the Aesthete, or – if that does not happen – at least indulges in friendship with him, because so many Aesthetes are charming people.'[18] An added benefit of this sort of relationship is that it produces a Grecian-styled paternity in which one sees an older undergraduate becoming fond of a younger student, helping 'to mould his growing soul – in fact, he shows an almost womanly constructiveness. One is reminded of the way in which the ancient Lacedaemonains [sic] exploited Greek Love, expecting the elder to pair not merely to inspirit the younger by means of his affection, but also to instruct him in the art of war.'[19] Clearly, Edward Perry Warren was not alone in his Victorian-leaning Greek ideal when he published the first volume of his *Defence of Uranian Love* in 1928, though with very different desired results.

Homosexual writers like W. H. Auden, Christopher Isherwood, Beverley Nichols and Cecil Beaton, to note only a few examples, all went to Oxford and Cambridge in the 1920s and 1930s and toyed with their so-called 'aesthetic' inclinations. According to Greenbridge, men like them could be identified, namely through common sartorial choices that included:

> brightly coloured coats, cut short and very tight in the waist, their grey flannel trousers will be of a conspicuously silver hue and flow loosely, their feet will be shod with gay suede shoes. They will speak with artificial voices of a somewhat high timbre, also they will walk with a mincing gait.[20]

Like Auden and Isherwood, Nichols himself conceded that he neither acquired a taste for an affected voice (said to be common among this set), nor did he indulge in any passion 'for dressing up' the way Beaton and his best friend Stephen Tennant did. The pair were amongst a select coterie of Bright Young Things who coloured their hair and wore makeup. Beaton began his career photographing this smart set, their environments and their fancy dress parties for which they were notorious. As Nichols reminisced: 'The Bright Young Things of the twenties never missed an opportunity to dress up … any excuse was good enough for putting a wig and painting one's face and roaring round the town. Cecil was always a ringleader in these expeditions, and I did not realize at the time that this passion for fancy dress was the first indication of his longing to design, to create beauty in line and colour'.[21] With acknowledgement, however, comes shame through Nichols's pen when he unflatteringly described how Beaton's laugh 'resembled the sounds made by an extremely fatigued corncrake, when he is amused it recalls an obscene laughing jackass'.[22] Mainstream and heterosexist culture does not possess exclusive rights over shame as it is too often deployed within the confines of queer culture itself.

Beaton dismissed his years spent in Cambridge and often claimed that life for him began in 1926, the year after he left St John's College, when he slowly began to forge his career as photographer. In a lecture he delivered in the USA, he stated: 'During the three years I spent at Cambridge, I put myself down to a mixture of studies, but I never

7.4 Cecil Beaton sitting in his student residence, Cambridge, 1922.

went to lectures. Instead I became a whole-hearted aesthete, joined the Theatre Club, designed costumes and scenery, and performed in the stage productions.'[23] Beaton was always in pursuit of self-promotion even in those early days at university. He would arrange to have photographs taken of himself in his rooms, have them sent off to newspapers, admitting when they were published: 'Few things thrill me more'.[24] Nichols once noted how early on Beaton had 'no real theatre in which to clothe his fancies, so he made a theatre of the drawing-room'.[25] While at Cambridge Beaton did not live in residence at St John's College, but resided at 47 Bridge Street [see Figure 7.4]. His charming, sloped-floor rooms with their white walls and exposed beams were a perfect background for Beaton's early theatrical talents. Walls were not left bare for long, but covered with Pamela Bianco illustrations in stark black frames that led Beaton to believe he was not in Cambridge but in Venice, a far more romantically appropriate location for his self-fashioning and artifice. Beaton spent much time and money on the refurbishing of his rooms, and his extravagance was far removed from his athletic contemporaries who roamed the university precincts.[26] On 3 May 1923 he acquired a gyp (the Cambridge term to designate a gentleman's gentleman), when Bill Butler arrived to care for the young Beaton. 'The room was full of sketchbooks. He remembered a smart man who came to see Cecil from time to time. Butler wondered what he was. Later he discovered: "It was his tailor from London".'[27] The study of self-fashioning through artifice was Beaton's true and only vocation while at university.

Through the looking glass: affectation and shame

Beaton had many friends and likely as many foes, but numerous are those who provided fascinating descriptions of him over the years. Interior decorator, socialite and friend David Herbert described Beaton in the following manner: 'Tall, thin and willowy, he had the most remarkable eyes: violet and piercing, set flat against his face and as far apart as a goat's ... he "walked delicately", unlike most Englishmen he used his hands expressively when talking'.[28] Tennant was more profound in his description, claiming Beaton always struggled to redesign himself into a better version – less cruel through his wit.[29] Beaton's cruelty was noted by many, and he recalled how Cocteau christened him 'Malice in Wonderland' and chided him for, according to him,

> spending my life in unreality made up of fun, too much fun and my interests are limited to the joys of certain superficial forms of beauty, to sensual delights only to a certain blunt degree, and with too many people, too many light quick sketches, quick fire articles and photographs galore. The crowded weeks gave place to others and I am under the delusion that I am 'living' so much more vitally than I should have if I had 'gone my own way'.[30]

The simple, yet repeated, use of 'too' serves as a linguistic designation for Beaton's artifice and excess, it *too* becomes the conduit for shame itself. In her celebrated essay 'Notes on "Camp"' Susan Sontag asserted that '[c]amp is a certain mode of aestheticism. It is one way of seeing the world as an aesthetic phenomenon. That way, the way of Camp, is not in terms of beauty, but in terms of the degree of artifice, of stylization'.[31] More often than not style and artifice have, strangely, connoted a lack or deceitful move away from substance and truth itself.

In the summer of 1927 Coward, whom Beaton looked up to, satirized the young man and the 'Bright Young Things' in his song 'I've been to a marvellous party', in which he sang: 'Dear Cecil arrived wearing armour /Some shells and a black feather boa'.[32] However, it was not simply at fancy dress parties that 'fancy' men were made fun of for their over-the-top stylizations or had to take care to avoid shame or retribution. The fear of suspicion was more broadly felt in the urban landscape in which men had to ensure proper sartorial comportment, at all costs. One London man, for example, recalled how he 'was always particularly circumspect on his own street. While he always wore his overcoat over his shoulders in the West End – "it was camp and a risqué thing to do" – his arms went in his sleeves when he got close to home.'[33]

Self-scrutiny, as we have seen in the previous chapter, was championed and formed an indelible facet of Coward's personality and self-fashioning, and served as repeated attacks against Beaton. Upon meeting him for the first time in April 1930 when the playwright was at sea, travelling with Venetia Montagu from New York to London, he assailed Beaton for the 'malicious' article he had written on one of his recent plays. Coward attacked asserting: '"You must expect to be attacked if you write such horrible things."... But there was so much truth in what they had to say that I could not deny it ... As for Noël Coward, the truth is that I've wanted to meet him for many years. I adore everything about his work: his homesick, sadly melodious tunes, his revues, his witty plays, his astringent acting ... Yet both came to the same conclusion: I was flobby, flabby and affected.'[34] On a second encounter on the same journey, Beaton was to draw him, and instead he was given a lesson on corporeal and sartorial management. Mocking his effeminate walk and voice, Coward reproached him: 'It is important not to let the public have a loophole to lampoon you'. Coward understood all too well the importance of the public persona for a homosexual man, advocating, at least on the surface, a distance between the private man and the public mask. Beaton remarked how Coward surveyed himself, looking at his 'façade' carefully, the very same façade used to perform his masculinity, off stage. Coward once again chastised Beaton, stating:

> You should appraise yourself ... Your sleeves are too tight, your voice is too high, and too precise. You mustn't do it. It closes so many doors ... It's hard, I know. One would like to indulge one's own taste. I myself dearly love a good match, yet I know it is overdoing it to wear tie, socks and handkerchief of the same colour. I take ruthless stock of myself in the mirror before going out. A polo jumper or unfortunate tie exposes one to danger.[35]

Again *too* discursively signified the shame of excess within a culture of homophobic panic. Coward's words are at once homophobic and cautionary and obliquely acknowledge the constant necessary negotiation between resistance and shame *bachelors of a different sort* performed. Further, the door to which he alluded tacitly acknowledged how the proverbial closet could affect perception and hence success within the public domain of celebrity. However, Beaton's own sense of shame and self-inflicted remorse began long before his chance meeting with Coward. In a conversation with Billee Le Bas regarding his feelings for and relationships with women, Beaton recalled how he simply preferred to limit himself to dancing with them. Regarding how he felt about men, this proved to be an altogether different and complicated matter. On another occasion Beaton wrote: 'My friendships with men are much more wonderful than with women. I've never been in love with women and I don't think I ever shall in the way that I have been in love with men. I'm really a terrible, terrible homosexualist and try so hard not to be. I try so terribly hard to be good and not cheap and horrid ... it's so much nicer just to be affectionate and sleep in the same bed but that's all. Everything else is repulsive and yet it's awfully difficult!'[36] Here the twin relationship between denial and shame taints the expressions and experiences of sexuality and subjectivity itself.

In 1926 Beaton was invited to a party at British *Vogue* editors Madge Garland and Dorothy Todd's home where he met socialites like actor Tom Douglas, Elizabeth Ponsoby and Cynthia Noble (Lady Gladwyn). At the party Freddie Ashton performed campy, 'shy-making imitations of various ballet dancers and Queen Alexandra, the sort of thing one is ashamed of and only does in one's bedroom in front of large mirrors when one is rather excited and worked up'.[37] It seems incongruous that a man who provided us with the extravagant designs for *My Fair Lady*, the countless theatrical landscapes of *haute couture* and numerous fantastical fancy dress parties should be so shy and ashamed. However, it demonstrates the ways in which shame and camp are the opposing sides of the same coin. As Christopher Reed asserts: 'Such anecdotes reveal a subculture that delighted in queerness and performance – indeed, in queerness *as* a form of performance that could challenge the shame associated with the usual dynamics of seeing deviance: inadvertent display or unwanted exposure'.[38] While Beaton's shame was palpable and visceral at Todd and Garland's soirée, it would help pave the way for Beaton's gradual acceptance of shame as an integral part to the way he staged his resistance to a world hostile to camp, artifice and effeminacy.

The path, however, was not necessarily always easy and Beaton even suffered homophobic aspersions at the hands of a woman like Virginia Woolf, long celebrated for her queer sense and sensibility. Woolf declined to sit for the photographer on the false pretence she was staying on in Sussex where she had already been for some time. In reality, as she later confessed to Vita Sackville-West, she had refused him precisely because of his 'style and manner' and claimed him simply to be 'a mere catamite' (the boy in Roman pederastic unions).[39] In short, it was the perceived effeminacy and so-called style (read: artifice) by which he performed his gender, a pose that exposed too easily his sexuality, apparent superficiality and lack of masculinity. Here, again, sexuality and aesthetics are all too easily conflated in a relationship degraded by even the most tolerant of luminaries. Woolf and Queen Mary were the only two cultural figures of note who dared refuse to sit for the photographer in his long, acclaimed career. Catherine Horwood claims that 'Beaton walked a tightrope between permissible eccentricity and outright theatricality during the late 1920s and 19230s. Photographs of him at home in his kitchen show that he cared little for current styling. For a homosexual of this period, it was only safe to wear more "outrageous" outfits in one's own home and those of a small circle of trusted friends.'[40] An interest in

7.5 Cecil Beaton. Self-Portrait in drag as Lady Mendl (Elsie de Wolfe) for Elsa Maxwell's costume party at the Waldorf, New York, 1 May 1934.

clothing was already seen as decidedly 'un-British'.[41] However, Beaton long enjoyed an unabashed relationship with fancy dress and at times outright drag sported either at his renowned parties at his home or while attending those hosted by his illustrious friends. On one occasion he took his costuming to a new exciting level. Beaton attended a costume party given by Elsa Maxwell at the Waldorf in New York on 1 May 1934 at which he elected not to dress as a fantastical character, but in drag as the celebrated interior decorator Lady Mendl (Elsie de Wolfe) [Figure 7.5]. Like Coward, Beaton understood the signifying power of dress. However, unlike Coward, Beaton unabashedly celebrated the limitless queer potential, the artifice that fashion provided for. Beaton's performance was a camp send-up of his alliance with design greats who decorated in a similar style and forged new terrain at an important historical juncture in the bodily and cultural politics of gender. The costume or more aptly the pose was not merely homage to a celebrity female designer from earlier in the century, but underpinned Beaton's own fascination with the interior world of design. Coward and Beaton provided portraits of deep contrast: for every act of self-scrutiny and closeting (acts of privatization) that Coward self-consciously performed, Beaton had the courage to go public with his resistance, to place front and centre his effeminacy, artifice and sexual otherness within the public domain. As such, Beaton layers the trans-gendered performance and historical significance of those whose instincts and workmanship enhanced the value and art of the modern interior, in other words, artifice itself. In this, as in all of Beaton's creative productions (of which drag formed a part), artifice as style operates as a locus of resistance as much to masculinist modernism as to homophobic panic. Fancy dress, however, was not always a requisite for attacks.

Looking back on the 1920s and the colourful characters that populated it, Coward once described the particular, very unique subset of the Bright Young Things. According to Coward they 'are just as determined to be bright as were their fathers and mothers; parapets are still walked at midnight, and dinner-jacketed young men are still falling or being pushed into swimming pools or the river of successful parties'.[42] Coward's less than subtle allusions were to Beaton and a specific event that left its mark on the young man as much as on the collective perceptions of the aesthete, the progeny of Wilde's maligned generation of queers. In his diary, Beaton recorded the event with a degree of indifference, boasting he was neither shaken by it nor did he make a fuss over it. The event to which both men referred, nevertheless, uncovers a seemly aspect of queer cultural life. In the summer of 1928 Beaton along with many others was invited to celebrate the coming-of-age of Lord Herbert. For the event, Beaton was accommodated by good friend Edith Oliver. While Beaton and his party walked the path along the river leading to the festivities, he recalled how 'beautiful the night scene was! How calm and visionary! But my reveries were short-lived'. Things quickly turned into a 'nightmare', when

> [o]ut of the darkness a group of tail-coated young men surrounded me and, without a world of explanation, hijacked me across the lawns at enormous pace towards the river. I remember my head was raised in a Guido Reni agony which seemed to be unending. In the panic that assailed me, the emotions of humiliation and shame were stronger than those of fear. The black night whirled past me, bat-like, as the phantasmorgia journey continued, until abruptly, with a vicious thrust from all my attackers, I was catapulted into the darkness. With a tremendous splash and plopping of stones, I found myself standing knee deep in the Nadder. Too stunned to know what to do, in my startled misery, I merely stood silent. This had the effect of a clever ruse: my enemies now became somewhat apprehensive lest their treatment of me should have ended in my complete disappearance. The group above me on the river's bank murmured, 'Do you think the bugger's drowned?'... Eventually, in a rather dead voice, I replied, 'Yes, the bugger's alive,' and I trudged up the stones ad mud into the comparative light of the lawns. My attackers had vanished ... 'Yes, it was a glorious ball. The best I've ever been to'. About one thing I was determined: the incident would never be mentioned by me. So far as I was concerned, it had never taken place.[43]

In Beaton's recollection shame and joy prove, at least on the surface, odd bedfellows. However, it is worth underlining how humiliation and shame of the experience in no way marred his experiences of and expressions of himself as a true aesthete. Here the joy of the aesthetic provides the core of his resistance, for, without it, surely his recollections and memorializing (themselves a function of this resistance) would have been vastly different. In Beaton's diary, shame never dampens the power of artifice, rather, like a good aesthete, it only serves to heighten its potency. After all, for someone well versed in the true power of artifice a 'glorious ball' is the only true antidote to the scaring pain of shame. Beaton in his artifice and flamboyance was never shy about expressing his queer masculinity. Although it would be tempting to cast this off as the silly machinations of pranksters, in light of the manner it seems to have affected Beaton, for better or for worse, it cannot be viewed as anything less than homophobic bullying, a concept we often conveniently misplace in the annals of history, queer or otherwise. In large measure, the reason is that homophobia is internalized as much as it projects, suppresses and denies not only within the victim but also within the culture that tolerates and advocates it. Looking back on the 1920s and discussing the idea that hindsight is 20/20 and often crueller than necessary, Beaton opined that '[t]olerance and a sense of the comic as well as the tragic ought to make us see, in the fashion and frivolities of any given epoch, the wonderful creativity that finds expression, conscious and unconscious, in clothes, songs, slang, dances, art – in short, in all that becomes history. I do not see the twenties as imbued with false nostalgia, but as a tonic period in modern life.'[44] In short, artifice was a, *the*, necessary mode of resistance.

Materializing the homosexual: The Green Bay Tree

As I noted in the previous chapter, the homosexual as a discursive entity could not be staged in the theatre until well after 1958. While it is undeniable that words are often burdened by and loaded with social, political and cultural force and resonance, we might also consider that the contours of homosexuality could, however, be articulated through other equally powerful conduits, those of material culture and the performances of and within interiors. Mardaunt Shairp defiantly portrayed the homosexual through the closeting guise of its own stereotype in *The Green Bay Tree: A Play in Three Acts* Mardaunt Shairp produced at the St Martin's Theatre, London, on 25 January 1933, The play narrates the story of Mr Dulcimer, a wealthy, gentleman who, throughout the play, never leaves the sanctuary of his luxurious home in Mayfair, an artificial world of his own devising, which the audience encounters as soon as the curtain rises. Soon after we are also introduced to Julian, his adopted son-protégé. The description of Dulcimer's Mayfair home is detailed and vivid; it also marks one of the most important techniques of characterization of the main character, given how he is regarded as a lover of luxury and material excess. Theatre scholar Nicholas de Jongh notes how from the outset of the play '[t]he audience is incited to believe that Julian's addiction to "luxury" and "pleasure" has contaminated him', terms that positioned together serve as clear indices of his queer inclinations.[45] Dulcimer and his home embodied the moral decay decried by Loos and Le Corbusier, a decline in civilization through the corruption of the modern interior (both unnatural and effeminate), the very heart of Western civilization.

What makes *The Green Bay Tree* particularly compelling is the attention to detail used to describe Dulcimer's Mayfair home and Julian's biological father's (Mr Owen's) home in the second act. The atmosphere of Dulcimer's salon is suffused with a tone 'of luxury and fastidiousness', the very clichéd emblems long held to identify the home of the aberrant. In a nod to the aesthetes of the late nineteenth century, Dulcimer is described as 'an artist' in the opening descriptive remarks: 'He is an artist in the sense that everything in the room has been chosen for its intrinsic value and given its absolutely right position in the general scheme of decoration. He never puts up anything because of its associations, nor leaves anything about because the room has been well-used.' In this calculated and thought-out manner, the room appears 'artificial', but at the same time 'it excites curiosity about the owner', whose home 'is a constant source of pleasure' for himself. Common with theories of the day, the salon and the home overall 'reflect his personality, his sensitiveness, and delicate appreciation of beauty'. Dulcimer is the embodiment of the modern aesthete, one who has not turned his back on the home, but rather has made it his sanctuary, coded as a feminizing enterprise, further implicating the central character in the queerness of his identity. 'Above all, the rational home abhorred all that the middle-class Victorian home had stood for, especially its emphasis on the aesthetic and the symbolic'.[46] As Sparke has importantly highlighted, the de-aestheticization of the home in general[47] suggested that men (fictive or real) like Dulcimer posed a threat to this new ethos of the rational, anaesthetized modern home merely by his suggestively, queer nature.

Dulcimer's salon, likened to an artist's room, includes a bowl of flowers placed on the grand piano positioned at such an angle that, when Dulcimer is seated at it, he has a perfect view of the entire room/stage, a means to furnish his omnipresence. A fireplace, downstage, is included on the other side of the room, as is a writing desk on which is placed a telephone. Finally, a side-table used for cocktails and dinner stands immediately behind a couch that is placed at right angles in front of the fireplace. The final useful instruction Shairp gives is that the room is limited in its ornamentation save for a 'decorative painting by a modern artist'.[48] Dulcimer enters the room immediately. His appearance is equally important in that he stands in for the *objets d'art* the room lacks; he stands in for the decorative detail, the embodiment of a lack. He is characterized as 'a man of about forty-five immaculately turned out, and wearing at present a double-breasted dinner jacket. He speaks exquisitely, in a clear voice, and with now and then a slight drawl. He has a habit of looking at you from under his eyes, and though a complete dilettante, he has an alert, vibrating personality. A man who could fascinate, repel, and alarm.'[49]

It is a lovely day in May, and Dulcimer calls out to his butler Trump and claims the 'room looks naked!'[50] To clothe the body of the room, fresh flowers are suggested, a queer allusion. Dulcimer intones that he is terribly over-dressed for preparing flowers and requires his gloves. Julian emerges from upstairs and into the room and feels compelled to describe a feeling he had that very afternoon. He is unable, however, as Dulcimer cuts him off by asserting:

> Dulcimer: Don't try then. Only poets can do justice to the spring, that cruel, terrifying time.
> Julian: Terrifying?
> Dulcimer: There is always something terrifying in all the remorselessness of nature, something shattering in all this re-assertion of the principle of life.
> Dulcimer: Choice is what separates the artist from the common herd. Nobody knows how to choose nowadays. I hope you will never forgo your prerogative of choice. Never do anything that is unconsidered, or take what is second best.[51]

Here man takes control over nature, artifice triumphs within Dulcimer's order of things; his mastery is such that he even controls human nature, as becomes painfully clear by the play's end. Choice and control become sinister bedfellows within Dulcimer's cunning theories of the art of life. He proclaims that he prefers 'to see Nature, controlled and at [his] feet'.[52] Also compelling in his scheme are the negative associations he conjures with the 're-assertion of the principle of life', perhaps we might conclude, an attack on the heterosexist expression of time, which privileges progeny, inheritance and legacy.

In the following scene we see the men prepared for dinner in appropriate attire; Shairp underscores the 'rather grotesque likeness between him [Julian] and Mr Dulcimer'.[53] Here again, culture, or more aptly artifice, seems to win out over nature, as Julian is not Dulcimer's biological heir; hence the reason for their 'grotesque', deceiving similitude. Rather than being celebrated, their likeness serves only to reinforce the missing biological link that in turn marks them out as different from within the heterosexual matrix. Their resemblance is a queer one, and as such is troubling and grotesque, an artificial aberration. Trouble begins to present itself for Dulcimer when the young man announces he has met a young woman with whom he has fallen in love, the unusual feeling he sought to express earlier in the day, when Dulcimer extolled the virtues of taking control over nature, or perhaps more aptly one's urges. Dulcimer winces at the notion of this love. Julian makes matters worse when he announces he wishes to marry Leo (a mannish nickname for his beloved Leonora Yale). Dulcimer swiftly dismisses his son's desires as yet another passing fancy, one that will slip away as quickly as it arrived. In response, Julian attacks his adopted father's theory about choice, cutting to the heart of Dulcimer's character by claiming that it is not about 'choosing', a notion he does not expect his guardian to understand. Dulcimer is an artist, a dilettante, a collector of things, who has successfully designed an aesthetic lifestyle of detachment free of emotion. Humans as much as objects are equally a part of the collection and interiors one forges, and Julian quickly admits that he recognizes he is dependent on Dulcimer, who in turn is prepared to offer him a trousseau and give him away at St Paul's, Knightsbridge. This act of kindness Julian acknowledges, but he also stipulates that it will be less than sufficient for a married life in which he also intends to pursue studies in medicine and quickly requests an increase in his monthly stipend. It is then revealed to Julian that the true cost of the marriage is, in fact, complete disinheritance. Indeed, Dulcimer asks the young man how he plans to support his wife, an idea he fathoms as 'an ugly middle-class term'.[54] Here we realize, as much as Julian does, that he has no rights, only privileges; after all, according to Dulcimer:

> I created you. I've made you what you are because I rescued you from a life of squalor. I chose you instinctively, just as I have chosen everything else in my life. It was a bold experiment, but I didn't make a mistake. You have always been a very delightful son and companion to me. But life with me and life with Leo are two very different things. You can't expect them to overlap.[55]

Julian is fashioned as the ultimate aesthetic creation. Dulcimer betrays the notion that humans are fundamentally no different from the objects that inhabit the spaces of our life-world; both populate and constitute a domestic landscape.

When Dulcimer first meets Leo their exchange is formal and cold, and, as one might expect from Dulcimer, aesthetically charged. Their initial conversation revolves around what ideal type of dog might occupy his interiors. Leo thoughtfully suggests a Borzoi, precisely because they are so 'decorative'. When Dulcimer surmises where he could precisely envision a dog on his rug he notices how Leo stares at him while he visually conceptualizes it. He turns to her and quips: 'That amuses you, doesn't it? But you professional people can never understand an artist.' Dulcimer's aristocratic disdain for 'professional people' is a clear allusion to the middle class and its moral compass, the very same that tried and convicted Wilde. Leo notes her own surprise that he has 'never gone in for decoration', but Dulcimer admits that he could never 'endure planning rooms for other people. My taste', he asserts, 'would have to be theirs'.[56] Choice and control once again commingle as ugly bedfellows at the hands of this decidedly queer man. Leo draws the final assault against Dulcimer's aesthetic life/style when she asks:

> Leo: (With a touch of sarcasm) Is he good with his needle, too?
> Dulcimer: No. I tried to teach him, but such gifts are not easily acquired. (Sensing her thought.) It doesn't quite meet with your approval, does it?
> Leo: I'm bound to say that I'm glad he won't want to embroider. But then, I'm so poor at sewing myself.
> Dulcimer: (indignantly). Sewing? Is that all you see in my work? (Rising and coming towards her.) I don't believe it! There is nothing Philistine about you, even though you have this dreadful obsession for dumb animals.

Dulcimer ranks needlework, privileging embroidery over *mere* sewing. However, it is also at this moment in their conversation that Leo begins to challenge Dulcimer's position and relationship with Julian. Dulcimer nonetheless wonders whether she would have thought they were father and son. She concludes she would have thought them related, given how Julian possesses many of his 'mannerisms', a not so subtle allusion to a supposedly inherent and visibly definable homosexual corporeality. She also wonders whether Julian is similar in any way to his biological father, whom she wishes to meet. This final gesture of defiance at the conclusion of Act One is an attempt to reinforce the heterosexual matrix in which inheritance, whether of mannerisms, culture or money, is conceived of as residing purely within the domain of biology, that is, the natural. Determined to marry Leo, Julian abandons the plush confines of the home of his upbringing.

Act Two begins with a description of contrasts in which the scene is set for Mr Owen's sitting room in Camden Town, three months later in the dead of summer. The room is meant to be small, neat and furnished simply and sparingly. The furniture is solid wood, absent of any decoration while 'the wallpaper is crude and the pictures and ornaments are chosen without taste'. The home gives Owen a sense of pride while his son abhors it and is ashamed; a marked contrast to the luxury he has grown accustomed to since the age of eleven when Dulcimer took him away from the very place he now finds himself. The windows of the parlour give way no longer to the controlled beauty of Mayfair gardens, but to advertising posters boasting 'Guinness is good for you'. A former alcoholic, Owen is now a reformed man, and has become a Christian minister, keenly aware of Julian's fondness for luxury which leads him, like everyone else, to search out 'Pleasure, pleasure, pleasure!'[57] For Owen, the perfect antidote for Julian's unfortunate longing for luxury, the result of twelve years' living with Dulcimer, is falling in love with Leo. According to him: 'The love of a good woman is the antidote to the evils of luxury'.[58] Heterosexuality serves as a cure, inoculates against the artifice of luxury. However, Julian's desire for luxury – his seemingly natural urges – is stronger than those for Leo and he rushes back to Dulcimer who quickly informs his prodigal son that there can be no room for Leo in his scheme. Dulcimer proclaims that Julian cannot be two different people at once: Julian Dulcimer on the one hand and a married man on the other. For her part, Leo cannot accept Julian has returned to Dulcimer's lair. She is distraught to find out the man she loves reaffirms Max Nordau's worst assumptions, that he 'isn't a real man at all, but only a bundle of sensations'.[59] True masculinity is antithetical to sensations, and Nordau was clear to warn that the home of the aesthete was riddled with myriad competing sensations that together conspire to affect the nervous wellbeing of a home's visitors let alone its occupant. She asks Dulcimer whether he has 'any conscience at all about keeping him from what is normal and healthy, what is best for him?' Dulcimer, however, is a self-professed 'materialist' and revels in his artifice. Owen, who joined Leo as part of her intervention, takes hold of Dulcimer's revolver and shoots him with it. With Dulcimer's death, Shairp reifies the long-held trope that the evil queer must die, a just punishment for his unnatural inclinations.

In the final scene of the play, we come full circle. Back in the dead Dulcimer's Mayfair home, Julian attends to the task of placing flowers in a vase, the very same sequence and dialogue as that which initiated the play. While the gloves and initial dialogue are identical, the performance has taken on a slightly different tinge of difference. As with all performative actions, something has changed, even if only slightly. It is, in fact, the *choice* of vase, which alerts us to the ultimate success of Dulcimer's *perverse* project. When Trump brings over the green vase preferred by Dulcimer, Julian dismisses it, and confidently claims: 'I like to make my own choice. Choice, Trump, is what distinguishes the artist from the common herd. I prefer the amber vase.' Shairp twists the ultimate outcome as the play's final act and scene by staging queer time and space. By ensuring Julian never leaves the home Dulcimer has perfectly orchestrated, he is never able to consummate the heterosexual union (the so-called natural progress of things), but rather is compelled to repeat – or renew – the material, aesthetic and hence queer programme set in motion by Dulcimer. As *The Times* in its review noted: 'The Victory is Dulcimer's, whose death mask looks down, a little extravagantly perhaps, from the wall'.[60] Culture has completely and utterly triumphed over nature, and in its wake solidified the belief that luxury begets degeneracy, begotten from one generation to another, regardless of biology. While it must be made clear that the perversion of the play underscores a stereotype through which to demonstrate moral decay, a means to assuage the Lord Chamberlain, it nevertheless sets itself up as a tale of resistance and a perversion of the social order through the very mechanism used against a queer (sexual and material) culture. As Matt Cook underlines, '[c]ritics were quick to spot the "repulsive" and "abnormal" implications and the *Weekend Review* was sure to highlight "the Anglo-Hellenic" "domesticity" of the lead character's "way of life"'.[61] Alan Sinfield asserts that 'by suppressing irregular sexuality the chamberlain did not eliminate it; on the contrary, he implied that it was always about to erupt into visibility'.[62] The so-called closet as an open secrete folds upon itself and marks a space of 'knowing by not knowing'.[63] It becomes the very apparatus of artifice that inadvertently exposes the hidden truths that supposedly lurk below; it is the very thing that allows queer material culture to be staged. In Shairp's play the closet works in odd and mysterious ways, threatening the very contours and stability of the so-called pre-ordained natural order of things. Although the play would fall into relative obscurity it certainly indulged a cultural milieu that saw artifice as unbecoming for a man.

Ashcombe: Love attained, love denied

> For me these years that followed were the gayest of my life.
> Cecil Beaton

In his preface to Ian Grant's *Great Interiors* from 1967 Beaton made an important claim when he stated that one's identity was a guide to understanding one's interior surroundings. The most 'satisfying' interiors, according to him, are those 'that conjure up an atmosphere, that sing, that dance, our judgement is affected by whether the creator has managed successfully to say what he originally intended'.[64] Indeed, if there is one example of a 'satisfying' interior that best reveals its owner, it surely must have been Beaton's Ashcombe. In April 1930 Beaton joined close Friends Rex Whistler and Edith Oliver at her country estate Daye House, for the weekend, a trip to the country that would set him on his greatest domestic and design adventure. As he described his first

7.6 Millar and Harris. Cecil Beaton posing outside Ashcombe, 1930.

impression of the Ashcombe estate in *Vogue*, the experience was nothing short of love at first sight/site. He retold countless times how: 'I walked under the arch and stood spellbound at the romantic beauty of the place, with its atmosphere of infinite peace and rather tragic beauty'.[65] Indeed, the atmosphere at Ashcombe Beaton conjured on numerous occasions was one steeped in beauty, if not also tinged by tragedy. He described the house and its grounds as though 'some royalty has been banished in a fairy-story',[66] adding a pinch of camp flavour to this ideal scene, one in which fairies and queens seem to reside. With Beaton they would, for at Ashcombe in the Wiltshire downs, he hosted myriad sorts of fancy costume parties, much to the dismay and amusement of the local townspeople. Already in the preface to his rich and vivid memorial dedicated to his home, *Ashcombe: The Story of a Fifteen-Year Lease*, which he wrote a few years after having been forced to give up the lease, Beaton betrays how 'living then you could still cherish the illusion that you might go on for ever leading your own private life, undisturbed by the international crises in the newspapers. This illusion was finally and irrevocably shattered in 1939' with the war.[67] As he quickly disclosed, and as will become increasingly apparent, throughout the fifteen years he lived there the house was a refuge, a sanctuary in times of trouble for Beaton, a space entirely of his own design. However, for Beaton, it 'was love at first sight … from the moment that [he] stood under the archway'.[68]

Initially, Beaton petitioned the owner to purchase the place but to no avail. Nevertheless, he did concede to leasing it out for a limited period. Beaton naively recalled how '[w]hen the lease of Ashcombe was handed over to me, I felt the place was mine for life'.[69] Beaton sweetened the deal, promising to renovate and modernize the interiors. On the property only two buildings remained from the reign of Henry VIII. Ashcombe was built in 1730, and Beaton immediately called upon Austrian architect Michael Rosenauer, on recommendation from Anita Loos (a mutual friend) as consultant for the renovation. Soon thereafter windows once bricked in were opened, plumbing was installed and rafters were replaced. Good friend Rex Whistler designed an ornamented stone doorway to the house, while decorative urns were placed on the parapet. Beaton's life-world was quickly seen through the prism of a fanciful Rococo style. Regular trips to the continent, thanks in part large to his work for *Vogue*, enabled him to indulge in his new passion of collecting for and decorating his new country home. Sontag asserts that 'many of the objects prized by camp are old-fashioned, out-of-date, démodé. It's not the love of the old as such. It's simply that the process of aging and deterioration provides the necessary detachment or arouses a necessary sympathy.'[70] On these trips Beaton acquired silver, gilded birdcages, Italian console tables, candlesticks for an entire household, elaborate mirrors and much other decorative *bric-à-brac* to fill his home. Many of

7.7 Millar and Harris. Cecil Beaton posing outside his studio at Ashcombe, 1930.

the objects, however, were not expensive. Rather, Beaton had a keen eye for extravagance on a limited budget. 'Materials were put to uses never intended. "Animal baize", as the felt is called which covers pantomime zebras and leopards, provided excellent carpeting, and other theatrical materials, originally invented to last for the run of a play, had to stand the test as curtains and sofa coverings'.[71]

In 1932, coincidentally the same year that Beaton penned his loving description of his English home for *Vogue*, Taylor Croft published a condemning tract on the vices of London city life, in which he paid particular attention to the homosexual. Croft detailed the typical home of the urning (homosexual) and described the figure in the following way:

> Though many of them, the more cultured, have extremely good taste, so that their flats and homes are among the most charming in London, among the less refined love of colour and feminine etceteras produces an effect of overcrowding and vulgarity. Their walls are papered or distempered in staring yellows or crimsons, their woodwork lacquered in brilliant hues, the curtains, perhaps, of black velvet with golden moons embroidered on them, and every available shelf crowded with tasselled match-boxes and silk dolls.[72]

Men like Beaton, whether in London or in the English countryside, delighted in their lavishly conceived homes and took no bother of such inflammatory texts. Beaton's newly acquired taste for the 'eccentric' and 'bizarre' was also a response to his familial home which he saw as lacking in sparkle, overcome by too much restrain and orderliness. It was also in keeping with what Reed has identified as the 'amusing style', an important recurrent motif in the homes of figures like the Sitwells, who were close friends and allies of Beaton. Reed notes how the style emerged in the interwar period and featured a whimsical approach to modernity that was in contradistinction to the severe heroic modernism advocated by continental masculinist architects.[73] Beaton was also influenced by the Baroness d'Erlanger (1874–1959), who saw herself as the patroness not only of the younger Beaton but also of Sergei Diaghilev. Beaton considered her 'a woman of remarkable magnetism and ingenuity who formulated much of the decorative taste of this period'.[74] Every object Beaton collected for his various rooms was punctuated with delight and pregnant with sensory purpose. As Sontag states, the artifice of '[c]amp sees everything in quotation marks. It's not a lamp, but a "lamp"; not a woman, but a "woman". To perceive Camp in objects and persons is to understand Being-as-Playing-a-Role. It is the farthest extension, in sensibility, of the metaphor of life as theatre'.[75] Beaton's home was the spatial product of hyperbolic abandon, theatrical in its artifice and excess. On the main floor, in the small room was a festival of colour and objects. Brocade couches and a Kent sofa mixed with French chairs and a Victorian armchair, while colours exploded through the strawberry ice-cream-coloured walls juxtaposed with turquoise-blue curtains. Although the room boasted numerous and impressive *objets d'art*, it also featured wall brackets for candles reminiscent of *La Dame aux Camélias* as well as an 'Eastern boy' from the eighteenth century carved out of silver wood.[76] The picture it lent was a far cry from the sober white spaces soon to make overtures on British soil.

Beaton's sisters' rooms became confectionery havens with 'ceiling[s] in the pink of raspberry ice-cream' while the 'fluffy carpets' were of the same material as used in fancy dress costumes for cowboys' trousers died cedar-wood pink. Curtains, beds and dressing tables were equally suggestive, done in turquoise-blue and white striped satin. Down the hall from their rooms was another bedroom done in white with white satin, a leopard-print carpet and a four-poster bed. A truly theatrical effect, however, was granted the greatest licence in Beaton's own bedroom, one of the last rooms to be decorated. Beaton asked friends, many artists themselves, to paint figures from the *commedia dell'arte* joined by 'baroque emblems, barley-sugar poles and flowered mirrors' [Figure 7.8] The overall effect he wanted was that of a circus, a surreal space of amusement, the result of which bemused many guests, a fact he relished. The most private of spaces became for Beaton the most theatrical. The

7.8 Cecil Beaton in Tyrolean suit posing in front of the bedroom murals, Ashcombe, early 1930s.

7.9 Possibly by Baron George Hoyningen-Huene. Cecil Beaton in his bed designed by friend and artist Rex Whistler, Ashcombe, 1930.

centrepiece of the room was a four-poster bed designed by Rex, executed by Savage's, the circus-roundabout-makers of King's Lynn, lending a degree of authenticity to the atmosphere, an effect appropriate to the room as Beaton conceptualized it [Figure 7.9]. In the first decades of the twentieth century the Harlequin, Pierrot and other *commedia dell'arte* or carnival figures were made famous anew by Diaghilev and the Ballets Russes and quickly became coded homosexual figures, particularly in light of their strategies of masquerade and deception.[77] Martin Green notes how the characters of Harlequin and Pierrot, in particular, enabled 'a private world of beauty and emotion that was hostile to the worlds of work and marriage'. Both resided in the realm of fantasy and provided a direct 'assault on realism',[78] and opened up unto a whole world of ambiguity, masquerade and artifice.

Across from the main house was a second building where Beaton created an ideal and fashionable studio in which to work [see Figure 7.10]. The space, which enjoyed enormous light through five expansive windows, was drenched in the glow of white. White walls, a white ceiling, white cubes, white sofas, white drums and white blossoms decorating

7.10 Cecil Beaton siting on a white sofa in his all-white studio, Ashcombe, early 1930s.

the tables. As Beaton confessed, '[t]he fashion for white rooms was just about to spread like a plague of anaemia, throughout the drawing rooms of the world. My studio must be entirely white. "Nothing," I explained, "can be so practical".'[79] Ostensibly Beaton had fallen victim to the dominating taste of his friend Syrie Maugham, who, as we saw in the previous chapter, worked with Coward. It is worth noting, however, the manner in which he described the 'spread' of the trend, equating it to a plague, linking disease and contagion to interior design. Further fascinating is how Beaton ostensibly reversed the relationship between disease and white as a potentially revealing colour. For Beaton, white functioned as plague, rather than as a conduit to the exposure of disease and a necessary antidote to Victorian and Edwardian excess. Maugham opened a store at the corner of Grosvenor Square to sell her designs and refurbished antiques, which Nichols had once described as 'a place that was filled with exquisite but faintly dubious objects of furniture that were liable, if examined too closely, to fall to pieces. However, they were examined too closely; Syrie's brilliance and charm attracted most of the attention to herself ... Hence an astonishing collection of old bits and pieces of French provençal armoires, Biedermeieere sofas, nineteenth-century Italian chests, etc, etc. – all most delicately "pickled" and tarted up – passed across the Atlantic, at fabulous prices, and slowly decomposed in the mansions of Long Island. After such a slightly acid paragraph I feel obliged to admit that Syrie had the most delicate and civilized touch in decoration of anybody I ever knew'. Oddly, he concluded, '[h]er sense of colour was impeccable'.[80] In another description of her style, Beaton again stated how she

> caught the 'no colour' virus and spread the disease around the world. Mrs Maugham is a woman with flair and a strong personal taste of her own. She is also one of the most energetic women of her day. Her indefatigable strength was now given to turning the world white, not only in winter but throughout the seasons of the year. With the strength of a typhoon she blew all colour before her. For the next decade Syrie Maugham bleached, pickled or scraped every piece of furniture in sight. White sheepskin rugs were strewn on the eggshell-surfaced floors, huge white sofas were flanked with white crackled-paint tables, white peacock feathers were put in white vases against a white wall'.[81]

Beaton further described how everything she did 'was so immaculate and hygienic'.[82] Under her spell, 'Mayfair drawing rooms looked like albino stage sets'.[83] One has to wonder if he was not including Coward's Gerald Road home in that category. These albino stage sets seem to provide, at least to Beaton, space for the moralizing dramas of hygiene and the new modernity that turned its back on the high artifice of brocade, velvet and fancy-dress decadence he delighted in. These whitewashed spaces seemed lifeless to Beaton, even if slightly stylish and functional enough to be used for his studio. The space of his studio did nonetheless give way to his unique form of decorative excess. The five windows were treated with a simple and inexpensive canvas. These, however, were heavily embroidered with mother of pearl buttons, twenty thousand in total. The effect was dazzling and reminiscent of a costermonger's costume.

From the outset Beaton distinctly wanted the house to 'be furnished in pale colours and lead the spirit of gaiety and masquerade'.[84] Indeed he achieved just that, a stage for parties and friendship, theatrical in its effects and epic in his entertaining glory. He described in whimsical terms how the 'blazing crisp satin curtains and freshly upholstered chairs, looking like lollipops, have a theatrical and sugary aspect to the erstwhile rustic interiors'. The playful nature also gave way to impressionable sensory memories; whether it was the '[t]hirty white doves and pigeons, fluttering and cooing under the ilex trees, [that] provided an unending symphony of sound and movement' or the 'smell of new calico, linen and of sawdust', a rusticated 'perfume' to Beaton that led an 'enjoyable excitement of taking possession of my first home. In memory it will never be entirely out of my nostrils'.[85] Memory and the domestic interior cohere on the surface of the body, inscribing it with the experiences of space itself, to the point of inhaling it. The deep impression left upon Beaton cannot be overstated, and for him the experience of decorating his home was only possibly comparable, not surprisingly, 'to the excitement of decorating for the theatre'.[86]

By his own modest admission Beaton was himself a 'bad housekeeper, and utterly extravagant'.[87] Food was often brought in directly from London. Floral arrangements were grand, took hours to prepare and were a significant part of the staged sensory effect. Although Beaton was 'a thoughtful and generous host, he also revelled in the peace of Ashcombe when he was alone. He was never lonely there; though he often felt pangs of stark loneliness in big cities. He went for long walks, sat in the sun, sketched in the studio, and sometimes hung his head between his legs and gazed at the view upside-down. He relished every moment of possessing the place.'[88] Christmas provided the first occasion for Beaton to host his family who initially held mixed reactions to the house and its whimsical interiors. Beaton described how:

> My father was quite baffled by the décor, and tripped over the dais on which Carousel bed was poised. Rubbing a sprained ankle, he complained that for his taste the house was too full of booby traps. By degrees my mother, forgetting Ashcombe's impracticabilities and its remoteness, made excellent suggestions for next summer in the garden; while Aunt Jessi, with eyes twinkling, oohed and aahed to my heart's delight.[89]

Three hours by car from London, Ashcombe was difficult to get to, and many were those who found themselves lost on their first visit. Most weekends Beaton invited people to stay from Saturday to Monday, fitting in as many as his 'small but expansive house' would allow for. It was not uncommon for Beaton to greet his travel-weary guests in a Tyrolean suit. Costume was such a major force in his life and one simply has to look at the photographs taken of him at Ashcombe to appreciate its role. While one must exercise considerable caution when assessing the sartorial costumes or interior designs of historical characters based exclusively on extant photographs, images of Beaton overwhelming celebrate his insatiable appetite for costume and fancy dress. As a photographer, fancy dress parties provided him with innumerable opportunities. He would often 'encourage [his] guests to bring fancy costume in their luggage so that [he] could photograph them against' the 'romantic background' that Ashcombe provided.[90] Fancy dress coupled with the atmosphere Beaton painstakingly constructed purposefully allowed guests to 'exchange reality for a complete escape into the realms of fantasy' and ignore the more seemly aspects of life.[91] Life at Ashcombe was theatre and theatre was reality. Here the distinction between fact and fantasy, indoor and outdoor, held no currency in the cultural and social life of

Beaton's country house. Burlesque operas and ballets were performed in the blank backdrop provided by the white drenched studio, while neighbours and people from the area would ogle and watch with amazement the comings and goings of his group of friends. Some of these parties became so elaborate that buses were laid on as a shuttle service for guests. On the occasion of one 'fête champêtre' co-hosted by Michael Duff, Beaton orchestrated a 'perversely sophisticated piece of rusticity'. Preparations took six weeks, decorations were imported from Paris and Milan and guests flew in from around the world.[92] It is not entirely surprising that, on occasion, neighbours would also stop by to 'enjoy the peep-show of seeing [Beaton's] preposterous decorations'.[93] In his moralizing text, Croft described how the city-dwelling homosexual was particularly fond of parties; they were, he described, the 'commonest medium of urning entertainment'. He argued that

> I am convinced that it is no exaggeration to say that there are homosexual parties in one part or another of London every evening, and some of them are extremely large. Occasionally, when women are invited, pretence of normality is made, but others become a mere orgy and sexual excesses are freely, even publicly indulged in. Urnings are fond of dancing together at these parties and many of them are dressed as girls, or in effeminate fancy dress of some sort. Older homosexuals are particularly fond of giving these parties, since they frequently enable them in the alcoholic abandonment of the occasion to satisfy themselves with younger men.[94]

Soon, Ashcombe was referred to as a nudist colony, with locals shocked and dismayed to see Beaton and his guests sunbathing, exposing themselves as if they were in Deauville or Venice. Every new guest was required to conform to one final ritual upon leaving Ashcombe: each guest was made to trace an outline of his or her hand. Some had painted nails included, while most had their signature signed across it [Figure 7.11]. 'By degrees an extraordinary collection was achieved.'[95] Now the guests' corporeal imprint became an integral part of the interior design, altering the visual culture of its inhabited landscape.

Performance, script, stage set, characters and costumes were not simply relegated to the theatre for Beaton, but comprised the very fibres of his version of a stage-set modernism. As Matt Houlbrook argues, the home offered an important and vital space in which many queer Londoners – equally extended to queers in the country – hosted parties and social events that allowed these men 'to dissolve rather than confirm the boundary between public and private'.[96] For Beaton, the public/private divide was, fundamentally, an artificial one. Much later in 1968, Arabella Boxer recalled how he used to entertain: 'Beaton seems to regard party-giving in theatrical terms, rather as one might think of mounting

7.11 Cecil Beaton in Tyrolean suit, standing in his bathroom surrounded by the hand outlines of his many friends who visited Ashcombe, early 1930s.

a new production. He provides the setting and assembles the cast, then expects the actors to do their bit. One is conscious of this, feeling uneasily aware that more is expected of one than just to look nice or behave well. As he says, "guests themselves have to participate, and by providing a stage for the guests you have done something constructive".'[97]

'I love you, Mr. Watson'

As already evident, Beaton's home played host to numerous guests, but one in particular would forever play a significant if not tragic role in the theatrical life at Ashcombe. In the summer of 1930, while in Vienna, Beaton met Peter Watson (1908–1956), best known for his formidable art collection, through a mutual friend, stage designer Oliver Messel (1904–1978). Messel and Watson set off from there on a trip to Venice and persuaded Beaton to join them. Watson, born as Victor William, went to St John's College, Oxford, and given his vast fortune he soon garnered for himself numerous friends. On the death of his father, when he came into his fortune, '[h]e ordered new suits and a vast black and orange Rolls Royce. His interests would change over the years and he would become a creative connoisseur of modern art, an intelligent and discreet patron to a new generation of painters, the financial baker of Cyril Connolly's *Horizon* and one of the founders of the Institute of Contemporary Arts'.[98] It was 'in the dark alleys' of Venice that Beaton 'foraged for junk and bought for Ashcombe old painted doors and cupboards and stone ornaments, to be sent home by *Petite Vitesse*' and fell in love with the decidedly handsome Watson.[99] Messel was also himself intrigued by Watson, which inspired great pangs of insecurity on the part of Beaton. On the last night of the trio's vacation together in Venice, Messel and Watson became lovers. Not dissuaded, Beaton felt he could still manage to win Watson's affections. 'Thus Cecil entered a period of obsession which was to dominate his life for the next four years. He imitated Peter in every respect. They wore the same clothes, the same scent and even talked in the same manner, so much so that Cecil's sisters never knew which one it was on the telephone'.[100] It was at Ashcombe, however, that Beaton was first overcome by despair, jealousy and rage. Messel and Watson in 1930 visited his country home, where he gave one bedroom to the two men. Again, on the last morning of their visit, Beaton knocked on their door, but it was locked. 'Cecil's heart "turned to stone". His mouth went dry and he could hardly speak for the rest of the day. The incident was particularly beastly as far as Cecil was concerned because he had gone to such lengths to make his first guests welcome. He could not believe they would do "such a thing under my roof"'.[101] The cat and mouse chase continued for some time and, in the summer of 1931, Beaton spent a lonely summer longing for Watson's calls and visits, which were few and far between. In a diary entry from that summer he recorded the torment of his situation, and how it was only at Ashcombe where he could find any solace.

> I felt lonely and unhappy and the terrible weather did not improve matters. My great comfort was lovely Ashcombe. What a thrill to return there and to find so much done. The dining-room curtains were up and divine. Each weekend brought vast improvements. I would travel down with the car packed to the skies with cupids, chairs and provisions, flowers and there were some heavenly parties, writing games in front of the fire, hysterical laughter around Edith. I was always very busy and tired'.[102]

Here the interior provided Beaton, not with a substitute, a transference as many would suggest, but rather a place of respite, joy, love and pleasure. Beaton's longing for Watson took its toll and while at Ashcombe he would experience the 'hysterical highs and desperate lows'. Although Watson never visited Ashcombe on his own and the two would never become lovers, Beaton made the most fuss and preparations for his arrivals.[103] Truman Capote once wrote to Beaton's biographer Hugo Vickers exposing the symbolism of Beaton's decorating choices: 'In Cecil's house there was a book on the desk – a nineteenth-century novel and a book mark in the place where one of the characters says "I love you, Mr Watson."'[104] For better or worse Ashcombe revealed the material cultures of love gained for a house and love lost for a man. Beaton was unable to retain the lease on Ashcombe and was forced to leave his beloved home in 1945. This caused far greater suffering for Beaton in the long term than had the numerous dramas associated with Watson. After all, Ashcombe was his first and only true love.

Interior as stage insinuates a place of artifice, a space for performance and theatricality, of fashioning one's self or one's character. Beaton was always engaged with his domestic spaces as sites of a continuous melodrama, tragedy or comedy, always new and always in a state of process and development, and certainly the site of many *gay* parties. Indeed, neither Beaton nor Ashcombe was ever static, nor did they sin the gravest of sins of all, of 'being boring'. Ashcombe was for Beaton a source of joy, creative fulfilment and a refuge. However, Beaton found a second house in the country, Redditch House, five miles east of Broadchalke, Wiltshire, which he purchased in 1948, and there, as at Ashcombe, Beaton set out on an elaborate refurbishing programme, transforming the house into a home fit to entertain such guests as Greta Garbo, with whom he had an infamous affair. In *Vogue* he described how Redditch House's 'finely proportioned rooms reflect the imaginative taste of the owner'.[105] In the same magazine he had contributed so many words and pictures, little was given by way of description of the lived spaces of Redditch House. Rather, Beaton provides the reader a litany of the work he is busily engaged with. The article, 'My Two Houses": Two Lives, Two Different Designs', is markedly more detached and reserved than the previous writings on Ashcombe, betraying the more functional aspects of his designs, and his new life there.[106] Unlike with Ashcombe, the decoration at Redditch 'seems to demand a certain respect, and I had to discard all the "amusing" rubbish, with which my previous country house was furnished'. Nonetheless, in the pictures one can clearly identify how, at least according to *Vogue*, Beaton 'has applied his usual ratio of one part formality to one part informality'. Eighteenth-century furniture was heavily represented throughout the house and was accompanied by heavy doses of chintz. The spaces were darker, decidedly more masculine and sober, a far cry from the 'amusing style' of the 1920s and early 1930s. Was this the style of maturation and social position or the sign of changing times? Indeed it was both. By this point Beaton had long enjoyed fame and fortune, and he set himself up at Redditch in a manner that befitted his position. Here he created an environment conducive to his numerous and varied projects. In his article on the country estate little ink is spent on describing the spaces and furniture on the part of Beaton – an odd thing when one considers the time he spent considering such things in his theatrical staging of portraits, stage sets and of course the lengthy and numerous descriptions of Ashcombe. Missing is the joy, delight and sheer splendour he once lavished on Ashcombe. Splendour has been replaced by respectability, joy by sober hues, gaiety gives way to social position, decadence to stature, the fashionability of white darkened by masculine burgundies and muted greens. His neighbours were now high-ranking members of the cultural and political elite, a long way from the exotic terrain Beaton once cultivated in Ashcombe where locals stood in amazement at the scenes of fantasy unravelling before their eyes. Beaton died at Redditch House in January 1980 and was buried in its churchyard, and, while he was very comfortable in this estate, it did not warrant an entire love story, as did his beloved Ashcombe.

In his descriptions of Ashcombe, Beaton effortlessly fused his own identity with that of the house, its interiors and its grounds through a self-conscious repetitive act of continuous narration. Whether in articles for *Vogue*, extracts from his autobiography or the book on Ashcombe, Beaton scripted the stage on which the comedy and tragedy of identity was performed. Unlike Coward, whose pose of indifference meant that his various interiors figured little if ever in his own self-conscious musings and recollections of his life, Beaton relished in the environments he created. Not unlike with Lord Gower, Beaton's mode of writing the interior functioned as an alternative autobiography: autobiography as interior; interior design as autobiography.

Queer by design

We often view Beaton as the 'gay' photographer who provided us with exceedingly glamorous and fashionable pictures of society's numerous doyennes. However, in this limited portrait, we also strip him of the political and cultural agency of resistance much of his material and domestic culture revealed; importantly this resistance was directed to the hetero-patriarchal culture of aggregation and bullying, the latter often following from the former. Here, I wish to conclude with one final remark by returning to an issue that has featured differently throughout this book, that of shame. Sedgwick in her ground-breaking and arousing work on shame has suggested the notion of 'queer performativity' as 'the name of a strategy for the production of meaning and being, in relation to the affect of shame and to the later and related fact of stigma'.[107] Six long decades after the Labouchere Amendment, the Wolfenden Report submitted that 'homosexual behaviour between consenting adults in private should no longer be a criminal offence'. The rationalization, not unlike the Labouchere Amendment, was public safety, reminding homosexuals and heterosexuals alike of the indefinite nature of the public/

7.12 Cecil Beaton and Rex Whistler painting *en plein air* on Ashcombe's grounds, c. 1930s.

private divide, where boundaries under the law were not clear-cut but equally subject to surveillance, scrutiny and policing. The report came some way to alleviating social pressures, though not far enough. It was in this new climate of debate that Beaton came out, as it were, to reveal what the experiences of homophobia, fear and shame meant growing up as a young homosexual male in Britain. He wrote:

> Of recent the tolerance towards the subject has made a nonsense of many of the prejudices for which I myself felt acutely as a young man. Even now I can only vaguely realize that it was only comparatively late in life that I would go into a room full of people without a feeling of guilt. To go into a room full of men, or to a lavatory in the Savoy, needed quite an effort. With success in my work this situation became easier. But when one realizes the damage, what tragedy has been brought on by this lack of sympathy to a very delicate and difficult subject, this should be a great time of celebration … For myself I am grateful. Selfishly I wish that this marvellous step forward could have been taken at an earlier age. It is not that I would have wished to avail myself of further licence, but to feel that one was not a felon and an outcast could have helped enormously during these difficult young years.[108]

Whether the events of that night of humiliation when he was tossed into the pond are accurate, I argue, is fundamentally inconsequential, for these form the residues of the affect of shame, no differently than the bullying he suffered at the hands of Evelyn Waugh while attending Heath Mount School. As Sedgwick points out: 'The forms taken by shame are not distinct "toxic" parts of a group or individual identity that can be excised; they are instead integral to and residual by which identity itself is formed. They are available for the work of metamorphosis, reframing, refiguration, transfiguration, of affective and symbolic loading and deformation, but perhaps all too potent for the work of purgation and deontological closure'.[109] Valerie Traub and David Halperin have suggested that attending to the unlikeable and seemly aspects of homosexuality, such as shame, might inadvertently provide the very basis for the material used in attacks against queers by the public at large. This has in turn 'led to an unofficial and informal ban on the investigation of certain unsettling or undignified aspects of homosexuality, specifically questions of emotion or affect, disreputable sexual histories or practices, dissident gender identities, outdated or embarrassing figures and moments from the lesbian-gay-queer past'.[110] Beaton's own experiences are a part of that history, experiences that seldom, if ever, make it into the glamorized narrative of his life and oeuvre.

Notes

1 C. Beaton, *Self-Portrait with Friends: The Selected Diaries of Cecil Beaton 1926–1974* (London: Weidenfeld and Nicolson, 1979), p. 45.

2 D. Cohen, *Households Gods: The British and Their Possessions* (New Haven and London: Yale University Press, 2006), p. 125.

3 Beaton, *Self-Portrait with Friends*, p. 42.

4 Ibid., p. 43.

5 Ibid., p. 71.

6 Ibid., p. 72.

7 Beaton in J. Ross, *Beaton in Vogue* (New York: Clarkson N. Potter, Inc., 1986), p. 158.

8 E. K. Sedgwick, 'Shame, Theatricality, and Queer Performativity: Henry James's The Art of the Novel', in David M. Halperin and Valerie Traub (eds.), *Gay Shame* (Chicago and London: University of Chicago Press, 2009), p. 50.

9 Ibid., p. 51.

10 P. Sparke, *As Long as It's Pink: The Sexual Politics of Taste* (London and San Francisco: Pandora, 1994), p. 105.

11 *The Modern Man*, 13 February 1909.

12 S. Gundle, *Glamour: A History* (Oxford and New York: Oxford University Press, 2008), p. 154.

13 T. Greenidge, *Degenerate Oxford: A Critical Study of Modern University Life* (London: Chapman and Hall, 1930), p. 1.

14 *Ibid.*, pp. 2–3.

15 *Ibid.*, p. 73.

16 B. A. Macfadden, *The Virile Powers of Superb Manhood: How Developed, How Lost, How Regained* (New York: Physical Culture Publishing, Co., 1900), pp. 13–15; see also J. Potvin, *Visual and Material Cultures Beyond Male Bonding, 1880–1914: Bodies, Boundaries, and Intimacy* (Aldershot and Burlington: Ashgate, 2008), pp. 18–26.

17 Greenidge, *Degenerate Oxford*, p. 83.

18 *Ibid.*, p. 99.

19 *Ibid.*, p. 101.

20 *Ibid.*, p. 108.

21 B. Nichols, *The Sweet and Twenties* (New York: British Book Centre, 1958), p. 210.

22 *Ibid.*, pp. 209–10.

23 In H. Vickers, *Cecil Beaton: The Authorized Biography* (London: Weidenfeld and Nicolson, 1985), p. 26.

24 In *ibid.*, p. 43.

25 Nichols, *The Sweet and Twenties*, p. 210.

26 Vickers, *Cecil Beaton*, pp. 28–31.

27 *Ibid.*, p. 35.

28 In *ibid.*, p. 98.

29 *Ibid.*, p. 97.

30 February 1935 in Vickers, *Cecil Beaton*, p. 181.

31 S. Sontag, 'Notes on Camp', in *Against Interpretation and Other Essays* (New York: Picard, 2001), p. 276.

32 Vickers, *Cecil Beaton*, p. 96.

33 M. Houlbrook, *Queer London: Perils and Pleasures in the Sexual Metropolis, 1918–1957* (Chicago and London: University of Chicago Press, 2005), p. 127.

34 Beaton, *Self-Portrait with Friends*, p. 12.

35 *Ibid.*, p. 12.

36 In Vickers, *Cecil Beaton*, p. 40.

37 In *ibid.*, p. 84.

38 C. Reed, 'Design for [Queer] Living: Sexual Identity, Performance, and Décor in British *Vogue*, 1922–1926', *GLQ*, vol. 12, no. 3 (2006), p. 380.

39 In Vickers, *Cecil Beaton*, p. 101.

40 C. Horwood, *Keeping Up Appearances: Fashion and Class between the Wars* (Stroud: The History Press, 2011), p. 148.

41 *Ibid.*, p. 149.

42 Coward in B. Day (ed.), *The Letters of Noël Coward* (London: Methuen Drama, 2007), p. 164.

43 Beaton, *Self-Portrait with Friends*, p. 7.

44 C. Beaton, *The Glass of Fashion* (London: Weidenfeld and Nicolson, 1954), p. 160.

45 N. de Jongh, *Not in Front of the Audience: Homosexuality on Stage* (London and New York: Routledge, 1992), p. 35.

46 Sparke, *As Long as It's Pink*, p. 79.
47 See *ibid.*, pp. 80–6.
48 M. Shairp, *The Green Bay Tree: A Play in Three Acts* (London: George Allen and Unwin Ltd, 1933), pp. 13–14.
49 *Ibid.*, p. 14.
50 *Ibid.*
51 *Ibid.*, p. 17.
52 *Ibid.*, p. 18.
53 *Ibid.*, p. 20.
54 *Ibid.*, p. 26.
55 *Ibid.*
56 *Ibid.*, p. 29.
57 *Ibid.*, p. 48.
58 *Ibid.*, p. 64.
59 *Ibid.*, p. 78.
60 *The Times*, 26 January 1933.
61 M. Cook, *Queer Domesticities: Homosexuality and Home Life in Twentieth Century London* (London: Palgrave, 2014).
62 A. Sinfield, 'Private Lives/Public Theater: Noël Coward and the Politics of Homosexuality', *Representations*, no. 36 (autumn 1991), p. 45.
63 M. P. Brown, *Closet Space: Geographies of Metaphor from the Body to the Globe* (London and New York: Routledge, 2000), p. 13.
64 Beaton in I. Grant, (ed.), *Great Interiors* (London: Weidenfeld and Nicolson, 1967), p. 7.
65 British *Vogue*, 1 March 1932.
66 *Ibid.*
67 C. Beaton, *Ashcombe: The Story of a Fifteen-Year Lease* (Wimborne: The Dovecote Press 1999 [1949]), n.p.
68 *Ibid.*, p. 5.
69 *Ibid.*, p. 13.
70 Sontag, 'Notes on Camp', p. 285.
71 Beaton, *Self-Portrait with Friends*, p. 27.
72 T. Croft, *The Clover Hoof: A Study of Contemporary London Vices* (London: Denis Archer, 1932), pp. 63–4.
73 See Reed 'Design for [Queer] Living'.
74 Beaton, *Ashcombe*, pp. 10–11.
75 Sontag, 'Notes on Camp', p. 280.
76 British *Vogue*, 1 March 1932.
77 T. T. Latimer, 'Balletomania: A Sexual Disorder?', *GLQ*, vol. 5, no. 2 (1999), p. 182.
78 M. Green, *Children of the Sun* (New York: Basic Books, 1976), p. 22.
79 Beaton, *Ashcombe*, pp. 12–13.
80 Nichols, *The Sweet and Twenties*, pp. 205–6.

81 Beaton, *The Glass of Fashion*, p. 208.
82 *Ibid.*, p. 209.
83 *Ibid.*
84 *Ibid.*, p. 10.
85 *Ibid.*, pp. 16, 15.
86 Beaton, *Ashcombe*, p. 16.
87 *Ibid.*, p. 29.
88 Vickers, *Cecil Beaton*, p. 160.
89 C. Beaton, *The Wandering Years, Diaries: 1922–1939* (London: Weidenfeld and Nicolson, 1961), pp. 223–4.
90 Beaton, *Ashcombe*, p. 32.
91 *Ibid.*, p. 33.
92 Beaton, *The Wandering Years*, pp. 243–5.
93 Beaton, *Ashcombe*, p. 48.
94 Croft, *The Clover Hoof*, pp. 67–8.
95 Beaton, *Ashcombe*, p. 47.
96 Houlbrook, *Queer London*, p. 129.
97 In Ross, *Beaton in Vogue*, p. 15.
98 Vickers, *Cecil Beaton*, p. 148.
99 Beaton, *Self-Portrait with Friends*, p. 27.
100 Vickers, *Cecil Beaton*, p. 149.
101 In *ibid.*, p. 150.
102 In *ibid.*, p. 154.
103 *Ibid.*, p. 155.
104 In *ibid.*, p. 147.
105 British *Vogue*, 15 October 1949.
106 British *Vogue*, 15 March 1963.
107 E. K. Sedgwick, 'Shame, Theatricality, and Queer Performativity: Henry James's The Art of the Novel', in David M. Halperin and Valerie Traub (eds.), *Gay Shame* (Chicago and London: University of Chicago Press, 2009), p. 58.
108 In Vickers, *Cecil Beaton*, p. 41.
109 Sedgwick, 'Shame, Theatricality, and Queer Performativity', p. 60.
110 D. M. Halperin and Valerie Traub (eds.), *Gay Shame* (Chicago and London: University of Chicago Press, 2009), p. 11.

8 ✧ Conclusion: manifesto for a queer home of one's own

CHRISTOPHER REED importantly reminds us that while Virginia Woolf may have popularized the expression 'a room of one's own', it was originally coined in a letter from writer Lytton Strachey to painter Duncan Grant.[1] Members of the Bloomsbury Group, these two *bachelors of a different sort* yearned for a space all their own, designed and defined on their own terms, set apart from the stifling strictures of hetero-patriarchy that surrounded them. What makes the men in this book exceptional and compelling is that they dared to appropriate normative codes of domesticity to forge a material culture and design aesthetic toward distinctly queer ends. Since the nineteenth century, to be a bachelor has all too commonly raised an eyebrow of suspicion. To be a *bachelor of a different sort*, therefore, has meant a challenge, inadvertent or direct, to the very assumptions that underpin the limits and potential of the modern interior. Whether Gower's idolatry of the diva-queen, Shannon and Ricketts's decadent aestheticism, Warren's outmoded Uranian recipe for all-male aeskesis, Morris and Lett's decorative inclinations, Coward's controlled performance of glamour or Beaton's fantastic and bold artifice, these men managed to construct Strachey's greatest wish, a room – and possibly a home – to call their own. Collectively these are the sins implicated in the queer expression of the modern interior. These men set out to establish spaces and communities outside of the normalizing ethos of domestic relations with its taken-as-given network of objects, spaces and familial bonds.

If one's identity is circumscribed by laws and amendments then queer designs, purchases, decorations, patterns, movements, bodily inscriptions and certainly sexual appetites are often viewed as excessive, that is, in excess of the law that binds and defines them. These sins of excess of the modern bachelor become the very signs of a continuous disavowal. As a result of the circumscriptions and legal strictures long applied to queer lives, this book has purposefully, and importantly,

Conclusion

moved queer identity and the experiences of the interior outside of the libidinal and orgasmic, while at the same avoiding denial or passing judgement of their importance within practices of lived-in, embodied space.

Queers are always placed in a position of having to justify their actions, often perceived to be excessive or their experiences deemed *too* particularized, unable to suggest or support a supposed and often privileged universal experience. External pressure compels one to rationalize or justify why these men and their interiors matter; this, however, serves only to spotlight the need to validate them against the background of universal ideals. An all too facile question that I have been asked is what makes queer men's lives more interesting or particularly important to have an entire book devoted to the subject? The answer is a rather simple though fundamental one: queers then and now continue to experience homophobia in real and tangibly physical ways, our experiences of the private and public often mitigated by the constant challenges of negotiating a place in society, in space itself, often against a backdrop of dismissal, denial or outright hostility. In short, what I am referring to here are the collective and personal experiences, both public and private, of the myriad techniques of shame. Queers make sense of space by making it uniquely our own as a vital means to allow for our embodied selves to take place, whether in, out or on the threshold of the proverbial closet.

Even in these times of so-called permissiveness, inclusion and tolerance, it is all too easy (frighteningly so) to take history and queer experiences for granted. Life is good now, why upset anyone, we might ask; a queer feeling of wanting to blend in or avoid drawing attention to oneself. These are remnants of shame we know all too well. Heterosexual men, while they may have their own challenges, have never been subjected to decades, even centuries of persecution on such a widespread socially, politically and religiously sanctioned level as homophobia. When amendments and laws are enforced, whether in the past or in the present, whether in Britain, Russia or in any other part of the world, which establish and restrict the limits of love, sex, public visibility and private space, one necessarily has a different and unique relationship to the modern interior and design. And one often feels the need to act out, even if only through the design of one's interiors. The modern interior is not now nor has it ever been free of social, cultural or political associations or burdens. As Sedgwick has asserted, queers are forced to 'patch together from fragments a community, a usable heritage, a politics of survival or resistance'.[2] *Lest we forget*, queers have long had (and in fact continue) to conceptualize our identities, our very (material) existence in wholly differing ways from our heterosexual cohorts, and, for this reason alone, these fragments beg exploration. My hope is that this book will serve to inspire future study and continue to piece together the myriad fragments of queerly lived-in spaces and modern identities.

It is not entirely unusual for straight people to look at 'queer' homes with pleasure, mystification, admiration and yet often tinged with a hint of condescension. 'It's all so gorgeous, but we could never spend that amount on a piece of bric-à-brac, we have a family, we have real concerns', is an all too common moralizing reproach when asked how much things cost in a so-called 'glamorous' queer home. Here, once again, shame and the decorative, shame and artifice, shame and excess filter perceptions, receptions and queer experiences of their own lives and life-choices. Shame and design make uneasy bedfellows and yet they comprise the politics of aesthetics of the modern interior. Shame erects walls. Shame clothes pain and suffering. Shame materializes phobia and panic. Yet shame also builds things of beauty, which in turn become the material cultures of resistance. Shame teaches. Shame activates. Shame, importantly, also resists; for it must in order for the queer subject to survive. Shame, like the visual and material culture of the modern interior, is both a public expression and private experience. Because shame was and more often than not remains an integral part of queer identity, spatial narratives are rich with socio-cultural and political implications and resonance, and speak to larger concerns beyond the particular case studies presented in this book.

Domestic spaces materialize the building of lives, as much as they are sites of ideological struggle, tension and resistance, the material stuff of identity. They form the landscape wherein knowledge is acquired and gender and sexual difference are coded, performed and circumscribed. The experiences and expressions of the modern interior are endless and there is much more than can be excavated and said about the queer experience of it. Toward this end, the archive as an important source of knowledge comes to mind here. The archives, however, are not always generous to those seeking the archaeological remnants of voices long lost or those still residing on the margins. Words, subject terms and search engines tend to fail us when pursuing the narratives and identities of the spaces of the interior. Within the physical and conceptual spaces of the archive, not unlike the modern interior itself, much is taken for granted within structures that tend toward normalizing material culture, history and the perceptions that condition knowledge. The archive is itself a modern interior equally charged with limitations and possibilities. It contains the mysteries of lives and spaces obscured by and over time. Like the approaches used in each case study here, the future lay in unlocking the door to the threshold to those stories. The key to understanding them is to acknowledge there are numerous ways to approach queer space; after all, if there is one lesson that queer theory has taught us, it is that difference is real, dynamic and boundless.

When I set out to research and write this book, my goal was certainly to uncover the narratives of design, domesticity and how gender and sexuality altered and were affected by these narratives. What I did not realize or intend to prove was the ways in which many of these men, while having left indelible marks on the history of art, design and culture, have all suffered in some form or other the shame that often accompanies the identity of the *bachelor of a different sort*. The descriptive interiors explored in this book are all unique and different, while all remaining *positively* queer. For me, the men in this book embodied the burdens of the masks we don, the public persona of gaiety that inevitably cloak the face of private shame. At the same time, these men and the spaces they designed also remind us of the power of and the pleasures associated with transcending limitations by engendering a world of beauty, not merely as an escape from the sundry and glib world we may inhabit, but by creating a thing or spaces of beauty for beauty's sake. This beauty, it must be said, is fundamentally modern, that is, the free expression of love, companionship, sexual pleasure and aesthetic fulfilment.

What better way to purge the true deadly sins of this world?

Notes

1 C. Reed (ed.), *Not at Home: The Suppression of Domesticity in Modern Art and Architecture* (London: Thames and Hudson, 1996), p. 149.
2 E. K. Sedgwick, *Epistemology of the Closet* (Berkeley: University of California Press, 1990), p. 81.

Select bibliography

Note that for the sake of brevity and a concern for space, articles in daily and weekly periodicals are not listed in the bibliography.

Primary sources

'A House Built for a Bachelor', *The Ideal Home*, October 1928.

'Art in the Home: Healthy Decoration in the Home', *The Artist*, 1 August 1884.

'The Art of Furnishing', *Cornhill Magazine*, January–June 1875.

'Artistic Decoration and the Middle-Class Home', *The Artist*, 1 September 1892.

Archer, T., *The Pauper, the Thief, and the Convict: Sketches of Some of Their Homes, Haunts and Habits*, London, Groombridge, 1865.

B., M. A., 'Lord Ronald Gower: Sculptor, Author and Dilettante', *English Illustrated Magazine*, no. 13, April–September 1895.

Balzac, H. de, *Le Cousin Pons*, Paris, Garnier, 1962 [1847].

Beaton, C., *The Glass of Fashion*, London, Weidenfeld and Nicolson, 1954.

Beaton, C., *The Wandering Years, Diaries: 1922–1939*, London, Weidenfeld and Nicolson, 1961.

Beaton, C., *Self-Portrait with Friends: The Selected Diaries of Cecil Beaton 1926–1974*, London, Weidenfeld and Nicolson, 1979.

Beaton, C., *Ashcombe: The Story of a Fifteen-Year Lease*, Wimborne, Dorset, The Dovecote Press, 1999 [1949].

Birnbaum, M., *Introductions: Painters, Sculptors and Graphic Artists*, New York, Frederic Fairchild Sherman, 1919.

Blair, The Rt Rev. Sir D. H., *In Victorian Days and Other Papers*, Freeport, NY, Books for Libraries Press, 1969 [1939].

Bourget, P., *Nouveaux essais de psychologie contemporaine*, Paris, Lemerre, 1888.

Brown, J. B., *The Home: In Its Relation to Man and to Society*, London, James Clarke and Co., 1883.

C., H. J., *The Art of Furnishing on Rational and Aesthetic Principles*, London, Henry S. King and Co., 1876.

Bibliography

Carpenter, E., *Homogenic Love and Its Place in a Free Society*, London, Redundancy Press, 1895.

Chambers, W. and R. Chambers, 'Scamping', *Chambers' Journal of Popular Literature, Science, and Art*, vol. 56, no. 787, 25 January 1879.

Coates, W., 'Furniture Today – Furniture Tomorrow', *The Architectural Review*, vol. lxxii, no. 428, July 1932.

Connolly, C., 'Genuine Arts & Crafts', *The Architectural Review*, vol. LXXI, no. 422, January 1932.

Cook, C., *The House Beautiful Essays on Beds and Tables, Stools and Candlesticks*, New York, Scribner, Armstrong and Company, 1878.

Coward, N., *Present Indicative*, Garden City and New York, Doubleday and Company, Inc., 1937.

Coward, N., 'Private Lives', in *Three Plays*, New York, Vintage, 1999 [1930].

De Goncourt, E., *La Maison d'un artiste*, 2 vols, Paris, G. Charpentier, 1881.

Delaney, P. J. G. (ed.), *Some Letters from Charles Ricketts and Charles Shannon to 'Michael Field' (1894–1902)*, Edinburgh, The Tragara Press, 1979.

Earp, T. W., 'Cedric Morris', *The Studio*, vol. xcvi, no. 427, October 1928.

Edis, R., *Decoration and Furniture of Town Houses*, London, Kegan Paul, 1881.

Ellis, H., *Studies in the Psychology of Sex*, New York, Random House, 1942 [1933].

Eye and Ear Memory: The Memory and Thought Series, Harrisburg and New York, James P. Downs Publisher, 1891.

Forster, E. M., *Maurice*, London and New York, Penguin Books, 1971.

Fry, R., 'The Artist as Decorator', in Christopher Reed (ed.), *A Roger Fry Reader*, Chicago and London, University of Chicago Press, 1996 [1917].

Gower, Lord R., *My Reminiscences*, 2 vols, London, Kegan Paul, Trench, Trübner, and Co. Ltd, 1883.

Gower, Lord R., *Last Days of Marie Antoinette: An Historical Sketch*, London, Kegan Paul, Trench and Co., 1885.

Gower, Lord R., *Bric À Brac or Some Photoprints Illustrating Art Objects at Gower Lodge, Windsor*, London, Kegan Paul, Trench and Co., 1888.

Grant, I (ed.), *Great Interiors*, preface by Cecil Beaton, London, Weidenfeld and Nicolson, 1967.

Hamilton, W., *The Aesthetic Movement in England*, London, Reeves and Turner, 1882.

Haweis, Mrs H. R., *The Art of Decoration*, London, Chatto and Windus, 1881.

Heard, H. J., 'Are You a Fop? A Social Study', *The Modern Man*, 2 January 1909.

Hemingway, E., *The Sun Also Rises*, New York, Scribner, 2006 [1926].

Holmes, C. J., *Self & Partners (Mostly Self)*, London and Toronto, Constable and Co., 1936.

Hunt, W. H., 'Aestheticism', in *Pre-Raphaelitism and the Pre-Raphaelite Brotherhood*, vol. ii. London, Macmillan, 1913.

Hussey, C., 'The Keep of Chilham Castle Kent: A Residence of Mr. Charles Shannon, R.A. and Charles Ricketts A.R.A', *Country Life*, vol. 55, 21 June 1924.

Huysmans, J.-K., *Against Nature* Oxford, Oxford World's Classics, 1998 [1884].

J., F. B., 'When a Man Entertains: What a Bachelor Should Do in the Position of Host', *Homes and Gardens*, June 1926.

Jackson, C. K., 'New Chivalry', *Artist*, 2 April 1894.

Johnson, T. B., 'Bachelor Leisure', *The Modern Man*, 16 January 1909.

Jones, O., *The Grammar of Ornament*, London, Day & Son, 1856.

Kingsley, C., *Two Years Ago*, London, Macmillan, 1881.

Le Corbusier, *Toward a New Architecture*, London, Architectural Press, 1927 [1923].

Le Corbusier, *Decorative Art Today*, Cambridge, MA, The MIT Press, 1987 [1925].

Leslie, J., B. Nicholson and N. Gabo (eds.), *Circle: International Survey of Constructivist Art*, London, Faber and Faber, 1937.

Lett-Haines, A., 'Towards an Appreciation of Modern Art', unpublished script, Tate, Tga 8317.7.1.5.

Lett-Haines, A., *Cedric Morris Retrospective*, Cardiff, National Museum of Wales, 1968.

Lewis, C. (ed.), *Self-Portrait: Taken from the Letters and Journals of Charles Ricketts, R.A.*, collected and compiled by T. Sturge Moore, London, Peter Davis, 1939.

Loftie, J., *A Plea for Art in the House: With Special Reference to the Economy of Collecting Works of Art, and the Importance of Taste in Education and Morals*, London, Macmillan and Co., 1876.

Loos, A., 'Crime and Ornament', in Melony Ward and Bernie Miller (eds.), *Crime and Ornament: The Arts and Popular Culture in the Shadow of Adolf Loos*, Toronto, YYZ Books, 2002 [1908].

Lowndes, Mrs B., *The Merry Wives of Westminster*, London, Macmillan and Co. Ltd, 1946.

Lubbock, M., 'Collections as Decoration', *Homes and Gardens*, May 1939.

M., W., 'When a Man's Single: How a Bachelor Has Furnished His Chambers', *House and Gardens*, May 1924.

Macfadden, B. A., *The Virile Powers of Superb Manhood: How Developed, How Lost, How Regained*, New York, Physical Culture Publishing, Co., 1900.

Miller, F., *Interior Decoration*, London, Wyman and Sons, 1885.

Moffat, C., 'Furnishing a Man's Room: A Woman's View of the Problem', *Homes and Gardens*, January 1939.

Moore, S. (ed.), *Works and Days, From the Journal of Michael Field*, London, J. Murray, 1933.

Morris, C., 'Concerning Flower Painting', *The Studio*, vol. cxxiii, no. 590, May 1942.

Nash, P., *Room and Book*, London and New York, Soncino Press and Charles Scribner's Sons, 1932.

Nichols, B., *The Sweet and Twenties*, New York, British Book Centre, 1958.

Nordau, M., *Degeneration*, New York, D. Appleton and Company, 1905.

Old Bachelors: Their Varieties, Characters, and Conditions, 2 vols, London, John Macrone, 1835.

Pater, W., *Marius the Epicurean*. New York: Penguin Books, Ltd, 1985 [1892].

Pater, W., *The Renaissance, Studies in Art and Poetry*, Oxford and New York, Oxford University Press, 1990.

Pater, W., *Imaginary Portraits: With the Child in the House and Gaston de Latour*, New York, Allworth Press, 1997.

Pater, W., *Greek Studies: A Series of Essays*, Whitefish, MT, Kessinger Publishing, 2004.

Patmore, D., 'Interior Decoration', *Journal of the Royal Society of Arts*, 18 January 1935.

Perks, S., *Residential Flats of All Classes Including Artisan's Dwellings: A Practical Treatise on the Planning and Arrangement*, London, B. T. Batsford, 1905.

Plato, *Symposium*, B. Jowett (trans.), Indianapolis, Bobbs-Merrill, 1956.

Raymond, J. P. and C. Ricketts, *Oscar Wilde: Recollections*, London, The Nonesuch Press, 1932.

Ricketts, C., *Beyond the Threshold*, Privately Published, Plaistow, 1929.

Ricketts, C., *Unrecorded Histories*, London, Martin Secker, 1933.

Riviere, J., 'Womanliness as Masquerade', in Victor Burgin, James Donald and Cora Kaplan (eds.), *Formations of Fantasy*, New York, Routledge, 1986 [1929].

Rothenstein, Sir J., *The Artists of the 1890's*, London, G. Routledge and Sons, Ltd, 1928.

Rothenstein, Sir W., *Men and Memories: Recollections of William Rothenstein, 1900–1922*, London, Faber & Faber Limited, 1932.

Ruskin, J., *Sesame and Lilies*, New Haven and London, Yale University Press, 2002 [1865].

Santayana, G., *The Sense of Beauty Being the Outlines of Aesthetic Theory*, London, Adam and Charles Black, 1896.

Shairp, M., *The Green Bay Tree: A Play in Three Acts*, London, George Allen and Unwin Ltd, 1933.

Shaw, B., *The Sanity of Art: An Exposure of the Current Nonsense about Artists being Degenerate*, London, The New Age Press, 1908.

Smithells, R. and S. J. Woods, *The Modern Home: Its Decoration, Furnishing, and Equipment*, Benfleet, Essex, F. Lewis (Publishers) Limited, 1936.

Speyer, M., 'The Hybrid Home: Mixing the Old with the New', *Homes and Gardens*, January 1936.

Stanley, R., 'Houses of the Future? Machines to Live in', *Homes and Gardens*, February 1928.

Stevenson, J. J., *House Architecture*, Vol. II: *House Planning*, London, Macmillan and Co., 1880.

Stoker, B., *Dracula*, N. Auerbach and D. J. Skal (eds.), New York and London, W. W. Norton, Inc., 1997 [1873].

Stokes, O., 'Dandies', *The Modern Man*, 13 February 1909.

Symonds, J. A., *A Problem in Greek Ethics Being an Inquiry into the Phenomenon of Sexual Inversion*, London, The Apeonatitita Society, 1908.

Symonds, J. A., *The Letters of John Addington Symonds*, H. M. Schueller and R. L. Peters (eds.), vol. 3, 1885–1893, Detroit, Wayne State University Press, 1969.

Symonds, J. A. and H. Ellis, *Sexual Inversion*, Basingstoke and New York: Palgrave Macmillan, 2008.

T, A. H., 'Art in the Middle-Class Home', *The Artist*, 1 November 1891.

Todd, D. and R. Mortimer, *The New Interior Decoration*, London, B. T. Batsford, 1929.

Townsend, H., 'A Scheme of Decoration for a Bachelor's Room', *The Studio*, vol. 16, 1899.

Veblen, T., *The Theory of Leisure Class: An Economic Study of Institutions*, New York, The Modern Library, 1934 [1899].

Warburton, J., *A Painter's Progress, Part of a Life, 1920–1987*, unpublished manuscript. Tate tga 986.2.20.

Warren, E. P. (aka A. L. Raile), *A Defence of Uranian Love*, Privately Printed, 3 vols 1928.

White, W. H., 'On Middle-Class Houses in Paris and Central London', address to the Royal Institute of British Architects, *Sessional Papers, 1877–78*, 19 November 1877.

Wilde, O., *Essays and Lectures by Oscar Wilde*, London, Methuen and Co., 1908.

Wilde, O., *Art and Decoration: Being Extracts from Reviews and Miscellanies*, London, Methuen & Co. Ltd, 1920.

Williamson, G. C., 'The Lord Ronald Sutherland-Gower: A Memorial Tribute', *Khaki*, 1916.

Wilson, J. G., 'About Bric-à-Brac', *The Art Journal*, vol. 46, 1878.

Winckelmann, J. J., *History of Ancient Art*, New York, F. Ungan, 1968.

Winckelmann, J. J., *Reflections on the Imitation of Greek Works in Painting and Sculpture*, La Salle, IL, Open Court, 1987.

Woollcombe, J., 'Noël Coward's "Cottage Interior"', *Homes and Gardens*, February 1937.

Secondary sources

Adams, A., *Architecture in the Family Way: Doctors, Houses, and Women, 1870–1900*, Montreal, McGill-Queen's University Press, 1996.

Ahmed, S., 'Orientations: Toward a Queer Phenomenology', *GLQ: A Journal of Lesbian and Gay Studies*, vol. 12, no. 4, 2006.

Aldrich, R., *The Seduction of the Mediterranean: Writing, Art and Homosexual Fantasy*, New York and London, Routledge, 1993.

Anderson, A., '"She weaves by night and day, a magic web with colours gay": Trapped in the *Gesamtkunstwerk* of the Dangers of Unifying Dress and Interiors', in J. Potvin and A. Myzelev (eds.), *Fashion, Interior Design and the Contours of Modern Identity*, Aldershot and Burlington, Ashgate, 2010.

Anderson, A., 'The "New Old School": Furnishing with Antiques in the Modern Interior – Frederic, Lord Leighton's Studio-House and Its Collections', *Journal of Design History*, vol. 24, no. 4, 2011.

Anderson, A., 'Lost Treasures, Lost Histories, Lost Memories: Reconstructing the Interiors of Lord Frederic Leighton's Studio-House', *Interiors*, vol. 2, issue 1, 2011.

Anderson, B., *Imagined Communities: Reflections on the Origin and Spread of Nationalism*, London, Verso, 1991.

Appadurai, A. (ed.), *The Social Life of Things: Commodities in Cultural Perspective*, Cambridge, Cambridge University Press, 1986.

Attfield, J., *A View from the Interior: Feminism, Women and Design*, London, Women's Press, 1988.

Attfield, J., *Wild Things: The Material Culture of Everyday Life*, Oxford and New York, Berg, 2000.

Banham, J., S. MacDonald and J. Porter, *Victorian Interior Style*, London, Cassell, 1995.

Bann, S., *The Clothing of Clio: A Study of the Representation of History in Nineteenth-Century Britain and France*, Cambridge, Cambridge University Press, 1984.

Barrett-Ducrocq, F., *Love in the Time of Victoria: Sexuality, Class and Gender in Nineteenth-Century London*, London and New York, Verso, 1989.

Bartlett, N., *Who Was That Man? A Present for Mr. Oscar Wilde*, London, Serpent's Tail, 1989.

Baudrillard, J., 'The System of Collecting', in J. Elsner and R. Cardinal (eds.), *The Cultures of Collecting*, London, Reaktion Books Ltd, 1994.

Baudrillard, J., *The System of Objects*, London, Verso, 1996.

Belk, R. W. and M. Wallendorf, 'Of Mice and Men: Gender Identity in Collecting', in S. M. Pearce (ed.), *Interpreting Objects and Collections*, London and New York, Routledge, 1994.

Bell, D. (ed.), *Pleasure Zones: Bodies, Cities, Spaces*, Syracuse, Syracuse University Press, 2001.

Bell, D. and G. Valentine (eds.), *Mapping Desire: Geographies of Sexualities*, London, Routledge, 1995.

Bibliography

Benjamin, W., *The Arcades Project*, Cambridge, MA, and London, The Belknap Press of Harvard University, 1999.

Berlant, L. and M. Warner, 'Sex in Public', *Critical Inquiry*, vol. 24, no. 2, winter 1998.

Betsky, A., *Queer Space: Architecture and Same-Sex Desire*, New York, William Morrow, 1997.

Binnie, J., *The Globalization of Sexuality*, London, Sage, 2004.

Bleys, R. C., *The Geographies of Perversion: Male-to-Male Sexual Behaviour Outside the West and the Ethnographic Imagination, 1750–1918*, New York, New York University Press, 1995.

Blindon, M., 'Jalons pour une géographie des homosexualités', *Espace Géographique*, vol. 2, no. 37, 2008.

Blythe, R., 'Sir Cedric Morris', in S. Hill (ed.), *People, Essays and Poems*, London, Hogarth Press, 1983.

Bourdieu, P., *The Field of Cultural Production*, New York, Columbia University Press, 1993.

Boym, S., *The Future of Nostalgia*, New York, Basic Books, 2001.

Brooker, P., *Bohemia in London: The Social Scene of Early Modernism*, Basingstoke, Palgrave Macmillan, 2004.

Brown, J., *Glamour in Six Dimensions*, Ithaca and London, Cornell University Press, 2009.

Brown, M. P., *Closet Space: Geographies of Metaphor from the Body to the Globe*, London and New York, Routledge, 2000.

Browning, F., *A Queer Geography*, New York, Noonday, 1998.

Bryden, I., *Domestic Space: Reading the Nineteenth-Century Interior*, Manchester, Manchester University Press, 1999.

Buckley, C., 'The Decorated Object: Gender, Modernism and the Design of Industrial Ceramics in Britain in the 1930s', in B. Elliott and J. Helland (eds.), *The Gender of Ornament: Women Artists and the Decorative Arts 1880–1935*, Aldershot and Burlington, Ashgate, 2002.

Bullen, J. B. (ed.), *Post-Impressionists in England*, New York and London, Routledge 1988.

Burdett, O. and E. H. Goddard, *Edward Perry Warren: The Biography of a Connoisseur*, London, Christopher's, 1941.

Callen, A., *Angel in the Studio: Women in the Arts and Crafts Movement 1870–1914*, London, Astragal Books, 1979.

Calloway, S., *Charles Ricketts: Subtle and Fantastic Decorator*, London, Thames and Hudson, 1979.

Calloway, S., 'Tout pour l'art: Ricketts, Charles Shannon and the Arrangement of a Collection', *Journal of the Decorative Art Society*, 81, 1984.

Calloway, S., 'Wilde and the Dandyism of the Senses', in P. Raby (ed.), *The Cambridge Companion to Oscar Wilde*, Cambridge, Cambridge University Press, 1997.

Calloway, S. and P. Delaney, *Charles Ricketts and Charles Shannon: An Aesthetic Partnership*. Catalogue, Orleans, Gallery Twickenham, 1979.

Camille, M., 'Editor's Introduction', *Art History Special Issue on Queer Collecting*, vol. 24, no. 2, April 2001.

Castle, T., *The Apparitional Lesbian: Female Homosexuality and Modern Culture*, New York, Columbia University Press, 1993.

Castle, T., *Noël Coward and Radclyffe Hall: Kindred Spirits*, New York, Columbia University Press, 1996.

Causey, A., 'Paul Nash as Designer', in J. Peto and D. Loveday (eds.), *Modern Britain 1929–1939*, London, Design Museum, 1999.

Chatto, B., 'Sir Cedric Morris, Artist-Gardener', in David Wheeler (ed.), *Hortus Revisited: A Twenty-First Birthday Anthology*, London, Frances Lincoln Limited, 2008.

Chauncey, Jr, G, *Gay New York: Gender, Urban Culture and the Making of the Gay Male World. 1890–1940*, New York, Basic Books, 1994.

Chauncey, Jr, G., 'Privacy Could Only Be in Public', in J. Sanders (ed.), *Stud: Architectures of Masculinity*, New York, Princeton Architectural Press, 1996.

Chudacoff, H., *The Age of the Bachelor: Creating an American Subculture*, Princeton, Princeton University Press, 1999.

Clarke, J. R., 'The Warren Cup of the Contexts for the Representations of Male-to-Male Lovemaking in Augustan and Early Julio-Claudian Art', *The Art Bulletin*, vol. 73, no. 2, June 1993.

Cohen, D., *Households Gods: The British and Their Possessions*, New Haven and London, Yale University Press, 2006.

Cohen, E., *Talk on the Wilde Side: Toward a Genealogy of a Discourse on Male Sexualities*, London and New York, Routledge, 1993.

Colomina, B., *Sexuality and Space*, New York, Princeton Architectural Press, 1992.

Colomina, B., *Privacy and Publicity: Modern Architecture as Mass Media*, Cambridge, Cambridge University Press, 1994.

Connell, R. W., *Masculinities*, Berkeley, University of California Press, 1995.

Cook, M., *London and the Culture of Homosexuality, 1885–1914*, Cambridge, Cambridge University Press, 2003.

Cook, M., 'Families of Choice? George Ives, Queer Lives and the Family', *Gender and History*, no. 22, April 2010.

Cook, M., 'Domestic Passions: Unpacking the Homes of Charles Shannon and Charles Ricketts', *Journal of British Studies*, vol. 51, no. 3, June 2012.

Cook, M., *Queer Domesticities: Homosexuality and Home Life in Twentieth Century London*, London, Palgrave, 2014.

Cooper, E., *The Sexual Perspective: Homosexuality and Art in the Last 100 Years in the West*, New York and London, Routledge, 1994.

Cooper, N., *The Opulent Eye: Late Victorian and Edwardian Taste in Interior Design*, London, The Architectural Press Ltd, 1976.

Corbett, D. P., *The World in Paint*, Philadelphia, Penn State University Press, 2004.

Corbett, D. P., 'Oedipus and the Sphinx: Visual Knowledge and Homosociality in the Ricketts Circle', *Visual Culture in Britain*, vol. 8, no. 1, summer 2007.

Craft, C., *Another Kind of Love: Male Homosexual Desire in English Discourse, 1850–1920*, Berkeley, University of California Press, 1994.

Croft, T., *The Clover Hoof: A Study of Contemporary London Vices*, London, Denis Archer, 1932.

Cromley, E. C., *Alone Together: A History of New York's Early Apartments*, Ithaca and London, Cornell University Press, 1990.

Crook, T., 'Craft and the Dialogics of Modernity: The Arts and Crafts Movement in Late-Victorian and Edwardian England', *The Journal of Modern Craft*, vol. 2, no. 1, March 2009.

Crow, T., *Modern Art in the Common Culture*, New Haven and London, Yale University Press, 1996.

Curtin, K., *We Can Always Call Them Bulgarians: The Emergence of Lesbians and Gay Men on the American Stage*, Boston, Alyson, 1987.

Darling, E., '"The scene in which the daily drama of personal life takes place": Towards the Modern Interior in Early 1930s Britain', in P. Sparke et al. (eds.), *Designing the Modern Interior: From the Victorians to Today*, Oxford and New York, Berg, 2009.

Darracott, J. (ed.), *The Ricketts and Shannon Collection*, New York and Cambridge, The Fitzwilliam Museum, 1979.

Darracott, J., *The World of Charles Ricketts*, London, Eyre Methuen, 1980.

David, H., *On Queer Street: A Social History of British Homosexuality 1895–1995*, London, HaperCollins Publishers, 1997.

Davidoff, L., 'The Separation of Home and Work? Landladies and Lodgers in the Nineteenth- and Twentieth-Century England', in S. Burman (ed.), *Fit Work for Women*, London, Croom Helm, 1979.

Davidoff, L., *The Family Story: Blood, Contract, and Intimacy, 1830–1960*, London and New York, Longman, 1999.

Davis, A. G. and P. M. Strong, 'Working without a Net: The Bachelor as a Social Problem', *Sociological Review*, vol. 25, 25 April 1977.

Davis, W., 'Homoerotic Art Collection from 1750 to 1920', *Art History*, vol. 24, no. 2, April 2001.

Davis, W., 'Lord Ronald Gower and the Offending Adam', in D. J. Getsey (ed.), *Sculpture and the Pursuit of a Modern Ideal in Britain, c. 1880–1930*, Aldershot, Ashgate Publishing Limited, 2004.

Dawson, G., *Soldier Heroes: British Adventure, Empire, and the Imagining of Masculinities*, New York and London, Routledge, 1994.

Day, B. (ed.), *The Letters of Noël Coward*, London, Methuen Drama, 2007.

Day, B., *The Essential Noël Coward Compendium: The Very Best of His Work, Life and Times*, London, Methuen Drama, 2009.

De Certeau, M., *The Practice of Everyday Life*, Berkeley, University of California Press, 1988.

De Jongh, N., *Not in Front of the Audience: Homosexuality on Stage*, London and New York, Routledge, 1992.

Delaney, P. J. G., *Charles Ricketts: A Biography*, Oxford and New York, Oxford University Press, 1990.

Dellamora, R., *Masculine Desire: The Sexual Politics of Victorian Aestheticism*, Chapel Hill and London, University of North Carolina Press, 1990.

Doan, L., *Fashioning Sapphism: The Origins of a Modern English Lesbian Culture*, New York, Columbia University Press, 2001.

Doan, L. and J. Garrity (eds.), *Sapphic Modernities: Sexuality, Women and National Culture*, New York, Palgrave Macmillan, 2006.

Douglas, M., *Purity and Danger: An Analysis of the Concepts of Pollution and Taboo*, London, Routledge, 1966.

Dowling, L., *Hellenism and Homo-sexuality in Victorian Oxford*, Ithaca and London, Cornell University Press, 1994.

Duncan, N., *Bodyspace: Destablizing Geographies of Gender and Sexuality*, London and New York, Routledge, 1996.

Edwards, J., 'Alfred Gilbert's Aestheticism: Homoeroticism, Artistic Identity and the New Sculpture', *Visual Culture in Britain*, vol. 2, no. 1, 2001.

Edwards, J., 'The Lessons of Leighton House: Aesthetics, Politics, Erotics', in J. Edwards and I. Hart (eds.), *Rethinking the Interior: Aestheticism and the Arts and Crafts Movement, 1867–1896*, Aldershot and Burlington, Ashgate, 2010.

Edwards, J. and I. Hart (eds.), 'Introduction: The Victorian Interior: A Collaborative Eclectic', in *Rethinking the Interior: Aestheticism and the Arts and Crafts Movement, 1867–1896*. Aldershot and Burlington, Ashgate, 2010.

Elliman, M. and F. Roll, *The Pink Plaque Guide to London*, London, GMP Publishers, 1986.

Elliott, B., 'Housing the Work: Women Artists, Modernism and the *maison d'artiste*: Eileen Gray, Romanie Brooks and Gluck', in B. Elliott and J. Helland (eds.), *Women Artist and the Decorative Arts, 1880–1935: The Gender of Ornament*, Aldershot and Burlington, Ashgate, 2002.

Elliott, B., *Benjamin for Architects*, New York and London, Routledge, 2011.

Ellmann, R., *Oscar Wilde*, London: Penguin, 1988.

Elsner, J. and R. Cardinal (eds.), *The Cultures of Collecting*, London, Reaktion Books Ltd, 1994.

Evangelista, S., '"Lovers and Philosophers at Once": Aesthetic Platonism in the Victorian "Fin de Siècle"', *The Yearbook of English Studies*, vol. 36, no. 2, 2006.

Farfan, P., 'Noël Coward and Sexual Modernism: *Private Lives* as Queer Comedy', *Modern Drama*, vol. 48, no. 5, winter 2005.

Felski, R., *The Gender of Modernity*, Cambridge, MA, Harvard University Press, 1995.

Ferry, E., 'Introduction', in P. Sparke et al. (eds.), *Designing the Modern Interior: From the Victorians to Today*, Oxford and New York, Berg, 2010.

Fischer, L., *Designing Women: Cinema, Art Deco and the Female Form*, New York, Columbia University Press, 2003.

Flanders, J., *Inside the Victorian Home: A Portrait of Domestic Life in Victorian England*, New York, W. W. Norton, 2004.

Forty, A., *Words and Buildings: A Vocabulary of Modern Architecture*, London, Thames & Hudson, 2000.

Foster, S., 'The Use of Personality: Allan Walton Textiles and Screen-Painting in the 1930s', *Things*, vol. 1, winter 1994.

Foster, H., 'Prosthetic Gods', *Modernism/Modernity*, vol. 4, no. 2, 1997.

Foucault, M., *History of Sexuality, Volume 2: The Uses of Pleasure*, New York, Vintage Books, 1990.

Foucault, M., 'Friendship as a Way of Life', in P. Rabinow (ed.), *Ethics: Subjectivity and Truth: The Essential Works of Michel Foucault, Volume One*, New York, The New Press, 1997.

Frank, I. (ed.), *The Theory of European Decorative Art: An Anthology of European and American Writings, 1750–1940*, New Haven and London, Yale University Press, 2000.

Friedman, A. T., *Women and the Making of the Modern House: A Social and Architecture History*, New York, Harry N. Abrams, 1998.

Furjan, H., 'The Specular Spectacle of the House of the Collector', *Assemblage*, no. 34, December 1997.

Fuss, D., *A Sense of an Interior: Four Writers and the Rooms that Shaped Them*, New York and London, Routledge, 2004.

Gere, C., *Nineteenth-Century Decoration: The Art of the Interior*, New York, H. N. Abrams, 1989.

Gere, C., 'A Picture of Green and Gray', *Country Life*, vol. 194, no. 28, 13 July 2000.

Gere, C. with L. Hoskins, *The House Beautiful: Oscar Wilde and the Aesthetic Interior*, Aldershot, Lund Humphries, 2000.

Gilbert, S. *Noël Coward and the Queer Feminine*, Diss. Toronto, University of Toronto, 2006.

Girouard, M., 'Chelsea's Bohemian Studio Houses', *Country Life*, 152, 23 November 1972.

Girouard, M., *Sweetness and Light: The 'Queen Anne' Movement 1860–1900*, Oxford, Oxford University Press, 1977.

Glick, E., 'The Dialectics of Dandyism', *Cultural Critique*, vol. 48, spring 2001.

Grace, D. and G. Reynolds (eds.), *Benton End Remembered: Cedric Morris and Arthur Lett-Haines, and the East Anglian School of Painting and Drawing*, London, Unicorn, 2002.

Green, M., *Children of the Sun*, New York, Basic Books, 1976.

Greenberg, C., 'Milton Avery', *Arts Magazine*, no. 32, December 1957.

Greenberg, C., 'Review of Exhibitions of Joan Miro, Fernand Léger, and Wassily Kandinsky', in John O'Brian (ed.), *The Collected Essays and Criticisms: Volume 1, Perceptions and Judgements, 1939–1944*, Chicago and London, University of Chicago Press, 1986.

Greenberg, D. F., *The Construction of Homosexuality*, Chicago and London, University of Chicago Press, 1988.

Greenidge, T., *Degenerate Oxford: A Critical Study of Modern University Life*, London, Chapman and Hall, 1930.

Greenwood, J., *The Wilds of London*, London, Chatto and Windus, 1874.

Greg, W. R., 'Are Women Redundant?', *National Review*, vol. 14, no. 28, April 1862.

Grier, K. C., *Culture & Comfort: People, Parlors, and Upholstry 1850–1930*, Amherst, University of Massachusetts Press, 1988.

Gronberg, T., 'Décoration: Modernism's Other', *Art History*, vol. 15, no. 4, December 1992.

Gronberg, T., 'The Inner Man: Interiors and Masculinity in Early Twentieth-Century Vienna', *Oxford Art Journal*, vol. 24, no. 1, 2001.

Grosskurth, P., *The Woeful Victorians: A Biography of John Addington Symonds*, New York, Random House 1964.

Grosz, E., *Architecture from the Outside: Essays in Virtual and Real Space*, Cambridge, MA, and London, MIT Press, 2001.

Groth, P., *Living Downtown: The History of Residential Hotels in the United States*, Berkeley, University of California Press, 1994.

Gundle, S., 'Hollywood Glamour and Mass Consumption in Postwar Italy', *Journal of Cold War Studies*, vol. 4, no. 3, summer 2002.

Gundle, S., *Glamour: A History*, Oxford and New York, Oxford University Press, 2008.

Halberstam, J., *Female Masculinities*, Durham, NC, Duke University Press, 1998.

Halberstam, J., *In a Queer Time and Place: Transgender Bodies, Subcultural Lives*, New York and London, New York University Press, 2005.

Halperin, D. M., *One Hundred Years of Homosexuality and Other Essays on Greek Love*, New York and London, Routledge, 1990.

Halperin, D. M., *Saint Foucault: Towards a Gay Hagiography*, Oxford and New York, Oxford University Press, 1995.

Halperin, D. M., 'How to Do the History of Male Homosexuality', *GLQ: The Journal of Lesbian and Gay Studies*, vol. 6, no. 1, 2000.

Halperin, D. M. and V. Traub (eds.), *Gay Shame*, Chicago and London, University of Chicago Press, 2009.

Hammill, G. L., *Sexuality and Form: Caravaggio, Marlowe and Bacon*, Chicago and London, University of Chicago Press, 2000.

Hanson, E., 'Undead', in D. Fuss (ed.), *Inside/Out, Lesbian Theories, Gay Theories*, New York, Routledge, 1991.

Harrison, C., *English Art and Modernism, 1900–1939*, New Haven and London, Yale University Press, 1994.

Hartzell, F., 'The Velvet Touch: Fashion, Furniture and the Fabric of the Interior', *Fashion Theory*, vol. 13 no. 1, 2009.

Hatt, M., 'The Male Body in Another Frame', *Journal of Philosophy and the Visual Arts*, 1993.

Hatt, M., 'Near and Far: Homoeroticism, Labour and Hamo Thornycroft's *Mower*', *Art History*, vol. 26, no. 1, February 2003.

Hatt, M., 'Space, Surface, Self: Homosexuality and the Aesthetic Interior', *Visual Culture in Britain*, vol. 8, no. 1, summer 2007.

Helland, J. 'Translating Textiles: "private palaces" and the Celtic Fringe, 1890–1910', in J. Potvin and A. Myzelev (eds.), *Fashion, Interior Design and the Contours of Modern Identity*, Aldershot and Burlington, Ashgate, 2010.

Henderson, S. R. 'Bachelor Culture in the Work of Adolf Loos', *Journal of Architectural Education*, vol. 55, no. 3, February 2002.

Henkinson, A., *Man of Wars: William Howard Russell of The Times*, London, Heinemann, 1982.

Herron, P., 'Tom Herron: A Biographical Note', *The Journal of Decorative Arts Society 1890–1940*, no. 4, 1980.

Heynen, H., 'Modernity and Domesticity: Tensions and Contradictions', in H. Heynen and G. Baydar (eds.), *Negotiating Domesticity*, New York, Routledge, 2005.

Hoare, P., *Noël Coward: A Biography*, New York, Simon & Schuster, 1995.

Hoare, P., *Oscar Wilde's Last Stand*, New York, Arcade Publishing, 1997.

Holzberger, G. and J. Saatkamp (eds.), *Persons and Places: Fragments of an Autobiography*, Cambridge, MA, MIT Press, 1986.

Horwood, C., *Keeping Up Appearances: Fashion and Class between the Wars*, Stroud, The History Press, 2011.

Houlbrook, M., *Queer London: Perils and Pleasures in the Sexual Metropolis, 1918–1957*, Chicago and London, University of Chicago Press, 2005.

Hyde, H. M., *The Trials of Oscar Wilde*, London, William Hodge and Company, 1948.

Hyde, H. M., 'Oscar Wilde and his Architect'. *Architectural Review*, vol. 109, no. 651, March 1951.

Innes, C., *Modern British Drama: The Twentieth Century*, Cambridge, Cambridge University Press, 2002.

Jackson, S., *Lines of Activity: Performance, Historiography, Hull-House Domesticity*, Ann Arbor, University of Michigan Press, 2000.

Jeremiah, D., *Architecture and Design for the Family in Britain, 1900–1970*, Manchester and New York, Manchester University Press, 2000.

Johnson, E. H. (ed.), *American Artists on Art: From 1940 to 1980*, Boulder, Westview Press, 1982.

Johnston, L. and R. Longhurst, *Space, Place and Sex: Geographies of Sexualities*, Lanham, Rowman and Littlefield, 2010.

Jordan, J. O., 'Domestic Servants and the Victorian Home', in M. Baumgarten and H. M. Daleski (eds.), *Homes and Homelessness in the Victorian Imagination*, New York, AMS Press 1998.

Joyce, S., 'Sexual Politics and the Aesthetics of Crime: Oscar Wilde in the Nineties', *ELH*, no. 69 2002.

Kinchin, J., 'Interiors: Nineteenth-Century Essays on the "Masculine" and the "Feminine" Room', in Pat Kirkham (ed.), *The Gendered Object*, Manchester and New York, Manchester University Press, 1996.

Kinsman, G., *The Regulation of Desire: Homo and Hetero Sexualities*, Montreal, New York and London, Black Rose Books, 1996.

Kirkham, P., *The Gendered Object*, Manchester and New York, Manchester University Press, 1996.

Kitchin, R., 'Sexing the City: The Sexual Production of Non-Heterosexual Space in Belfast, Manchester and San Francisco', *City*, vol. 6, no. 2, 2002.

Koestenbaum, W., *The Queen's Throat: Opera, Homosexuality and the Mystery of Desire*, New York, Da Capo Press, 1993.

Koven, S., *Slumming: Sexual and Social Politics in Victorian London*, Princeton, Princeton University Press, 2004.

Kuzmanovic, N., *John Paul Cooper: Designer and Craftsman of the Arts and Crafts Movement*, Phoenix Hill and New York, Sutton, 1999.

Lane, C., *Burdens of Intimacy: Psychoanalysis and Victorian Masculinity*, Chicago, Chicago University Press, 1999.

Latimer, T. T., 'Balletomani a: A Sexual Disorder?', *GLQ*, vol. 5, no. 2, 1999.

Latimer, T. T., *Women Together/Women Apart*, New Brunswick, Rutgers University Press, 2005.

Lesley, C., G. Payne and S. Morley, *Noël Coward and His Friends*, New York, William Morrow, 1979.

Light, A., *Forever England: Femininity, Literature and Conservativism between the Wars*, London, Routledge, 1991.

Logan, T., *The Victorian Parlour*, Cambridge, Cambridge University Press, 2001.

Macleod, D. S., *Art and the Victorian Middle-Class: Money and the Making of Cultural Identity*, New York and Cambridge, Cambridge University Press, 1996.

Mangan, J. A. and J. Walvin (eds.), *Manliness and Morality: Middle Class Masculinity in Britain and America, 1800–1940*, Manchester, Manchester University Press, 1987.

Marcus, S., *Apartment Stories: City and Home in Nineteenth-Century Paris and London*, Berkeley, Los Angeles and London, University of California Press, 1999.

Marcus, S., *Between Women: Friendship, Desire, and Marriage in Victorian England*, Princeton, Princeton University Press, 2007.

Marcus, S., 'At Home with the Other Victorians: The History of Homosexuality as the History of Domesticity', *South Atlantic Quarterly*, vol. 108, no. 1, winter 2009.

Marra, K., 'A Lesbian Marriage of Cultural Consequence: Elisabeth Marbury and Elsie de Wolfe, 1886–1933', *Theatre Annual: A Journal of Performance Studies*, no. 47, fall 1994.

McCormick, J., *George Santayana: A Biography*, New Brunswick, Transaction Publishers, 2003.

McCormack, J. H., *The Man who Was Dorian Gray*, London, Palgrave, 2000.

McKenna, K., 'An Insatiable Appetite for Style: The World of Photographer-Costume Designer Cecil Beaton', *Los Angeles Times*, 19 February 1989.

McKenna, N., *The Secret Life of Oscar Wilde*, New York, Basic Books, 2005.

McNeil, P., 'Designing Women: Gender, Sexuality and the Interior Decorator, c. 1890–1940', *Art History*, vol. 17, no. 4, December 1990.

McNeil, P., 'Crafting Queer Spaces: Privacy and Posturing', in J. Potvin and A. Myzelev (eds.), *Fashion, Interior Design and the Contours of Modern Identity*, Aldershot and Burlington, Ashgate, 2010.

Meyer, R., 'Big, Middle-Class Modernism', *October*, no. 131, winter 2010.

Miller, D., *Home Possessions: Material Culture Behind Closed Doors*, Oxford and New York, Berg, 2001.

Milne-Smith, A., 'A Flight to Domesticity? Making a Home in the Gentlemen's Clubs of London, 1880–1914', *Journal of British Studies*, no. 45, October 2006.

Moran, M., 'Walter Pater's House Beautiful and the Psychology of Self-Culture', *English Literature in Transition, 1880–1920*, vol. 50, no. 3, 2007.

Morphet, R., *Cedric Morris*, London, Tate Gallery, 1984.

Mosse, G. L., *The Images of Man: The Creation of Modern Masculinity*, Oxford and New York, Oxford University Press, 1996.

Neve, C. and T. Venison, 'A Painter and His Garden: Cedric Morris at Benton End', *Country Life*, 17 May 1979.

Newton, C., *Victorian Designs for the Home*, London, V and A Publications, 1999.

Noble, G., 'Accumulating Being', *International Journal of Cultural Studies*, vol. 7, no. 2, 2004.

Osgerby, B., 'The Bachelor Pad as Cultural Icon: Masculinity, Consumption and Interior Design in American Men's Magazines, 1930–65', *Journal of Design History*, vol. 18, no. 1, spring 2005.

Oswin, N., 'Critical Geographies and the Uses of Sexuality: Deconstructing Queer Space', *Progress in Human Geography*, vol. 32, no. 1, 2008.

'The Outsider: Cedric Morris as Painter and Gardener', *Country Life*, 26 April 1984.

Painter, C., *Contemporary Art and the Home*, Oxford and New York, Berg, 2002.

Pearce, S. M. (ed.), *Interpreting Objects and Collections*, London, Routledge, 1994.

Pearce, S. M., *On Collecting: An Investigation into Collecting in the European Tradition*, London and New York, Routledge, 1995.

Perrot, M. (ed.), *A History of Private Life: IV From the Fires of Revolution to the Great War*, Cambridge, MA, and London: The Belknap Press of Harvard University Press, 1990.

Pick, D., *Faces of Degeneration: A European Disorder*, Cambridge, Cambridge University Press, 1989.

Pollock, G., *Vision and Difference: Femininity, Feminism and the Histories of Art*, London and New York, Routledge, 1988.

Polloni, J., 'The Warren Cup: Homoerotic Love And Symposial Rhetoric In Silver', *Art Bulletin*, vol. 81, no. 1, March 1999.

Potts, A., *Flesh and the Ideal: Winckelmann and the Origins of Art History*, New Haven and London, Yale University Press, 1994.

Potvin, J., 'Vapour and Steam: The Victorian Bath, Homosocial Health and Male Bodies on Display', *Journal of Design History*, vol. 18, no. 4, winter 2005.

Potvin, J., 'Perversely Mystical: Towards a Queer Semiology of Breton Male Bodies', *Genders*, issue 41, spring 2005.

Potvin, J., *Visual and Material Cultures Beyond Male Bonding, 1880–1914: Bodies, Boundaries, and Intimacy*, Aldershot and Burlington, Ashgate, 2008.

Potvin, J., 'The Aesthetics of Community: Queer Interiors and the Desire for Intimacy', in J. Potvin and A. Myzelev (eds.), *Material Cultures, 1740–1920: The Meanings and Pleasures of Collecting*, Aldershot and Burlington, Ashgate, 2009.

Potvin, J., 'The Aesthetics of Community: Charles Shannon and Charles Ricketts and the Art of Domesticity', in J. Edwards and I. Hart (eds.), *Rethinking the Interior: Aestheticism and the Arts and Crafts Movement, 1867–1896*, Aldershot and Burlington, Ashgate, 2010.

Potvin, J., 'The Velvet Masquerade: Fashion, Interior Design and the Furnished Body', in J. Potvin and A. Myzelev (eds.), *Fashion, Interior Design and the Contours of Modern Identity*, Aldershot and Burlington, Ashgate, 2010.

Potvin, J. and A. Myzelev (eds.), *Material Cultures, 1740–1920: The Meanings and Pleasures of Collecting*, Aldershot and Burlington, Ashgate, 2009.

Prettejohn, E. (ed.), *After the Pre-Raphaelites: Art and Aestheticism in Victorian England*, New Brunswick, Rutgers University Press, 1999.

Rault, J., *Eileen Gray and the Design of Sapphic Modernity: Staying In*, Burlington and Aldershot, Ashgate, 2011.

Reed, C. (ed.), *Not at Home: The Suppression of Domesticity in Modern Art and Architecture*, London, Thames and Hudson, 1996.

Reed, C., 'Immanent Domain: Queer Space in the Built Environment', *Art Journal*, vol. 55, no. 4, winter 1996.

Reed, C., *A Roger Fry Reader*, Chicago and London, University of Chicago Press, 1996.

Reed, C., *Bloomsbury Rooms: Modernism, Subculture, and Domesticity*, New York, Yale University Press, 2004.

Reed, C., 'A Vogue that Dare not Speak Its Name: Sexual Subculture During the Editorship of Dorothy Todd, 1922–26', *Fashion Theory*, vol. 10, no. 1/2, 2006.

Reed, C., 'Design for [Queer] Living: Sexual Identity, Performance, and Décor in British *Vogue*, 1922–1926', *GLQ*, vol. 12, no. 3, 2006.

Rendell, J., *The Pursuit of Pleasure: Gender, Space and Architecture*, New Brunswick, Rutgers University Press, 2002.

Reynolds, G. and D. Grace (eds.), *Benton End Remembered: Cedric Morris, Arthur Lett-Haines and the East Anglian School of Painting and Drawing*, London, Unicorn Press, 2002.

Rice, C., 'Rethinking Histories of the Interior', *The Journal of Architecture*, no. 9, autumn 2004.

Rice, C., *The Emergence of the Interior*, London and New York, Routledge, 2007.

Robb, G., *Strangers: Homosexual Love in the Nineteenth Century*, London and New York, W. W. Norton and Company, 2003.

Roper, M. and J. Tosh (eds.), *Manful Assertions: Masculinities in Britain since 1880*, New York, Routledge, 1983.

Rosner, V., *Modernism and the Architecture of Private Life*, New York, Columbia Press, 2005.

Ross, J., *Beaton in Vogue*, New York, Clarkson N. Potter, Inc., 1986.

Russel, J., *File on Coward*, London, Methuen, 1987.

Rybczynski, W., *Home: A Short History of an Idea*, New York, Viking, 1986.

Saisselin, R., *The Bourgeois and the Bibelot*, New Brunswick, Rutgers University Press, 1984.

Sarnoff, I. and S. Sarnoff, *Intimate Creativity: Partners in Love and Art*, Madison, The University of Wisconsin Press, 2002.

Schaffer, T., '"A Wilde Desire Took Hold of Me": The Homoerotic History of *Dracula*', in N. Auerbach and D. J. Skal (eds.), *Dracula*, New York and London, W. W. Norton, Inc., 1997.

Schaffer, T., *Forgotten Female Aesthetes: Literary Culture in Late Victorian Britain*, Charlottesville and London, University Press of Virginia, 2000.

Schmiechen, J. A., 'The Victorians, the Historians, and the Idea of Modernism', *The American Historical Review*, vol. 93, no. 2, April 1988.

Sedgwick, E. K., *Between Men: English Literature and Male Homosocial Desire*, New York, Columbia University Press, 1985.

Sedgwick, E. K., *Epistemology of the Closet*, Berkeley, University of California Press, 1990.

Sedgwick, E. K., *Tendencies*, Durham NC, Duke University Press, 1993.

Sedgwick, E. K., 'Shame, Theatricality, and Queer Performativity: Henry James's The Art of the Novel', in D. M. Halperin and V. Traub (eds.), *Gay Shame*, Chicago and London, University of Chicago Press, 2009.

Seremetakis, C. N., *The Senses Still: Perception and Memory as Material Culture in Modernity*, Boulder, Westview Press, 1994.

Service, A., *Edwardian Interiors: Inside the Homes of the Poor, the Average and the Wealthy*, London, Barrie and Jenkins, 1982.

Shields, R. (ed.), *Places on the Margin: Alternative Geographies of Modernity*, London and New York, Routledge, 1991.

Short, B., D. Gilbert and D. Matless (eds.), *Geographies of British Modernity: Space and Society in the Twentieth Century*, Oxford, Blackwell Publishing, 2003.

Simmel, G., *The Sociology of Georg Simmel*, New York, The Free Press, 1950.

Sinfield, A., 'Private Lives/Public Theater: Noël Coward and the Politics of Homosexuality', *Representations*, no. 36, autumn 1991.

Sinfield, A., *The Wilde Century: Effeminacy, Oscar Wilde and the Queer Moment*, New York, Columbia University Press, 1994.

Slater, D., *Consumer Culture and Modernity*, Cambridge, Polity Press, 1997.

Sloan, J., 'Quarrels and Coteries in the 1890s', *Yearbook of English Studies*, vol. 36, no. 2, 2006.

Snyder, K. V., *Bachelors, Manhood, and the Novel*, Cambridge, Cambridge University Press, 1999.

Sontag, S., 'Notes on Camp', in *Against Interpretation and Other Essays*, New York, Picard, 2001.

Soros, S. W. (ed.), *E. W. Goodwin Aesthetic Movement Architect and Designer*, New Haven and London, Yale University Press, 1999.

Sox, D., *Bachelors of Art: Edward Perry Warren and the Lewes House Brotherhood*, London, Fourth Estate, 1991.

Sparke, P., *As Long as It's Pink: The Sexual Politics of Taste*, London and San Francisco, Pandora, 1994.

Sparke, P., *The Modern Interior*, London, Reaktion Press, 2008.

Sparke, P. and S. McKellar (eds.), *Interior Design and Identity*, Manchester, Manchester University Press, 2004.

Stephenson, A., 'Refashioning Modern Masculinity: Whistler, Aestheticism and National Identity', in D. P. Corbett and L. Perry (eds.), *English Art 1860–1914, Modern Artists and Identity*, New Brunswick, Rutgers University Press, 2001.

Stephenson, A., 'Staging Authenticity: Tourist Spaces and Artistic Inscription in Inter-war English Art', *Visual Culture in Britain*, vol. 4, no. 1, 2003.

Stephenson, A., 'Precarious Poses: The Problem of Artistic Visibility and Its Homosocial Performances in Late Nineteenth-Century London', *Visual Culture in Britain*, vol. 8, no. 1, summer 2007.

Stewart, S., *On Longing: Narratives of the Miniature, the Gigantic, the Souvenir, the Collection*, Baltimore and London, The Johns Hopkins University Press, 1984.

Syme, A., *A Touch of Blossom: John Singer Sargent and the Queer Flora of Fin-de-Siècle Art*, University Park, Pennsylvania State University Press, 2010.

Tamagne, F. *A History of Homosexuality in Europe: Berlin, London, Paris 1919–1939*, vol. ii, New York, Algora Publishing, 2004.

Taylor, W. M., 'Characterizing the Inhabitant in Robert Kerr's "The Gentleman's House, 1864"', *Design Issues*, vol. 18, no. 3, summer 2002.

Tickner, L., *Modern Life and Modern Subjects: British Art in the Early Twentieth Century*, New Haven and London, Yale University Press, 2000.

Tillyard, S. K., *The Impact of Modernism, 1900–1920: Early Modernism and the Arts and Crafts Movement in Edwardian England*, London and New York, Routledge, 1988.

Tosh, J., 'The New Man? The Bourgeois Cult of Home', *History Today*, December 1996.

Tosh, J., *A Man's Place: Masculinity and the Middle-Class Home in Victorian England*, New Haven and London, Yale University Press, 1999.

Trilling, J., *The Language of Ornament*, London, Thames & Hudson, 2001.

Troy, N. J., *Modernism and the Decorative Arts in France: Art Nouveau to Le Corbusier*, London and New Haven, Yale University Press, 1991.

Tufnell, B. et al. *Cedric Morris and Let-Haines: Teaching and Life*, Norwich and Cardiff, Norfolk Museums and Archaeology, 2003.

Turner, V., *The Ritual Process: Structure and Anti-Structure*, New York, Aldine de Gruyter, 1995.

Vanita, R., *Sappho and the Virgin Mary: Same-Sex Love and the English Literary Imagination*, New York, Columbia University Press, 1996.

Venison, T., 'The Painter's Living Legacy', *Country Life*, 9 February 2006.

Verity, F. T., E. T. Hall, G. C. Horsley and W. S. Sparrow (eds.), *Flats, Urban Houses and Cottage Homes: A Companion Volume to 'The British Home To-Day'*, London, Hodder and Stoughton, 1906.

Vicinus, M., *Intimate Friends: Women Who Loved Women, 1778–1928*, Chicago, University of Chicago Press, 2004.

Vickers, H., *Cecil Beaton: The Authorized Biography*, London, Weidenfeld and Nicolson, 1985.

Vidal-Naquet, P., *The Black Hunter: Forms of Thought and Forms of Society in the Greek World*, Baltimore and London, The Johns Hopkins University Press, 1981.

Walkley, G., *Artists' Houses in London 1764–1914*, Aldershot, Scolar Press, 1994.

Ward-Jackson, P., 'Lord Ronald Gower, Gustave Doré and the Genesis of the Shakespeare Memorial at Stratford-on-Avon', *Journal of the Warburg and Courtauld Institute*, vol. 50, 1987.

Weeks, J., *Coming Out: Homosexual Politics in Britain from the Nineteenth Century to the Present*, London, Quartet Books, 1977.

Wigley, M., 'Untitled: The Housing of Gender', in B. Colomina (ed.), *Sexuality and Space*, New York, Princeton Architectural Press, 1992.

Wigley, M., 'White-Out: Fashioning the Modern [Part 2]', *Assemblage*, no. 22, December 1993.

Wigley, M., 'White Out: Fashioning the Modern', in D. Fausch et al. (eds.), *Architecture in Fashion*, Princeton, Princeton Architectural Press, 1994.

Wigley, M., *White Walls, Designer Dresses: The Fashioning of Modern Architecture*, Cambridge, MA, and London, The MIT Press, 2001.

Wilson, E., 'A Note on Glamour', *Fashion Theory*, vol. 11, no. 1, 2007.

Wollen, P., *Raiding the Icebox: Reflections on Twentieth-Century Culture*, Bloomington and Indianapolis, Indiana University Press, 1993.

Index

Abbott, Berenice 165
Aesthetic Movement 59, 74, 84, 85, 95, 107
affect 5, 29, 47, 55, 59, 73, 106, 213, 281–2
Allen, Adrianne 228
Antoinette, Marie 30, 39, 46, 49, 50, 53–4, 64, 67–75, 79 ftnt. 89
Archer, Thomas 21
Aristotle 138
Art Deco 204, 206, 226, 227
Arts and Crafts 86, 95, 116, 175
Ashton, Freddie 258
Auden, W. H. 254

Bakst, Leon 191
Ballets Russes 272
Balzac, Honoré de 72–4
  Le Cousin Pons (1847) 72–4
Banting, John 188–9
Barnes, Djuna 165
Baroness d'Erlanger 270
Bas, Billee Le 257
Baudelaire, Charles 170
Beardsley, Aubrey 100
Beaton, Cecil 6, 8, 29, 31, 208, 215, 217, 234, 246–50, 254–61, 267–82, 286
  Ashcombe 31, 267–82
  Redditch House 279–80
Beerbohm, Max 98
Bell, Clive 177
Bell, Vanessa 176, 183
Benjamin, Walter 18, 67, 73, 92, 171
Bernhardt, Sarah 60
Bianco, Pamela 255
Billing, Noël Pemberton 200
Blair, Rt Rev. Sir David Hunter 59, 62–4

Blanche, Jacques-Émile 91, 95
Bliss, Mary 141
Bloomsbury Group 24, 95, 175, 176–7, 183, 191, 286
Blythe, Ronald 162
Bourget, Paul 57
Bousfield, Daphne 188–9
Boxer, Arabella 276
Bradley, Katherine 97–8, 101, 103, 104
Braithwaite, Lilian 202
bric-à-brac 15–16, 43–44, 46–9, 53, 55, 58–9, 65–7, 73–5, 110, 173, 217, 224, 269, 288
Bright Young Things 31, 250–6, 260
Brinkworth, Ian 181
British Museum 96
Broadway 213, 227, 235, 240
Brown, Eric 100
Brown, Ford Maddox 95
Brown, John Baldwin 143–4
Browning, Oscar 140
Burne-Jones, Edward 95
Butts, Mary 165

Calthrop, Gladys 202, 207, 215, 217
Cambridge University 14, 62, 250, 254–5
camp 28, 31, 185, 208, 213, 258, 259, 268–70
Capote, Truman 278
Carpenter, Edward 5–6, 142
Carpenter, Ellis 184, 186
Casa d'Arte Braglia 168
Cézanne, Paul 171, 177, 247
Chatto, Beth 188
Chavannes, Puvis de 96, 105
Clark, Sir Kenneth 104, 105–6

Cleveland Street scandal 23, 117
closet 11, 23, 25, 27, 31, 58, 65–6, 91, 119, 121, 132, 142, 154, 210–11, 240, 257, 161, 267
Coates, Wells 236–8
Cocteau, Jean 246, 256
collecting 10, 30, 43, 44, 46–9, 53–8, 65–75, 84, 85, 92, 102, 104–12, 122, 133, 188, 264, 269
commedia dell'arte 271, 272
Constance, Duchess of Westminster 49, 60, 62
Cook, Clarence 47
Cooper, Edith 97–8, 101, 104
Coward, Noël 6, 29, 31, 199–241, 250, 252, 256–7, 259–60, 273–4, 280, 286
  Bitter Sweet (1930) 211
  Design for Living (1933) 201, 227, 230–5, 238, 240
  111 Ebury Street 199, 206, 208, 227, 234
  17 Gerald Road 206, 217, 274
  Goldenhurst 216–17
  Private Lives (1930) 201, 214, 218, 227–30, 231
  The Vortex (1924) 202–4, 205, 206, 227
Cranach, Lucas
  Adam and Eve (1526) 138
Croft, Taylor 270, 276
Cross, Paul Odo 187–8
Cubism 172
Cunard, Nancy 165

David, Jacques Louis 69
Davis, Sir Edmund 104
Deacon, Hetty (Ester) 90
Descartes, René
  cogito 3, 5
Diaghilev, Sergei 270, 272
The Dial 99
Dietrich, Marlene 211
Dobson, Frank 181, 189
Dossetter, Edward 45
Douglas, Lord Alfred (Bosie) 75, 113, 200
Douglas, Tom 258
Downman, John 49
Dreier, Katherine 174
Duchamp, Marcel 165
Duff, Michael 276

East Anglian School of Painting and Drawing (EASPD) 163, 178, 181–3, 186
Edis, Robert 85, 117
Ellis, Havelock 97, 150

excess 27, 28, 29, 57, 59, 72, 110, 113, 115, 117, 119, 121, 153, 177, 191, 201, 203, 212, 227, 234, 240, 257, 262, 270, 273, 276, 286–7, 288
Exhibition of British Industrial Arts in the Home 235–6

Fitzwilliam Museum (Cambridge) 102
Fontanne, Lynn 214–15, 217, 218, 230
Forster, E. M. 5–6, 121
  Maurice 5
Fothergill, John 140
Fragonard, Jean-Honoré 102
Franklin, Maud 97
Freud, Lucien 163, 178
Freud, Sigmund 65–6, 72, 204, 233, 235
Friesz, Othon 165
Fry, Roger 95, 104, 140, 174–5, 176
  Omega workshop 95, 175, 176
Fusato, Angelo 64
Futurism 172

Gainsborough, Thomas 49
Galeries L. and P. Rosenberg 96
Garbo, Greta 279
Garland, Madge 258
Gauguin, Paul 171
Gesamtkunstwerk 98
Gielgud, John 205
Gill, C. F. 114
Godwin, Edward Williamson 60
Goncourt, Edmond de 57, 99, 210
Gosse, Edmund 64
Gower, Lord Ronald 6, 8, 29–30, 39–46, 48–55, 59, 62, 67–75, 80 ftnt. 120, 85, 280, 286
  Bric À Brac (1888) 41, 44, 45–6, 51–3
  Gower Lodge 39–41, 43, 45, 51–3, 69
  Stafford House 42–3
Grant, Duncan 176, 183, 286
Gray, John 99–100
Great Exhibition (1851) 236
Greenberg, Clement 192
Greenbridge, Terrence 251–4
Greenwood, James 14
Gris, Juan 165
Grosvenor Gallery 86
Group X 168
Guggenheim, Peggy 165

Hale, Kathleen 165, 188
Hall, Radclyffe 204, 209, 216
  The Well of Loneliness (1928) 204

Index

Hambling, Maggi 178
Hamilton, Stella 181
Hamilton, Walter 59
Harrison, Mrs Burton 67
Haweis, Mrs H. R. 85
Hayes, Millie 178
Hemmingway, Ernest 165–6
Hepburn, Katherine 217
Herbert, David 256, 260
Hertz, Louis 55
Hichens, Robert 190
Hill, Oliver 236
Hind, Lewis 91–2
Hird, Frank 73, 75
Hodgkins, Frances 161, 162, 174, 178, 181
Hokusai, Katsushika 96, 97
Hollywood 213, 238
Holman-Hunt, William 56–7, 95
Holmes, Sir Charles John 100–1
House Beautiful 57, 74
Housman, Laurence 100
Huysmans, Joris-Karl 3, 189
  A rebours (1884) 3, 127 ftnt. 95, 189

Impressionism 170, 172, 174
Industrial Revolution 11, 55, 236
International Health Exhibition (1884) 58, 117
Isherwood, Christopher 254
Ives, George 148

Jackson, Charles Kains 147–9, 154, 155
Jarman, Derek 204
Joan of Arc 69–70

Kant, Emmanuel 20, 93, 152
King George V 200, 204–5
King Henry VIII 269
Konody, P. G. 173

Labouchere Amendment 22, 24, 26, 56, 100, 113–17, 120, 200, 202, 210, 280
Lanchester, Elsa 238
Langtry, Lillie 60, 62
Lanvin 214
Laughton, Charles 238
Lawrence, Gertrude 215, 217, 218, 228
Lawrence, Sir Thomas 49
Le Corbusier 176, 191, 224–5, 235, 236, 238, 262
Lee, Thomas Sterling 97
Léger, Fernand 165
Leighton, Lord Frederic 56

Lesley, Cole 205
Lett-Haines, Arthur 6, 8, 29, 31, 161–8, 178–92, 200, 223
  Benton End 182–91
  The Bowgie 162
  East Anglian School of Painting and Drawing (EASPD) 163, 178, 181–3, 186
  The Pound 178–82, 184, 191
Lewis, Cecil 92, 100, 102, 104, 106, 108
Lewis, Wyndham 168, 175
Lhote, André 165
Lincoln, Gertrude Aimee 162
Lindsay, Sir Coutts 86
Lindsay, Lady Harriett 86
Littell, E. T. 19
Loftie, John 47, 48–9
London Artists Association 168, 171
Loos, Anita 269
Loraine, Lorn 205, 207, 221
Lord Chamberlain 204, 240, 267
Loss, Adolf 207, 224, 225, 238, 262
Lowndes, Mrs Marie Adelaide Belloc 49–50, 67
Lunt, Alfred 214, 217, 218, 230, 231, 234

Macfadden, Bernarr Aldolphus 252
Mackay, Williamson 64
MacLennan, Michael Lewis 81
Madame Tussaud 69
Madarassi, Luca 68
Marinetti, Fillipo Tommaso 168
Marshall, John 6, 134–6, 141, 149
Mason, Charles Spurrier 113
masturbation 3
Matisse, Henri 163, 191, 230
Maugham, Somerset W. 225
Maugham, Syrie 214, 216–18, 223, 225–6, 234, 273–4
Mavor, Sidney 113
Maxwell, Elsa 259
memory 5, 7, 8, 14, 45, 56, 84, 102, 104, 155, 164, 199, 274
Merrill, George 5–6
Messel, Oliver 277–8
Miles, Frank 43–4, 60, 62, 190
Millais, Sir John Everett 49, 95
Miller, Fred 85
The Modern Man (Magazine) 3
Molyneux, Edward 217, 228
Montagu, Venetia 257
Moore, Thomas Sturge 97, 99, 118
Morgan, Glyn 162, 184, 189

Morris, Sir Cedric 6, 8, 29, 31, 161–75, 178–92, 200, 223
  Benton End 182–91
  The Bowgie 162
  East Anglian School of Painting and Drawing (EASPD) 163, 178, 181–3, 186
  The Pound 178–82, 184, 191
Morris, William 95
Mortimer, Raymond 177
Munnings, Sir Alfred 181
Munro, Alexander 51
Museum of Fine Arts (Boston) 134

Nash, Paul 176–7
National Gallery of Canada 100
National Portrait Gallery (London) 81, 100
Nichols, Beverley 200, 204, 209, 214, 225, 254, 255, 273
Nicholson, Ben 168
Nicholson, Winifred 168
Noble, Cynthia (Lady Gladwyn) 258
Noble, Matthew 39
Nordau, Max 57–8, 104, 110, 266
Novello, Ivor 205, 212, 215
Nutt, A. Y. 51

Oliver, Edith 260, 267
Olivier, Laurence 228
Omega workshop 95, 175, 176
Order of Chaeronea 148
Oxford University 14, 59–60, 62, 74, 134, 142, 152, 154, 250, 253, 254, 277

Parker, Charles 113
Parker, William 113
Parsons, Harold 137
Pater, Walter 104, 126 ftnt. 67, 152–3, 154–5
Patmore, Derek 26
Perks, Sydney 21
Perrin, Raoul 64
Pevsner, Nikolaus 176
phenomenology 6
Picasso, Pablo 168, 170, 171, 247
The Picture Hire, Limited 170
Plato 138, 142, 156
  Symposium 138, 142
Poiret, Paul 191
Ponsoby, Elizabeth 258
Post-Impressionism 86, 171, 174
Poynter, Edward 60
Pre-Raphaelite Brotherhood 95
Prince of Wales 64, 167

Proust, Marcel
  mémoire involontaire 7
  mémoire volontaire 7

Queen Alexandra 258
Queen Mary 258
Queen Victoria 39, 43, 49, 50, 51, 55
Quilter, Harry 57

Raffalovitch, André 100
Ray, Man 165
resistance 4, 7, 24, 27, 28, 29, 240, 250, 258, 259–61, 267, 280, 287–9
Reynolds, Gwyneth 185
Reynolds, Sir Joshua 49
Ricketts, Charles 5, 6, 11, 25, 29–30, 44, 81, 83–112, 116, 118–23, 137, 161, 163, 187, 286
  Lansdowne House 95, 104, 107
  Townshend House 105, 107
  The Vale 97–101, 118
Rijn, Rembrandt van 102, 107
Riviere, Joan 235
Rodin, August 138, 140
  Le Baiser (1899) 138
Rosenauer, Michael 269
Ross, Robbie 90, 104, 140, 200
Rossetti, Dante Gabriel 95, 96
Rothenstein, Sir William 95, 97, 99, 118, 139–40
Rubens, Peter Paul 96, 102
Ruskin, John 18, 82, 116, 143

Sackville-West, Vita 258
Sala, George Augustus 45
Santayana, George 140, 153–4, 155
Sargent, John Singer 189
Savage, Marmion
  The Bachelor of Albany (1847) 19
Seccombe, Thomas 59–60
senses 3, 5, 6, 7, 8, 47, 99, 102, 104, 114, 274–5
Seven and Five Society 168
Shairp, Mardaunt
  The Green Bay Tree (1933) 249–50, 261–7
shame 4, 7, 10, 11, 24, 27, 29, 72, 91, 120, 121, 154, 156, 192, 200, 201, 208, 212, 213, 240, 248, 250, 252, 254, 256–61, 280–2, 287–9
Shannon, Charles 5, 6, 11, 25, 29–30, 44, 81, 83–112, 116, 118–23, 161, 163, 187, 286
  Lansdowne House 95, 104, 107
  The Man with the Greek Vase (1916) 111–12

Townshend House 105, 107
The Vale 97–101, 118
Sheckelton, Captain Frank 75, 80 ftnt. 120
Sheperd, Martha 140
Sisson, Margery 181
Skeeping, John 179
Société Anonyme 168, 174
Somerset, Lord Arthur 117
spermatorrhea 3
Stafford House 42–3, 45
Stein, Gertrude 247
Stevenson, J. J. 20
Stoker, Bram 119–20
  Dracula (1897) 119–20
Stonewall 25
Stratchey, Lytton 286
Sully, James 153
Swabe, Maurice 113
Symmonds, John Addington 7, 64, 90–1, 97, 142, 147

The Tate (London) 165, 184
Taylor, Alfred 6, 8, 11, 113–20, 122–3, 132, 210
Teleny (1893) 25
Tennant, Stephen 254, 256
Tiepolo, Giovanni Battista 102
Todd, Dorothy 177, 258
Toklas, Alice B. 247
Tree, Iris 165
Twyseden, Lady Tuff 165

Ulrichs, Karl Heinrich 142

Valentino, Rudolph 215
Venice Biennale 168
Victor, Prince Albert 117
Vorticism 95, 204

Warburton, Joan 162, 179, 181, 185
Warner, Kathleen Arnold 140–1
Warren, Edward Perry 6, 29, 31, 121, 131–57, 183, 254
  A *Defence of Uranian Love* (1928) 31, 132, 141–57, 254, 286
  Lewes House 132, 134, 136–43, 144, 151, 154–6, 184
  Lewes House brotherhood 137, 148
  The Prince Who Did Not Exist (1904) 141
Watson, Peter 277–9
Watteau, Jean-Antoine 102
Waugh, Evelyn 282
Whistler, James McNeill 97, 112
Whistler, Rex 267, 269, 272
Wilde, Oscar 6, 8, 11, 19, 29–30, 31, 43–4, 56, 58, 59–64, 65, 73, 74–5, 78 ftnt. 78, 81, 83–4, 85, 86, 87, 91, 94, 95, 97, 99, 112, 113–23, 132, 152, 154, 175, 190, 200, 202, 208, 211–12, 232, 240, 250, 252, 260, 265
  The Importance of Being Earnest (1895) 19
  The Picture of Dorian Gray (1891) 44, 65, 81, 99, 127 ftnt. 95
  The Portrait of Mr W. H. (1889) 44
  trials 23, 49, 113–23, 132, 151, 154, 156, 210, 212
Wilson, James Grant 47–8
Wilson, John Chapman 205, 216, 217, 218
Winckelmann, Johann Joachim 150–1, 152, 154–5, 156
Wolfe, Elsie de 25, 259
Wolfenden Report xv, 22, 23–4, 26, 280–1
Wood, Christopher 181
Woolf, Virginia 258, 286

Yeats, W. B. 121

EU authorised representative for GPSR:
Easy Access System Europe, Mustamäe tee 50,
10621 Tallinn, Estonia
gpsr.requests@easproject.com